Common Errors in English Usage

THIRD EDITION

Paul Brians

*Professor Emeritus of English,
Washington State University*

WILLIAM, JAMES & CO.

Sherwood, Oregon

Dedication

For my wife, Paula Elliot. Her sharp
editorial eye, sense of style and support
have helped make this book what it is.

Publisher	Jim Leisy (james_leisy@wmjasco.com)
Acquisition Editor	Bill Hoffman
Production Editors	Tom Sumner
	Jaron Ayres
	Stephanie Welch

Printed in the U.S.A.

Rights and Permissions
William, James & Co., Portland Office
2154 NE Broadway, Suite 100
Portland, Oregon 97232

Library of Congress Cataloging-in-Publication Data

Brians, Paul.
  Common errors in English usage / Paul Brians, Professor Emeritus of English,
Washington State University. -- Third Edition.
    pages cm
  ISBN 978-1-59028-263-2 (alk. paper)
  1. English language--Usage--Dictionaries. 2. English language--Errors of usage--
Dictionaries. 3. English language--United States--Idioms--Dictionaries. I. Title.
  PE1464.B75 2013
  421'.1--dc23
                          2013027318

Contents

Foreword   iv
   by Mignon Fogarty, "Grammar Girl"

Introduction   vi

Common Errors in English Usage:
   Alphabetical Listing   1

Category Listings   329
   Commonly Confused Expressions   329
   Of Foreign Origin   334
   Grammar, Spelling & Style   335
   Homonyms   338
   Commonly Misspelled   339
   Mangled Expressions   345
   Inexact Words & Phrases   348
   Pronunciation   351
   Problem Prepositions   352
   Redundancies   353
   Commonly Misused Expressions   354
   American English vs. British English   357
   Misheard Expressions   358

Appendix: Phrasal Verbs vs. Nouns   361

Foreword

Like Paul Brians, I have taken the foolish step of issuing regular public commentary on English usage. In my experience, there's no better way to liven up a week (and raise your blood pressure) than to write 1000 words on a contentious usage point, release those words on the Web, and sift through the inevitable barrage of comments.

Unlike Brians and many of my other comrades, I do not hold a graduate degree in English, literature, or other such discipline. I merely find language fun and can't seem to restrain myself from sharing my weekly discoveries. Therefore, I stand on the shoulders of giants—an apt phrase despite its cliché status.

I rarely take a *Grammar Girl* podcast live without at least quadruple-checking my main thesis, and *Common Errors in English Usage* has quickly become one of my most valued fact-checking resources. In addition, I reach for *Common Errors* almost daily to find the answers to smaller questions, and in fact, I have already used the book multiple times while writing this foreword. Would Brians capitalize Web? (Yes.) Which way does the mark above the *e* in *cliché* lean? (Right.) And just out of curiosity, what is that mark called again? (An acute accent mark.)

Whereas I may yammer on about the exceptions to a rule (or supposed rule) and the nuances of dissenting arguments, Brians confidently takes a stand. Although he does quickly note when there is controversy, he never shies away from issuing an opinion, and that makes his book a valuable resource for anyone seeking quick, reliable answers.

He has a gift for writing a clear, concise, and yet entertaining entry: "Unless you are going to claim credit for accomplishments you had in previous incarnations, you should refer to your *vita*, not your *vitae*." He strikes a sensible balance between the prescriptive and descriptive extremes: "*Incentivize* is even more widely used [than *incent*], but strikes many people as an ugly substitute for *encourage*." And he peppers his writing with helpful memory tricks: "Just remember that *X* in *except* excludes things—they tend to stand out, be different." Brilliant!

When the corners of this book are worn off, the spine is broken, and the fuzzy edges are spiked with Post-it® notes marking your most used pages, don't forget to write Brians a note of thanks. By distilling reams of rules and opinions into a usable, entertaining reference book, he's made all our lives a little easier.

—Mignon Fogarty,
Grammar Girl
QuickAndDirtyTips.com

Introduction

Prescription vs. description

The concept of errors in English usage is a fuzzy one. Language experts like to distinguish between two opposed approaches to the subject: theoretically prescriptivists work from rigid rules and traditions and seek to impose their views of correctness on the writing and speaking public, while descriptivists simply note the prevailing patterns of writers and speakers and report their results without in any way judging them.

But in fact it is not so easy to distinguish between these two approaches to usage: all prescriptivists rely heavily on usage patterns to develop their prescriptions and are willing to make exceptions to general "rules"; and even the most laissez-faire descriptivist will admit that "hte" is a typographical error for "the," that "Heineken remover" is based on a mishearing of "Heimlich maneuver," and that "perverbial" is not just a variant spelling of "proverbial"—it's a mistake.

Reserving judgment

Many teachers of composition feel that covering a paper with red ink just discourages and paralyzes students (in fact, I've found a standard pencil arouses much less anxiety than a red pen). The dominant philosophy of teaching students to write argues that only abundant practice can lead to improved writing. Errors naturally diminish as students read and write more.

This is very true. No list of errors—no matter how diligently memorized—can make you into a fine writer. Nothing beats lots of reading and writing. But the sad truth is that few students read or write much these days, and most of it is done in the anarchic setting of e-mail and texting, where "correctness" is scorned. It is not uncommon for students to make it all the way through school without having their writing thoroughly scrutinized and critiqued until they encounter disaster in the form of a picky professor, editor, or boss. Many businesses consider standard English usage a prime requirement for employment in responsible positions. Would-be schoolteachers are particularly harshly judged if their English is sub-par.

Linguistic discrimination

Much of the tension surrounding debates about usage has to do with concern for various groups—minorities and immigrants in particular—who often suffer discrimination as a result of their deviations from dominant language patterns. Prescriptivism is viewed by many language experts as the equivalent of imperialist tyranny, or to use the jargon of the moment, linguistic hegemony.

It's true that the dominant patterns in English can exclude some very lively and creative language, and that a good deal of wonderful poetry, fiction, and drama has been written in nonstandard dialects. But in almost every case writers who are able to effectively wield the dialect they grew up speaking have also mastered standard English. To take only one of many examples, Langston Hughes brilliantly played the lively Harlem dialect of his character Jesse B. Semple against his own persona's rather formal diction in a long series of classic columns for the *Chicago Defender*.

If you have no access to standard English, a dialect can trap you. If you apply for an executive position by saying "I heared t'other day you done got some jobs open," chances are good you'll be directed to try farther down the corporate hierarchy. It may be deplorable, but the fact is that our language is judged all the time by employers, friends, and potential dates. When some teachers evade the issue by declaring all dialects equal, they set their students up for bitter disappointment in the world outside school. By all means celebrate the variety of Englishes abounding in the world today—but everyone deserves to know what sorts of usage variations may cause them trouble.

Errors, confusions, and non-errors

Errors in usage are a lot like errors in table manners. There are tiny deviations from standard practice few people will notice or care about, like using your salad fork to eat a steak, or using "decimate" to mean "destroy." Saying "I got my dandruff up" rather than "my dander" is more like trying to stab chunks of sweet-and-sour pork with the sharpened end of a chopstick—likely to raise eyebrows. But it's the equivalent of falling face-first into the mashed potatoes when some poor soul refers to a man as "circusized."

An English usage guide is like that really close friend who dares to tell you that there's some spinach stuck between your teeth.

And then there are people who insist you should never drink white wine with red meat; they're like those who heap contempt on split infinitives. Humor them if you must, but most of us feel they're dead wrong. Many linguistic bugaboos of this sort are included in this book so you can be reassured that not all the people who condemn your usage know what they're talking about.

Standard and nonstandard English

Entries are not simply divided into "correct" and "erroneous." The label "standard English" is frequently applied to patterns that sophisticated writers and speakers tend to use. This definition is to some extent circular: we consider them sophisticated partly because they use that kind of English. But standard English is what counts; it's what your own usage may be compared with. It's up to you to decide whether, after learning the dominant pattern, you want to blend in or use a different wording that appeals to you more. I had to rack my brains for a long time to understand the distinction some people make between "which" and "that," but I finally decided that I didn't give a fig about what they thought and generally ignore the distinction in my own writing. Guidelines for usage don't have to be regarded as iron chains dragging you down. You can still choose your own style.

When a usage is labeled as belonging to a dialect, it may be regional, ethnic, or national. Rather than stigmatize any particular group, I don't try to label these dialectical variations beyond indicating that they differ from standard usage. If you're "down to home," by all means greet your brother-in-law with "Look what the cat drug in!" But in writing your college admissions essay you'd be wiser to use "dragged" as in, "Although I love opera now, I was dragged to my first one protesting loudly."

By no means the majority of the usages discussed in this book are dialectical, however. It also covers technical and business jargon, pretentious but mistaken coinages created by highly educated speakers, and usages that are common but offensive to certain communities.

A special problem is the differences between standard American usage and standard United Kingdom usage, which is also largely followed in Canada, Australia, and some other countries. This particular usage guide is aimed primarily at Americans, but often notes when patterns are different elsewhere.

Who says?

Because of current trends in English studies, the folks you find patrolling the usage beat are not likely to be trained linguists these days; and I'm no exception. I have a Ph.D. in comparative literature, not in English composition. But I love good writing and encourage it in my students. I first got the idea of writing about usage while studying the mangled language on restaurant menus, and you'll find several examples of that sort of thing in this book.

Common Errors in English Usage does not merely enshrine my personal preferences, however. I've consulted dictionaries and other usage manuals and consulted with colleagues more expert than myself. Web search engines have been a very handy tool for confirming the extent to which many errors have spread. Unlike the editors of some distinguished usage guides, I don't have a formal board of consultants; but I do have something that functions rather like one. This project began in 1997 as a Web site called *Common Errors in English* (http://public.wsu.edu/~brians/errors/), and since then it's earned many positive reviews, received numerous awards, and attracted more than 15 million visitors, thousands of whom have written to me with thanks or suggestions.

The Web site contains a list of "More Errors," many of which are too bizarre to be included here, but too entertaining to be omitted there. The Web site is also where you'll find an e-mail link if you want to write me.

If you think having a teacher criticize your writing is hard to bear, imagine being open to constant carping by the pickiest people in existence. Though I don't always agree with my correspondents, I've learned a lot from them. They've tipped me off to common errors that have escaped the notice of other usage guide authors and sometimes argued me out of my own prejudices against usages that turned out to be more standard than I had thought.

This book is thus the result of an ongoing conversation among people from all over the world and all walks of life who care about the language, and I owe those contributors a profound debt. Although *Common Errors in English* is not particularly aimed at non-native speakers, many correspondents struggling to learn English have found its explanations of the differences between seemingly similar words and phrases helpful.

You may find certain words or phrases criticized here listed in dictionaries. Note carefully labels like *dial.* (dialectical), *nonstandard,* and *obsolete* before assuming that the dictionary is endorsing them. The primary job of a dictionary is to track how people actually use language. Dictionaries differ among themselves on how much guidance to usage they provide; but the goal of a usage guide like this is substantially different: to protect you against patterns regarded as nonstandard by substantial numbers of well-educated people.

What's different about this usage guide?

Common Errors in English Usage is unusual in a number of other ways besides having originated on the World Wide Web.

Because it concentrates on the most common errors, it's much shorter—and not incidentally, cheaper—than most, though I include some oddities that I consider especially interesting or which are simply pet peeves of mine.

This guide makes no pretense to exhaustively exploring complex topics, limiting itself to pointing out the most commonly encountered problems and giving hints for avoiding them, using a minimum of technical terminology. This is the equivalent of a first-aid manual, not of the *Physician's Desk Reference.*

It avoids discussing most common misspellings, leaving the correction of such slips to your spelling checker, concentrating instead on linguistic confusions your computer won't catch.

It discusses many casual, slangy forms that are beneath the notice of some of the more high-toned usage guides.

It incorporates up-to-date comments on words and phrases from the world of the Internet and from other technologies.

It provides illustrative examples written in the sort of English familiar to most people likely to use this book. When writing a book about common errors, it would be pointless to select learned examples a general audience would not relate to.

It also places the primary discussion of words and phrases alphabetically under their erroneous forms, so you don't need to know the correct forms to look them up. A cross-reference is given at the expected location to guide you if you do know the correct form.

It's written in a chatty, informal tone designed to take the edge off what could otherwise be an unpleasant barrage of criticism. It makes abundant use of the first- and second-person voice to create the effect of an informal chat rather than a pompous lecture.

And from time to time, it tries to entertain. People often write to tell me that they laugh as well as groan as they make their way through what I've written. I hope you find this book fun to read as well as informative.

A Note on the Third Edition

This edition of *Common Errors in English Usage* follows the great success of the first two editions, published in 2002 and 2009. In the intervening years I have continued to add entries and tinker with the old ones. This new edition contains over 300 entirely new entries and over 75 revised ones, along with several new cartoons selected and captioned by Tom Sumner. Some of the revisions expand or clarify the old explanations, and in some cases I have simply changed my mind.

As always, I am deeply grateful to the thousands of readers who have written to me, many of them offering ideas and suggestions which have found their way into this edition.

If you enjoy *Common Errors in English Usage*, you may want to sign up for the *Common Errors in English Usage Calendar*, delivered free by e-mail daily, at http://tinyurl.com/commonerrorscalendar. You can also read more extended essays on language and usage on the *Common Errors in English Usage* blog at http://tinyurl.com/commonerrorsblog.

—*P.B.*

Common Errors in English Usage

a/an

If the word following begins with a vowel sound, the word you want is "an": "Have an apple, Adam." If the word following begins with a consonant, but begins with a vowel sound, you still need "an": "An X-ray will show whether there's a worm in it." It is nonstandard and often considered sloppy speech to utter an "uh" sound in such cases.

The same rule applies to initialisms like "NGO" (for "non-governmental organization"). Because the letter *N* is pronounced "en," it's "an NGO" but when the phrase is spoken instead of the abbreviation, it's "a non-governmental organization."

When the following word definitely begins with a consonant sound, you need "a": "A snake told me apples enhance mental abilities."

Note that the letter *Y* can be either a vowel or a consonant. Although it is sounded as a vowel in words like "pretty," at the beginning of words it is usually sounded as a consonant, as in "a yolk."

Words beginning with the letter *U* and starting with a *Y* consonant sound, like "university" and "utensil," also take an "a": "a university" and "a utensil." But when an initial *U* has a vowel sound, the word is preceded by "an": it's "an umpire," "an umbrella," and "an understanding."

See also "historic: an historic vs. a historic."

a cappella/acapella, a capella

See "acapella, a capella/a cappella."

A.D.

"A.D." does not mean "after death," as many people suppose. "B.C." stands for the English phrase "before Christ," but "A.D." stands confusingly for a Latin phrase: *anno domini* ("in the year of the Lord"—the year Jesus was born). If the calendar actually changed with Jesus' death, then what would we do with the years during which he lived? Since Jesus was probably actually born around 6 B.C. or so, the connection of the calendar with him can be misleading.

Many Biblical scholars, historians, and archeologists prefer the less sectarian designations "before the Common Era" (B.C.E.) and "the Common Era" (C.E.).

Traditionally "A.D." was placed before the year number and "B.C." after, but many people now prefer to put both abbreviations after the numbers.

All of these abbreviations can also be spelled without their periods.

a historic/an historic
See "historic: an historic vs. a historic."

à la/ala
See "ala/à la."

a lot/alot
See "alot/a lot."

abject
"Abject" is always negative—it means "hopeless," not "extreme." You can't experience "abject joy" unless you're being deliberately paradoxical.

able to
People are able to do things, but things are not able to be done: you should not say, "the budget shortfall was able to be solved by selling brownies."

about
"This isn't about you." What a great rebuke! But conservatives sniff at this sort of abstract use of "about," as in "I'm all about good taste" or "successful truffle-making is about temperature control"; so it's better to avoid it in very formal English.

absorbtion/absorption
Although it's "absorbed" and "absorbing," the correct spelling of the noun is "absorption."

But note that scientists distinguish between "absorption" as the process of swallowing up or sucking in something and "adsorption" as the process by which something adheres to the surface of something else without being assimilated into it. Even technical writers often confuse these two.

abstruse/obtuse
Most people first encounter "obtuse" in geometry class, where it labels an angle of more than 90 degrees and less than 180. Imagine what sort of blunt arrowhead that kind of angle would make and you will understand why it also has a figurative meaning of "dull, stupid." But people often mix the word up with "abstruse," which means "difficult to understand."

When you mean to criticize something for being needlessly complex or baffling, the word you need is not "obtuse," but "abstruse."

academia
Although some academics are undoubtedly nuts, the usual English-language pronunciation of "academia" does not rhyme with "macadamia." The third syl-

lable is pronounced "deem." Just say "academe" and add "ee-yuh."

However, there's an interesting possibility if you go with "ack-uh-DAME-ee-yuh": although some people will sneer at your lack of sophistication, others will assume you're using the Latin pronunciation and being learned.

acapella, a capella/a cappella

In referring to singing unaccompanied by instruments, the traditional spelling is the Italian one, *a cappella*: two words, two *P*s, two *L*s. The Latin spelling *a capella* is learned, but in the realm of musical terminology, we usually stick with Italian. The one-word spelling "acapella" is widely used by Americans, including by some performing groups, but musical experts generally regard this as an error.

Even at the Women's Barbell Academy it is not pronounced "ack-uh-DAME-ee-yuh."

accede/exceed

If you drive too fast, you exceed the speed limit. "Accede" is a much rarer word meaning "give in, agree."

accent marks

In what follows, "accent mark" will be used in a loose sense to include all diacritical marks that guide pronunciation. Operating systems and programs differ in how they produce accent marks, but it's worth learning how yours works. Writing them in by hand afterwards looks amateurish.

Words adopted from foreign languages sometimes carry their accent marks with them, as in "fiancé," "protégé," and "cliché." As words become more at home in English, they tend to shed the marks: "Café" is often spelled "cafe." Unfortunately, "résumé" seems to be losing its marks one at a time (*see also* "vitae/vita").

Many computer users have not learned their systems well enough to understand how to produce the desired accent and often insert an apostrophe (curled) or foot mark (straight) after the accented letter instead: "cafe'" or "cafe'." This is both ugly and incorrect. The same error is commonly seen on storefront signs.

So far we've used examples containing acute (right-leaning) accent marks. French and Italian (but not Spanish) words often contain grave (left-leaning) accents; in Italian it's a *caffè*. It is important not to substitute one kind of accent for the other.

The diaeresis over a letter signifies that it is to be pronounced as a separate syllable: "noël" and "naïve" are sometimes spelled with a diaeresis, for instance. The umlaut, which looks identical, modifies the sound of a vowel, as in German *Fräulein* (girl), where the accent mark changes the "frow" sound of *Frau* (woman) to "froy." Rock groups like Blue Öyster Cult scattered umlauts about nonsensically to create an exotic look.

Spanish words not completely assimilated into English—like *piñata* and *niño*—retain the tilde, which tells you that an *N* is to be pronounced with a *Y* sound after it.

In English-language publications accent marks are often discarded, but the acute and grave accents are the ones most often retained.

accept/except
If you offer me Godiva chocolates I will gladly accept them—except for the candied violet ones. Just remember that the *X* in "except" excludes things—they tend to stand out, be different. In contrast, just look at those two cozy *C*'s snuggling up together. Very accepting. And be careful; when typing "except" it often comes out "expect."

access/get access to
"Access" is one of many nouns that's been turned into a verb in recent years. Conservatives object to phrases like, "You can access your account online." Substitute "use," "reach," or "get access to" if you want to please them.

accessory
There's an "ack" sound at the beginning of this word, though some mispronounce it as if the two *C*'s were to be sounded the same as the two *SS*'s.

accidently/accidentally
You can remember this one by remembering how to spell "accidental." There are quite a few words with "-ally" suffixes (like "incidentally"), which are not to be confused with words that have "-ly" suffixes (like "independently"). "Incidental" is a word, but "independental" is not.

according to/per
See "per/according to."

accurate/precise
In ordinary usage, "accurate" and "precise" are often used as rough synonyms, but scientists like to distinguish between them. Accurate measurements reflect true values; but precise measurements are close to each other, even if all of them are wrong in the same way. The same distinction applies in scientific contexts to the related words "accuracy" and "precision."

This distinction is not likely to come up outside of contexts where it is understood, but science writers might want to be aware that the general public will not understand this distinction unless it's explained.

acronyms and apostrophes

One unusual modern use of the apostrophe is in plural acronyms, like "ICBM's," "NGO's," and "CD's." Since this pattern violates the rule that apostrophes are not used before an *S* indicating a plural, many people object to it. It is also perfectly legitimate to write "CDs," etc. Likewise for "50s." But the use of apostrophes with initialisms like "learn your ABC's" and "mind your P's and Q's" is now so universal as to be acceptable in almost any context.

Note that "acronym" was used originally only to label pronounceable abbreviations like "NATO," but is now generally applied to all sorts of initialisms. Be aware that some people consider this extended definition of "acronym" to be an error.

See also "apostrophes."

acrosst/accrossed/across

In some dialects, "acrosst" is a common misspelling of "across." Also, the chicken may have *crossed* the road, but did so by walking *across* it.

actionable/doable

"Actionable" is a technical term referring to something that provides grounds for a legal action or lawsuit. People in the business world have begun using it as a fancy synonym for "doable" or "feasible." This is both pretentious and confusing.

"In actual fact, I think I'm very well spoken."

"Well, actually . . ."

actual fact/actually

"In actual fact" is an unnecessarily complicated way of saying "actually."

ad nauseum/ad nauseam

Seeing how often *ad nauseam* is misspelled makes some people want to throw up. English writers also often mistakenly half-translate the phrase as *ad nausea*.

This Latin phrase comes from a term in logic, the *argumentum ad nauseam*, in which debaters wear out the

The carousel, the calliope— they both went on ad nauseam.

opposition by just repeating arguments until they get sick of the whole thing and give in.

adapt/adopt

You can adopt a child or a custom or a law; in these cases you are making the object of the adoption your own, accepting it. If you adapt something, however, you are changing it.

add/ad

"Advertisement" is abbreviated "ad," not "add."

add/plus

See "plus/add."

added bonus/bonus

People who avoid redundancies tend to object to the extremely popular phrase "added bonus" because a bonus is already something additional. Speakers who use this phrase probably think of "bonus" as meaning something vaguely like "benefit." The phrase is so common that it's unlikely to cause you real problems.

More people frown on the similarly redundant "and plus": "I was fired, and plus I never got my last paycheck." Just say "and" or "plus."

See also "redundancies."

addicting/addictive

Do you find beer nuts *addicting* or *addictive*? "Addicting" is a perfectly legitimate word, but much less common than "addictive," and some people will scowl at you if you use it.

adieu/ado

See "without further adieu/without further ado."

administer/minister

You can minister to someone by administering first aid. Note how the "ad" in "administer" resembles "aid" in order to remember the correct form of the latter phrase. "Minister" as a verb always requires "to" following it.

administrate/administer

Although it is very popular with administrators and others, many people scorn "administrate" as an unnecessary substitute for the more common verb form "administer."

admission/admittance

"Admission" is a much more common word than "admittance" and is a good choice for almost all contexts. You may gain admission or admittance to a college, but you'll probably be dealing with its admissions office. When "admittance" is used, it's most likely to refer to physical entry into some place or other, as is indicated by signs saying "No Admittance."

In electronics, admittance is the opposite of impedance.

adopt/adapt

See "adapt/adopt."

adopted/adoptive

Some people seem to think that "adoptive" is just a more fancy word than "adopted" and write about "the adoptive child." But the two words have different meanings. Parents who do the adopting are adoptive, children are adopted.

Don't call people adopting children "adaptive," though. Adaptive parents would be parents that could adapt themselves to changing circumstances.

When a city, club, or other organization adopts you, it also is adoptive.

adultry/adultery

"Adultery" is often misspelled "adultry," as if it were something every adult should *try*. This spelling error is likely to get you snickered at. The term does not refer to all sorts of illicit sex: at least one of the partners involved has to be married for the relationship to be adulterous.

advance/advanced

When you hear about something in advance, earlier than other people, you get *advance* notice or information. "Advanced" means "complex," "sophisticated" and doesn't necessarily have anything to do with the revealing of secrets.

adverse/averse

The word "adverse" turns up most frequently in the phrase "adverse circumstances," meaning difficult circumstances, circumstances which act as an adversary; but people often confuse this word with "averse," a much rarer word, meaning having a strong feeling against, or aversion toward.

advice/advise

"Advice" is the noun, "advise" the verb. When a columnist advises people, she gives them advice.

adviser/advisor

"Adviser" and "advisor" are equally fine spellings. There is no distinction between them.

advocate for/advocate

When they are acting as advocates for a cause, people often say they are "advocating for," say, traffic safety. This is not as widely accepted as "campaigning for" or "working toward." Saying you are "advocating for the blind" leaves a lot of listeners wondering what it is you advocate for them. If you can substitute "advocate" for "advocate for," you should do so: "I advocate for higher pay for teachers" becomes "I advocate higher pay for teachers."

aesthetic/ascetic

People often encounter these two words first in college, and may confuse one with the other although they have almost opposite connotations. "Aesthetic" (also spelled "esthetic") has to do with beauty, whereas "ascetic" has to do with avoiding pleasure, including presumably the pleasure of looking at beautiful things.

St. Francis had an ascetic attitude toward life, whereas Oscar Wilde had an esthetic attitude toward life.

affect/effect

There are five distinct words here. When "affect" is accented on the final syllable (a-FECT), it is usually a verb meaning "have an influence on": "The million-dollar donation from the industrialist did not affect my vote against the Clean Air Act."

Occasionally a pretentious person is said to affect an artificial air of sophistication. Speaking with a borrowed French accent or ostentatiously wearing a large diamond ear stud might be an affectation. In this sort of context, "affect" means "to make a display of or deliberately cultivate."

Another unusual meaning is indicated when the word is accented on the first syllable (AFF-ect), meaning "emotion." In this case the word is used mostly by psychiatrists and social scientists—people who normally know how to spell it.

The real problem arises when people confuse the first spelling with the second: "effect." This too can be two different words. The more common one is a noun: "When I left the stove on, the *effect* was that the house filled with smoke." When you *affect* a situation, you have an *effect* on it.

Less common is a verb meaning "to create": "I'm trying to *effect* a change in the way we purchase widgets." No wonder people are confused. Note especially that the proper expression is not "take affect" but "take effect"—become effective. Hey, nobody ever said English was logical: just memorize it and get on with your life.

The stuff in your purse? Your personal *effects*.

The stuff in movies? Sound *effects* and special *effects*.

"Affective" is a technical term having to do with emotions; the vast majority of the time the spelling you want is "effective."

affluence/effluence

Wealth brings affluence; sewage is effluence.

Afghan/Afghani

The citizens of Afghanistan are Afghans. Similarly, it's Afghan food, Afghan politics, and Afghan afghans. The only time to use "Afghani" is in reference to the unit of Afghan currency by that name. Afghans spend Afghanis.

African-American

There have been several polite terms used in the US to refer to persons of African descent: "colored," "negro," "Black," and "African-American." "Colored" is definitely dated, though "people of color" is now widely used with a broader meaning, including anyone with non-European ancestry, sometimes even when their skin is not discernibly darker than that of a typical European. A few contemporary writers like to defy convention by referring to themselves as "negro." "Black," formerly a proudly assertive label claimed by young radicals in the 1960s, is now seen by some people as a racist insult. Some people insist on capitalizing "Black," but others prefer "black." The safest and most common neutral term is "African-American," but Americans sometimes misuse it to label people of African descent living in other countries or even actual Africans. To qualify as an "African-American" you have to be an American.

afterwards/afterwords

Like "towards," "forwards," and "homewards," "afterwards" ends with *-wards*.

"Afterwords" are sometimes the explanatory essays at the ends of books or speeches uttered at the end of plays or other works. They are made up of *words*.

aggravate vs. irritate

Some people claim that "aggravate" can only mean "make worse" and should not be used to mean "irritate"; but the latter has been a valid use of the word for four centuries, and "aggravation" means almost exclusively "irritation."

agnostic/atheist

Both agnostics and atheists are regularly criticized as illogical by people who don't understand the meaning of these terms. An agnostic is a person who believes that the existence of a god or gods cannot be proven or known. Agnosticism is a statement about the limits of human knowledge. It is an error to suppose that agnostics perpetually hesitate between faith and doubt: they are confident they cannot know the ultimate truth. Similarly, atheists believe there are no gods. Atheists need not be able to disprove the existence of gods to be consistent just as believers do not need to be able to prove that gods do exist in order to be regarded as religious. Both attitudes have to do with beliefs, not knowledge.

"Agnostic" is often used metaphorically of any refusal to make a judgment, usually on the basis of a lack of evidence; people can be agnostic about acupuncture, for instance, if they believe there is not enough evidence one way or another to decide its effectiveness.

agreeance/agreement

When you agree with someone you are in agreement.

ahold/hold

In standard English you just "get hold" of something or somebody.

aide/aid

In American English, an *aide* is a personal assistant (nurse's aide, presidential aide) but an inanimate object or process is always an *aid* (hearing aid, first aid).

ain't/am not/isn't/aren't

"Ain't" has a long and vital history as a substitute for "isn't," "aren't," and so on. It was originally formed from a contraction of "am not" and is still commonly used in that sense. Even though it has been universally condemned as the classic "mistake" in English, everyone uses it occasionally as part of a joking phrase or to convey a down-to-earth quality. But if you always use it instead of the more "proper" contractions you're sure to be branded as uneducated.

aisle/isle

An aisle is a narrow passageway, especially in a church or store; an isle is an island. Propose to the person you're stranded on a desert isle with and maybe you'll march down the aisle together after you're rescued.

ala/à la

If you offer pie *à la mode* on your menu, be careful not to spell it "ala mode" or—worse—"alamode." The accent over the first "a" is optional in English, although this is an adaptation of the French phrase *à la mode de* meaning "in the manner of." The one-word spelling used to be common, but as people became more sensitive to preserving the spelling of originally French phrases, it fell out of favor. In whose manner is it to plop ice cream on your pie? Nobody really knows, but it's yummy. Stick with the two-word spelling in all other uses of the phrase *à la* as well.

all

Put this word where it belongs in the sentence. In negative statements, don't write, "All the pictures didn't show her dimples" when you mean, "The pictures didn't all show her dimples."

all and all/all in all

"The dog got into the fried chicken, we forgot the sunscreen, and the kids started whining at the end, but all in all the picnic was a success." "All in all" is a traditional phrase which can mean "all things considered," "after all," or "nevertheless." People unfamiliar with the traditional wording often change it to "all and all," but this is nonstandard.

all be it/albeit

"Albeit" is a single word meaning "although": "Rani's recipe called for a table-spoon of saffron, which made it very tasty, albeit rather expensive." It should not be broken up into three separate words as "all be it," just as "although" is not broken up into "all though."

all for not/all for naught

"Naught" means "nothing," and the phrase "all for naught" means "all for nothing." This is often misspelled "all for not" and occasionally "all for knot."

all goes well/augurs well

Some folks who don't understand the word "augur" (to foretell based on omens) try to make sense of the common phrase "augurs well" by mangling it into "all goes well." "Augurs well" is synonymous with "bodes well."

all of the sudden/all of a sudden

An unexpected event happens not "all of *the* sudden" but "all of *a* sudden."

all ready/already

"All ready" is a phrase meaning "completely prepared," as in, "As soon as I put my coat on, I'll be all ready." "Already," however, is an adverb used to describe something that has happened before a certain time, as in, "What do you mean you'd rather stay home? I've already got my coat on."

all right/alright

See "alright/all right."

all the farther/as far as

In some American dialects it is not uncommon to hear sentences such as "Abilene is all the farther the rustlers got before the posse caught up with them." The strangely constructed expression "all the farther" should be replaced with the much more straightforward "as far as."

all together/altogether

See "altogether/all together."

alleged, allegedly

Seeking to avoid prejudging the facts in a crime and protect the rights of the accused, reporters sometimes over-use "alleged" and "allegedly." If it is clear that someone has been robbed at gunpoint, it's not necessary to describe it as an alleged robbery nor the victim as an alleged victim. This practice insultingly casts doubt on the honesty of the victim and protects no one. An accused perpetrator is one whose guilt is not yet established, so it is redundant to speak of an "alleged accused." If the perpetrator has not yet been identified, it's pointless to speak of the search for an "alleged perpetrator."

allegory

See "parallel/symbol."

alliterate/illiterate

Pairs of words with the same initial sound *alliterate*, like "wild and wooly." Those who can't read are *illiterate*.

alls/all

"Alls I know is . . ." may result from anticipating the *S* in "is," but the standard expression is "All I know is. . . ."

11

allude/elude

You can allude (refer) to your daughter's membership in the honor society when boasting about her, but a criminal tries to elude (escape) captivity. There is no such word as "illude."

allude/refer

To allude to something is to refer to it indirectly, by suggestion. If you are being direct and unambiguous, you are referring to the subject rather than alluding to it.

allusion/illusion

An allusion is a reference, something you allude to: "Her allusion to flowers reminded me that Valentine's Day was coming." In that English paper, don't write "literary illusions" when you mean "allusions." A mirage, hallucination, or magic trick is an illusion. (Doesn't being fooled just make you *ill*?)

allusive/elusive/illusive

When the defense lawyer alludes to his client's poor mother, he is being *allusive*. When the mole keeps eluding the traps you've set in the garden, it's being *elusive*. We also speak of matters that are difficult to understand, identify, or remember as elusive. Illusions can be *illusive*, but we more often refer to them as *illusory*.

almost

Like "only," "almost" must come immediately before the word or phrase it modifies: "She almost gave a million dollars to the museum" means something quite different from, "She gave almost a million dollars to the museum." Right? So you shouldn't write, "There was almost a riotous reaction when the will was read" when what you mean is, "There was an almost riotous reaction."

almost always/most always

See "most always/almost always."

along the same vein/in the same vein, along the same line

The expressions "in the same vein" and "along the same line" mean the same thing ("on the same subject"), but those who cross-pollinate them to create the hybrid "along the same vein" sound a little odd to those who are used to the standard expressions.

alot/a lot

Perhaps this common spelling error began because there does exist in English a word spelled "allot" which is a verb meaning to apportion or grant. The correct form, with "a" and "lot" separated

How much space should you allot for Farmer Howard's shipment of hay? A lot!

by a space is perhaps not often encountered in print because formal writers usually use other expressions such as "a great deal," "often," etc.

You shouldn't write "alittle" either. It's "a little."

aloud/allowed

If you think Grandma allowed the kids to eat too much ice cream, you'd better not say so aloud, or her feelings will be hurt. "Aloud" means "out loud" and refers to sounds (most often speech) that can be heard by others. But this word is often misused when people mean "allowed," meaning "permitted."

already/all ready

See "all ready/already."

alright/all right

The traditional form of this phrase has become so rare in the popular press that many readers have probably never noticed that it is actually two words. But if you want to avoid irritating conservatives you'd better tell them that you feel "all right" rather than "alright."

altar/alter

An altar is that platform at the front of a church or in a temple; to alter something is to change it.

alterior/ulterior

When you have a concealed reason for doing something, it's an *ulterior* motive.

alternate/alternative

Although UK authorities disapprove, in US usage, "alternate" is frequently an adjective, substituted for the older "alternative": "an alternate route." "Alternate" can also be a noun; a substitute delegate is, for instance, called an "alternate." But when you're speaking of "every other" as in "our club meets on alternate Tuesdays," you can't substitute "alternative."

altho, tho/although

The casual spellings "altho" and "tho" are not acceptable in formal or edited English. Stick with "although" and "though."

altogether/all together

"Altogether" is an adverb meaning "completely," "entirely." For example: "When he first saw the examination questions, he was altogether baffled." "All together," in contrast, is a phrase meaning "in a group." For example: "The wedding guests were gathered all together in the garden." Undressed people are said in informal speech to be "in the altogether" (perhaps a shortening of the phrase "altogether naked").

alumnus/alumni

We used to have "alumnus" (male singular), "alumni" (male plural), "alumna" (female singular), and "alumnae" (female plural); but the latter two are now popular only among older female graduates, with the first two terms becoming unisex. However, it is still important to distinguish between one alumnus and a stadium full of alumni. Never say, "I am an alumni," if you don't want to cast discredit on your school. Many avoid the whole problem by resorting to the informal abbreviation "alum."

Alzheimer's disease/old-timer's disease
See "old-timer's disease/Alzheimer's disease."

AM/PM
"AM" stands for the Latin phrase Ante Meridiem—which means "before noon"—and "PM" stands for Post Meridiem: "after noon." Although digital clocks routinely label noon "12:00 PM" you should avoid this expression not only because it is incorrect, but because many people will imagine you are talking about midnight instead. The same goes for "12:00 AM." You can say or write "twelve noon," "noon sharp," or "exactly at noon" when you want to designate a precise time.

It is now rare to see periods placed after these abbreviations: "A.M."; but in the US, in formal writing it is still preferable to capitalize them, though the lowercase "am" and "pm" are now so popular they are not likely to get you into trouble. The lowercase forms are standard usage in the UK.

Occasionally computer programs encourage you to write "AM" and "PM" without a space before them, but others will misread your data if you omit the space. The nonstandard habit of omitting the space is spreading rapidly, and should be avoided in formal writing.

am not/isn't/aren't/ain't
See "ain't/am not/isn't/aren't."

amature/amateur
Most of the words we've borrowed from the French that have retained their "-eur" endings are pretty sophisticated, like "restaurateur" (notice, no *N*) and "auteur" (in film criticism), but "amateur" attracts amateurish spelling.

ambiguous/ambivalent
Even though the prefix "ambi-" means "both," "ambiguous" has come to mean "unclear, undefined," while "ambivalent" means "torn between two opposing feelings or

"I feel ambiguous about my progress improving my vocabulary. Sometimes I feel I've made great progress, and other times I feel I have not."

"I'll just say it's not very ambiguous to me."

views." If your attitude cannot be defined into two polarized alternatives, then you're ambiguous, not ambivalent.

ambivalent/indifferent

If you feel pulled in two directions about some issue, you're ambivalent about it; but if you have no particular feelings about it, you're indifferent.

American

Some Canadians and more Latin Americans are understandably irritated when US citizens refer to themselves simply as "Americans." Canadians (and only Canadians) use the term "North American" to include themselves in a two-member group with their neighbor to the south, though geographers usually include Mexico in North America. When addressing an international audience composed largely of people from the Americas, it is wise to consider their sensitivities.

However, it is pointless to try to ban this usage in all contexts. Outside of the Americas, "American" is universally understood to refer to things relating to the US. There is no good substitute. Brazilians, Argentineans, and Canadians all have unique terms to refer to themselves. None of them refer routinely to themselves as "Americans" outside of contexts like the "Organization of American States." Frank Lloyd Wright promoted "Usonian," but it never caught on. For better or worse, "American" is standard English for "citizen or resident of the United States of America."

among/between

See "between/among."

among/within

See "within/among."

amongst/among

Although "amongst" has not aged nearly as badly as "whilst," it is still less common in standard speech than "among."

amoral/immoral

"Amoral" is a rather technical word meaning "unrelated to morality" or "indifferent to morality." When you mean to denounce someone's behavior, call it "immoral."

amount/number

This is a vast subject. I will try to limit the *number* of words I expend on it so as not to use up too great an *amount* of space. The confusion between the two categories of words relating to amount and number is so pervasive that those of us who still distinguish between them constitute an endangered species; but if you want to avoid our ire, learn the difference. *Amount* words relate to quantities of things that are measured in bulk; *number* to things that can be counted.

In the second sentence above, it would have been improper to write "the amount of words" because words are discrete entities that can be counted, or numbered.

Here is a handy chart to distinguish the two categories of words:

amount	number
quantity	number
little	few
less	fewer
much	many

You can eat *fewer* cookies, but you drink *less* milk. If you ate too *many* cookies, people would probably think you've had too *much* dessert. If the thing being measured is being considered in countable units, then use *number* words. Even a substance that is considered in bulk can also be measured by number of units. For instance, you shouldn't drink too *much* wine, but you should also avoid drinking too *many* glasses of wine. Note that here you are *counting glasses*. They can be numbered.

The most common mistake of this kind is to refer to an "amount" of people instead of a "number" of people.

Just to confuse things, "more" can be used either way: you can eat more cookies *and* drink more milk.

Exceptions to the less/fewer pattern are references to units of time and money, which are usually treated as amounts: less than an hour, less than five dollars. Only when you are referring to specific coins or bills would you use fewer: "I have fewer than five state quarters to go to make my collection complete."

ampitheater/amphitheater

The classy way to pronounce the first syllable of this word is "amf-," but if you choose the more popular "amp-" remember that you still have to include the *H* after the *P* when spelling it. UK-standard writers spell it "amphitheatre," of course.

amuse/bemuse

See "bemuse/amuse."

an/and

It's easy to type "and" when you mean "an." A spelling checker won't catch the mistake.

an historic/a historic

See "historic: an historic vs. a historic."

analog/analogue

See "'lite' spelling."

analogous

Even though "analogy" is spoken with a soft *G*, use a hard *G* in pronouncing "analogous" so that it sounds like the beginning of the word "gust." Many people mistakenly use a soft *G*, which sounds like the beginning of the word "just."

analogy
See "parallel/symbol."

ancestor/descendant
When Albus Dumbledore said that Lord Voldemort was "the last remaining ancestor of Salazar Slytherin," more than one person noted that he had made a serious verbal bumble; and in later printings of *Harry Potter and the Chamber of Secrets* author J. K. Rowling corrected that to "last remaining descendant." People surprisingly often confuse these two terms with each other. Your great-grandmother is your ancestor; you are her descendant.

anchors away/anchors aweigh
Anchors are "weighed" by being gathered up on chains. The correct expression is "anchors aweigh."

and/or
The legal phrase "and/or," indicating that you can either choose between two alternatives or choose both of them, has proved irresistible in other contexts and is now widely acceptable though it irritates some readers as jargon. However, you can logically use it only when you are discussing choices which may or may not both be done: "Bring chips and/or beer." It's very much overused where simple "or" would do, and it would be wrong to say, "you can get to the campus for this morning's meeting on a bike and/or in a car." Choosing one eliminates the possibility of the other, so this isn't an and/or situation.

and also/and, also
"And also" is redundant; say just "and" or "also."

and plus
See "redundancies."

anecdote/antidote
A humorist relates "anecdotes." The doctor prescribes "antidotes" for children who have swallowed poison. Laughter may be the best medicine, but that's no reason to confuse these two with each other.

angel/angle
People who want to write about winged beings from Heaven often miscall them "angles." A triangle has three angles. The Heavenly Host is made of angels. Just

The angel came in at an odd angle.

remember the adjectival form: "angelic." If you pronounce it aloud you'll be reminded that the *E* comes before the *L*.

annihilate
See "decimate/annihilate, slaughter, etc."

another words/in other words
When you reword a statement, you can preface it by saying "in other words." The phrase is not "another words."

anteclimax/anticlimax
When an exciting build-up leads to a disappointing end, the result is an anticlimax—the opposite of a climax. The prefix "anti-" is used to indicate opposition whereas the prefix "ante-" is used to indicate that something precedes something else; so be careful not to misspell this word "anteclimax."

anticlimatic/anticlimactic
This word has to do with climaxes, not climate, so the word is "anticlimactic."

antidote/anecdote
See "anecdote/antidote."

antihero
In literature, theater, and film an antihero is a central character who is not very admirable: weak, lazy, incompetent, or mean-spirited. However, antiheroes are rarely actually evil, and you should not use this word as a synonym for "villain" if you want to get a good grade on your English lit paper.

antisocial/asocial
See "asocial/antisocial."

anxious/eager
Most people use "anxious" interchangeably with "eager," but its original meaning had to do with worrying, being full of anxiety. Perfectly correct phrases like "anxious to please" obscure the nervous tension implicit in this word and lead people to say less correct things like, "I'm anxious for Christmas morning to come so I can open my presents." Traditionalists frown on anxiety-free anxiousness. Say instead you are eager for or looking forward to a happy event.

any
Instead of saying, "He was the worst of any of the dancers," say, "He was the worst of the dancers."

any other number of/any number of other
When there are a lot of possible alternatives, we may say there are any number of them: "There are any number of other colors I would have preferred to this sickening lime green."

This expression often gets scrambled into "any other number of."

any where/anywhere
"Anywhere," like "somewhere" and "nowhere," is always one word.

anymore/any more
In the first place, the traditional (though now uncommon) spelling is as two words: "any more" as in "We do not sell bananas any more." In the second place, it should not be used at the beginning of a sentence as a synonym for "nowadays." In certain dialects of English it is common to utter phrases like "anymore you have to grow your own if you want really ripe tomatoes," but this is guaranteed to jolt listeners who aren't used to it. Even if they can't quite figure out what's wrong, they'll feel that your speech is vaguely clunky and awkward. "Any more" always needs to be used as part of an expression of negation except in questions like "Do you have any more bananas?" Now you won't make that mistake any more, will you?

Some Americans now distinguish between the one-word and two-word versions. "Anymore" is recommended for uses meaning "nowadays," and "any more" for other uses. Examples: "I don't bet on horses anymore" vs. "I don't want any more neckties." This distinction is not universally observed by any means. In the UK, the two-word spelling is still preferred.

anyone/any one
When it means "anybody," "anyone" is spelled as a single word: "anyone can enter the drawing."

But when it means "any single one," "any one" is spelled as two words: "any one of the tickets may win."

anytime/any time
Though it is often compressed into a single word by analogy with "anywhere" and similar words, "any time" is traditionally a two-word phrase.

anyways/anyway
"Anyways" at the beginning of a sentence usually indicates that the speaker has resumed a narrative thread: "Anyways, I told Matilda that guy was a lazy bum before she ever married him." It also occurs at the end of phrases and sentences, meaning "in any case": "He wasn't all that good-looking anyways." A slightly less rustic quality can be imparted to these sentences by substituting the more formal "anyway." Neither expression is a good idea in formal written English. The two-word phrase "any way" has many legitimate uses, however: "Is there any way to prevent the impending disaster?"

anywheres/anywhere
"Anywheres" is a dialectical variation on the standard English word "anywhere."

apart/a part
Paradoxically, the one-word form implies separation while the two-word form

implies union. Feuding roommates decide to live *apart*. Their time together may be *a part* of their lives they will remember with some bitterness.

apiece/a piece

When you mean "each" the expression is "apiece": these pizzas are really cheap—only ten dollars apiece." But when "piece" actually refers to a piece of something, the required two-word expression is "a piece": "This pizza is really expensive—they sell it by the slice for ten dollars a piece."

Despite misspellings in popular music lyrics, the expression is not "down the road apiece"; it's "down the road a piece."

apostrophes

First let's all join in a hearty curse of the grammarians who inserted the wretched apostrophe into possessives in the first place. It may well have been a mistake. In Medieval English possessive nouns ended with an *-ES* or *-YS*. Eventually the vowel before the *S* disappeared, and we were left with forms like "Johns hat." Some 17th-century writers took the result to be an abbreviation and decided that the simple "s" of possession in a phrase like "Johns hat" must have been formed out of a contraction of the more "proper" "John his hat." One theory is that since in English we mark contractions with an apostrophe, some scholars did so, and we were stuck with "John's hat." Their purported error can be a handy reminder: if you're not sure whether a noun ending in *S* should be followed by an apostrophe, ask yourself whether you could plausibly substitute "his" or "her" for the *S*.

The exception to this pattern involves personal pronouns indicating possession like "his," "hers," and "its." For more on this point, see the entry for "its/it's."

Get this straight once and for all: when the *S* is added to a word simply to make it a plural, no apostrophe is used (except in expressions where letters or numerals are treated like words, like "mind your P's and Q's" and "learn your ABC's").

Apostrophes are also used to indicate omitted letters in real contractions: "do not" becomes "don't."

Why can't we all agree to do away with the wretched apostrophe? Because its two uses—contraction and possession—have people so thoroughly confused that they are always putting in apostrophes where they don't belong, in simple plurals ("cucumber's for sale") and family names when they are referred to collectively ("the Smith's").

The practice of putting improper apostrophes in family names on signs in front yards is an endless source of confusion. "The Brown's" is just plain wrong. (If you wanted to suggest "the residence of the Browns" you would have to write "The Browns'," with the apostrophe *after* the *S*, which is there to indicate a plural number, not as an indication of possession.) If you simply want to indicate that a family named Brown lives here, the sign out front should read simply "The Browns." When a name ends in an *S* you need to add an *ES* to make it plural: "The Adamses."

No apostrophes for simple plural names or names ending in *S*, OK? I get irritated when people address me as "Mr. Brian's."

What about when plural names are used to indicate possession? "The Browns' cat" is standard (the second *S* is "understood"), though some prefer "the Browns's cat." The pattern is the same with names ending in *S*: "the Adamses' cat" or—theoretically—"the Adamses's cat." However, because these standard forms can seem awkward, "the Adams' cat" is widely accepted, with one *S* indicating both plural number and possession.

Apostrophes are often mistakenly omitted in common expressions such as "at arm's length" and "at wits' end." Note that the position of the apostrophe before or after the *S* depends on whether the word is a plural form ending in *S*. You hold someone at the length of your arm (singular), but are at the end of your wits.

Other examples: "the people's choice," "for old times' sake," and "for heaven's sake." Why is the place name in England "Land's End" but the American corporation "Lands' End"? It was just a mistake, and now the company is stuck with its misplaced apostrophe.

Apostrophes are also misplaced in common plural nouns on signs: "Restrooms are for customer's use only." Who is this privileged customer to deserve a private bathroom? The sign should read "for customers' use."

For ordinary nouns, the pattern for adding an apostrophe to express possession is straightforward. For singular nouns, add an apostrophe plus an *S*: "the duck's bill." If the singular noun happens to end in one *S* or even two, you still just add an apostrophe and an *S*: "the boss's desk."

For plural nouns which end in *S*, however, add only the apostrophe: "the ducks' bills." But if a plural noun does not end in S, then you follow the same pattern as for singular nouns by adding an apostrophe and an *S*: "the children's menu."

In names which end in *S* the possessive plural is usually formed by simply adding an apostrophe: "the Joneses' house" It's most often "in Jesus' name." "In Jesus's name" is acceptable, but those three syllables ending in *S* next to each other sound awkward.

It is not uncommon to see the *S* wrongly apostrophized even in verbs, as in the mistaken "He complain's a lot."

Unfortunately, some character sets do not include proper curled apostrophes, including basic HTML and ASCII. If you do not turn off the "smart quotes" feature in your word processor, the result will be ugly gibberish in your writing which will make it hard to read.

But if you wish to create a true apostrophe in HTML ['] instead of a straight "foot mark" ['], you can write this code: **’**.

Another problem involving smart quotes arises when you need to begin a word with an apostrophe, as in "the roaring '20s" or "give 'em a break." Smart quotes will curl those opening apostrophes the wrong way.

There's more than one way to solve this problem, but here are the easiest ones in Microsoft Word: 1) for Windows users, hold down the Ctrl key and hit the apostrophe key twice, 2) for Mac users, hold down the Option and Shift keys and hit the right square bracket key. If all else fails, you can type a pair of single quotation marks and delete the first one.

See also "acronyms and apostrophes."

appauled/appalled

Those of us named Paul are appalled at the misspelling of this word. No *U*, two *L*'s please. And it's certainly not "uphauled"!

appose/oppose

These two spellings originally meant the same thing, but now "appose" is a rare word having to do with placing one thing close to or on something else (compare with *juxtapose*). It mainly occurs today as an error spelling-checkers won't catch when the word intended is "oppose," meaning to be against something. If you object to a proposed course of action, you are opposed (not "apposed") to it.

appraise/apprise

When you estimate the value of something, you appraise it. When you inform people of a situation, you apprise them of it.

apropos/appropriate

"Apropos," (anglicized from the French phrase "à propos") means relevant, connected with what has gone before; it should not be used as an all-purpose substitute for "appropriate." It would be inappropriate, for example, to say "Your tuxedo was perfectly apropos for the opera gala." Even though it's not pronounced, be careful not to omit the final *S* in spelling "apropos."

Arab/Arabic/Arabian

Arabs are a people whose place of ethnic origin is the Arabian Peninsula.

The language which they speak, and which has spread widely to other areas, is Arabic. "Arabic" is not generally used as an adjective except when referring to the language or in a few traditional phrases such as "gum arabic" and "arabic numerals." Note that in these few phrases the word is not capitalized. Otherwise it is "Arab customs," "Arab groups," "Arab countries," etc.

A group of Arab individuals is made of Arabs, not "Arabics" or "Arabians." The noun "Arabian" by itself normally refers to Arabian horses. The other main use of the word is in referring to the collection of stories known as *The Arabian Nights*.

However, the phrase "Saudi Arabian" may be used in referring to citizens of the country of Saudi Arabia, and to aspects of the culture of that country. But it is important to remember that there are many Arabs in other lands, and that this phrase does not refer properly to them. Citizens of Saudi Arabia are often referred to instead as "Saudis," although strictly speaking this term refers to members of the Saudi royal family and is usually journalistic shorthand for "Saudi Arabian government."

It is also important not to treat the term "Arab" as interchangeable with "Muslim." There are many Arabs who are not Muslims, and the majority of Muslims are not Arab. "Arab" refers to an ethnic identity, "Muslim" to a religious identity.

The standard pronunciation of "Arab" in American English is "AIR-rub." Unless you are referring to the character in *West Side Story* called "A-rab" (with the second syllable rhyming with "cab"), you'll sound better educated if you stick with the standard version.

aren't/ain't/am not/isn't
See "ain't/am not/isn't/aren't."

arrant/errant
In modern English "arrant" is usually used to describe someone notorious, thoroughly shameless: an arrant villain, an arrant thief. It has a rather old-fashioned air to it, and is often used in antique phrases like "an arrant knave."

"Errant" is also an antique word, now used exclusively to mean "wandering," especially in the phrase "a knight errant" (a wandering knight). As here, it usually follows the noun it modifies. Although you can argue that "arrant" also used to have this meaning, most readers will regard its use in this sense today not as learned, but as mistaken.

"No, I do not want to watch that Dudley Moore movie again . . . you see, I have Arthur-*itis."*

arthuritis/arthritis
If there were such a word as "arthuritis" it might mean the overwhelming desire to pull swords out of stones; but that ache in your joints is caused by "arthritis."

artic/arctic
Although some brand names have incorporated this popular error, remember that the Arctic Circle is an arc. By the way, Ralph Vaughan Williams called his suite drawn from the score of the film *Scott of the Antarctic* the *Sinfonia Antartica*, but that's Italian, not English.

artical/article
The correct spelling is "article."

23

artisanal/artesian

For the past half-century foodies have referred to foods and drinks made in small batches by hand using traditional methods as artisanal—made by artisans: workers in handicrafts. The term has also been extended to a wide variety of other handmade products. Dictionaries agree that the word should be pronounced "ARR-tizz-uh-nul" with the accent on the first syllable and the second syllable rhyming with "fizz." Just say "artisan" and add "-ul."

Diners and restaurant workers alike commonly confuse the pronunciation of its first three syllables with that of "artesian"—"arr-TEE-zhun"—which is an adjective to describe water which spurts out of the earth under natural pressure. In this word the accent falls on the second syllable, pronounced like "tea." A spring such as this is called an "artesian spring" or "artesian well."

If you hand-bottle water from a natural spring in your backyard I suppose you could call the result artisanal artesian water.

as

In some American dialects it is common to say things like "I see lots of folks as hasn't got the sense to come in out of the rain." In standard English, the expression would be "folks that" or "folks who."

as best as/as best

You can try to be as good as you can be, but it's not standard to say that you do something "as best as you can." You need to eliminate the second "as" when "good" changes to "best." You can try to do something as best you can. You can also do the best that you can (or even better, the best you can).

Unlike asbestos removal, "as best as" removal is easy, and you don't have to wear a hazmat suit.

as far as/all the farther

See "all the farther/as far as."

as far as/as far as . . . is concerned

Originally people used to say things like "As far as music is concerned, I especially love Baroque opera." Recently they have begun to drop the "is concerned" part of the phrase. Perhaps this shift was influenced by confusion with a similar phrase, "as for." "As for money, I don't have any," is fine; "As far as money, I don't have any," is clumsy.

as follow/as follows

"My birthday requests are as follows." This standard phrase doesn't change number when the items to follow grow from one to many. It's never correct to say "as follow."

as if/like

See "like/as if."

as less as possible

The expression is not "as less as possible," but "as little as possible."

as of yet/yet

"As of yet" is a windy and pretentious substitute for plain old English "yet" or "as yet," an unjustified extension of the pattern in sentences like "as of Friday the 27th of May."

as per/in accordance with

"Enclosed is the shipment of #2 toggle bolts as per your order of June 14" writes the businessman, unaware that not only is the "as" redundant, he is sounding very old-fashioned and pretentious. The meaning is "in accordance with," or "in response to the request made"; but it is better to avoid these cumbersome substitutes altogether: "Enclosed is the shipment of bolts you ordered June 14."

as such

The expression "as such" has to refer to some status mentioned earlier. "The CEO was a former drill sergeant, and as such expected everyone to obey his orders instantly." In this case "such" refers back to "former drill sergeant." But often people only imply that which is referred to, as in "The CEO had a high opinion of himself and as such expected everyone to obey his orders instantly." Here the "such" cannot logically refer back to "opinion." Replace "as such" with "therefore."

ascared/scared

The misspelling "ascared" is probably influenced by the spelling of the synonym "afraid," but the standard English word is "scared."

ascent/assent

"Assent" is a noun or verb meaning "agreement" or "consent." "Ascent" is a noun meaning "climb." When you get people to agree with you, you gain their assent. When you climb a mountain, you make an ascent.

ascetic/aesthetic

See "aesthetic/ascetic."

ascribe/subscribe

If you agree with a theory or belief, you *subscribe* to it, just as you subscribe to a magazine.

Ascribe is a very different word. If you ascribe a belief to someone, you are attributing the belief to that person, perhaps wrongly.

ashfault/asphalt

"Ashfault" is a common misspelling of "asphalt."

Asian/Oriental
See "Oriental/Asian."

ask/question
See "question/ask."

ask/request
See "request/ask."

asocial/antisocial
Someone who doesn't enjoy socializing at parties might be described as either "asocial" or "antisocial," but "asocial" is too mild a term to describe someone who commits an antisocial act like planting a bomb. "Asocial" suggests indifference to or separation from society, whereas "antisocial" more often suggests active hostility toward society.

aspect/respect
When used to refer to different elements of or perspectives on a thing or idea, these words are closely related, but not interchangeable. It's "in all respects," not "in all aspects." Similarly, one can say "in some respects" but not "in some aspects." One says "in this respect," not "in this aspect." One looks at all "aspects" of an issue, not at all "respects."

assent/ascent
See "ascent/assent."

assess
"Assess" is a transitive verb; it needs an object. You can assess your team's chances of winning the bowl game, but you cannot assess that they are playing better than last year. "Assess" is not an all-purpose synonym of "judge" or "estimate." Most of the time if you write "assess that" you are making a mistake. The errors arise when "that" is being used as a conjunction. Exceptions arise when "that" is a pronoun or adverb: "How do you assess that?" "I assess that team's chances as good."

assumably/presumably
The correct word is "presumably."

assure/ensure/insure
To "assure" a person of something is to make him or her confident of it. According to Associated Press style, to "ensure" that something happens is to make certain that it does, and to "insure" is to issue an insurance policy. Other authorities, however, consider "ensure" and "insure" interchangeable. To please conservatives, make the distinction. However, it is worth noting that in older usage these spellings were not clearly distinguished.

European "life assurance" companies take the position that all policy-holders are mortal and someone will definitely collect, thus assuring heirs of some income. American companies tend to go with "insurance" for coverage of life as well as of fire, theft, etc.

asterick/asterisk

Some people not only spell this word without its second *S*, they say it that way too. It comes from Greek *asteriskos*: "little star." Tisk, tisk, remember the "-isk"; "asterick" is icky.

In countries where the *Asterix* comics are popular, that spelling gets wrongly used for "asterisk" as well.

astrology/astronomy

Modern astronomers consider astrology an outdated superstition. You'll embarrass yourself if you use the term "astrology" to label the scientific study of the cosmos. In writing about history, however, you may have occasion to note that ancient astrologers, whose main goal was to peer into the future, incidentally did some sound astronomy as they studied the positions and movements of celestial objects.

aswell/as well

No matter how you use it, the expression "as well" is always two words, despite the fact that many people seem to think it should be spelled "aswell." Examples: "I don't like plastic trees as well as real ones for Christmas." "Now that we've opened our stockings, let's open our other presents as well."

at all

Some of us are irritated when a grocery checker asks, "Do you want any help out with that at all?" "At all" is traditionally used in negative contexts: "Can't you give me any help at all?" The current pattern of using the phrase in positive offers of help unintentionally suggests aid reluctantly given or minimal in extent. As a way of making yourself sound less polite than you intend, it ranks right up there with "no problem" instead of "you're welcome."

at home/to home

See "to home/at home."

atheist/agnostic

See "agnostic/atheist."

athiest/atheist

An atheist is the opposite of a theist. *Theos* is Greek for "god." Make sure the *TH* is followed immediately by an *E*.

athlete

Tired of people stereotyping you as a dummy just because you're a jock? One way to impress them is to pronounce "athlete" properly, with just two syllables, as "ATH-leet" instead of using the common mispronunciation "ATH-uh-leet."

ATM machine/ATM

"ATM" means "Automated Teller Machine," so if you say "ATM machine" you are really saying "Automated Teller Machine machine."

attain/obtain

"Attain" means "reach" and "obtain" means "get." You attain a mountaintop, but obtain a rare baseball card. "Attain" usually implies a required amount of labor or difficulty; nothing is necessarily implied about the difficulty of obtaining that card. Maybe you just found it in your brother's dresser drawer.

Some things you obtain can also be attained. If you want to emphasize how hard you worked in college, you might say you attained your degree; but if you want to emphasize that you have a valid degree that qualifies you for a certain job, you might say you obtained it. If you just bought it from a diploma mill for fifty bucks, you definitely only *obtained* it.

attribute/contribute

When trying to give credit to someone, say that you *attribute* your success to their help, not *contribute*. (Of course, a politician may attribute his success to those who contribute to his campaign fund, but probably only in private.)

au contraire

See "on the contraire/au contraire, on the contrary, to the contrary."

augur/auger

An "augur" was an ancient Roman prophet, and as a verb the word means "foretell"—"their love augurs well for a successful marriage." Don't mix this word up with "auger," a tool for boring holes.

See also "all goes well/augurs well."

aural/oral

"Aural" has to do with things you hear, "oral" with things you say, or relating to your mouth.

autobiography/biography

When you write the story of your own life, you write an *autobiography*; but when you write the story of someone else's life, it's just a plain old *biography*.

avaidable/available

Many people mispronounce and misspell "available" as "avaidable," whose peculiar spelling seems to be influenced by "avoidable," a word that has opposite connotations.

"Avaidable" is avoidable; avoid it.

avenge/revenge

When you try to get vengeance for people who've been wronged, you want to avenge them. You can also avenge a wrong itself: "He avenged the murder by taking vengeance on the killer." Substituting "revenge" for "avenge" in such contexts is very common, but frowned on by some people. They feel that if you seek revenge in the pursuit of justice you want to avenge wrongs, not revenge them.

averse/adverse
See "adverse/averse."

avocation/vocation
Your "avocation" is just your hobby; don't mix it up with your job: your "vocation."

Rose was prepared to take out her revenge with a vengeance.

away/a way
"Jessica commented on my haircut in a way that made me think maybe I shouldn't have let my little sister do it for me." In this sort of context, "a way" should always be two distinct words, though many people use the single word "away" instead. If you're uncertain, try substituting another word for "way": "in a manner that," "in a style that." If the result makes sense, you need the two-word phrase. Then you can tell Jessica to just go away.

awe, shucks/aw, shucks
"Aw, shucks," is a traditional folksy expression of modesty. An "aw-shucks" kind of person declines to accept compliments. "Aw" is an interjection roughly synonymous with "oh." "Awe" is a noun which most often means "amazed admiration." So many people have begun to misspell the familiar phrase "awe, shucks," that some writers think they are being clever when they link it to the expression "shock and awe." Instead, they reveal their confusion.

awhile/a while
When "awhile" is spelled as a single word, it is an adverb meaning "for a time" ("stay awhile"); but when "while" is the object of a prepositional phrase, like "Lend me your monkey wrench for a while," the "while" must be separated from the "a." (But if the preposition "for" were lacking in this sentence, "awhile" could be used in this way: "Lend me your monkey wrench awhile.")

ax/ask
The dialectical pronunciation of "ask" as "ax" suggests to most people that the speaker has a substandard education. You should avoid it in formal speaking situations.

axel/axle
The centers of wheels are connected by axles. An axel is a tricky jump in figure skating named after Axel Paulson.

back/forward/up in time

For most people you move an event forward by scheduling it to happen sooner, but other people imagine the event being moved forward into the future, postponed. This is what most—but not all—people mean by saying they want to move an event back—later. Usage is also split on whether moving an event up means making it happen sooner (most common) or later (less common). The result is widespread confusion. When using these expressions make clear your meaning by the context in which you use them. "We need to move the meeting forward" is ambiguous; "we need to move the meeting forward to an earlier date" is not.

Just to confuse things further, when you move the clock ahead in the spring for daylight saving time, you make it later; but when you move a meeting ahead, you make it sooner. Isn't English wonderful?

backseat/back seat

Although you will often see people writing about the "backseat" of a car, the standard and still most common spelling of the noun form is as two words: "back seat." "Small children should ride in the back seat." "In a crisis, planning takes a back seat to immediate action."

The one-word adjective "backseat" is appropriate when it describes where something is. "The backseat area is cramped in this model." "Don't be a backseat driver." Conservatives prefer the hyphenated spelling "back-seat" for this sort of use: the back-seat area, a back-seat driver.

backslash/slash

This is a slash: /. Because the top of it leans forward, it is sometimes called a "forward slash."

This is a backslash: \. Notice the way it leans back, distinguishing it from the regular slash.

Slashes are often used to indicate directories and subdirectories in computer systems such as Unix and in World Wide Web addresses. Unfortunately, many people, assuming "backslash" is some sort of technical term for the regular slash, use the term incorrectly, which risks confusing those who know enough to distinguish between the two but not enough to realize that Web addresses rarely contain backslashes.

backup/back up

To "back up" is an activity; "back up your computer regularly"; "back up the truck to the garden plot and unload the compost."

A "backup" is a thing or describes a thing: "keep your backup copies in a safe place." Other examples: a traffic backup, sewage backup, backup plan, backup forces.

Older writers often hyphenated this latter form ("back-up"), but this is now rare. *See also* "phrasal verbs vs. nouns."

backward/backwards

As an adverb, either word will do: "put the shirt on backward" or "put the shirt on backwards." However, as an adjective, only "backward" will do: "a backward glance." When in doubt, use "backward."

backyard/back yard

The thing itself is a two-word phrase: you grow vegetables in your back yard. The adjective form that describes the location of something behind your house is a single word: you have a backyard vegetable garden.

bad/badly

In informal speech "bad" is sometimes used as an adverb: "the toilet was leaking pretty bad" or "my arm hurt so bad I thought it was broken." In formal writing, "badly" is preferred in both contexts.

bail/bale

You bail the boat and bale the hay.

In the expression "bail out" meaning to abandon a position or situation, it is nonstandard in America to use "bale," though that spelling is widely accepted in the UK. The metaphor in the US is to compare oneself when jumping out of a plane to a bucket of water being tossed out of a boat, though that is probably not the origin of the phrase.

bailout/bail out

Whether you are bailing out a rowboat or a bank, use the two-word spelling to describe the action of doing it (the verb form): "we need to bail out the boat before we can go fishing."

But to label the activity itself (the noun form), use the one-word spelling: "this bailout is going to be expensive."

See also "phrasal verbs vs. nouns."

baited breath/bated breath

Although the odor of the chocolate truffle you just ate may be irresistible bait to your beloved, the proper expression is "bated breath." "Bated" here means "held, abated." You do something with "bated breath" when you're so tense you're holding your breath.

baldfaced, boldfaced/barefaced

The only one of these spellings recognized by the *Oxford English Dictionary* as meaning "shameless" is "barefaced." Etymologies often refer to the prevalence of beards among Renaissance Englishmen, but beards were probably too common to be considered deceptively concealing. It seems more likely that the term derived from the widespread custom at that time among the upper classes of wearing masks to social occasions where one would rather not be recognized.

ball/bawl

To "bawl" is to cry out loudly, so when you break down in tears you bawl like a baby and when you reprimand people severely you bawl them out. Don't use "ball" in these sorts of expressions. It has a number of meanings, but none of them have to do with shouting and wailing unless you're shouting "play ball!"

baloney/bologna

See "bologna/baloney."

barb wire/bob wire/barbed wire

In some parts of the country this prickly stuff is commonly called "barb wire" or even "bob wire." When writing for a general audience, stick with the standard "barbed wire."

BAR-B-Q, barbeque/barbecue

Casual restaurants like to advertise "BAR-B-Q" and you often see the spelling "barbeque" and variations like "barbaque," but the standard form is "barbecue."

bare/bear

There are actually three words here. The simple one is the big growly creature (unless you prefer the Winnie-the-Pooh type). Hardly anyone past the age of 10 gets that one wrong. The problem is the other two. Stevedores bear burdens on their backs and mothers bear children. Both mean "carry" (in the case of mothers, the meaning has been extended from carrying the child during pregnancy to actually giving birth). But strippers bare their bodies—sometimes bare-naked. The confusion between this latter verb and "bear" creates many unintentionally amusing sentences; so if you want to entertain your readers while convincing them that you are a dolt, by all means mix them up. "Bear with me," the standard expression, is a request for forbearance or patience. "Bare with me" would be an invitation to undress. "Bare" has an adjective form: "The pioneers stripped the forest bare."

No one wondered what she had said; it was, "Bear with me."

barter/haggle

When you offer to trade your vintage jeans for a handwoven shirt in Guatemala, you are engaged in *barter*—no money is involved. One thing (or service) is traded for another.

But when you offer to buy that shirt for less money than the vendor is asking, you are engaged in *haggling* or *bargaining*, not bartering.

base/bass

Like Big Mouth Billy Bass, things musical are usually "bass": bass guitars, bass drums, bass clefs. Don't use the more common word "base" in such contexts.

based around, based off of/based on

You can build a structure around a center; but bases go on the bottom of things, so you can't base something *around* something else.

Similarly, you can build something off of a starting point, but you can't base anything *off of* anything. Something is always based *on* something else.

basises/bases

The plural of "basis" is "bases," pronounced "BAY-sees" (not to be confused with *Baywatch*).

basicly/basically

There are "-ly" words and "-ally" words, and you basically just have to memorize which is which. But "basically" is very much overused and is often better avoided in favor of such expressions as "essentially," "fundamentally," or "at heart."

bated breath/baited breath

See "baited breath/bated breath."

bazaar/bizarre

A "bazaar" is a market where miscellaneous goods are sold. "Bizarre," in contrast, is an adjective meaning "strange, weird." Let all those *A*'s in "bazaar" remind you that this is a Persian word denoting traditional markets.

bear/bare

See "bare/bear."

beat/bead

In American English when you focus narrowly on something or define it carefully you "get a bead" or "draw a bead" on it. In this expression the term "bead" comes from the former name for the little metal bump on the end of a gun barrel which helped the shooter aim precisely at a target. "Beat" is often mistakenly substituted for "bead" by people who imagine that the expression has something to do with matching the timing of the person or activity being observed, catching up with it.

beaurocracy/bureaucracy

The French *bureaucrats* from whom we get this word worked at their *bureaus* (desks, spelled *bureaux* in French) in what came to be known as *bureaucracies*.

because/due to the fact that

See "due to the fact that/because."

because/since
See "since/because."

beckon call/beck and call
This is a fine example of what linguists call "popular etymology." People don't understand the origins of a word or expression and make one up based on what seems logical to them. "Beck" is just an old, shortened version of "beckon." If you are at people's beck and call it means they can summon you whenever they want: either by gesture (beck) or speech (call).

began/begun
In modern English "began" is the simple past tense of "begin": "he began to study for the test at midnight."

But the past participle form—preceded by a helping verb—is "begun": "By morning, he had begun to forget everything he'd studied that night."

beginning a sentence with a conjunction
See "conjunction, beginning a sentence with a."

beginning of time
Stephen Hawking writes about the beginning of time, but few other people do. People who write "from the beginning of time" or "since time began" are usually being lazy. Their grasp of history is vague, so they resort to these broad, sweeping phrases. Almost never is this usage literally accurate: people have not fallen in love since time began, for instance, because people arrived relatively late on the scene in the cosmic scheme of things. When I visited Ferrara several years ago I was interested to see that the whole population of the old city seemed to use bicycles for transportation, cars being banned from the central area. I asked how long this had been the custom and was told "We've ridden bicycles for centuries." Since the bicycle was invented only in the 1890s, I strongly doubted this (no, Leonardo da Vinci did not invent the bicycle—he just drew a picture of what one might look like—and some people think that picture is a modern forgery). If you really don't know the appropriate period from which your subject dates, you could substitute a less silly but still vague phrase such as "for many years," or "for centuries"; but it's better simply to avoid historical statements if you don't know your history.

begs belief/beggars belief
You beggar people by impoverishing them, reducing them to beggary. This term now survives mainly in metaphorical expressions such as "it beggars description" (exhausts my ability to describe it) or "it beggars belief" (exhausts my ability to believe it).

People who aren't familiar with this meaning of the word "beggar" often substitute "beg," saying of something implausible that it "begs belief." This makes no sense, for it implies that the story is trying to persuade you to believe it.

begs the question

An argument that improperly assumes as true the very point the speaker is trying to argue for is said in formal logic to "beg the question." Here is an example of a question-begging argument: "This painting is trash because it is obviously worthless." The speaker is simply asserting the worthlessness of the work, not presenting any evidence to demonstrate that this is in fact the case. Since we never use "begs" with this odd meaning ("to improperly take for granted") in any other phrase, most people now suppose the phrase implies something quite different: that the argument demands that a question about it be asked—*raises* the question. Although using the expression in its original sense is now rare, using it in the newer sense will cause irritation among traditionalists.

behaviors/behavior

"Behavior" has always referred to patterns of action, including multiple actions, and did not have a separate plural form until social scientists created it. Unless you are writing in psychology, sociology, anthropology, or a related field, it is better to avoid the use of "behaviors" in your writing.

being that/because

Using "being that" to mean "because" is nonstandard, as in "Being that the bank robber was fairly experienced, it was surprising that he showed the teller his ID card when she asked for it." "Being as how" is even worse. If "because" or "since" are too simple for your taste, you could use "given that" or "in that" instead.

Belated Happy Birthday/Happy Belated Birthday

See "Happy Belated Birthday/Belated Happy Birthday."

belief/believe

People can't have religious "believes"; they have religious beliefs. If you have it, it's a belief; if you do it, you believe.

belief toward/belief in

You may have a positive attitude toward an idea, but you have a belief *in* it.

below table/table below

When calling your readers' attention to an illustration or table further on in a text, the proper word order is not "the below table" but "the table below."

bemuse/amuse

When you bemuse someone, you confuse them, and not necessarily in an entertaining way. Don't confuse this word with "amuse."

It was an act that left the audience both bemused and amused.

beside/besides

"Besides" can mean "in addition to" as in "besides the puppy chow, Spot scarfed up the filet mignon I was going to serve for dinner." "Beside," in contrast, usually means "next to." "I sat beside Cheryl all evening, but she kept talking to Jerry instead." Using "beside" for "besides" won't usually get you in trouble, but using "besides" when you mean "next to" will.

better

When Chuck says, "I better get my research started; the paper's due tomorrow," he means "I *had* better," abbreviated in speech to "I'd better." The same pattern is followed for "he'd better," "she'd better," and "they'd better."

between

"Between 1939 to 1945" is obviously incorrect to most people—it should be "between 1939 and 1945"—but the error is not so obvious when it is written thus: "between 1939–1945." In this case, the "between" should be dropped altogether. Also incorrect are expressions like "there were between 15 to 20 people at the party." This should read "between 15 and 20 people."

between/among

The "-tween" in "between" is clearly linked to the number two, but, as the *Oxford English Dictionary* notes, "In all senses, between has, from its earliest appearance, been extended to more than two." We're talking about Anglo-Saxon here—*early*. Pedants have labored to enforce "among" when there are three or more objects under discussion, but largely in vain. Very few speakers naturally say, "A treaty has been negotiated among Britain, France, and Germany."

between you and I/between you and me

"Between you and me" is preferred in standard English.
See also "I/me/myself."

beyond the pail/beyond the pale

A pale is originally a stake of the kind which might make up a palisade, or enclosure. The uncontrolled territory outside was then "beyond the pale." The expression "beyond the pale" came to mean "bizarre, beyond proper limits"; but people who don't understand the phrase often alter the last word to "pail."

The area of Ireland called "the Pale" inside the Dublin region formerly controlled by the English is often said to have been the inspiration for this expression, but many authorities challenge that explanation.

bias/biased

A person who is influenced by a bias is *biased.* The expression is not "they're bias," but "they're biased." Also, many people say someone is "biased toward" something or someone when they mean biased *against.* To have a bias toward something is to be biased in its favor.
See also "prejudice/prejudiced."

Bible

Whether you are referring to the Jewish Bible (the Torah plus the Prophets and the Writings) or the Protestant Bible (the Jewish Bible plus the New Testament), or the Catholic Bible (which contains everything in the Jewish and Protestant Bibles plus several other books and passages mostly written in Greek in its Old Testament), the word "Bible" must be capitalized. Remember that it is the title of a book, and book titles are normally capitalized. An oddity in English usage is, however, that "Bible" and the names of the various parts of the Bible are not italicized or placed between quotation marks.

Even when used metaphorically of other sacred books, as in "The Qur'an is the Bible of the Muslims," the word is usually capitalized; although in secular contexts it is not: "*Physicians' Desk Reference* is the pharmacists' bible." "Biblical" may be capitalized or not, as you choose (or as your editor chooses).

Those who wish to be sensitive to the Jewish authorship of the Jewish Bible may wish to use "Hebrew Bible" and "Christian Scriptures" instead of the traditionally Christian nomenclature: "Old Testament" and "New Testament." Modern Jewish scholars sometimes use the Hebrew acronym "Tanakh" to refer to their Bible, but this term is not generally understood by others.

bicep/biceps

A biceps is a single muscle with two attaching tendons at one end. Although "bicep" without the *S* is often used in casual speech, this spelling is frowned on in medical and anatomical contexts.

biography/autobiography

See "autobiography/biography."

bit/bitten

When Walter Brennan in *To Have and Have Not* asks "Was you ever bit by a dead bee?" the effect is to illustrate his folksy, semiliterate way of speaking. The traditional way to phrase this question would be "Were you ever stung by a dead bee?"

The simple past form of "bite" is "bit," as in "Their dog bit the paper carrier." But the past participle is "bitten," as in "The paper carrier was bitten by their dog."

In common expressions about becoming enthusiastic about something, like "bit by the genealogy bug" the verb should technically be "bitten," but "bit" is so common that it's not likely to be noticed. In other contexts where you are not sure which one works best, try "bitten." If it sounds OK, go with it.

biweekly/semiweekly

Technically, a biweekly meeting occurs every two weeks and a semiweekly one occurs twice a week; but so few people get this straight that your club is liable to disintegrate unless you avoid these words in the newsletter and stick with "every other week" or "twice weekly." The same is true of "bimonthly" and "semimonthly," though "biennial" and "semiannual" are less often confused with each other.

bizarre/bazaar

See "bazaar/bizarre."

blatant

The classic meaning of "blatant" is "noisily conspicuous," but it has long been extended to any objectionable obviousness. A person engaging in blatant behavior is usually behaving in a highly objectionable manner, being brazen. Unfortunately, many people nowadays think that "blatant" simply means "obvious" and use it in a positive sense, as in "Kim wrote a blatantly brilliant paper." Use "blatant" or "blatantly" only when you think the people you are talking about should be ashamed of themselves.

blindsighted/blindsided

When you are struck by surprise from an unexpected direction, you are *blindsided*, as if from your blind side. Do not be confused by the many punning titles using the deliberate misspelling "blindsighted" and use the latter spelling for this meaning.

block/bloc

"Block" has a host of uses, including as the spelling in the phrase "block of time." But for groups of people and nations, use the French spelling *bloc*: "bloc of young voters," "Cold War-era Eastern bloc of nations." Don't be confused by punning names for groups and Web sites like "Writer's Bloc."

blog/post

Ships used to chart their progress by heaving overboard a chunk of wood (the "log") trailing a line and measuring how much of it unspooled in a given length of time. This allowed them to record the rate of the ship's progress through the water. The resulting figures were recorded in a "log-book," which was later abbreviated to "log." The word's meaning shifted from the device floating in the water to the book in which progress was recorded. "Log" also became a verb, referring to the process of making entries in a log-book. In modern times the word drifted away from seafaring matters to refer to any record of progress created out of periodic entries.

Around the turn of the millennium, keepers of journals on the World Wide Web began to shorten the term "Web log" to "blog," and to refer to the activity of keeping a blog as "blogging." The common term referring to a single entry in a blog is "post" (short for "posting"). But "post" is also a verb: you post an entry to your blog. Amidst all this overlapping terminology many confused people have begun to refer to the individual entries as "blogs," writing "I made a new blog today" when they mean "I put a new post on my blog today."

blonde/blond

Few people will care which spelling you use, but there are some interesting points to observe about "blonde" and "blond."

In the original French and in traditional English usage, "blonde" is female and "blond" is male: it's "a blonde woman" and "a blond man."

Hair itself has no gender in English, but we usually use the female spelling in the phrase "blonde hair." Similarly, furniture made of light-colored wood is most often referred to as "blonde."

When someone is referred to as "a blonde" we almost always think of a woman, even if the spelling used is "a blond." Feminists point out that typically only women are reduced to their hair color in this way, and that it can be offensive. Note that there is a whole category of "blonde jokes" stereotyping these women as air-headed. However, when the word refers specifically to hair color in a useful way, no one is likely to object: "She is a blonde with very light skin, so she has to use a lot of sunscreen."

Oddly, we rarely use the French masculine spelling *brunet*. Anyone can have brunette hair, although "brunettes" like "blondes" are usually assumed to be women.

blunt/brunt

Some people mistakenly substitute the adjective "blunt" for the noun "brunt" in standard expressions like "bear the brunt." "Brunt" means "main force."

boarders/borders

Boarders are residents in a boarding house or school paying for their room and board (food), fighters who board ships, or more recently, people who go snowboarding a lot. You can also board animals, though usually only people are called "boarders." All of these have some connection with boards: hunks of wood (the planks of a table, the deck of a ship, a snowboard).

All uses having to do with boundaries and edges are spelled "border": border collies, Doctors Without Borders, borderline disorders, border guard.

boast your confidence/bolster your confidence

A bolster is a large pillow, and when you bolster something you support it as if you were propping it up with a pillow. Thus the expression is "bolster your confidence." People unfamiliar with the word sometimes say instead "boast your confidence." They may also be confusing this saying with "boost your confidence."

boatload/buttload

See "buttload/boatload."

bob wire

See "barb wire/bob wire/barbed wire."

bologna/baloney

"Bologna" is the name of a city in Italy, pronounced "boh-LOAN-ya." But although in English the sausage named after the city is spelled the same, it is pronounced "buh-LOAN-ee" and is often spelled "baloney." Either spelling is acceptable for the sliced meat product.

Then there is the expression "a bunch of baloney." "Baloney" in this case probably originated as a euphemism for "BS." When it means "nonsense," the standard spelling is "baloney." People who write "bunch of bologna" are making a pun or are just being pretentious.

bon a petite/bon appétit

The traditional French phrase to utter when you serve the food is *bon appétit*: "good appetite" (and pronounced "bone ah-puh-TEE"). It implies "may you enjoy your food with a good appetite." (For some reason I think this is fine but get irritated when a waiter tells me "enjoy!")

You see all sorts of misspellings of this phrase: "bon a petite," "bon à petite," "bon á petite," "bona petite," "bonapetite," "bon a petit," etc. All of these are *bon à rien*—good for nothing.

bonafied/bonafide

Bona fide is a Latin phrase meaning "in good faith," most often used to mean "genuine" today. It is often misspelled as if it were the past tense of an imaginary verb: "bonafy."

bonds/bounds

In expressions like "beyond the bounds of credibility" and "beyond the bounds of decency" the word "bounds" is short for "boundaries," and means "limits." Many people transform these sayings by substituting "bonds" for "bounds," evidently thinking of people straining against restraints, even going so far as to speak of the bonds of credibility being stretched or broken. This usage makes a sort of sense, but it is not traditional.

bonus/added bonus

See "added bonus/bonus."

boost in the arm/shot in the arm

Early in the 20th century it used to be common for people feeling a bit run-down to go to the doctor to get injected with a stimulant. By 1916 this remedy had led to a saying according to which a positive stimulation of almost any kind could be called "a real shot in the arm."

We still use this expression in a wide variety of ways. It can refer to an increase of business in a company, to a stimulus administered to the economy, to the hopes of a sports franchise or a politician running for office.

A simpler way of expressing the idea is to refer to a stimulus as a "boost." Examples: "the flowers on my birthday gave my spirits a real boost," "the large donation by the pharmaceutical company gave his campaign a major boost," "the President is looking for ways to boost the economy."

It's easy to understand how these two expressions came to be confused with each other in the popular form "a boost in the arm." After all, we go to the doctor for a booster shot. But the boost in this expression is a shove from underneath to raise the whole body, not a needle in the biceps. It makes more sense to stick with the traditional expression "a shot in the arm" or to simply use "boost."

bored of/bored with
It's "bored with."

born/borne
This distinction is a bit tricky. When birth is being discussed, the past tense of "bear" is usually "born": "I was born in a trailer—but it was an Airstream." Note that the form used here is passive: you are the one somebody else—your mother—bore. But if the form is active, you need an *E* on the end, as in "Midnight has *borne* another litter of kittens in Dad's old fishing hat" (Midnight did the bearing).

But in other meanings not having to do with birth, "borne" is always the past tense of "bear": "My brother's constant teasing about my green hair was more than could be borne."

born out of/born of
This distinction is a bit tricky. When birth is being discussed, the past participle of "bear" is usually "born": "I was born in a trailer—but it was an Airstream." Note that the form used here is passive: you are the one somebody else—your mother—bore. But if the form is active, you need an *E* on the end, as in "Midnight has borne another litter of kittens in Dad's old fishing hat" (Midnight did the bearing).

But in other meanings not having to do with birth, "borne" is always the past participle of "bear": "My brother's constant teasing about my green hair was more than could be borne."

The simple past tense of "bear" when no helping verb is involved is of course "bore": "Yesterday my wife bore twins."

The dialectical form "borned" is not standard English.

borrow/loan
In some dialects it is common to substitute "borrow" for "loan" or "lend," as in "Borrow me that hammer of yours, will you, Jeb?" In standard English the person providing an item can loan it; but the person receiving it borrows it.

See also "lend/loan."

both
"Both" refers to two items only. It is easy in speech to absent-mindedly add items to an initial pair and wind up saying things like "I like both mangos and papayas and Asian pears." Try to avoid this when writing.

How do you use "both" in a possessive construction? It's not easy. "It's both of our home town" sounds awkward. Better to restructure the sentence and say "it's the home town of both of us."

People occasionally say things like "I phoned both them," when they mean "I phoned both of them," or "I phoned them both."

both/each

There are times when it is important to use "each" instead of "both." Few people will be confused if you say, "I gave both of the boys a baseball glove," meaning "I gave both of the boys baseball gloves" because it is unlikely that two boys would be expected to share one glove; but you risk confusion if you say, "I gave both of the boys $50." It is possible to construe this sentence as meaning that the boys shared the same $50 gift. "I gave each of the boys $50" is clearer.

both of them/the both of them
See "the both of them/both of them."

bought/brought
If you pay for something, you've *bought* it; if you bring something you've *brought* it. These two words are probably interchanged most often out of mere carelessness. A spelling checker won't catch the switch, so watch out for it.

boughten/bought
"Bought," not "boughten," is the past tense of "buy." "Store-bought," a colloquial expression for "not home-made," is already not formal English; but it is not improved by being turned into "store-boughten."

bounce/bounds
A leaky ball may be out of bounce, but when it crosses the boundary line off the basketball court or football field it goes out of *bounds*. Similarly, any action or speech that goes beyond proper limits can be called "out of bounds": "Mark thought that it was out of bounds for his wife to go spelunking with Tristan, her old boyfriend."

bound/heading
See "heading/bound."

bounds/bonds
See "bonds/bounds."

bourgeois
In the original French, a *bourgeois* was merely a free inhabitant of a *bourg*, or town. Through a natural evolution it became the label for members of the property-owning class, then of the middle class. As an adjective it is used with contempt by bohemians and Marxists to label conservatives whose views are not sufficiently revolutionary. The class made up of bourgeois (which is both the singular and the plural form) is the bourgeoisie. Shaky spellers are prone to leave out the *E* from the middle because "eoi" is not a natural combination in English; but these words have remarkably enough retained their French pronunciation: "boorzh-WAH" and "boorzh-WAH-zee." The feminine form, *bourgeoise*, is rarely encountered in English.

bouyant/buoyant

Buoys are buoyant. In the older pronunciation of "buoyant" as "bwoyant" this unusual spelling made more sense. Now that the pronunciation has shifted to "boyant" we have to keep reminding ourselves that the *U* comes before the *O*. The root noun, however, though often pronounced "boy" is more traditionally pronounced "BOO-ee."

bow

When it shoots arrows, plays your violin, or secures your shoelaces, "bow" rhymes with "go." When it's a respectful bending of the body or the front end of a ship, it rhymes with "cow" and sounds just like the "bough" on a tree.

brainchild

Some people misuse "brainchild," as in "Steve Jobs is the brainchild behind the iPhone." A brainchild is not a person, but the child (product) of someone's brain. So the iPhone is the brainchild of Steve Jobs.

brake/break

You brake to slow down; if your brakes fail and you drive through a plate-glass window, you will break it.

bran new/brand new

The scarecrow in *The Wizard of Oz* (the book) was given "bran-new" brains composed literally of bran, but for everyone else the expression should be "brand new."

brand names

Popular usage frequently converts brand names into generic ones, with the generic name falling into disuse. Few people call gelatin dessert mix anything other than "Jell-O," which helps to explain why it's hard to find Royal Gelatin on the grocery shelves. All facial tissues are "Kleenex" to the masses, all photocopies "Xeroxes." Such commercial fame is, however, a two-edged sword: sales may be lost as well as gained from such over-familiarity. Few people care whether their "Frisbee" is the genuine Wham-O brand original or an imitation. Some of these terms lack staying power: "Hoover" used to be synonymous with "vacuum cleaner," and the brand name was even transmuted into a verb: "to hoover" (these uses are still common in the UK). Most of the time this sort of thing is fairly harmless, but if you are a motel operator offering a different brand of whirlpool bath in your rooms, better not call it a "Jacuzzi."

brang/brung/brought

In some dialects the past tense of "bring" is "brang" and "brung" is the past participle; but in standard English both are "brought."

breach/breech

Substitute a *K* for the *CH* in "breach" to remind you that the word has to do

43

with breakage: you can breach (break through) a dam or breach (violate the terms of) a contract. As a noun, a breach is something broken off or open, as in a breach in a military line during combat.

"Breech," however, refers to rear ends, as in "breeches" (slang spelling "britches"). Thus "breech cloth," "breech birth," or "breech-loading gun."

"Once more unto the breach, dear friends," means "let's charge into the gap in the enemy's defenses," not "let's reach into our pants again."

breakup/break up

A breakup is what happens when two people break up. The one-word form is the result, whereas the two-word form is the action that leads to it.

breath/breathe

When you need to breathe, you take a breath. "Breathe" is the verb, "breath" the noun.

breeches

The most common pronunciation of this word referring to pants rhymes with "itches." The more phonetic spelling "britches" is perfectly acceptable.

brilliant/genius

See "genius/brilliant."

bring/take

When you are viewing the movement of something from the point of arrival, use "bring." "When you come to the potluck, please bring a green salad." Viewing things from the point of departure, you should use "take": "When you go to the potluck, take a bottle of wine."

Britain/Briton

A British person is a Briton; only the country can be referred to as "Britain."

British/English

See "English/British."

broach/brooch

A decorative pin is a "brooch" even though it sounds like "broach"—a quite different word. Although some dictionaries now accept the latter spelling for jewelry, you risk looking ignorant to many readers if you use it.

broke/broken

When you break something, it's broken, not "broke," though a person or organization which has run out of money can be said in informal speech to be "broke." Otherwise, use "broke" only as the simple past tense of "break," without a helping verb: "Azfar broke the record," but "The record was broken by Azfar."

brought/brung/brang

See "brang/brung/brought."

brussel sprout/brussels sprout

These tiny cabbage-like vegetables are named after the Belgian city of Brussels, which has an *S* on the end. The correct spelling is "brussels sprout."

build off of/build on

You build on your earlier achievements, you don't build off of them.

bullion/bouillon

Gold bricks are bullion. Boil down meat stock to get bouillon. It's an expensive mistake to confuse bouillon with bullion in a recipe.

bully pulpit

We occasionally still use the old positive meaning of the word "bully" when congratulating somebody (sincerely or sarcastically) by saying "Bully for you!" A century ago "bully" meant "good," "great."

Billy, after years of theological studies and training, was more than disappointed to learn what was really meant by a "bully pulpit."

That's why Theodore Roosevelt called the American presidency a "bully pulpit," meaning that it provided him an outstanding platform from which to preach his ideas. The expression is often misused by writers who mistakenly think it has something to do with preaching at people in a bullying way.

bumrush/bum's rush

A 1987 recording by the rap group Public Enemy popularized the slang term "bumrush" as a verb meaning "to crash into a show hoping to see it for free," evidently by analogy with an earlier usage in which it meant "a police raid." In the hip-hop world to be "bumrushed" (also spelled as two words) has evolved a secondary meaning, "to get beaten up by a group of lowlifes, or 'bums.'" However, older people are likely to take all of these as mistakes for the traditional expression "bum's rush," as in "Give that guy the bum's rush," i.e., throw him out unceremoniously, treating him like an unwanted bum. It was traditionally the bum being rushed, whereas in the newer expressions the bums are doing the rushing. It's good to be aware of your audience when you use slang expressions like this, to avoid baffling listeners.

buoyant/bouyant

See "bouyant/buoyant."

burned/burnt
See "-ed/-t."

but . . . however/but, however
Since "but" and "however" perform the same function in a sentence, it's not appropriate to use them together. Suppose you have written "but the cake he made for my birthday, however, was his old girlfriend's favorite flavor, not mine." Revise this to use just one or the other. For instance: "but the cake he made for my birthday was . . ." or "the cake he made made for my birthday, however, was. . . ."

butt naked/buck naked
The standard expression is "buck naked," and the contemporary "butt naked" is an error that will get you laughed at in some circles. However, it might be just as well if the new form were to triumph. Originally a "buck" was a dandy, a pretentious, overdressed show-off of a man. Condescendingly applied in the US to Native Americans and black slaves, it quickly acquired negative connotations. To the historically aware speaker, "buck naked" conjures up stereotypical images of naked "savages" or—worse—slaves laboring naked on plantations. Consider using the alternative expression "stark naked."

buttload/boatload
The original expression (meaning "a lot"), both more polite and more logical, is "boatload."

by/'bye/buy
These are probably confused with each other more often through haste than through actual ignorance, but "by" is the common preposition in phrases like "you should know by now." It can also serve a number of other functions, but the main point here is not to confuse "by" with the other two spellings: "'bye" is an abbreviated form of "goodbye" (preferably with an apostrophe before it to indicate the missing syllable), and "buy" is the verb meaning "purchase." "Buy" can also be a noun, as in "that was a great buy." The term for the position of a competitor who advances to the next level of a tournament without playing is a "bye." All others are "by."

by accident/on accident
See "on accident/by accident."

by far and away/by far, far and away
You could say that Halloween is by far your favorite holiday, or you can say that it's far and away your favorite holiday; but if you combine the two expressions and say "by far and away" you'll annoy some people and puzzle others who can't figure out why it doesn't sound quite right.

by in large/by and large
The expression is "by and large." Some also write erroneously "by enlarge."

by the same token/on the same token

See "on the same token/by the same token."

---

cacao/cocoa

Technically speaking, the plant is called a "cacao tree" and the seeds and the chocolate powder made from them are called "cocoa." These spellings are often swapped, but in contexts where botanical names matter, it's better to stick with "cacao tree."

Neither of these should be confused with "coca," the source of cocaine.

cache/cachet

"Cache" comes from the French verb *cacher*, meaning "to hide," and in English is pronounced exactly like the word "cash." But reporters speaking of a cache (hidden hoard) of weapons or drugs often mispronounce it to sound like *cachet*—"ca-SHAY"—a word with a very different meaning: originally a seal affixed to a document, now a quality attributed to anything with authority or prestige. Rolex watches have *cachet*.

caddy-corner/catty-corner, cater-corner, kitty-corner

This expression, meaning "diagonally opposite," was formed from a misspelling in English of the French word *quatre* ("four") prefixed to "corner." Although the word has nothing to do with cats or kittens, in various dialects all three spellings are acceptable: "catty," "cater," or "kitty."

But unless you have somebody holding your golf clubs permanently stationed in the corner of your room, you shouldn't use the spelling "caddy corner."

Caesar/Ceasar

See "Ceasar/Caesar."

callous/callused

Calling someone "callous" is a way of metaphorically suggesting a lack of feeling similar to that caused by calluses on the skin; but if you are speaking literally of the tough build-up on a person's hand or foot, the word you need is "callused."

calls for/predicts

> *Glendower:* I can call spirits from the vasty deep.
> *Hotspur:* Why, so can I, or so can any man;
> But will they come when you do call for them?
> —Shakespeare: *Henry IV, Part 1*

Newspeople constantly joke that the weather service is to blame for the weather, so we shouldn't be surprised when they tell us that the forecast "calls for" rain when what they mean is that it "predicts" rain. Remember, wherever you live, the weather is uncalled for.

calm, cool, and collective/calm, cool, and collected

Unless you're living in an unusually tranquil commune, you wouldn't be "calm, cool, and collective." The last word in this traditional phrase is "collected," in the sense of such phrases as "let me sit down a minute and collect my thoughts." If you leave out "cool" the last word still has to be "collected."

Calvary/cavalry

"Calvary," always capitalized, is the hill on which Jesus was crucified. It means "hill of skulls." Soldiers mounted on horseback are cavalry.

can goods/canned goods

Is there a sign at your grocery store that says "can goods"? It should say "canned goods."

Canadian geese/Canada geese

"Canadian geese" would be any old geese that happen to be in Canada. What people usually mean to refer to when they use this phrase is the specific species properly called "Canada geese."

cannot/can not

These two spellings are largely interchangeable, but by far the most common is "cannot"; and you should probably use it except when you want to be emphatic: "No, you can *not* wash the dog in the Maytag."

See also "may/might."

canon/cannon

"Canon" used to be such a rare word that there was no temptation to confuse it with "cannon": a large piece of artillery. The debate over the literary canon (a list of officially approved works) and the popularity of Pachelbel's *Canon* (an imitative musical form commonly called a round) have changed all that—confusion is rampant. Just remember that the big gun is a "cannon." All the rest are "canons." Note that

Pachelbel's cannon fired off even more rounds than his Canon.

there are metaphorical uses of "cannon" for objects shaped like large guns, such as a horse's "cannon bone."

can't . . . too

In many contexts, "can't" followed by "too" can be confusing. "You can't put too much garlic in this stew" could mean "be careful not to put too much garlic in this soup" or "there's no limit to how much garlic you could put in this soup—use lots!"

canvas/canvass

Heavy cloth, whether in the frame of a painting or on the floor of a boxing ring, is canvas, with one *S*.

To survey ballots or voters is to canvass them, with two *S*'s.

capeesh/capisce

"Capisce?" is American pseudo-Italian slang for "understand?" and functions rather like "know what I mean?" In Italian this form would be used only in a formal setting; the typically casual American-style contexts would require *capischi*.

Since American slang uses the wrong spelling by Italian standards anyway, it probably doesn't matter that it's often misspelled as "capeesh"; but "kapeesh" is really uncool: there's no *K* in Italian.

In formal Italian, *capisce* is pronounced "cah-PEE-shay," but in slangy Italian and English it's "cah-PEESH."

capital/capitol

A "capitol" is almost always a building. Cities which serve as seats of government are capitals spelled with an *A* in the last syllable, as are most other uses of the word as a common noun. The only exceptions are place names alluding to capitol buildings in some way or other, like "Capitol Hill" in DC, Denver, or Seattle (the latter named either after the hill in Denver or in hopes of attracting the Washington State capitol building). Would it help to remember that Congress with an *O* meets in the Capitol with another *O*?

capitalization

Proper nouns (names of people and places: "Frederick," "Paris") and proper adjectives ("French," "Biblical") must be capitalized. Many people used to casual online writing patterns have begun to omit capital letters throughout their writing, even at the beginning of sentences when writing in more formal contexts. Unless your correspondent is someone that you know prefers the all-lower-case approach, to be taken seriously you should take the trouble to hit that Shift key when necessary. Particularly watch out for this sloppy habit in writing timed examinations. A teacher who has devoted 20 years to the study of Chinese art flinches when she sees her cherished subject demoted to "chinese."

caramel/Carmel

Take Highway 1 south from Monterey to reach the charming seaside town of Carmel, of which Clint Eastwood was formerly mayor. Dissolve sugar in a little water and cook it down until the sugar turns brown to create caramel. A nationwide chain uses the illiterate spelling "Karmelkorn™," which helps to perpetuate the confusion between these two words.

carat/caret/carrot/karat

"Carrots" are those crunchy orange vegetables Bugs Bunny is so fond of, but this spelling gets misused for less familiar words which are pronounced the same but have very different meanings. Precious stones like diamonds are weighed in carats. The same word is used to express the proportion of pure gold in an alloy, though in this usage it is sometimes spelled "karat" (hence the abbreviation "20K gold"). A caret is a proofreader's mark showing where something needs to be inserted, shaped like a tiny pitched roof. It looks rather like a French circumflex, but is usually distinct from it on modern computer keyboards. Carets are extensively used in computer programming. Just remember, if you can't eat it, it's not a carrot.

card shark/cardsharp

Although he may behave like a shark, the slick, cheating card player is a "cardsharp."

care less

See "could care less/could not care less."

careen/career

A truck careening down the road is swerving from side to side as it races along, whereas a truck careering down the road may be simply traveling very fast. But because it is not often clear which meaning a person intends, confusing these two words is not likely to get you into trouble.

A cardsharp may also be a sharp dresser.

caret/carrot/karat/carat

See "carat/caret/carrot/karat."

caring

Most people are comfortable referring to "caring parents," but speaking of a "caring environment" is jargon, not acceptable in formal English. The environment may contain caring people, but it does not itself do the caring.

Carmel/caramel

See "caramel/Carmel."

carousal/carousel

A carousal is a wild drunken party.

When you encounter a "carousal horse," a "baggage carousal," or a "carousal CD player," what is meant is "carousel."

If you've been invited to a "carousal party" don't head for the liquor store until you're sure you haven't just been invited to ride on a merry-go-round.

carrot/karat/carat/caret

See "carat/caret/carrot/karat."

carrot on a stick/the carrot or the stick

Authoritative dictionaries agree—the expression refers to offering to reward a stubborn mule or donkey with a carrot or threatening to beat it with a stick and not to a carrot being dangled from a stick. For me, the clincher is that no one actually cites the form of the "original expression." In what imaginable context would it possibly be witty or memorable to say that someone or something had been motivated by a carrot on a stick? Why not an apple on a stick, or a bag of oats? Boring, right? Not something likely to pass into popular usage. This saying belongs to the same general family as "You can draw more flies with honey than with vinegar." It is never used except when such contrast is implied.

case and point/case in point

The example before us is a "case in point," not "case and point."

cast dispersions/cast aspersions

"Aspersions" is an unusual word whose main meaning is "false or misleading accusations," and its only common use is in the phrase "cast aspersions." To disperse a crowd is to break it up and scatter it, which perhaps leads some people to mistakenly associate "cast" ("throw") with "disperse" but the expression is "cast aspersions."

catalog/catalogue

See "'lite' spelling."

Catch-22

People familiar with Joseph Heller's novel are irritated when they see "Catch-22" used to label any simple hitch or problem rather than this sort of circular predicament: you can't get published until you have an agent, and you can't get an agent until you've been published. "There's a catch" will do fine for most other situations.

"Here's a Catch-22: I can never remember how to use phrases correctly."

"Yes, I see."

catched/caught

The standard past tense form of "catch" in modern English is not "catched," but "caught."

Catholic religion

See "religion."

Caucasian

"Caucasian" is an outdated term originally used to refer to some or all of the people of Europe, North Africa, the Horn of Africa, and Central and South Asia. It was invented in the early 19th century by Johann Friedrich Blumenbach, who felt the Caucasian "race" was best exemplified by people living in the Caucasus mountains of Georgia. It is widely misused today as a synonym for "white." Although the concept of "race" is still widely popular, contemporary scientists have generally rejected the concept as simplistic and misleading.

The term is better avoided except in reference to people actually from the Caucasus.

cavalry/Calvary
See "Calvary/cavalry."

cay/quay/key
See "quay/cay/key."

CD-ROM disk/CD-ROM

"CD-ROM" stands for "compact disc, read-only memory," so adding another "disc" or "disk" is redundant. The same goes for "DVD" (from "Digital Video Disc" or "Digital Versatile Disc"—there are non-video versions). Don't say "give me that DVD disk," just "give me that DVD."

Ceasar/Caesar

Did you know that German "Kaiser" is derived from the Latin "Caesar" and is pronounced a lot more like it than the English version? We're stuck with our illogical pronunciation, so we have to memorize the correct spelling. (The Russians messed up the pronunciation as thoroughly as the English, with their "Czar.") Throughout America thousands of menus are littered with "Ceasar salads," which should be "Caesar salads"—named after a restaurateur, not the Roman ruler (but they both spelled their names the same way).

cease the day/seize the day

The classical Latin phrase *carpe diem*—usually translated as "seize the day"—means "act now," "there's no time like the present."

It has to do not with ceasing, but with acting.

celibate/chaste

Believe it or not, you can be celibate without being chaste, and chaste without being celibate. A celibate person is merely unmarried, usually (but not always) because of a vow of celibacy. The traditional assumption is that such a person is not having sex with anyone, which leads many to confuse the word with "chaste," denoting someone who does not have illicit sex. A woman could have wild sex twice a day with her lawful husband and technically still be chaste, though the word is more often used to imply a general abstemiousness from sex and sexuality. You can always amuse your readers by misspelling the latter word as "chased."

Celtic

Because the Boston Celtics basketball team pronounces its name as if it began with an *S*, Americans are prone to use this pronunciation of the word as it applies to the Bretons, Cornish, Welsh, Irish, and Scots; but the dominant pronunciation among sophisticated US speakers is "keltik." Just remember: "Celts in kilts."

Interestingly, the Scots themselves often use the *S* pronunciation, notably in referring to the Glasgow soccer team, the "Celtic Football Club."

cement/concrete

People in the building trades distinguish cement (the gray powder that comes in bags) from concrete (the combination of cement, water, sand, and gravel which becomes hard enough in your driveway to drive your car on). In contexts where technical precision matters, it's probably better to speak of a "concrete sidewalk" rather than of a "cement sidewalk."

censor/censure/sensor/censer

To *censor* somebody's speech or writing is to try to suppress it by preventing it from reaching the public. When guests on network TV utter obscenities, broadcasters practice censorship by bleeping them.

To *censure* someone, however, is to officially denounce an offender. You can be censured as much for actions as for words. A lawyer who destroyed evidence which would have been unfavorable to his client might be censured by the bar association.

A device which senses any change like changes in light or electrical output is a *sensor*. Your car and your digital camera contain sensors.

A *censer* is a church incense burner.

center around/center on/revolve around

Two perfectly good expressions—"center on" and "revolve around"—get conflated in this nonsensical neologism. When a speaker says his address will "center around the topic of" whatever, my interest level plummets.

center of attraction/center of attention

"Center of attraction" makes perfect sense, but the standard phrase is "center of attention."

cents

On a sign displaying a cost of 29 cents for something, the price can be written as ".29," as "$.29," or as "29¢," but don't combine the two forms. ".29¢" makes no sense, and "$.29¢" is worse.

century names
See "hundreds/century."

ceremonial/ceremonious
"Ceremonial" and "ceremonious" are often considered synonyms, and can indeed be used interchangeably in many contexts. But there are some cases in which one is better than the other.

If you are talking about the performance of a ceremony, the word you will usually want is "ceremonial" as in "ceremonial offering," "ceremonial garb," or "ceremonial dance." Sikhs traditionally wear ceremonial daggers.

"Ceremonious" is mostly used to describe formal behavior which often has little or no connection with a literal ceremony: "ceremonious manners," "ceremonious welcome," or "ceremonious speech."

chai tea/chai
Chai is simply the word for "tea" in Hindi and several other Asian languages. Indians often brew their tea with lots of milk and spices (called *masala*—they call this drink *masala chai*); and that's what most people in the West know as "chai." Since everyone likely to be attracted by the word "chai" already knows it's a tea-based drink, it's both redundant and pointless to call the product "chai tea."

chaise longue
When English speakers want to be elegant they commonly resort to French, often mangling it in the process. The *entrée*, the dish served before the *plat*, usurped the latter's position as main dish. And how in the world did French *lingerie* (originally meaning linen goods of all sorts, later narrowed to underwear only), pronounced—roughly—"LANZH-uh-ree," come to be English "LAWNZH-uh-ray"? *Quelle horreur! Chaise longue* (literally "long chair"), pronounced—roughly—"SHEZZ lohng" with a hard *G* on the end, became in English "SHAYZ long." Many speakers, however, confuse French *chaise* with English "chase" and French *longue* with English "lounge" (understandable since the article in question is a sort of couch or lounge), resulting in the mispronunciation "chase lounge." We may imagine the French as chasing each other around their lounges, but a *chaise* is just a chair.

chalk it up/chock it up
See "chock it up/chalk it up."

chalk-full/chock-full, chuck-full
Originally a person or thing stuffed to the point of choking was "choke-full." In modern speech this expression has become "chock-full," or in less formal American English, "chuck-full." Chalk has nothing to do with it.

champ at the bit/chomp at the bit
See "chomp at the bit/champ at the bit."

Champaign/Champagne

Champaign is the name of a city and county in Illinois.

Champagne is a region of France that produces the sparkling wine of this name.

Chanukah, Hanukkah

See "Hanukkah, Chanukah."

chaste/celibate

See "celibate/chaste."

chauvinist/male chauvinist, sexist

Nicolas Chauvin of Rochefort became a laughingstock in Napoleon's army for his exaggerated nationalism, and his name gave rise to the term "chauvinism," which characterizes people who wildly overestimate the excellence and importance of their own countries while denigrating others. The word was then broadened to cover an exaggerated belief in the superiority of one's own kind in other respects. Following this pattern, feminists in the 1970s invented the term "male chauvinist" to label people who considered women inferior to men. Unfortunately, this was the context in which many people first encountered "chauvinism" and not understanding that it had a broader meaning, dropped the "male," thinking that "chauvinist" was a synonym for "sexist." This misunderstanding is so widespread that only occasionally will you encounter someone who knows better, but in formal writing it is wise to avoid the abbreviated form in this restricted meaning. However, if you do intend the older meaning of the word, it's also a good idea to make that clear from your context, for a great many of your readers will assume you are talking about sexism.

cheap at half the price/cheap at twice the price

"Cheap at half the price" implies the price is too high. The only logical version of this common phrase is "cheap at twice the price."

cheap, expensive

See "expensive, cheap."

cheat/gyp

See "gyp/cheat."

Check/Czech

Pronounce the name of the country which broke away from the former Czechoslovakia to form the Czech Republic as "check," but don't spell it that way. Its citizens are Czechs.

chemicals

Markets offering "organic" produce claim it has been raised "without chemicals." News stories fret about "chemicals in our water supply." This common error in usage indicates quite clearly the lamentable level of scientific literacy in our population. Everything on earth save a few stray subatomic particles and various kinds of energy (and—if you believe in it—pure spirit) is composed of chemicals. Pure water consists of the chemical dihydrogen oxide. Vitamins and minerals are chemicals. In the broadest sense, even simple elements like nitrogen can be called chemicals. Writers who use this term sloppily contribute to the obfuscation of public debate over such serious issues as pollution and malnutrition.

"Guaranteed not to be free of chemicals!"

Chicano/Latino/Hispanic

"Chicano" means "Mexican-American," and not all the people denoted by this term like it. When speaking of people living in the US from various other Spanish-speaking countries, "Chicano" is an error for "Latino" or "Hispanic." Only "Hispanic" can include people with a Spanish as well as with a Latin American heritage; and some people of Latin American heritage object to it as ignoring the Native American element in that population. Only "Latino" could logically include Portuguese-speaking Brazilians, though that is rarely done.

chick/chic

Something fashionable can be labeled with the French adjective *chic*, but it is definitely not *chic* to spell the word "chick" or "sheek."

Cherie in her stylish egg shell cap—très chic!

chock it up/chalk it up

"Chalk it up" is a very old expression that goes back to the custom of writing a customer's outstanding charges on a chalkboard, especially in a bar. Today it means to give credit in a more general sense, as in the expression "chalk it up to experience" (credit it to experience, add it to your account of experiences). A successful team may chalk up another win.

You chock a vehicle parked on a slope by slipping a wedge called a "chock" behind its wheels.

chomp at the bit/champ at the bit

"Champ at the bit" is the only common use of this old word meaning "gnash," and it conjures up a restless horse chewing on its bit, eager to get underway. Its unfamiliarity makes some people mistakenly substitute the slangy "chomp."

choose/chose

You chose tequila last night; you choose aspirin this morning. "Chose" is the past tense, "choose" the present.

chrispy/crispy

There are a lot of menus, signs, and recipes out there featuring "chrispy chicken." Is this misspelling influenced by the *CH* in "chicken" or the pattern in other common words like "Christmas"? At any rate, the proper spelling is "crispy."

chunk/chuck

In casual conversation, you may get by with saying, "Chuck [throw] me that monkey wrench, will you?" But you will mark yourself as illiterate beyond mere casualness by saying instead, "Chunk me that wrench." This is a fairly common substitution in some dialects of American English.

Church/church

Catholics routinely refer to their church as the Church, with a capital *C*. This irritates the members of other churches, but is standard usage. When "Church" stands by itself (that is, not as part of a name like "First Methodist Church"), capitalize it only to mean "Roman Catholic Church." Note that protestant theologians and other specialists in religion do refer to the whole body of Christians as "the Church," but this professional usage is not common in ordinary writing.

See also "religion."

cite/site/sight

You *cite* the author in an endnote; you visit a Web *site* or the *site* of the crime, and you *sight* your beloved running toward you in slow motion on the beach (a sight for sore eyes!).

You travel to see the *sights*. It's called not "siteseeing" but *sightseeing*.

clamor/clamber

To clamor for something is to loudly demand it. An enthusiastic audience may clamor for an encore; and an angry populace may clamor for a leader's resignation.

As its spelling hints, "clamber" is related to "climb." To clamber is to climb strenuously. You can clamber up the steep bank of a river, or up a tower.

classic/classical

"Classical" usually describes things from ancient Greece or Rome, or things from analogous ancient periods like classical Sanskrit poetry. The exception is classical music, which in the narrow sense is late 18th- and 19th-century music by the likes of Mozart, Haydn, and Beethoven, and in the broader sense formal concert music of any period in the West or traditional formal music from other cultures, like classical ragas.

"Classic" has a much looser meaning, describing things that are outstanding examples of their kind, like a classic car or even a classic blunder.

classmate/fellow classmate
See "fellow classmate/classmate."

cleanup/clean up
"Cleanup" is usually a noun: "The cleanup of the toxic waste site will cost billions of dollars." "Clean" is a verb in the phrase "clean up": "You can go to the mall after you clean up your room."

clench/clinch
"Clench" and "clinch" are related words, but they are not interchangeable.

You clench a fist or teeth.

You clinch a deal or a victory. A reliable person comes through in the clinch.

Bent-over nails are sometimes said to be clenched, but are more often clinched.

cliché/clichéd
One often hears young people say, "That movie was so cliché!" "Cliché" is a noun, meaning an over-familiar phrase or image. A work containing clichés is clichéd.

click/clique
Students lamenting the division of their schools into snobbish factions often misspell "clique" as "click." In the original French, *clique* was synonymous with *claque*—an organized group of supporters at a theatrical event who tried to prompt positive audience response by clapping enthusiastically.

climactic/climatic
"Climactic" and "anticlimactic" have to do with climaxes, "climatic" with climate. There is no such word as "anticlimatic."

climax/crescendo
See "crescendo/climax."

close/clothes
Because the *TH* in "clothes" is seldom pronounced distinctly, it is often misspelled "close." Just remember the *TH* in "clothing," where it is obvious. Clothes are made of cloth. Rags can also be cloths (without an *E*).

close proximity/close/in proximity to

A redundancy: "in proximity to" means "close to."

closed-minded/close-minded

"Closed-minded" might seem logical, but the traditional spelling of this expression is "close-minded." The same is true for "close-lipped" and "close-mouthed."

coarse/course

"Coarse" is always an adjective meaning "rough, crude." Unfortunately, this spelling is often mistakenly used for a quite different word, "course," which can be either a verb or a noun (with several different meanings).

coat strings/coat tails

A person deriving unearned benefits by being attached to another is riding on his or her coat tails. This expression derives from the long tails on men's old-fashioned coats.

A person clinging to another's apron strings is excessively dependent on him or her, like a small child hanging on to its mother's clothing.

These two expressions are often mistakenly blended. The result is statements such as "she hoped to succeed by clinging to her boss's coat strings" and "he is still clinging to his mother's coat strings." Some coats have strings, but "coat strings" is not standard usage in either of these sorts of expressions.

cocoa/cacao

See "cacao/cocoa."

coffee clutch/coffee klatsch, coffee klatch

"Coffee klatsch" comes from German *Kaffeeklatsch* meaning "coffee chat." This is a compound word of which only one element has been translated, with the other being left in its original German spelling.

Many people anglicize the spelling further to "coffee klatch" or "coffee clatch." Either one is less sophisticated than "coffee klatsch," but not too likely to cause raised eyebrows.

"Coffee clutch" is just a mistake except when used as a deliberate pun to label certain brands of coffee-cup sleeves or to name a cafe.

If you find Walter's weightlifting wonderful, be sure to catch his coffee clutch.

coiffeur/coiffure

The guy who does your hair is a "coiffeur," just as the person who drives a car is a "chauffeur," and a restaurant owner is a "restaurateur." The *-eur* suffix occurs regularly in occupation names which we have borrowed from the French. In French all of these would be male, though Americans often refer to female restaurateurs and chauffeurs. But it less acceptable to refer to a female hairdresser as a coiffeur.

When the coiffeur has finished, the end product—your hairdo—is your "coiffure."

coincidentally/ironically

See "ironically/coincidentally."

cold slaw/cole slaw

The popular salad made of shredded cabbage was originally "cole slaw," from the Dutch for "cabbage salad." Because it is served cold, Americans have long supposed the correct spelling to be "cold slaw"; but if you want to sound more sophisticated go with the original.

coliseum/Colosseum

The standard spelling for an outdoor stadium is "coliseum," but the one in Rome is called the "Colosseum." Also note that the name of the specific construction in Rome is capitalized.

collaborate/corroborate

People who work together on a project collaborate (share their labor); people who support your testimony as a witness corroborate (strengthen by confirming) it.

collective plural

In UK English it is common to see statements like "Parliament have raised many questions about the proposal" in which because Parliament is made up of many individuals, several of whom are raising questions, the word is treated as if it were plural in form and given a plural verb. This is the proper-noun form of what is called the "collective plural." Many UK authorities object when this pattern is applied to organization names if the organization is being discussed as a whole and not as a collection of individuals. According to them, "The BBC have been filming in Papua New Guinea" should be "The BBC has been filming. . . ."

This sort of collective plural applied to the names of organizations is almost unheard of in the US, and in fact strikes most Americans as distinctly weird, with an exception being the occasional sports team with a singular-form name like the Utah Jazz, the Miami Heat, the Orlando Magic, or the Seattle Storm. There's a sarcastic saying, "The Utah Jazz are to basketball what Utah is to jazz."

Another occasional exception is singular performing group names that are sometimes treated as plural, like The Who and The Clash, though such groups are also often referred to the singular. It's almost as common to write "The Who rule" as "The Who rules."

Colombia/Columbia

Although both are named after Columbus, the US capital is the District of Columbia, whereas the South American country is Colombia.

colons/semicolons

Colons have a host of uses, mostly to connect what precedes them with what follows them. Think of the two dots of a colon as if they were stretched out to form an equal sign, so that you get cases like this: "He provided all the ingredients: sugar, flour, butter, and vanilla." There are a few exceptions to this pattern, however. One unusual use of colons is in between the chapter and verses of a Biblical citation, for instance, "Matthew 6:5." In bibliographic citation a colon separates the city from the publisher: "New York: New Directions, 1979." It also separates minutes from hours in times of day when given in figures: "8:35."

It is incorrect to substitute a semicolon in any of these cases. Think of the semicolon as erecting a little barrier with that dug-in comma under the dot; semicolons always imply separation rather than connection. A sentence made up of two distinct parts whose separation needs to be emphasized may do so with a semicolon: "Mary moved to Seattle; she was sick of getting sunburned in Los Angeles." When a compound sentence contains commas within one or more of its clauses, you have to escalate to a semicolon to separate the clauses themselves: "It was a mild, deliciously warm spring day; and Mary decided to walk to the fair." The other main use of semicolons is to separate one series of items from another—a series within a series, if you will: "The issues discussed by the board of directors were many: the loud, acrimonious complaints of the stockholders; the abrupt, devastating departure of the director; and the startling, humiliating discovery that he had absconded with half the company's assets." Any time the phrases that make up a series contain commas—for whatever reason—they need to be separated by semicolons.

Many people are so terrified of making the wrong choice that they try to avoid colons and semicolons altogether; but formal writing often requires their use, and it's wise for serious writers to learn the correct patterns.

Colorado

"Colorado" is one of three states whose names are commonly mispronounced by non-Westerners. The third syllable should sound like "rad," not "rod."

See also "Oregon" *and* "Nevada."

Columbia/Colombia

See "Colombia/Columbia."

coma/comma

Some people write of patients languishing in a comma, and others refer to inserting a coma into a sentence. A long-term unconscious state is a *coma*; the punctuation mark is a *comma*.

come with

In some American dialects it is common to use the phrase "come with" without specifying with whom, as in "We're going to the bar. Want to come with?"

This sounds distinctly odd to the majority of people, who would expect "come with us."

commas

What follows is not a comprehensive guide to the many uses of commas, but a quick tour of the most common errors involving them.

The first thing to note is that the comma often marks a brief pause in the flow of a sentence, and helpfully marks off one phrase from another. If you write "I plan to see Shirley and Fred will go shopping while we visit" your readers are naturally going to think the announced visit will be to both Shirley and Fred until the second half surprises them into realizing that Fred is not involved in this visit at all. A simple comma makes everything clear: "I plan to see Shirley, and Fred will go shopping while we visit." People who read and write little have trouble with commas if they deal with English primarily as a spoken language, where emphasis and rhythm mark out phrases. It takes a conscious effort to translate the rhythm of a sentence into writing using punctuation.

Not many people other than creative writers have the occasion to write dialogue, but it is surprising how few understand that introductory words and phrases have to be separated from the main body of speech in direct address: "Well, what did you think of that?" "Good evening, Mr. Nightingale."

Commas often help set off interrupting matter within sentences. The proper term for this sort of word or phrase is "parenthetical." There are three ways to handle parenthetical matter. For asides sharply interrupting the flow of the sentence (think of your own examples) use parentheses. For many other kinds of fairly strong interjections, dashes—if you know how to type them properly—work best. Milder interruptions, like this, are nicely set off with commas. Many writers don't realize that they are setting off a phrase, so they begin with the first comma but omit the second, which should conclude the parenthetical matter. Check for this sort of thing in your proofreading.

A standard use for commas is to separate the items in a series: "cats, dogs, and gerbils." Authorities differ as to whether that final comma before the "and" is required. Follow the style recommended by your teacher, editor, or boss when you have to please them; but if you are on your own, I suggest you use the final comma. It often removes ambiguities.

A different kind of series has to do with a string of adjectives modifying a single noun: "He was a tall, strong, handsome, but stupid man." But when the adjective becomes an adverb modifying another adjective instead of the noun, then no comma is used: "He was wearing a garish bright green tie." A simple test: if you could logically insert "and" between the adjectives in a series like this, you need commas.

English teachers refer to sentences where clauses requiring some stronger punctuation are instead lightly pasted together with a comma as "comma splices." Here's an example: "He brought her a dozen roses, he had forgotten she was allergic to them." In this sentence the reader needs to be brought up sharply and reoriented mid-sentence with a semicolon; a comma is too weak to do the trick. Here's a worse example of a comma splice: "It was a beautiful day outside, she remembered just in time to grab the coffee mug." There is no obvious logical connection between the two parts of this sentence. They don't belong in the same sentence at all. The comma should be a period, with the rest being turned into a separate sentence.

Some writers insert commas seemingly at random: "The unabridged dictionary, was used mainly to press flowers." When you're not certain a comma is required, read your sentence aloud. If it doesn't seem natural to insert a slight pause or hesitation at the point marked by the comma, it should probably be omitted.

See also "colons/semicolons" *and* "hyphens & dashes."

company names with apostrophes

Some company names which have a possessive form use an apostrophe before the *S* and some don't: "McDonald's" does and "Starbucks" doesn't. "Macy's" idiosyncratically uses a star for its apostrophe. Logo designers often feel omitting the apostrophe leads to a cleaner look, and there's nothing you can do about it except to remember which is standard for a particular company. But people sometimes informally add an *S* to company names with which they are on familiar terms: "I work down at the Safeway's now" (though in writing, the apostrophe is likely to be omitted). This is not standard usage.

compare and contrast/compare

Hey kids, here's a chance to catch your English teacher in a redundancy! To compare two things is to note their similarities and their differences. There's no need to add "and contrast."

compare to/compare with

These are sometimes interchangeable, but when you are stressing similarities between the items compared, the most common word is "to": "She compared his home-made wine to toxic waste." If you are examining both similarities and differences, use "with": "The teacher compared Steve's exam with Robert's to see whether they had cheated."

complement/compliment

Originally these two spellings were used interchangeably, but they have come to be distinguished from each other in modern times. Most of the time the word people intend is "compliment": nice things said about someone ("She paid me the compliment of admiring the way I shined my shoes"). "Complement," much less common, has a number of meanings associated with matching or completing. Complements supplement each other, each adding something the others lack, so we can say that "Alice's love for entertaining and Mike's love for washing dishes complement each other." Remember, if you're not making nice to someone, the word is "complement."

A complement can also be the full number of something needed to make it complete: "my computer has a full complement of video-editing programs." If it is preceded by "full" the word you want is almost certainly "complement."

complementary/complimentary

When paying someone a compliment like "I love what you've done with the kitchen!" you're being complimentary. A free bonus item is also a complimentary gift. But items or people that go well with each other are complementary.

In geometry, complementary angles add up to 90°, whereas supplementary ones add up to 180°.

a completely different/a whole 'nother

See "a whole 'nother/a completely different."

comprised of/composed of

Although "comprise" is used primarily to mean "to include," it is also often stretched to mean "is made up of"—a meaning that some critics object to. The most cautious route is to avoid using "of" after any form of "comprise" and substitute "is composed of" in sentences like this: "Jimmy's paper on Marxism was composed entirely of sentences copied off the Marx Brothers Home Page."

There's a lot of disagreement about the proper use of "comprise," but most authorities agree that the whole comprises the parts: "Our pets comprise one dog, two cats, and a turtle." The whole comes first, then "comprise" followed by the parts. But there's so much confusion surrounding the usage of this word that it may be better to avoid it altogether.

comptroller

Although it is less and less often heard, the traditional pronunciation of "comptroller" is identical with "controller." The *Oxford English Dictionary*, indeed, considers "comptroller" to have begun as a misspelling of "controller"—back in the 16th century.

concensus/consensus

You might suppose that this word had to do with taking a census of the participants in a discussion, but it doesn't. It is a good old Latin word that has to do with arriving at a common sense of the meeting, and the fourth letter is an "S."

Speaking of a "general consensus" is extremely common, though strictly speaking it's a redundant expression since a consensus is by definition a general agreement.

concerning/worrisome, troubling

People commonly say of things that are a cause for concern that they are "concerning": "My boyfriend's affection for his pet rattlesnake is concerning." This is not standard English. There are many better words that mean the same thing including "worrisome," "troubling," and "alarming."

concerted effort
One cannot make a "concerted effort" all by one's self. To work "in concert" is to work together with others. The prefix "con-" means "with." One can, however, make a concentrated effort.

concrete/cement
See "cement/concrete."

confident/confidant/confidante
In modern English "confident" is almost always an adjective. Having studied for a test you feel confident about passing it. You're in a confident frame of mind. This spelling is often misused as a noun meaning "person you confide in," especially in the misspelled phrase "close confident."

The spelling "confidante" suggests that such a close friend might be a female, and conservatives prefer to confine its use to refer to women. But this spelling is also very common for males, and the spelling "confidant" is also used of both males and females. Either one will do in most contexts, but the person you trust with your deep secrets is not your "confident."

conflicted/conflicting feelings
Phrases like "conflicted feelings" or "I feel conflicted" are considered jargon by many and out of place in formal writing. Use "I have conflicting feelings" instead, or write "I feel ambivalent."

Confusionism/Confucianism
This spelling error isn't exactly an English error, but it's very common among my students. Confucius is the founder of Confucianism. His name is not spelled "Confucious," and his philosophy is not called "Confusionism." When you spot the confusion in the latter term, change it quickly to "Confucianism."

congradulations/congratulations
I fear that all too many seniors are being "congradulated" for *grad*uating from high school by people who don't know that this word should be spelled "congratulations." Try a search for this misspelling on your favorite Web search engine and be prepared to be astonished.

conjunction, beginning a sentence with a
It offends those who wish to confine English usage in a logical straitjacket that writers often begin sentences with "and" or "but." True, one should be aware that many such sentences would be improved by becoming clauses in compound sentences; but there are many effective and traditional uses for

beginning
sentences thus.
One example
is the reply

"And how about ending a sentence with a preposition?"

"Yes, a preposition is a perfectly fine word to end a sentence with."

to a previous assertion in a dialogue:
"But, my dear Watson, the criminal
obviously wore expensive boots or he
would not have taken such pains to
scrape them clean." Make it a rule to
consider whether your conjunction
would repose more naturally within
the previous sentence or would lose
in useful emphasis by being demoted
from its position at the head of a new sentence.

connaisseur/connoisseur

Some complain that English "connoisseur" is a misspelling of French *connaisseur*; but when we borrowed this word from the French in the 18th century, it was spelled *connoisseur*. Is it our fault the French later decided to shift the spelling of many *OI* words to the more phonetically accurate *AI*? Of those Francophone purists who insist we should follow their example I say, let 'em eat *bifteck*.

connote/denote

The literal meaning of a word is its *denotation*; the broader associations we have with a word are its *connotations*. People who depend on a thesaurus or a computer translation engine to find synonyms often choose a word with the right denotation but the wrong connotations.

"Determined" and "pig-headed" both denote stubbornness; but the first connotes a wise adherence to purpose and the second connotes foolish rigidity.

"Boss" and "Chief Executive Officer" (CEO) can refer to the same office; but the first is less admiring and likely to connote the view of employees lower down in the company—nobody wants to be thought of as "bossy." Higher executives would be more likely to speak admiringly of a "CEO."

I often write "insufficiently complex" at the bottom of student papers instead of "simple-minded." Although they denote essentially the same quality, the connotations of the first are less insulting.

conscience, conscious, consciousness

Your conscience makes you feel guilty when you do bad things, but your consciousness is your awareness. If you are awake, you are conscious. Although it is possible to speak of your "conscious mind," you can't use "conscious" all by itself to mean "consciousness."

See also "unconscience/unconscious."

consensus/concensus

See "concensus/consensus."

conservativism/conservatism

The conservative spelling of this word is "conservatism."

contact/contract

If you touch a sick person, you have *contacted* him or her; but if you catch the disease, you have *contracted* it.

contaminates/contaminants

When run-off from a chemical plant enters the river it *contaminates* the water; but the goo itself consists of *contaminants*.

continual/continuous

"Continuous" refers to actions that are uninterrupted: "My upstairs neighbor played his stereo continuously from 6:00 PM to 3:30 AM." Continual actions, however, need not be uninterrupted, only repeated: "My father continually urges me to get a job."

contrary/contrast

The phrases "on the contrary" and "to the contrary" are used to reply to an opposing point. Your friend tells you she is moving to New York and you express surprise because you thought she hated big cities. She replies, "On the contrary, I've always wanted to live in an urban area."

When a distinction is being made that does not involve opposition of this sort, "in contrast" is appropriate. "In New York, you don't need a car. In Los Angeles, in contrast, you can't really get along without one, though you won't need a snow shovel."

Here's a simple test: if you could possibly substitute "that's wrong" the phrase you want is "on the contrary" or "to the contrary." If not, then use "in contrast."

contrasts/contrasts with

"With" must not be omitted in sentences like this: "Julia's enthusiasm for rugby contrasts with Cheryl's devotion to chess."

contribute/attribute

See "attribute/contribute."

conversate/converse

"Conversate" is what is called a "back-formation" based on the noun "conversation." But the verb for this sort of thing is "converse."

convince/persuade

Some people like to distinguish between these two words by insisting that you persuade people until you have convinced them; but "persuade" as a synonym for "convince" goes back at least to the 16th century. It can mean both to attempt to convince and to succeed. It is no longer common to say things like "I am persuaded that you are an illiterate fool," but even this usage is not in itself wrong.

cope up/cope with
When you can't keep up with your work you may not be able to cope with your job; but you never "cope up" with anything. In casual speech we say "I can't cope" but in formal writing "cope" is normally followed by "with."

copy and paste/cut and paste
See "cut and paste/copy and paste."

copywrite/copyright
You can copyright writing, but you can also copyright a photograph or song. The word has to do with securing *rights*.

core/corps/corpse
Apples have cores. A corps is an organization, like the Peace Corps. A corpse is a dead body, a carcass.

coronate/crown
A person is crowned, not coronated. "Coronate" is improperly derived from "coronation," but "crown" is the original and still standard form of the verb.

But don't be in too big a hurry to declare that there is "no such word": "coronate" means "crown-shaped," and has various uses in biology.

corroborate/collaborate
See "collaborate/corroborate."

cortage/cortege
"Cortage" is a common misspelling of "cortege."

costumer/customer
Just what would a "costumer service" do? Supply extra-shiny spangles for a Broadway diva's outfit? But this phrase is almost always a typographical error for "customer service," and it appears on an enormous number of Web pages. Be careful not to swap the *U* and *O* when you type "customer."

could care less/could not care less
Clichés are especially prone to scrambling because they become meaningless through overuse. In this case an expression that originally meant "it would be impossible for me to care less than I do because I do not care at all" is rendered senseless by being transformed into the now-common "I could care less." Think about it: if you could care less, that means you care some. The original already drips sarcasm, so it's pointless to argue that the newer version is ironic. People who misuse this phrase are just being careless.

could give a damn/couldn't give a damn

If you don't care at all about something, the standard popular expression is "I couldn't give a damn." People often say instead "I could give a damn," which should logically mean they care. Note that we say "I don't give a damn," not "I give a damn" unless it's set in some kind of negative context such as "do you really think I give a damn?" or "do I look like I give a damn?'

The same goes for parallel expressions where the last word is "darn" or some other expletive.

Just remember that in *Gone with the Wind* Clark Gable told Vivien Leigh, "Frankly, my dear, I don't give a damn."

could of, should of, would of/could have, should have, would have

This is one of those errors typically made by a person more familiar with the spoken than the written form of English. A sentence like "I would have gone if anyone had given me free tickets" is normally spoken in a slurred way so that the two words "would have" are not distinctly separated, but blended together into what is properly rendered "would've." Seeing that *V* tips you off right away that "would've" is a contraction of "would have." But many people hear "would of" and that's how they write it. Wrong.

Note that "must of" is similarly an error for "must have."

See also "verb tense."

council/counsel/consul

The first two words are pronounced the same but have distinct meanings. An official group that deliberates, like the Council on Foreign Relations, is a "council"; all the rest are "counsels": your lawyer, advice, etc. A consul is a local representative of a foreign government.

countries/states

See "states/countries."

coupe de gras/coup de grace

A *coupe de gras* (pronounced "coop duh grah") would be a cup of fat; what is intended is the French fencing term *coup de grace* (pronounced "coo duh grahss"), the final blow that puts the defeated victim out of his misery.

couple/couple of

Instead of "She went with a couple sleazy guys before she met me," write "a couple *of* guys" if you are trying to sound a bit more formal. Leaving the "of" out is a casual, slangy pattern.

No, Puss in Boots does not want to deliver a cup of fat. Puss in Boots wants to deliver a coup de grace.

69

course/coarse
See "coarse/course."

coursing through veins/cursing through veins
See "cursing through veins/coursing through veins."

cowered/coward
"Coward" and "cower" may seem logically connected. But "coward"—a noun used to scornfully label a fearful person—is derived from a French root, and "cower"—a verb meaning to crouch down, often fearfully—is derived from an entirely different Nordic one. "Cowered" is just the past tense of "cower" and should not be used as a spelling for the label given to a timid person. It's always "a coward" and "the coward."

"Cowered" is also occasionally used improperly when "cowed"—meaning "intimidated"—is meant. It is not related etymologically to either "coward" or "cowered."

cowtow/kowtow
You can tow a cow to water, but you can't make it drink. But the word that means bowing worshipfully before someone comes from the Chinese words for knocking one's head on the ground, and is spelled "kowtow."

Cracker Jacks/Cracker Jack
"Crackerjack" is an old slang expression meaning "excellent," and the official name of the popcorn confection is also singular: "Cracker Jack." People don't pluralize its rival Poppycock as "Poppycocks," but they seem to think of the individual popped kernels as the "jacks." A similarly named candy is "Good and Plenty." All three have descriptive names describing qualities and shouldn't be pluralized. A way to remember this: in "Take Me Out to the Ball Game" "Cracker Jack" rhymes with "back."

crafts
When referring to vehicles, "craft" is both singular and plural. Two aircraft, many watercraft, etc. Do not add an S.

But when referring to hobbies and skills such as "woodcrafts" or "arts and crafts" adding an S in the plural form is standard.

crape/crepe
In modern English "crape" refers to thin, crinkled paper or cloth. Black crape was traditionally associated with mourning. A crepe is a thin flat French pancake. Most Americans pronounce the two words the same, to rhyme with "ape." If you want to spell it the French way, you'll need to add a circumflex over the first E: *crêpe*, and pronounce it to rhyme with "step." Even if you use the French form you're likely to sound the final S in plural *crêpes*, though a real French speaker would leave it silent.

credible/credulous

"Credible" means "believable" or "trustworthy." It is also used in a more abstract sense, meaning something like "worthy": "She made a credible lyric soprano." Don't confuse "credible" with "credulous," a much rarer word which means "gullible." "He was incredulous" means "he didn't believe it" whereas "he was incredible" means "he was wonderful" (but use the latter expression only in casual speech).

Although you will commonly see it said of some far-fetched story either that "it strains credulity" or that "it strains credibility," the latter is more traditional. Something that strains credulity would be beyond the powers of even a very gullible person to believe. This form of the saying isn't very effective because a credulous person isn't straining to believe things anyway. Such a person believes easily without thinking. It makes more sense to say that something too weird or wild to be credible "strains credibility."

See also "incredible" *and* "begs belief/beggars belief"

creeped/crept

The standard past tense of "creep" is "crept." "Creeped" is used mostly in the slang expression "creeped out" to describe the reaction of someone to something weird or disgusting.

crescendo/climax

When something is growing louder or more intense, it is going through a crescendo (from an Italian word meaning "growing"). Traditionalists object to its use when you mean "climax." A crescendo of cheers by an enthusiastic audience grows until it reaches a climax, or peak. "Crescendo" as a verb is common, but also disapproved by many authorities. Instead of "the orchestra crescendos," write "the orchestra plays a crescendo."

crevice/crevasse

Crevices are by definition tiny, like that little crevice between your teeth where the popcorn hulls always get caught. A huge crack in a glacier is given the French spelling: *crevasse.*

crick/creek

The dialectical pronunciation and spelling of "creek" as "crick" is very popular in some parts of the US, but the standard pronunciation of the word is the same as that of "creak."

criteria/criterion

There are several words with Latin or Greek roots whose plural forms ending in *A* are constantly mistaken for singular ones. You can have one criterion or many criteria. Don't confuse them.

See also "data/datum" *and* "media/medium."

criticism

Beginning literature or art history students are often surprised to learn that in such contexts "criticism" can be a neutral term meaning simply "evaluating a work of literature or art." A critical article about *The Color Purple* can be entirely positive about Alice Walker's novel. Movie critics write about films they like as well as about films they dislike: writing of both kinds is called "criticism."

critique/criticize

A critique is a detailed evaluation of something. The formal way to request one is "give me your critique," though people often say informally "critique this"— meaning "evaluate it thoroughly." But "critique" as a verb is not synonymous with "criticize" and should not be routinely substituted for it. "Josh critiqued my backhand" means Josh evaluated your tennis technique but not necessarily that he found it lacking. "Josh criticized my backhand" means that he had a low opinion of it.

You can write criticism on a subject, but you don't criticize *on* something, you just criticize it.

crochet/crotchet/crotchety

Although all of these words are derived from a common ancestor meaning "hook" and are related to "crook," they have taken on different meanings in modern English. Those who do needlework with a crochet hook *crochet*. Your peculiar notions are your *crotchets*. And a crabby old person like Bob Cratchit's boss is *crotchety*. There are various other technical uses for "crotchet," but people who use them usually know the correct spelling. Just remember that "crochet" goes only with goods made with a crochet hook.

croissant

The fanciful legend which attributes the creation of the croissant to Christian bakers celebrating a 17th-century victory over the Turks is widely recounted but almost certainly untrue, since there is no trace of the pastry until a century later. Although its form was probably not influenced by the Islamic crescent, the word *croissant* most definitely is French for "crescent." Pastries formed from the same dough into different shapes should not be called "croissants." If a customer in your bakery asks for a *pain au chocolat* ("PAN oh-show-co-LA"), reach for that rectangular pastry usually mislabeled in the US a "chocolate croissant."

crowbar/wrecking bar

A crowbar is a straight bar with one end only slightly bent and sharpened into a beak. Often the beak is split, giving the tool its name from its resemblance to a crow's foot.

The tool with the much more pronounced hook on the end—designed for prying loose boards and drawing nails— may be considered a type of crowbar, but among people in construction and the hardware trade it is called a "wrecking bar."

crown/coronate

See "coronate/crown."

crucifiction/crucifixion

One might suppose that this common misspelling was a product of skepticism were it not for the fact that it most often occurs in the writings of believers. The word should make clear that Jesus was affixed to the cross, not imply that his killing is regarded as a fiction.

crucifix/cross

A crucifix is a cross with an image of the crucified Christ affixed to it. Reporters often mistakenly refer to someone wearing a "crucifix" when the object involved is an empty cross. Crucifixes are most often associated with Catholics, empty crosses with Protestants.

cue/queue

"Cue" has a variety of meanings, but all uses of "queue" relate to its original French meaning of "tail," which becomes a metaphor for a line (beware, however: in French *queue* is also rude slang for the male sex organ). Although a few dictionaries accept "cue" as an alternative spelling for the braided tail some people make of their hair or a waiting line, traditionally both are *queues*: "Sun Yat Sen ordered that all Chinese men should cut off their queues," "I have over 300 movies in my Netflix queue."

currant/current

"Current" is an adjective having to do with the present time. It can also be a noun naming a thing that, like time, flows: electrical current and currents of public opinion. "Currant" refers only to little fruits.

currently/presently

See "presently/currently."

currently, continuously/ongoingly

See "ongoingly/currently, continuously."

cursing through veins/coursing through veins

To *course* is to run. The most familiar use of this meaning of the word is in "racecourse": a place where races are run. When the blood runs strongly through your veins, it *courses* through them. Metaphorically we speak of strong emotions like fear, exhilaration, and passion as coursing through our veins.

Some people mistakenly substitute "curse" and think these feelings are *cursing* through their veins. This might make some sort of sense with negative emotions, but note that the expression is also used of positive ones. Stick with *coursing*.

curve your appetite/curb your appetite

A "curb" was originally a device used to control an unruly horse. Already in the

18th century people were speaking by analogy of controlling their appetites as "curbing" them. You do not "curve" your hunger, appetite, desires, etc. You curb them.

cut and dry/cut and dried

Many people mishear the standard expression meaning "set," "not open to change," as "cut and dry." Although this form is listed in the *Oxford English Dictionary*, it is definitely less common in sophisticated writing. The dominant modern usage is "cut and dried." When used to modify a noun, it must be hyphenated: "cut-and-dried plan."

cut and paste/copy and paste

Because "cut and paste" is a familiar phrase, many people say it when they mean "copy and paste" in a computer context. This can lead to disastrous results if followed literally by an inexpert person. If you mean to tell someone to duplicate something rather than move it, say "copy." And when you are moving bits of computer information from one place to another, the safest sequence is often to copy the original, paste the copy elsewhere, and only then delete (cut) the original.

cut of tea/cup of tea

An astounding number of people write "cut of tea" when they mean "cup of tea," especially in phrases like "not my cut of tea" instead of "not my cup of tea." This saying is not about fine distinctions between different ways the tea's been harvested; it just refers to the ordinary vessel from which you drink the stuff.

Is this mistake influenced by the expression "the cut of his jib" or is it just a goofy typo?

cut the muster/cut the mustard

Some people insist that the original phrase is "cut the muster" rather than the seemingly nonsensical "cut the mustard." This etymology seems plausible at first. Its proponents often trace it to the American Civil War. We do have the analogous expression "to pass muster," which probably first suggested this alternative; but although the origins of "cut the mustard" are somewhat obscure, the latter is definitely the form used in all sorts of writing throughout the 20th century. No advocate of the rival form has ever documented an authentic instance of its use in a 19th-century context. Common sense would suggest that a person cutting a muster is not someone being selected as fit, but someone eliminating the unfit.

Sometimes even mustard cuts the mustard.

dairy/diary
A common typo that won't be caught by your spelling checker is swapping "dairy" and "diary." Butter and cream are dairy products; your journal is your diary.

damped/dampened
When the vibration of a wheel is reduced it is damped, but when you drive through a puddle your tire is dampened. "Dampened" always has to do with wetting, if only metaphorically: "The announcement that Bob's parents were staying home after all dampened the spirits of the party-goers." The parents are being a wet blanket.

dander/gander
See "gander/dander."

dangling and misplaced modifiers
Dangling and misplaced modifiers are discussed at length in usage guides partly because they are very common and partly because there are many different kinds of them. But it is not necessary to understand the grammatical details involved to grasp the basic principle: words or phrases which modify some other word or phrase in a sentence should be clearly, firmly joined to them and not dangle off forlornly on their own.

Sometimes the dangling phrase is simply too far removed from the word it modifies, as in "Sizzling on the grill, Theo smelled the Copper River salmon." This makes it sound like Theo is being barbecued, because his name is the nearest noun to "sizzling on the grill." We need to move the dangling modifier closer to the word it really modifies: "salmon." "Theo smelled the Copper River salmon sizzling on the grill."

Sometimes it's not clear which of two possible words a modifier modifies: "Felicia is allergic to raw apples and almonds." Is she allergic only to raw almonds, or all almonds—even roasted ones? This could be matter of life and death. Here's a much clearer version: "Felicia is allergic to almonds and raw apples." "Raw" now clearly modifies only "apples."

Dangling modifiers involving verbs are especially common and sometimes difficult to spot. For instance, consider this sentence: "Having bought the harpsichord, it now needed tuning." There is no one mentioned in the sentence who did the buying. One way to fix this is to insert the name of someone and make the two halves of the sentence parallel in form: "Wei Chi, having bought the harpsichord, now needed to tune it." If you have a person in mind, it is easy to forget the reader needs to be told about that person; but he or she can't be just "understood."

Here's another sentence with a dangling modifier, in this case at the end of a sentence: "The retirement party was a disaster, not having realized that Arthur had been jailed the previous week." There is nobody here doing the realizing. One fix: "The retirement party was a disaster because we had not realized that Arthur had been jailed the previous week."

Using passive verbs will often trip you up: "In reviewing Gareth's computer records, hundreds of hours spent playing online games were identified." This sort of thing looks fine to a lot of people and in fact is common in professional writing, but technically somebody specific needs to be mentioned in the sentence as doing the identifying. Inserting a doer and shifting to the active voice will fix the problem. While we're at it, let's make clear that Gareth was doing the playing: "The auditor, in checking Gareth's computer records, identified hundreds of hours that he had spent playing online games."

Adverbs like "almost," "even," "hardly," "just," "only," and "nearly" are especially likely to get stuck in the wrong spot in a sentence. "Romeo almost kissed Juliet as soon as he met her" means he didn't kiss her—he only held her hand. True, but you might want to say something quite different: "Romeo kissed Juliet almost as soon as he met her." The placement of the modifier is crucial.

See also "only."

daring-do/derring-do

The expression logically should be "feats of daring-do" because that's just what it means: deeds of extreme daring. But through a chain of misunderstandings explained in the *Oxford English Dictionary*, the standard form evolved with the unusual spelling "derring-do," and "daring-do" is an error.

dashes

See "hyphens & dashes."

data/datum

There are several words with Latin or Greek roots whose plural forms ending in *A* are constantly mistaken for singular ones. "Datum" is so rare now in English that people may assume "data" has no singular form. Many American usage communities, however, use "data" as a singular and some have even gone so far as to invent "datums" as a new plural. This is a case where you need to know the patterns of your context. An engineer or scientist used to writing "the data is" may well find that the editors of a journal or publishing house insist on changing this phrase to "the data are." Usage is so evenly split in this case that there is no automatic way of determining which is right; but writers addressing an international audience of nonspecialists would probably be safer treating "data" as plural.

See also "criteria/criterion" *and* "media/medium."

dateline/deadline

The word "dateline" is used today mainly to label the bit of text at the top of a printed news story that indicates where and—often, but not always—when it was written. For instance, after a headline about events in Kenya, the dateline might read "NAIROBI, Kenya, June 2, 2013."

Probably because this rather obscure word has been popularized by its use for the name of an NBC television news show, some people confuse it with "deadline," which is most often the date by which something must be accomplished. You can miss deadlines, meet deadlines, or have to deal with short deadlines—but not datelines.

daylight savings time/daylight saving time
The official term is "daylight saving time," not "savings time."

de rigueur
The French phrase *de rigueur* means "required," "mandatory" (usually according to custom, etiquette, or fashion). It's one of those tricky words like "liqueur" with a *U* before the *E* and another one after it. It is misspelled in a host of ways (*de rigeur, de rigor, derigor*, etc.) It is pronounced duh-ree-GUHR. Like other incompletely adopted foreign phrases, it is usually italicized in print.

deaf/hearing-impaired
See "hearing-impaired/deaf."

deal
Popular expressions like "not that big a deal" and "what's the deal?" in which "deal" stands vaguely for something like "situation" are fine in casual spoken English, but inappropriate in formal writing.

Even in casual speech, it's better to leave out the "of" in "not that big of a deal."

deal-breaker/show-stopper
See "show-stopper/deal-breaker."

dealed/dealt
The standard past tense of "deal" is not "dealed" but "dealt." The only exception is the rhyming expression "wheeled and dealed," which is not formal English.

death nail/death knell, nail in the coffin
"Death nail" is a result of confusing two expressions with similar meanings.

The first is "death knell." When a large bell (like a church bell) rings—or tolls—it *knells*. When a bell is rung slowly to mark the death of someone, it is said to sound the death knell. But "death knell" is more often used figuratively, as in "his arrest for embezzlement sounded the death knell for Rob's campaign to be state treasurer."

Another way to describe the final blow that finishes someone or something off is "put the last nail in the coffin," as in "a huge budget cut put the last nail in the coffin of the city's plan to erect a statue of the mayor's dog." Something not yet fatal but seriously damaging can be said to "drive another nail" in its coffin.

debrief

"Debrief" has leaked out of the military and national security realms into the business world, where people seem pretty confused about it. When you send people out on missions, you brief them—give them information they'll need. When they come back, you *debrief* them by asking them what they did and found out. Note that in both cases it's not the person doing the actual work but the boss or audience that does the briefing and debriefing. But people commonly use "debrief" when they mean "report."

The verb "brief" comes originally from law, where someone being given a legal brief (instructions on handling a case) can be said to have been briefed. Debriefing has nothing to do with underwear.

decade names

There's no requirement for the apostrophe before the *S* in decade names like 50s and 60s, since there are no omitted letters, though it's also acceptable to include one. The term may be written "'50s" since "19" is being omitted, but "50s" is fine too. Writers who wish to have their references to decades clearly understood in the 21st century would be well advised not to omit the first two digits.

Note that you may have to turn off "smart quotes" in your word processor to get a leading apostrophe like the one in "'50s" to curl correctly unless you know how to type the character directly. Or you can just type two apostrophes in a row and delete the first one.

decent/descent/dissent

"Decent" (rhymes with "recent") is used to label actions, things, or people that are respectable, appropriate, satisfactory, or kind.

The word to use when discussing ancestry is "descent" (rhymes with "we sent"). Somebody whose ancestors came from Brazil is of Brazilian descent.

Occasionally this latter word is confused with "dissent," which means "disagreement."

deceptively

If you say of a soldier that he is "deceptively brave" you might be understood to mean that although he appears cowardly he is

Fernando took it as a compliment when they called him "deceptively brave." Little did he know . . .

actually brave, or that although he appears brave he is actually cowardly. This ambiguity should cause you to be very careful about using "deceptive" and "deceptively" to make clear which meaning you intend.

decimate/annihilate, slaughter, etc.

This comes under the heading of the truly picky. Despite the fact that most dictionaries have caved in, some of us still remember that when the Romans killed one out of every 10 (*decem*) soldiers in a rebellious group as an example to the others, they decimated them. People sensitive to the roots of words are uncomfortably reminded of that 10 percent figure when they see the word used instead to mean "annihilate," "obliterate," etc. You can usually get away with using "decimate" to mean "drastically reduce in numbers," but you're taking a bigger risk when you use it to mean "utterly wipe out."

deep-seeded/deep-seated

Those who pine for the oral cultures of Ye Olden Dayes can rejoice as we enter an era where many people are unfamiliar with common expressions in print and know them only by hearsay.* The result is mistakes like "deep-seeded." The expression has nothing to do with a feeling being planted deep within one, but instead refers to its being seated firmly within one's breast: "My aversion to anchovies is deep-seated." Compounding their error, most people who misuse this phrase leave the hyphen out. Tennis players may be seeded, but not feelings.

defamation/deformation

Someone who defames you, seeking to destroy your reputation (making you ill-famed), is engaging in defamation of character. Only if someone succeeded in actually making you a worse person could you claim that they had deformed your character.

defence/defense

If you are writing for a British publication, use "defence," but the American "defense" has the advantages of greater antiquity, similarity to the words from which it was derived, and consistency with words like "defensible." The pronunciation used in sports which accents the first syllable ("DEE-fense") should not be used when discussing military, legal, or other sorts of defense.

People in sports use "defense" as a verb meaning "defend against," as in "the team couldn't defense that strategy." Outside of sports talk, "defense" is never a verb.

definate/definite

Any vowel in an unstressed position can sometimes have the sound linguists call a *schwa*: "uh." The result is that many people tend to guess when they hear

---

* The notion that English should be spelled as it is pronounced is widespread, but history is against the reformers in most cases. Pronunciation is often a poor guide to spelling. The veneration of certain political movements for the teaching of reading through phonics is nicely caricatured by a t-shirt slogan I've seen: "Hukt awn fonix."

this sound, but "definite" is definitely the right spelling. Also common are various misspellings of "definitely," including the bizarre "defiantly."

defuse/diffuse

You defuse a dangerous situation by treating it like a bomb and removing its fuse; to diffuse, in contrast, is to spread something out: "Bob's cheap cologne diffused throughout the room, wrecking the wine-tasting."

degrade/denigrate/downgrade

See "downgrade/degrade/denigrate."

degree titles

When you are writing phrases like "bachelor's degree," "master of arts degree" and "doctor of philosophy degree" use all lower-case spelling. Less formally, these are often abbreviated to "bachelor's," "master's," and "doctorate": "I earned my master's at Washington State University."

The only time to capitalize the spelled-out forms of degree names is when you are specifying a particular degree's name: "Master of English Composition." However, the abbreviations BA, MA, and PhD are all capitalized. In modern usage periods are not usually added.

Be careful not to omit the apostrophes where needed. Some schools have adopted a spelling of "Masters" without an apostrophe, and if you work for one of them you may have to adopt this non-standard form for institutional work; but usage guides uniformly recommend the apostrophe.

deities/dieties

See "dieties/deities."

deja vu

In French *déjà vu* means literally "already seen" and usually refers to something excessively familiar. However, the phrase—sans accent marks—was introduced into English mainly as a psychological term indicating the sensation one experiences when feeling that something has been experienced before when this is in fact not the case. If you feel strongly that you have been previously in a place where you know you have never before been, you are experiencing a sensation of deja vu. English usage is rapidly sliding back toward the French meaning, confusing listeners who expect the phrase to refer to a false sensation rather than a factual familiarity, as in "Congress is in session and talking about campaign finance reform, creating a sense of deja vu." In this relatively new sense, the phrase has the same associations as the colloquial "same old same old" (increasingly often misspelled "sameo sameo" by illiterates). A common misspelling by those who know a little French is "deja vous."

Baseball player Yogi Berra famously mangled this expression in his redundant statement, "It's like deja vu all over again." Over the ensuing decades clever writers would allude to this blunder in their prose by repeating the phrase "deja vu all over again," assuming that their readers would catch the allusion and share a chuckle with them. Unfortunately, recently the phrase has been worn to a frazzle and become all but substituted for the original, so that not only has it become a very tired joke indeed—a whole generation has grown up thinking that Berra's malapropism is the correct form of the expression. Give it a rest, folks!

Democrat Party/Democratic Party

Certain Republican members of Congress have played the childish game in recent years of referring to the opposition as the "Democrat Party," hoping to imply that Democrats are not truly democratic. They succeed only in making themselves sound ignorant, and so will you if you imitate them. The name is "Democratic Party." After all, we don't say "Republic Party."

demure/demur

A quiet, reserved person is demure. Its second syllable begins with a kittenish "mew": "de-MYURE."

The verb *demur* has several meanings, but is now used in a sense derived from law to describe the action of someone who resists acting as requested or answering a question. Its second syllable sounds like the "mur" in "murmur": "duh-MURR." Note that it is not spelled with a final *E*. It is used mainly in legal contexts and in journalism, and is unfamiliar enough to many people that they mix it up with the adjective *demure*. An example of correct use: "If they ask me to make Danish pastries again, I'm going to demur." Demurs are usually mild, not loud, vehement refusals.

denied of/denied

If you are deprived of your rights you are denied them; but that's no reason to confuse these two expressions with each other. You can't be "denied of" anything.

denote/connote

See "connote/denote."

depends/depends on

In casual speech, we say, "It depends who plays the best defense," but in writing follow "depends" with "on."

depravation/deprivation

There is a rare word spelled "depravation" which has to do with something being depraved, corrupted, perverted.

But the spelling you're more likely to need is "deprivation," which has to do with being deprived of desirable things like sleep or chocolate.

depreciate/deprecate

To depreciate something is to actually make it worse, whereas to deprecate something is simply to speak or think of it in a manner that demonstrates your low opinion of it.

See also "downgrade/degrade/denigrate."

derring-do/daring-do
See "daring-do/derring-do."

descent
See "decent/descent/dissent."

descendant/ancestor
See "ancestor/descendant."

desert/dessert
Perhaps these two words are confused partly because "dessert" is one of the few words in English with a double *S* pronounced like *Z* ("brassiere" is another). That impoverished stretch of sand called a "desert" can only afford one *S*. In contrast, that rich gooey extra thing at the end of the meal called a "dessert" indulges in two of them. The word in the phrase "he got his just deserts" is confusingly pronounced just like "desserts."

desirable/desirous
When you desire something, you are desirous of it. The thing you desire is desirable.

despite/in spite of
See "in spite of/despite."

deviant/deviate
The technical term used by professionals to label someone whose behavior deviates from the norm is "deviate," but if you want to tease a perv friend you may as well call him a "deviant"—that's what almost everybody else says. In your sociology class, however, you might want to stick with "deviate."

device/devise
"Device" is a noun. A can-opener is a device. "Devise" is a verb. You can devise a plan for opening a can with a sharp rock instead. Only in law is "devise" properly used as a noun, meaning something deeded in a will.

devote/devout
If you are devoted to a particular religion, you are *devout*, not *devote*. You may be a devout Christian, a devout Catholic, a devout Jew, a devout Buddhist, etc.

"Devote" (with no final *D*) is a verb, something you do rather than something you are. You may devote a lot of your time to working at a food bank, or building model airplanes, for instance.

If you are enthusiastically dedicated to an activity, a cause or person, you are *devoted* to it. You can be devoted to your gardening, to collecting money for Unicef, or to your pet. You can be a devoted father, husband, or a devoted runner or knitter. You can be a devoted fan of the Seattle Storm. If you have a lot of fans, you may have a devoted following. The devotion involved need not be religious.

dew/do/doo/due

The original pronunciation of "dew" and "due" rhymed with "pew," but American pronunciation has shifted toward pronouncing all of these words alike, and the result is much confusion in standard phrases. On a damp morning there is dew on the grass. Doo on the grass is the result of failing to pick up after your dog. The most common confusion is substituting "do" for "due" (owing) in phrases like "credit is due," "due to circumstances," and "bill is due."

"Do" is normally a verb, but it can be a noun with meanings like "party," "hairdo," and "dos and don'ts." Note that in the last phrase it is not necessary to insert an apostrophe before the *S*, and that if you choose to do so you'll wind up with two apostrophes awkwardly close together: "don't's."

diaeresis

See "accent marks."

dialate/dilate

The influence of "dial" causes many people to mispronounce and misspell "dilate" by adding an extra syllable.

dialogue/discuss

"Dialogue" as a verb in sentences like "The Math Department will dialogue with the Dean about funding" is commonly used jargon in business and education settings, but abhorred by traditionalists. Say "have a dialogue" or "discuss" instead.

diary/dairy

See "dairy/diary."

did/done

See "done/did."

died after

See "killed after/killed in, killed by, died after."

dieties/deities

This one is always good for a laugh. The gods are deities, after the Latin *deus*, meaning "god."

Just four weeks on the South Beach Diet, and the deity looked great!

differ/vary

"Vary" can mean "differ," but saying "our opinions vary" makes it sound as if they were changing all the time when what you really mean is "our opinions differ." Pay attention to context when choosing one of these words.

different than/different from/different to

Americans say "Scuba-diving is different from snorkeling," the British often say "different to" (though most UK style guides disapprove), and many say "different than," though to some of us this sounds weird. However, though certain conservatives object, you can usually get away with "different than" if a full clause follows: "Your pashmina shawl looks different than it used to since the cat slept on it."

differently abled, physically challenged/disabled

These rather awkward euphemisms for "disabled" have attracted widespread scorn and mockery. They have achieved some limited currency, but it's generally safer to use "disabled."

diffuse/defuse

See "defuse/diffuse."

digestive track/digestive tract

It may seem logical to think of your guts as forming a track through your body, but the correct spelling is "digestive tract."

dike/dyke

In the US the barrier preventing a flood is called a "dike." "Dyke" is a term for a type of lesbian, generally considered insulting but adopted as a label for themselves by some lesbians.

dilate/dialate

See "dialate/dilate."

dilemma/difficulty

A dilemma is a difficult choice, not just any difficulty or problem. Whether to invite your son's mother to his high school graduation when your current wife hates her is a dilemma. Cleaning up after a hurricane is just a problem, though a difficult one.

"Dilemna" is a common misspelling of "dilemma."

dire straights/dire straits

When you are threading your way through troubles as if you were traversing a dangerously narrow passage, you are in "dire straits." The expression and the band by that name are often transformed by those who don't understand the word "strait" into "dire straights."

See also "straight/strait."

directions

Compass points like "north," "east," "south," and "west" are not capitalized when they are mere directions: the geese fly south for the winter and the sun sets in the west.

Capitalize these words only in the names of specific places identifiable on a map: Alabama is in the Deep South (the region which includes the Southern States) and Santa Claus lives at the North Pole.

The same pattern holds for the adjectival forms. It's a southern exposure, but Southern hospitality. Note that "The Westward Movement" (now often called the "Westward Expansion") refers to a specific series of migrations toward a specific region in the western part of the US.

"Yes, and when I turn around it becomes an Eastward Expansion!"

"Your Westward Expansion is expanding!"

disabled/differently abled, physically challenged
See "differently abled, physically challenged/disabled."

disasterous/disastrous
"Disastrous" has only three syllables, and is pronounced *diz-ASS-truss*. Because of its relationship to the word "disaster" many people insert an extra second syllable when speaking the word aloud, or even when writing it, resulting in "disasterous." Not a disastrous error, but it can be an embarrassing one.

disburse/disperse
You *disburse* money by taking it out of your purse (French *bourse*) and distributing it. If you refuse to hand out any money, the eager mob of beggars before you may *disperse* (scatter).

disc/disk
"Compact disc" is spelled with a *C* because that's how its inventors decided it should be rendered; but a computer hard disk is spelled with a *K*. In modern technological contexts, "disks" usually reproduce data magnetically, while "discs" (CD-ROMs, DVDs, etc.) reproduce it "optically," with lasers.

disconcerning/concerning, discerning
This odd word looks like it might be an error for "disconcerting," but people who use it seem mostly to mean something like "discerning" (perceiving) or "concerning" (in the sense of "being of concern," itself widely considered an error).

discreet/discrete
The more common word is "discreet," meaning "prudent, circumspect": "When arranging the party for Agnes, be sure to be discreet; we want her to be surprised." "Discrete" means "separate, distinct": "He arranged the guest list into two discrete groups: meat-eaters and vegetarians." Note how the *T* separates the two *E*'s in "discrete."

discretion/disgression
See "disgression/discretion."

discretion is the better part of valor

In Shakespeare's *Henry IV, Part I* when Prince Hal finds the cowardly Falstaff pretending to be dead on the battlefield, the prince assumes he has been killed. After the prince leaves the stage, Falstaff rationalizes "The better part of Valour, is Discretion; in the which better part, I haue saued my life" (spelling and punctuation from the *First Folio,* Act 5, Scene 3, lines 3085–3086).

Falstaff is saying that the best part of courage is caution, which we are to take as a joke. Truly courageous people may be cautious, but caution is not the most important characteristic of courage.

This passage is loosely alluded to in the saying "discretion is the better part of valor," which is usually taken to mean that caution is better than rash courage or that discretion is the best *kind* of courage. Only Shakespeare scholars are likely to be annoyed by this usage.

However, those who take "discretion" in this context to mean the quality of being discreet—cautiously quiet—are more likely to annoy their readers.

Much more of a problem are misspellings like "descretion," "disgression," "digression," and "desecration." Unless you are deliberately punning, stick with "discretion."

discuss/dialogue

See "dialogue/discuss."

discussed/disgust

"Discussed" is the past tense of the verb "discuss." Don't substitute for it the noun "disgust" in such sentences as "The couple's wedding plans were thoroughly discussed."

disease names

The medical profession has urged since the 1970s the dropping of the possessive *S* at the end of disease names which were originally named after their discoverers ("eponymous disease names"). The possessive is thought to confuse people by implying that the persons named actually had the disease. Thus "Ménière's syndrome" became "Ménière syndrome," Bright's disease" became "Bright disease" and "Asperger's syndrome" became "Asperger syndrome."

But the public has not always followed this rule. "Alzheimer disease" is still widely called "Alzheimer's disease" or just "Alzheimer's." Only among professionals is this really considered a mistake.

"Down syndrome," named after John Langdon Down—originally written "Down's syndrome"—has been so often mistakenly written without its apostrophe as "Downs syndrome" that many people conclude that the syndrome's discoverer must have been named "Downs."

Although some professionals write "Huntington disease"—originally "Huntington's chorea"—many still write "Huntington's." But another popular name for this illness is "Woody Guthrie's disease" because the folksinger actually had it, though one also occasionally sees "Woody Guthrie disease."

Lou Gehrig's disease, named after its most famous sufferer, always bears an apostrophe-*S* because professionals prefer the rather more cumbersome but nonpossessive "amyotrophic lateral sclerosis" (ALS).

The best practice is to follow the pattern prevalent in your social context. If you are a medical professional, you'll probably want to avoid the possessive forms.

"Legionnaires' disease" has its apostrophe at the end of the first word because it was first recognized among a group of American Legion members celebrating the American Bicentennial. Specialists consider it a severe form of Legionellosis, caused by the bacterium *Legionella pneumophila*.

Lyme disease should never be written "Lyme's disease" because it is not named after a person at all, but after the village of Lyme, Connecticut.

disembark the vessel/disembark

Announcements on many boats and ships tell passengers when to "disembark the vessel." This wording makes some of those listening wince.

To "disembark" is to get off a marine vessel or put something or someone off a vessel. The crew disembarks the passengers. On a cargo vessel they may disembark the cargo. It's the stuff on the ship, not the ship itself, which gets disembarked.

People sensitive to the history of words know that a "bark" is a boat or ship. The word is related etymologically to "barge."

It would be better to simply tell the passengers to get off the vessel, leave it, or go ashore. But "disembark the vessel" is so well established in the industry that it's not likely to go away any time soon. Meantime, it can bother you too.

disgression/discretion

Discretion has to do with being discreet or with making choices. A lot of people hear it and get influenced by the quite different word "digression" which is used to label in-stances of people wandering off the point. The result is the nonword "disgression." The expression is "you can do it at your own *discretion*."

Also wrong but less common—and pretty funny—is "at your own desecration."

disinterested/uninterested

A bored person is uninterested. Do not confuse this word with the much rarer "disinter-ested," which means "objective, neutral."

"Perhaps I should state it more exactly: I'm not disinterested; I'm uninterested."

87

disk/disc
See "disc/disk."

disk/drive
See "drive/disk."

disperse/disburse
See "disburse/disperse."

displeased/unpleased
See "unpleased/displeased."

dispose/dispose of
If you want to get rid of your stuff you may dispose *of* it on Freecyle or Craigslist. A great many people mistakenly dispose of the "of" in this phrase, writing sentences like "Dispose your unwanted mail in the recycling bin." You can also use "dispose of" to mean "deal with" ("you can dispose of your royalties as you see fit") or "demolish an opposing argument" ("the defense attorney disposed of the prosecutor's case in less than five minutes").

"Dispose" without "of" works differently, depending on the meaning. Whereas to dispose of your toy soldiers you might take them to a pawnshop, to dispose your toy soldiers you would arrange them for battle. Most politicians are disposed *to* talk at length.

disremember/forget
"Disremember" is an old synonym for "forget," but it is often considered dialectical today, not standard English.

disrespect
The hip-hop subculture revived the use of "disrespect" as a verb. In the meaning "to have or show disrespect," this usage has been long established, if unusual. However, the new street meaning of the term, ordinarily abbreviated to "dis," is slightly but significantly different: to act disrespectfully or—more frequently—insultingly toward someone. In some neighborhoods "dissing" is defined as merely failing to show sufficient terror in the face of intimidation. In those neighborhoods, it is wise to know how the term is used; but an applicant for a job who complains about having been "disrespected" elsewhere is likely to incur further disrespect . . . and no job. Street slang has its uses, but this is one instance that has not become generally accepted.

dissemble/disassemble
People who dissemble are being dishonest, trying to hide what they are really up to. This is an uncommon word, often misused when "disassemble" is meant. People who disassemble something take it apart—they are doing the opposite of assembling it.

dissent
See "decent/descent/dissent."

diswraught/distraught
"Diswraught" is a common misspelling of "distraught."

dived/dove
See "dove/dived."

divide by half/divide in half
If you are talking about dividing numbers or objects into two equal parts, the expression to use is "divide in half," not "divide by half."

Technically, to divide a number by half is the same as to multiply it by two. *See also* "multiply by double/double, multiply by 2."

do/doo/due/dew
See "dew/do/doo/due."

do respect/due respect
When you preface your critical comments by telling people "with all due respect" you are claiming to give them the respect they are due—that which is owed them. Many folks misunderstand this phrase and misspell it "all do respect" or even "all-do respect." You shouldn't use this expression unless you really do intend to be as polite as possible; all too often it's used merely to preface a deliberate insult.

do to/due to
This expression, meaning "because of," is often misspelled "do to." Some authorities urge substituting "because" in formal writing; but it's not likely to get you into trouble.

doctorial/doctoral
"Doctoral" is occasionally misspelled—and often mispronounced—"doctorial."

documentated/documented
The proper form is "documented."

doesn't/don't
See "don't/doesn't."

**doggy dog world/
dog-eat-dog world**
The punning name of the popular rap star Snoop Doggy Dogg did a lot to spread this misspelling. The

Wouldn't it be nicer if it really were a doggy dog world?

original image is of a cannibalistically competitive world in which people turn on each other, like dogs eating other dogs.

dogma/doctrine

Although in many contexts "dogma" and "doctrine" are used interchangeably, in technical theological contexts "dogma" has a narrower meaning: a doctrine which has given official status by a religious body. Especially in the Catholic Church dogmas are required beliefs whereas many other less firmly established beliefs are only doctrines.

Nonspecialists writing about religion often ignore the distinction, and call a doctrine which has not received such official status a "dogma." Since only some doctrines are dogmas but all dogmas are doctrines and since "dogma" often has negative connotations, it's safer in non-technical religious contexts to stick with "doctrine."

dolly/handcart

A dolly is a flat platform with wheels on it, often used to make heavy objects mobile or by an auto mechanic lying on one under a car body. Many people mistakenly use this word to designate the vertically oriented, two-wheeled device with upright handles and horizontal lip. This latter device is more properly called a "handcart" or "hand truck."

*She's confusing her words again—
last night she couldn't sleep and
was crying for her handcart."*

dominate/dominant

The verb is "dominate"; the adjective is "dominant." The dominant chimpanzee tends to dominate the others.

done/did

The past participle of "do" is "done," so it's not "they have did what they promised not to do" but "they have done. . . ." But without a helping verb, the word is "did." Nonstandard: "I done good on the test." Standard: "I did well on the test."

done/finished

Some claim "dinner is done; people are finished." I pronounce this an antiquated distinction rarely observed in modern speech. Nobody really supposes the speaker is saying he or she has been roasted to a turn. In older usage people said, "I have done," to indicate they had completed an action. "I am done" is not really so very different.

don't/doesn't

The opposite of "do" is "do not," usually contracted to "don't."

The opposite of "does" is "does not," usually contracted to "doesn't."

"I do," "you do," "we do," "they do," "the birds do." "It does," "she does," "he does," "the flock does."

So in standard English it's "I don't," "you don't," "we don't," "the birds don't" and "it doesn't," "he "doesn't," and "the flock doesn't."

But in many American dialects, "don't" is used in contexts where "doesn't" is standard: "she don't drive," "it don't make no sense," "the boss don't treat us right."

This is one of those patterns which is likely to make you sound less well educated and less sophisticated than standard English speakers. If you're trying to shake off your dialect, learning when to use "doesn't" is important.

You can usually tell when "doesn't" is more appropriate by expanding the contracted form to two words: "does not." It's not "she do not appreciate my singing," but "she does not appreciate it," so it should be "she doesn't appreciate it."

But in popular song lyrics "don't" prevails: "she don't like the lights," "he don't love you like I love you," "it don't come easy."

donut/doughnut
"Donut" is popular in advertising, but for most purposes spell it "doughnut."

do's and don'ts/dos and don'ts
One unusual use of apostrophes is to mark plurals of words when they are being treated as words, as in "pro's and con's," although plain old "pros and cons" without apostrophes is fine. But "don't" already has one apostrophe in it, and adding another looks awkward in the phrase "do's and don't's," so people wind up being inconsistent and writing "do's and don'ts." This makes no logical sense. You can also skip the extra apostrophes and write "dos and don'ts," unless you're afraid that "dos" will remind your readers of MS-DOS (but that unlamented operating system is now only a distant memory).

dosed/dozed
See "dozed/dosed."

double
See "multiply by double/double, multiply by 2."

double negatives
It is not true, as some assert, that double negatives are always wrong; but the pattern in formal speech and writing is that two negatives equal a mild positive: "He is a not untalented guitarist" means he has some talent. In informal speech, however, double negatives are intended as negatives: "He ain't got no talent" means he is a lousy musician. People are rarely confused about the meaning of either pattern, but you do need to take your audience into account when deciding which pattern to follow.

One of the funniest uses of the literary double negative is Douglas Adams' description of a machine dispensing "a substance almost, but not quite, entirely unlike tea."

double possessive

In "that dog of Bob's is ugly," there are two indicators of possession: "of" and "Bob's." Although this sort of expression is common in casual speech, in formal writing it's better to stick with just one: "Bob's dog is ugly."

doubt that/doubt whether/doubt if

If you really doubt that something is true (suspect that it's false), use "doubt that": "I doubt that Fred has really lost 25 pounds." If you want to express genuine uncertainty, use "whether": "I doubt whether we'll see the comet if the clouds don't clear soon." "Doubt if" can be substituted for "doubt whether," though it's considered somewhat more casual, but don't use it when you mean "doubt that."

doubtlessly/doubtless

Leave off the unnecessary "-ly" in "doubtless."

doughnut/donut

See "donut/doughnut."

douse/dowse

You douse a fire with water; you dowse for water with a dowsing rod. Unless you are discussing the latter practice, the word you want is "douse."

dove/dived

Although "dove" is a common form of the past tense of "dive," a few authorities consider "dived" preferable in formal writing.

To put it informally, the dove dove.

down the pipe/ down the pike

People in the northeastern US know that a pike is a highway, but others who don't understand the term mistakenly substitute the seemingly logical "pipe."

down the shoot/ down the chute

It is not uncommon to see people writing "down the shoot" when they mean "down the chute."

A chute is a sloping channel things move down along. It comes from the French word for "to fall."

But if you are a shipper of Chinese groceries you could shoot cans of bamboo shoots down a chute to the loading dock.

"Chute" is also short for "parachute," but people rarely misspell it in that sense.

downfall/drawback

A downfall is something that causes a person's destruction, either literal or figurative: "expensive cars were Fred's downfall: he spent his entire inheritance on them and went bankrupt." A drawback is not nearly so drastic, just a flaw or problem of some kind, and is normally applied to plans and activities, not to people: "Gloria's plan to camp on Mosquito Island had just one drawback: she had forgotten to bring her insect repellent." Also, "downfall" should not be used when the more moderate "decline" is meant; reserve it for ruin, not to designate simple deterioration.

downgrade/degrade/denigrate

Many people use "downgrade" instead of "denigrate" to mean "defame, slander." "Downgrade" is entirely different in meaning. When something is downgraded, it is lowered in grade (usually made worse), not just considered worse. "When the president of the company fled to Rio with $15 million, its bonds were downgraded to junk bond status." "Degrade" is much more flexible in meaning. It can mean to lower in status or rank (like "downgrade") or to corrupt or make contemptible; but it always has to do with actual reduction in value rather than mere insult, like "denigrate." Most of the time when people use "downgrade" they would be better off instead using "insult," "belittle," or "sneer at."

While we're at it, let's distinguish between "deprecate," meaning "disapprove," and "depreciate," which, like "downgrade," is not a mere matter of approval or opinion but signifies an actual lowering of value.

dozed/dosed

You can be dosed with a drug (given a dose of it), but if it makes you drowsy you may find you have dozed off.

dozen of/dozen

Why isn't it "a dozen of eggs" when it's standard to say "a couple of eggs"? The answer is that "dozen" is a precise number word, like "two" or "hundred"; we say "two eggs," "a hundred eggs," and "a dozen eggs."

"Couple" is often used less precisely, to mean "a few," so it isn't treated grammatically as an exact number. "A couple eggs" is less standard than "a couple of eggs."

"Dozens of eggs" is standard because you're not specifying how many dozens you're talking about.

dragged/drug

See "drug/dragged."

drank/drunk

Many verbs in English change form when their past tense is preceded by an auxiliary ("helping") verb: "I ran, I have run." The same is true of "drink." Don't say "I've drank the beer" unless you want people to think you are drunk. An even more common error is "I drunk all the milk." It's "I've drunk the beer" and "I drank all the milk."

drastic/dramatic

"Drastic" means "severe" and generally has negative or frightening associations. Drastic measures are not just extreme, they are likely to have harmful side-effects. Don't use this word or "drastically" in a positive or neutral sense. A drastic rise in temperature should be seen as downright dangerous, not just surprisingly large. Often when people use phrases like "drastic improvement," they mean "dramatic" instead.

drawback/downfall

See "downfall/drawback."

dreamt/dreamed

See "-ed/-t."

dredge/drudge/trudge

You use machinery to scoop stuff up from underwater—called a *dredge*—to dredge up gunk or debris from the bottom of a river or lake. Metaphorically, you also dredge up old memories, the past, or objects buried in the mess in your room.

To *drudge* is to do hard, annoying work; and a person who does such work can also be called a "drudge." If you find yourself saying "drudge up" about anything you're trying to uncover you almost certainly should be using "dredge up" instead.

When you slog laboriously up a hill, you *trudge* up it. Trudging may be drudgery; but the act of walking a difficult path is not drudging, but trudging.

And you cooks wondering whether dredging a chicken breast with flour has anything to do with river-bottom dredging will be relieved to know it does not. The two words have completely different origins ("sprinkling" vs. "scooping").

dribble/drivel

"Dribble" and "drivel" originally meant the same thing: drool. But the two words have become differentiated. When you mean to criticize someone else's speech as stupid or pointless, the word you want is "drivel."

drier/dryer

A clothes *dryer* makes the clothes *drier.*

drips and drabs/dribs and drabs

Something doled out in miserly amounts is provided in "dribs and drabs." A drib is a smaller relative of a dribble. Nobody seems to be sure what a drab is in this sense, except that it's a tiny bit larger than a drib.

Since the origin of the phrase is obscure, people try to substitute a more familiar word for the unusual word "drib" by writing "drips and drabs." But that's not the traditional formula.

drive/disk

A hard drive and a hard disk are much the same thing; but when it comes to removable computer media, the drive is the machinery that turns and reads the disk. Be sure not to ask for a drive when all you need is a disk.

drownding/drowning

Before you are drowned, you are "drowning," without the extra *D*. Later, you have not "drownded." You've "drowned."

drudge/trudge/dredge

See "dredge/drudge/trudge."

drug/dragged

"Well, look what the cat drug in!" Unless you are trying to render dialectical speech to convey a sense of down-home rusticity, use "dragged" as the past tense of "drag."

drunk/drank

See "drank/drunk."

dual/duel

"Dual" is an adjective describing the two-ness of something—dual carburetors, for instance. A "duel" is a formal battle intended to settle a dispute.

Dueling pistols—not exactly dual purpose!

duck tape/duct tape

A commercial firm has named its product "Duck Tape," harking back to the original name for an adhesive tape made of "duck" linen or cotton (a sort of a light canvas fabric).

It is now usually called "duct tape," for its supposed use in connecting ventilation and other ducts (which match its current silver color). Note that modern building codes consider duct tape unsafe for sealing ducts, particularly those that convey hot air.

due/dew/do/doo

See "dew/do/doo/due."

due to/do to

See "do to/due to."

due to the fact that/because

Although "due to" is now a generally acceptable synonym for "because," "due to the fact that" is a clumsy and wordy substitute that should be avoided in formal writing. "Due to" is often misspelled "do to."

duly/dully

To do something "dully" is to do it in a dull manner. Too often people use this word when they mean "duly," which means "properly." Something duly done is done properly; something done dully is just a bore.

DVD

See "CD-ROM disk/CD-ROM."

dwelt/dwelled

See "-ed/-t."

dyeing/dying

If you are using dye to change your favorite t-shirt from white to blue you are *dyeing* it; but if you don't breathe for so long that your face turns blue, you may be *dying*.

dyke/dike

See "dike/dyke."

e.g./i.e.

When you mean "for example," use "e.g." It is an abbreviation for the Latin phrase *exempli gratia*. When you mean "that is," use "i.e." It is an abbreviation for the Latin phrase *id est*. Either can be used to clarify a preceding statement; the first by example, the second by restating the idea more clearly or expanding upon it. Because these uses are so similar, the two abbreviations are easily confused. If you just stick with good old English "for example" and "that is" you won't give anyone a chance to sneer at you. If you insist on using the abbreviation, perhaps "example given" will remind you to use "e.g.," while "in effect" suggests "i.e."

Since "e.g." indicates a partial list, it is redundant to add "etc." at the end of a list introduced by this abbreviation.

each

"Each" as a subject is always singular: think of it as equivalent to "every one." The verb whose subject it is must also be singular. Some uses, like "To keep them from fighting, each dog has been given its own bowl," cause no problem. No one is tempted to say "have been given." But when a prepositional phrase with a plural object intervenes between subject and verb, we are likely to be misled into saying things like "Each of the children have to memorize their own locker combinations." The subject is "each," not "children."

The tendency to avoid specifying gender by using "their" adds pressure toward plurality; but the correct version of this sentence is "Each of the children has to memorize his or her own locker combination." One can avoid the entire problem by pluralizing throughout: "All the children have to memorize their own locker combinations" (*see also* "they/their (singular)" for more on this point). In many uses, however, "each" is not the subject, as in "We each have our own favorite flavor of ice cream," which is correct because "we," not "each," is the subject of the verb "have."

"Each other" cannot be a subject, so the question of verb number does not arise; but the number of the possessive creates a problem for some writers. "They gazed into each other's eyes" is correct and "each others' eyes" is incorrect because "each other" is singular. Reword to "each gazed into the other's eyes" to see the logic behind this rule. "Each other" is always two distinct words separated by a space although it functions grammatically as a sort of compound word.

See also "both/each."

eager/anxious
See "anxious/eager."

early adopter
An "early adopter" is a person who quickly adopts something new—usually a technological innovation. If you just have to rush out and buy the latest and coolest gadget, you're an early adopter. If it meant anything, an "early adapter" would be someone who reworked something first for his or her own purposes; but most of the time this version of the phrase is just a mistake.

earmarks/hallmark
The distinguishing cuts made into an animal's ear are its earmarks. They work like brands to mark ownership. Originally gold and silver articles assayed at Goldsmith's Hall in London received a "Hall-Mark" to certify them as genuine. In modern usage "earmarks" and "hallmark" are used in many other contexts and mean pretty much the same thing, except that we say "it has all the earmarks" of someone or something, and a certain characteristic is "the hallmark" of someone or something. Although a great many people pluralize this expression too, traditionally an item can have only one hallmark.

We speak today of parts of bills being earmarked when legislators set aside certain expenditures in them for particular purposes which benefit the legislators' own constituencies. They lay claim to public resources just as a shepherd would earmark a sheep to lay claim to it. Note that no one hallmarks a bill. If we said a bill bore Senator Blowhard's hallmark, we would mean that it bore some characteristic pattern by which we could recognize his influence on it.

Earth/earth/Moon/moon

Soil is lower-case "earth." And in most uses even the planet itself remains humbly in lower-case letters: "peace on earth." But in astronomical contexts, the Earth comes into its own with a proud initial capital, and in science fiction it drops the introductory article and becomes "Earth," just like Mars and Venus. A similar pattern applies to Earth's satellite: "shine on, harvest moon," but "from the Earth to the Moon." Because other planets also have moons, it never loses its article.

easedrop/eavesdrop

The area under the eaves right next to the front of a building used to be called the "eavesdrop," and somebody listening in secretively from such a position came to be called an "eavesdropper." Unfortunately, so few people distinctly pronounce the *V* in "eavesdrop" that many are misled into misspelling it "easedrop."

ecology/environment

"Ecology" is the study of living things in relationship to their environment. The word can also be used to describe the totality of such relationships; but it should not be substituted for "environment" in statements like "Improperly discarded lead batteries harm the ecology." It's not the relationships that are being harmed, but nature itself: the batteries are harming the environment.

economic/economical

Something is *economical* if it saves you money; but if you're talking about the effect of some measure on the world's economy, it's an *economic* effect.

ecstatic

Pronounced "eck-STA-tic," not "ess-TA-tic."

ect./etc.

"Etc." is an abbreviation for the Latin phrase *et cetera*, meaning "and others." (*Et* means "and" in French too.) Just say "et cetera" out loud to yourself to remind yourself of the correct order of the *T* and *C*. Also to be avoided is the common mispronunciation "excetera." "And etc." is a redundancy.

-ed/-t

You have *learnt* your lessons only in UK-influenced countries; you've *learned* them in the US. There are several common verbs which often have "T" endings in Britain which seem a little quaint and poetic in American English, where we prefer "-ED." Other examples: "dreamt/dreamed," "dwelt/dwelled," "leant/leaned," "leapt/leaped," and "spelt/spelled." However, the following alternatives are both common in the US: "burned/burnt" and "kneeled/knelt."

edge on/egg on

When you egg people on to do something you are inciting them to do something, often something risky. So why isn't the expression "to edge"? After all, you're pushing them toward the edge—trying to get them to do something edgy.

In fact the people who use "edge" in this way have both logic and history on their side. The oldest spelling of this verb meaning "incite" is "egge" pronounced "edge," and the spellings "edge" and "egg" coexisted for a long time before "egg" edged out its rival. Now, however, saying someone is edged on to do something is likely to be regarded as a mistake.

eek/eke

If you're startled by a snake that sneaks past you in a creek, you might squeak "eek!" "Eek" is just a noise you make when frightened.

But if you are barely squeaking by on a slim salary, you're trying to eke out a living. The original meaning of "eke" was "increase," but today it is used mainly in phrases having to do with supplementing or stretching resources or otherwise obtaining with difficulty: lost campers eke out their food until they are found, in a down market a few stocks eke out gains, and struggling athletic teams eke out narrow victories.

effect/affect
See "affect/effect."

effluence/affluence
See "affluence/effluence."

efforting/trying

Among the new verbs created out of nouns, "efforting" is one of the most bizarre and unnecessary, and has been met with a chorus of objections. You are not "efforting" to get your report in on time; you are *trying* to do so. Instead of saying "we are efforting a new vendor," say "we are trying to find a new vendor."

"I'm efforting to improve my English."   *"Well, keep trying."*

ei/ie

The familiar rule is that English words are spelled with the "I" before the "E" unless they follow a "C," as in "receive." But it is important to add that words in which the vowel sound is an "A" like "neighbor" and "weigh" are also spelled with the "E" first. And there are a few exceptions like "counterfeit," "either," "neither," "forfeit," "height," "leisure," "seize," "seizure," and "weird."

either/or, neither/nor

When making comparisons, "either" goes with "or" and "neither" with "nor": "I want to buy either a new desktop computer or a laptop, but I have neither the cash nor the credit I need."

"Either" often gets misplaced in a sentence: "He either wanted to build a gambling casino or a convent" should be "He wanted to build either a gambling casino or a convent." In this example, both things are wanted, so "either" comes after the verb.

But if the action is different in regard to the things compared, the "either" has to come before the verb: "He wanted either to build a casino or remodel a convent." Here two different actions are being compared, so the "either" has to precede both actions.

either are/either is
As a subject, "either" is singular. It's the opposite of "both" and refers to one at a time: "Either ketchup or mustard is good on a hot dog." But if "either" is modifying a subject in an "either . . . or" phrase, then the number of the verb is determined by the number of the second noun: "Either the puppy or the twins seem to need my attention every other minute."

elapse/lapse
Both these words come from a Latin root meaning "to slip." "Elapse" almost always refers to the passage of time. "Lapse" usually refers to a change of state, as in lapsing from consciousness into unconsciousness. Here are examples of the correct uses of these words you might get in the mail: "Six months have elapsed since your last dental appointment" and "You have allowed your subscription to *Bride Magazine* to lapse." Occasionally "lapse" can be used as a synonym of "elapse" in the sense "to slip away." Substituting one for the other is dangerous, however, if you are a lawyer. Insurance policies and collective bargaining agreements do not elapse when they expire; they lapse.

electorial college/electoral college
It's "electoral."

electrocute/shock
To electrocute is to kill using electricity. If you live to tell the tale, you've been shocked, but not electrocuted. For the same reason, the phrase "electrocuted to death" is a redundancy.

elegy/eulogy
A speech praising the deceased person at a funeral is a eulogy. An elegy is a poetic form, usually with a sad or thoughtful subject. It can also be a poem on any subject written in the form called "elegiac couplets." Unless it's in verse, the speech at a funeral isn't an elegy.

elicit/illicit
The lawyer tries to elicit a description of the attacker from the witness. "Elicit" is always a verb. "Illicit," in contrast, is always an adjective describing something illegal or naughty.

ellipses

Those dots that come in the middle of a quotation to indicate something omitted are called an "ellipsis" (plural "ellipses"): "Tex told Sam to get the . . . cow out of the bunk house." Here Tex's language has been censored, but you are more likely to have a use for ellipses when quoting some source in a paper: "Ishmael remarks at the beginning of *Moby-Dick*, 'some years ago . . . I thought I would sail about a little'—a very understated way to begin a novel of high adventure." The three dots stand for a considerable stretch of prose that has been omitted. If the ellipsis ends your sentence, some editorial styles require four dots, the first of which is a period: From the same paragraph in *Moby-Dick*: "almost all men . . . cherish very nearly the same feelings. . . ." Note that the period in the second ellipsis has to be snug up against the last word quoted, with spaces between the other dots.

Some modern styles do not call for ellipses at the beginning and ending of quoted matter unless not doing so would be genuinely misleading, so check with your teacher or editor if you're uncertain whether to use one in those positions. It is never correct to surround a quoted single word or short phrase with ellipses: "Romeo tells Juliet that by kissing her again his 'sin is purged'" (note, by the way, that I began the quotation after the first word in the phrase "my sin is purged" in order to make it work grammatically in the context of the sentence).

When text is typeset, the spaces are often but not always omitted between the dots in an ellipsis. Since modern computer printer output looks much more like typeset writing than old-fashioned typewriting, you may be tempted to omit the spaces; but it is better to include them and let the publisher decide whether they should be eliminated.

An ellipsis that works perfectly well on your computer may "break" when your text is transferred to another if it comes at the end of a line, with one or more of the dots wrapping around to the next line. To avoid this, learn how to type "non-breaking spaces" between the dots of ellipses: in Word for Windows it's Control-Shift-Spacebar; on a Mac, it's Option-Spacebar.

When writing HTML code to create a Web page, make a nonbreaking space with this code: ** **

elude/allude

See "allude/elude."

email/e-mail

Although the spelling "email" is extremely popular, some people prefer "e-mail," which follows the same pattern as "e-commerce." The *E* stands for "electronic."

embaress/embarrass

You can pronounce the last two syllables as two distinct words as a jog to memory, except that then the word may be misspelled "embareass," which isn't right either. You also have to remember the double *R* in "embarrass."

embedded/imbedded
See "imbedded/embedded."

emergent/emergency
The error of considering "emergent" to be the adjectival form of "emergency" is common only in medical writing, but it is becoming widespread. "Emergent" properly means "emerging" and normally refers to events that are just beginning—barely noticeable rather than catastrophic. "Emergency" is an adjective as well as a noun, so rather than writing "emergent care," use the homely "emergency care."

emigrate/immigrate
To "emigrate" is to leave a country. The *E* at the beginning of the word is related to the *E* in other words having to do with going out, such as "exit." "Immigrate," in contrast, looks as if it might have something to do with going in, and indeed it does—it means to move into a new country. The same distinction applies to "emigration" and "immigration." Note the double *M* in the second form. A migrant is someone who continually moves about.

eminent/imminent/immanent
By far the most common of these words is "eminent," meaning "prominent, famous." "Imminent," in phrases like "facing imminent disaster," means "threatening." It comes from Latin *minere*, meaning "to project or overhang." Think of a mine threatening to cave in. Positive events can also be imminent: they just need to be coming soon. The rarest of the three is "immanent," used by philosophers to mean "inherent" and by theologians to mean "present throughout the universe" when referring to God. It comes from Latin *manere*, "remain." Think of God creating man in his own image.

When a government exercises its power over private property it is drawing on its eminent status in society, so the proper legal phrase is "eminent domain."

empathy/sympathy
If you think you feel just like another person, you are feeling *empathy*. If you just feel sorry for another person, you're feeling *sympathy*.

Sometimes people say they "emphasize" with someone when they mean they "empathize" with him or her.

emphasize on/emphasize
You can place emphasis on something or you can emphasize it, but you can't emphasize *on* it or stress *on* it, though you can *place* stress on it.

emulate/imitate
People generally know what "imitate" means, but they sometimes don't under-

stand that "emulate" is a more specialized word with a purely positive function, meaning to try to equal or match. Thus if you try to climb the same mountain your big brother did, you're emulating him; but if you copy his habit of sticking peas up his nose, you're just imitating him.

Some behavior is worth neither emulating nor imitating.

en masse/in mass
See "in mass/en masse."

en route/in route
See "in route/en route."

enamored by/enamored of
If you're crazy about ferrets, you're enamored of them. It is less common but still acceptable to say "enamored with"; but if you say you are enamored by ferrets, you're saying that ferrets are crazy about you.

end result
Usually a redundancy. Most of the time plain "result" will do fine.

endemic/epidemic
"Endemic" is in danger of losing its core meaning through confusion with "epidemic." An *endemic* condition is one characteristic of a particular region, population, or environment: "sore thumbs are endemic among teen textmessagers." A condition need not affect a majority or even a very large number of people in a population to be endemic. In biology, an endemic disease is one that is maintained locally without the need for outside influence: "Cholera is endemic in Kolkata." It keeps recurring there, but still only a small minority of the population gets cholera.

An *epidemic* condition is widespread, rampant: "Overindulgence in fatty foods is epidemic throughout the world." The dominance of the noun "epidemic" ("the threat of a flu epidemic") may make people reluctant to use it as an adjective ("flu may become epidemic") but both uses are legitimate. It's best to stick with "epidemic" unless you have a specific need for the technical term "endemic."

ending a sentence with a preposition
The prohibition against ending a sentence with a preposition is a fine example of an artificial "rule" that ignores standard usage. The famous witticism usually attributed to Winston Churchill makes the point well: "This is the sort of English up with which I cannot put."

endnotes/footnotes
See "footnotes/endnotes."

endquote/unquote
Some people get upset at the common pattern by which speakers frame a

quotation by saying "quote . . . unquote," insisting that the latter word should logically be "endquote"; but illogical as it may be, "unquote" has been used in this way for about a century, and "endquote" is nonstandard.

engine/motor
People who work on them distinguish between the electrically powered unit called the "motor" and the engine which it starts; but even in auto-parts stores the stuff which by that logic should be called "engine oil" is marketed as "motor oil." Similarly, the English go motoring on motorways. In everyday American discourse, the terms are often interchangeable (you can buy a powerful engine for your motorboat), but you may embarrass yourself if you don't make the distinction when talking to your mechanic.

English/British
Americans tend to use the terms "British" and "English" interchangeably, but Great Britain is made up of England plus Scotland and Wales. If you are referring to this larger entity, the word you want is "British." Britons not from England resent being referred to as "English."

enjoy to/enjoy -ing
The expression "enjoy to" (or "enjoyed to") is nonstandard, influenced by "like to." You don't enjoy to jog; you either enjoy jogging or like to jog.

enormity/enormousness
Originally these two words were synonymous, but "enormity" for a time got whittled down to meaning something monstrous or outrageous. That meaning has largely vanished from contemporary usage, with the two words both meaning "hugeness." But some of us wish you wouldn't refer to the "enormity" of the Palace of Versailles unless you wish to express horror at this embodiment of Louis XIV's ego.

enquire/inquire
These are alternative spellings of the same word. "Enquire" is perhaps slightly more common in the UK, but either is acceptable in the US.

ensuite
Americans who have wandered chilly London hallways in the middle of the night in search of a toilet will appreciate learning the peculiar British meaning of the word "ensuite."

In French, a set of two rooms or more forming a single accommodation can be advertised as rooms *en suite* (forming a suite). But the single word French word *ensuite* means something entirely different: "then, later." Around the middle of the 20th century English landlords and hoteliers began to anglicize the phrase, placing it before the noun, so that traditional "rooms en suite" became "en suite rooms." Ads read "bath ensuite" or "toilet ensuite" as if the phrase meant "in the suite." The phrase "en suite" came to be used solely to designate bathrooms attached to a bedroom.

Following standard English patterns, they hyphenated the phrase as "en-suite bath" and often made the phrase into a single word: "ensuite bath." These have become standard British usage; but hoteliers often go a step further by writing "all rooms ensuite" (Americans would write "all rooms with bath").

It is clearly nonstandard to use "ensuite" as if it were a noun synonymous with "toilet" or "bathroom": "I went to the ensuite to take a shower." You may puke on your suit, but not into "the ensuite."

ensure/insure/assure

See "assure/ensure/insure."

enthuse

"Enthuse" is a handy word and "state enthusiastically" is not nearly so striking; but unfortunately "enthuse" is not acceptable in the most formal contexts.

entitled/titled

Some people argue that you should say a book is "titled" such-and-such rather than "entitled." But no less a writer than Chaucer is cited by the *Oxford English Dictionary* as having used "entitled" in this sense, the very first meaning of the word listed by the *OED*. It may be a touch pretentious, but it's not wrong.

entomology/etymology

Entomology is the study of insects, like ants ("ant" looks like "ent-") but etymology is the study of the history of words (from Greek, originally meaning "the true meaning of words").

envelop/envelope

To wrap something up in a covering is to envelop it (pronounced "en-VELL-up"). The specific wrapping you put around a letter is an envelope (pronounced variously, but with the accent on the first syllable).

envious/jealous

Although these are often treated as synonyms, there is a difference. You are envious of what others have that you lack. Jealousy, on the other hand, involves wanting to hold on to what you *do* have. You can be jealous of your boyfriend's attraction to other women, but you're envious of your boyfriend's CD collection.

enviroment/environment

The second *N* in "environment" is seldom pronounced distinctly, so it's not surprising that it is often omitted in writing. If you know the related word "environs," it may help remind you.

environment/ecology

See "ecology/environment."

epic/epoch

An "epoch" is a long period of time, like the Pleistocene Epoch. It often gets mixed up with "epic" in the sense of "large-scale." Something really big has "epic proportions," not "epoch proportions."

epicenter

The precise location where the earth slips beneath the surface in an earthquake is its hypocenter (or focus) and the spot up on the surface where people feel the quake is its epicenter. Geologists get upset when people use the latter word, designating a point rather removed from the main action, as if it were a synonym of "epitome" and meant something like "most important center." The British spell it "epicentre."

epigram/epigraph/epitaph/epithet

An epigram is a pithy saying, usually humorous. Mark Twain was responsible for many striking, mostly cynical epigrams, such as "Always do right. That will gratify some of the people, and astonish the rest." (Unfortunately, he was also responsible for an even more famous one that has been confusing people ever since: "Everyone is a moon, and has a dark side which he never shows to anybody." It's true that the moon keeps one side away from the earth, but—if you don't count the faint glow reflected from the earth—it is not any darker than the side that faces us. In fact, over time, the side facing us is darkened slightly more often because it is occasionally eclipsed by the shadow of the earth.)

An epigraph is a brief quotation used to introduce a piece of writing or the inscription on a statue or building.

An epitaph is the inscription on a tombstone or some other tribute to a dead person.

In literature, an epithet is a term that replaces or is added to the name of a person, like "clear-eyed Athena," in which "clear-eyed" is the epithet. You are more likely to encounter the term in its negative sense, as a term of insult or abuse: "The shoplifter hurled epithets at the guard who had arrested her."

epitomy/epitome

Nothing makes you look quite so foolish as spelling a sophisticated word incorrectly. Taken directly from Greek, where it means "abridgement," "epitome" is now most often used to designate an extremely representative example of the general class: "*Snow White* is the epitome of a Disney cartoon feature." Those who don't misspell this word often mispronounce it, misled by its spelling, as "EP-i-tohm," but the proper pronunciation is "ee-PIT-o-mee." The word means "essence," not "climax," so instead of writing "the market had reached the epitome of frenzied selling at noon," use "peak" or a similar word.

eponymous/self-titled

It has become popular among certain critics to call recordings named after their performing artists "eponymous." Thus the album by the Beatles titled *The*

Beatles would be an eponymous album. (Don't remember it? It's the one most people call *The White Album*; the title was embossed on the cover rather than printed on it.) This pretentious term is not only so obscure as to be almost useless, these writers are not using it in its original sense; it was the person who was eponymous, not the thing named after the person. I prefer the usage of critics who call such recordings "self-titled." It's an awkward phrase, but at least it's easy for the reader to figure out what is meant.

equally as/equally, as

It is redundant to follow "equally" with "as." If you have written "using a tanning bed is equally as harmful as sunbathing" you should drop the "equally": "using a tanning bed is as harmful as sunbathing." If you've written "equally as delicious is their *dulce de leche* ice cream," drop the "as": "equally delicious is their *dulce de leche* ice cream."

equivocate/equate

Some people mistakenly use "equivocate" when they mean "equate," "She equivocates rock to popular music generally" should be "equates rock to popular music generally" (though there are many kinds of popular music that are not rock). When something is being compared to something else as its equal, the word you want is "equate."

In modern English "equivocate" usually refers to the action of speaking misleadingly, privately meaning one thing but intentionally giving a different impression to listeners. It is also used in a broader sense of being evasive in speech. Politicians who say "I am not planning to run" while privately thinking "If I get enough encouragement I will definitely run" are equivocating.

When Shakespeare's witches assure Macbeth that he cannot be killed by any man "born of woman" they are equivocating because they know he will be killed by Macduff, who technically was not "born" but torn from his dying mother's womb in a crude cesarean section. Use this term only when deception or evasion is involved.

Conversely, to be "unequivocal" is to be straightforward, unambiguously saying what you mean.

-er/-est

The suffix "-est" is normally used only when comparing three or more items. If I have three pigs, I say "This is the fattest one." But when only two items are involved, it is traditional to use the suffix "-er." If I have two pigs, then I say "This is the fatter one."

In casual English it is very common to use "-est" for comparisons involving only two items, but it is good to remember the pattern when writing or speaking formal English.

errant/arrant

See "arrant/errant."

error/err

When you commit an error you err. The expression is "to *err* is human."

-es

Latin-derived terms whose singular form ends in "-is" (like "thesis") and whose plural forms end in "-es" (like "theses") have the final syllables of their plural forms pronounced "eez." This pattern causes some people to do the same with other words without a Latin singular "-is" form, like "processes" whose last syllable should properly be pronounced like "says."

"Yes, Puss, 'to error' is human, but first of all, you got the expression wrong; and secondly, you're not even human."

especially/expecially

See "expecially/especially."

espouse/expound/expand

The core meaning of "espouse" is "marry." When you espouse an idea or cause in public you are proclaiming that you are wed to it; you are promoting it as yours.

When you expound an idea you are explaining it. Theoretically you could expound an idea that you don't personally espouse. "Expound" was traditionally used mainly to refer to detailed examinations of complex or obscure systems of thought, but it is most often used today to mean "to speak at length about" and frequently occurs in the phrase "expound on": "the senator expounded on his love for the traditional family farm."

Sometimes in such contexts it would be more appropriate to use "expand on," which means "to speak at further length about." "Expand" in this sense lacks the systematic analytical connotations of "expound."

You never "espouse on" an idea; you just espouse it.

espresso/expresso

See "expresso/espresso."

et al.

"Et al." is a scholarly abbreviation of the Latin phrase *et alia*, which means "and others." It is commonly used when you don't want to name all the people or things in a list, and works in roughly the same way as "etc." "The reorganization plan was designed by Alfred E. Newman, General Halftrack, Zippy the Pinhead, et al.; and it was pretty useless." The "al." in this phrase needs a period after it to indicate it is an abbreviation of *alia*; but it is incorrect to follow "et" with a period.

etc.
See "ect./etc."

-eth
In older English "-eth" performed the same function as S in the third person singular present of verbs, as in "my cup runneth over." People jokingly trying to make speech sound antique often add "-eth" randomly to plurals, tenses, and person with which it never belonged. Unless you are trying to make your characters sound stupid, don't have them say things like "my cookies crumbleth," "the window broketh," or "you charmeth me."

ethics/morals/morale
Strictly speaking, ethics are beliefs: if you have poor ethics, you have lax standards; but your morals are your behavior: if you have poor morals, you behave badly. You can have high standards but still fail to follow them: strong ethics and weak morals. "Morale" formerly had both these meanings and you will find them attached to the word in some dictionaries, but you would be wise to avoid it in either of these senses in modern writing. By far the most common current use of "morale" is to label your state of mind, particularly how contented you are with life. A person with low morals is bad; but a person with low morale may be merely depressed.

ethnic
It's misleading to refer to minority groups as "ethnics" since everyone has ethnicity, even a dominant majority.

ever so often/every so often
In British-Irish English people sometimes speak of something that happens frequently as happening "ever so often." But when something happens only occasionally, it happens *every* so often.

every (plural vs. singular)
"Every," "everybody," "everyone," and related expressions are normally treated as singular in American English: "Every woman I ask out tells me she already has plans for Saturday night." However, constructions like "everyone brought their own lunch" are widely accepted now because of a desire to avoid specifying "his" or "her."

See also "they/their (singular)."

every since/ever since
The expression is not "every since" but "ever since."

everyday

"Everyday" is a perfectly good adjective, as in "I'm most comfortable in my everyday clothes." The problem comes when people turn the adverbial phrase "every day" into a single word. It is incorrect to write "I take a shower everyday." It should be "I take a shower every day."

everyone/every one

"Everyone" means "everybody" and is used when you want to refer to all the people in a group: "Everyone in my family likes spaghetti carbonara."

He wore his hat every day, but it was no everyday hat.

But if you're referring to the individuals who make up a group, then the phrase is "every one." Examples: "God bless us, every one" (may each individual in the group be blessed). "We wish each and every one of you a Merry Christmas" (every single one of you). In the phrase "each and every one" you should never substitute "everyone."

For "everyone" as singular or plural, see "every (plural vs. singular)."

everytime/every time

"Every time" is always two separate words.

evidence to/evidence of

You can provide evidence to a court, even enough evidence to convict someone; but the standard expression "is evidence of" requires "of" rather than "to" in sentences like this: "Driving through the front entrance of the Burger King is evidence of Todd's inexperience in driving." You can also omit the pronoun altogether by using "evidences" or "evidenced": "his driving evidences (or evidenced) his inexperience."

evoke/invoke

"Evoke" and "invoke" are close together in meaning, and are often confused with each other.

The action of "invoking" is usually more direct and active. It originally involved calling upon or summoning up a god or spirit. An invocation calls upon whatever is invoked to do something or serve a function. "Invoke" now can also be used to mean "to appeal to, to cite": "in his closing argument, the lawyer invoked the principle of self-defense."

"Evoke" is usually less purposefully active, more indirect, often used to mean "suggest." If you *invoke* the spirit of Picasso, you're trying to summon his soul up from the grave; but if your paintings *evoke* the spirit of Picasso, it means their style reminds viewers of that artist's work.

exacerbate/exasperate
See "exasperate/exacerbate."

exact revenge/extract revenge
See "extract revenge/exact revenge."

exact same/exactly the same
In casual speech we often say things like, "The shirt he gave me was the exact same kind I'd thrown away the week before"; but in formal English the phrase is "exactly the same," as in, "The shirt he gave me was exactly the same kind I'd thrown away the week before."

exaggerated/over-exaggerated
See "over-exaggerated/exaggerated."

exalted/exulted
To exult is to be extremely joyful whereas to exalt is to raise something in esteem or power or to intensify something. The adjectival forms are "exultant" and "exalted."

Something supremely admirable has exalted status.

People who have celebrated with great joy about an event have exulted in it. The spelling "exulted" should be used only for the past tense of the verb "exult": "The candidate exulted in her victory."

Neither word has an "H" in it.

exasperate/exacerbate
People get exasperated (irritated); situations get exacerbated (made worse).

excape/escape
The proper spelling is "escape." Say it that way too.

exceed/accede
See "accede/exceed."

except/accept
See "accept/except."

exception proves the rule
The Latin original of this saying dates back over two millennia to Cicero. It means if you make an exception to a rule, a rule must exist. If you say "in case of fire students may use the emergency exits" it is clear that the rule is that normally students are not supposed to use those exits. Few people understand this point and they misuse the phrase "the exception proves the rule" to mean that a rule is not really a rule unless there is an exception to it. This makes no sense. It's better to simply avoid this misleading phrase.

exceptional/exceptionable
If you take exception (object) to something, you find it "exceptionable." The

more common word is "exceptional," applied to things that are out of the ordinary, usually in a positive way: "These are exceptional Buffalo wings."

excrable/execrable

When you execrate (detest) something, you find it execrable. The second syllable is not often clearly pronounced, but that's no excuse for leaving it out when you spell the word.

execute on/execute

In the business world you'll see statements like "we need to execute on the strategy we planned." "Execute" all by itself can mean "carry out." The "on" is completely unnecessary.

Perhaps these people are influenced by another meaning of the word "execute": to carry out a sentence of death. Are they thinking there is something too final about "execute" unless they add "on" to make it active?

Most of the time "act on" or "carry out" would be better than "execute on."

exhileration/exhilaration

"Exhilaration" is closely related to "hilarious," whose strongly accented *A* should help remind you of the correct spelling.

exited/excited

A lot of people get so excited when they're typing that they mistakenly write they are "exited," and their spelling checkers don't tell them they've made an error because "exited" is actually a word, meaning "went out of an exit." Excitement makes you *excited*.

exorcise/exercise

You can try to exorcise evil spirits using an exorcist; but when you give your body a workout, it's exercise.

expand

See "espouse/expound/expand."

expatriot/expatriate

An expatriot would be somebody who used to be a patriot, but that's not how people use the term. Instead, it is a common misspelling of "expatriate," meaning someone who chooses to live abroad.

expecially/especially

A spelling checker will catch the common misspelling "expecially," but there are also many people who mispronounce "especially" with the first syllable sounding like "ex-" even when they know that the correct spelling begins with "es-."

expensive, cheap

A costly item is expensive, but the price itself is not expensive; neither does a cheap item have a cheap price. Prices are high or low, not expensive or cheap.

explicitly/implicitly

To be explicit about something is to be clearer than to merely imply it, so it's not surprising that people wanting to make clear that they really trust someone often mistakenly say that they trust the person "explicitly." But the traditional expression is that you trust someone "implicitly" because your trust is so strong that you don't need to say anything explicitly—it goes without saying.

exponential growth

Something grows exponentially when it repeatedly grows by multiples of some factor in a rapidly accelerating fashion. Don't use the word loosely to refer to an ordinary rapid, but steady, rate of growth.

See also "orders of magnitude."

expound

See "espouse/expound/expand."

expressed/express

One of the meanings of "express" is "explicit": "Izaak claimed that his old boss had given him express permission to shop on eBay for fishing rods during work hours." Some people feel the word should be "expressed," and that form is not likely to get anyone into trouble; but if you use it you should not presume to correct others who stick with the traditional form: "express permission" (or orders, or mandate, or whatever).

expresses that/says that

"In her letter Jane expresses that she is getting irritated with me for not writing" should be corrected to "In her letter Jane says that. . . ." You can express an idea or a thought, but you can't ever express *that*. In technical terms, "express" is a transitive verb and requires an object.

expresso/espresso

I've read several explanations of the origin of this word: the coffee is made expressly for you upon your order, or the steam is expressed through the grounds, or (as most people suppose—and certainly wrongly) the coffee is made at express speed. One thing is certain: the word is "espresso," not "expresso."

While you're at an American espresso stand, you might muse on the fact that both *biscotti* and *panini* are plural forms, but you're likely to baffle the *barista* if you ask in correct Italian for a *biscotto* or a *panino*.

extend/extent

People often write "to a great extend" or "to a lesser extend." "Extend" is a verb only, and should not be used as a noun. It's "to a great *extent*," and "to a lesser *extent*."

extended, extensive

"Extended" has to do with time, "extensive" with space. An extended tour lasts a long time; an extensive tour covers a lot of territory.

extract revenge/exact revenge

The use of a rare sense of "exact" confuses people, but the traditional phrase is "exact revenge," not the seemingly more logical "extract revenge" or "enact revenge."

extramural/intermural/intramural

See "intermural/intramural/extramural."

extremely/majorly

See "majorly/extremely."

exulted/exalted

See "exalted/exulted."

Marsha was very exact when it came to exacting revenge.

---

fabulous

See "incredible."

face the piper/pay the piper, face the music

When it comes time to accept the consequences of your actions you may have to pay the piper or face the music, but you don't have to "face the piper."

factoid

The "-oid" ending in English is normally added to a word to indicate that an item is not the real thing. A humanoid is not quite human. Originally "factoid" was an ironic term indicating that the "fact" being offered was not actually factual. However, CNN and other sources took to treating the "-oid" as if it were a mere diminutive and using the term to mean "trivial but true fact." As a result, the definition of "factoid" is hopelessly confused and it's probably better to avoid using the term altogether.

fair/fare

When you send your daughter off to camp, you hope she'll fare well. That's why you bid her a fond farewell. When you want to see how something will work out, you want to see how it fares. "Fair" as a verb is a rare word meaning "to smooth a surface to prepare it for being joined to another."

faithful/fateful

That decisive, highly significant day is not "faithful" but "fateful." Although the phrase "fateful day" can refer to a day significant in a positive way ("the fateful day that I first met the my lovely wife"), "fatal" is always negative ("the fatal day that I first tried to ride my bike 'no hands'").

false sense of hope/sense of false hope
See "sense of false hope/false sense of hope."

family name
See "last name/given name/first name."

fantastic
See "incredible."

far and few between/few and far between
The common expression "few and far between" is often carelessly flipped.

far be it for me/far be it from me
The mangled expression "far be it for me" is probably influenced by a similar saying: "it's not for me to say." The standard expression is "far be it *from* me" (may this possibility be far away from me).

fare/fair
See "fair/fare."

farther/further
Some authorities (like the Associated Press) insist on "farther" to refer to physical distance and on "further" to refer to an extent of time or degree, but others treat the two words as interchangeable except for insisting on "further" for "in addition" or "moreover." You'll always be safe in making the distinction; some people get really testy about this.

fastly/fast
"Fastly" is an old form that has died out in English. Interest in soccer is growing fast, not "fastly."

fatal/fateful
A "fatal" event is a deadly one; a "fateful" one is determined by fate. If there are no casualties left lying at the scene—whether mangled corpses or failed negotiations—the word you are seeking is "fateful." The latter word also has many positive uses, such as "George fondly remembered that fateful night in which he first met the woman he was to love to his dying day."

fateful/faithful
See "faithful/fateful."

fathom/phantom
See "phantom/fathom."

faun/fawn
A faun is a part-goat, part human-shaped mythological being. The most famous faun in modern literature is Mr. Tumnus in C.S. Lewis' *Narnia* novels.

A fawn is a young deer; and to fawn over someone is to show exaggerated affection or admiration for someone, usually to gain some advantage.

faze/phase

"Faze" means to embarrass or disturb, but is almost always used in the negative sense, as in "The fact that the overhead projector bulb was burned out didn't faze her." "Phase" is a noun or verb having to do with an aspect of something. "He's just going through a temperamental phase." "They're going to phase in the new accounting procedures gradually." Unfortunately, *Star Trek* confused matters by calling its ray pistols "phasers." Too bad they aren't "fazers" instead.

fearful/fearsome

To be "fearful" is to be afraid. To be "fearsome" is to cause fear in others. Remember that someone who is fierce is fearsome rather than fearful.

Febuary/February

Few people pronounce the first *R* in "February" distinctly, so it is not surprising that it is often omitted in spelling. This poor month is short on days; don't further impoverish it by robbing it of one of its letters.

federal (capitalization)

Some governmental style guidelines call for "federal" to be capitalized whenever it refers to a function or part of the federal government of the United States. However, in most contexts it is capitalized only in the titles of agencies like the "Federal Bureau of Investigation" and the "Federal Reserve." If you are not required to follow governmental guidelines it's "the federal budget," "federal courts," and "federal employees." Of course, in the titles of publications the word is capitalized like any other noun; and if the source you are quoting capitalizes it, you should preserve the capitalization.

feel stress/stress on

See "stress on/feel stress."

feelings for/feelings about

When someone says "I'm developing feelings for you," the message is "I'm falling in love with you." Feelings *for* are always positive feelings. In contrast, feelings *about* something or someone can be either positive or negative: "I've got a bad feeling about this."

feet/foot

See "foot/feet."

feint/faint

A feint, whether in chess or on the battlefield, is a maneuver designed to divert the opponent's attention from the real center of attack. A feint is a daring move. Do not use this very specialized word in the expression "faint of heart" (or "faint at heart"), which implies timidity.

fell swoop/fowl swoop
See "fowl swoop/fell swoop."

fellow classmate/classmate
Some redundancies are so common that few people notice them, but it's worthwhile to be aware of them. A good example is "fellow classmate." "Fellow" and "-mate" perform the same function. It's better to say simply "classmate."

The same is true of the equally redundant "fellow shipmate," " fellow roommate," "fellow co-worker," "fellow comrade," and "fellow colleague."

Even worse is "fellow peer." Your fellows are your peers: same thing. The only people who should speak of fellow peers are members of the British peerage referring to others of their social class.

female/woman
When referring to an adult female of the human species it sounds weird and may even be considered insulting to use the noun "female" instead of "woman." "The female pointed the gun at the cop" should be "the woman pointed the gun at the cop."

In the case of the related adjectives some people argue that since we say—for instance—"male doctor" we should always say "female doctor" rather than "woman doctor." It may be inconsistent, but the pattern of referring to females as women performers, professionals, etc. is very traditional, dating back at least to the 14th century. People who do this cannot be accused of committing an error.

Technical adjectival uses defining gender like "female genes" are fine (but don't confuse them with "women's jeans").

few/little
See "amount/number."

few and far between/far and few between
See "far and few between/few and far between."

fewer/less
See "amount/number."

fiance/fiancee
Your fiance is the man you plan to marry; your fiancee (or fiancée) is the woman you plan to marry.

fiery/firey
See "firey/fiery."

Filipinos/Philippines
See "Philippines/Filipinos."

fill the bill/fit the bill
See "fit the bill/fill the bill."

film
In this digital age we rarely use actual "film" to make movies or videos. Yet we still refer to movies as "films." Events where new productions are played via DVDs or other disc-based media are referred to as "film festivals." Language often lags behind technical changes like this. Modern phones have no dials, but we still "dial" numbers. It's usually useless to complain about this sort of thing, but to speak of "filming" an event when you are actually making a video of it seems wrong to me; but then if you are using a modern digital camera you are likely say you are "taping" it, which is technically not right either—though it is widely accepted usage despite the fact that most dictionaries do not recognize it.

See also "tape, record."

film/video
See "video/film."

finalize/finish, put into final form
"Finalize" is very popular among bureaucrats, but many people hate it. Avoid it unless you know that everyone in your environment uses it too.

fine toothcomb/fine-tooth comb
Brush your teeth, but don't comb them. Although the spelling "fine tooth-comb" is common enough to be listed as a variant in dictionaries, it looks pretty silly to people who prefer the traditional expression used to describe examining a territory or subject minutely: going over it with a "fine-tooth comb"—a comb with fine teeth. Some people prefer "fine-toothed comb."

finished/done
See "done/finished."

firey/fiery
It's "fire," so why isn't it "firey"? If you listen closely, you hear that "fire" has two distinct vowel sounds in it: "fi-er." Spelling the adjective "fiery" helps to preserve that double sound.

first annual
Some people get upset when the "first annual" occurrence of some event is announced, arguing that it doesn't become annual until it's been repeated. But "first annual" simply means "the first of what is planned to be an annual series of events"—it's a fine expression.

first come, first serve/first come, first served

It might seem logical to put both verbs in the same form, as in "first come, first serve," but actually the phrase means something like "the first to come will be the first to be served." Early comers do not do the serving; they are served.

first floor/ground floor

In the US, the first floor of a building is also the ground floor, but in Europe the first floor is the floor above the ground floor, and the second floor is the one above that. This is important information for novice American travelers trying to find their hotel rooms.

first name

See "last name/given name/first name."

first person

Some teachers frown on the first-person voice in student writing, striking out "I," "me," and "myself" whenever they encounter them; but although there are times when it is inappropriate to call attention to yourself, writing something like "public displays of affection are disgusting" is not more modest than "public displays of affection disgust me." The impersonal form arrogantly implies that you are the final authority and that all right-minded people must agree with you. The phrase "the author" substituted for "I" is no longer generally used even in the most formal writing. When you are arguing for a theory or opinion, it is often best to stand squarely behind it by using the first-person voice.

See also "I/me/myself."

firstable/first of all

The odd word "firstable" seems to be based on a mishearing of the expression "first of all."

fiscal/physical

In budget matters, it's the *fiscal* year, relating to *finances* with an *F*. The middle syllable of "physical" is often omitted in pronunciation, making it sound like the unrelated word "fiscal." Sound that unaccented *I* distinctly.

fit the bill/fill the bill

Originally a "bill" was any piece of writing, especially a legal document (we still speak of bills being introduced into Congress in this sense). More narrowly, it also came to mean a list such as a restaurant "bill of fare" (menu) or an advertisement listing attractions in a theatrical variety show such as might be posted on a "billboard." In 19th-century America, when producers found short acts to supplement the main attractions, nicely filling out an evening's entertainment, they were said in a rhyming phrase to "fill the bill." People who associate bills principally with shipping invoices frequently transform this expression, meaning "to meet requirements or desires," into "fit the bill." They are thinking of bills as if they were orders, lists of requirements. It is both more logical and more traditional to say "fill the bill."

fits to a tee/fits to a t
A t-shirt can be called a "tee," so it makes a sort of sense that a properly fitting garment could be said to "fit to a tee," but the original expression is actually "fit to a t." The "t" may refer to a drafting t-square, though that is uncertain.

flair/flare
"Flair" is conspicuous talent: "She has a flair for organization." "Flare" is either a noun meaning flame or a verb meaning to blaze with light or to burst into anger.

flak/flack
"Flak" is WW II airman's slang for shells being fired at you in the air, so to catch a lot of flak is to feel in danger of being shot down. However, most civilians these days have never heard of "flak," so they use "flack" instead, which originally meant "salesman" or "huckster." You need to worry about this only if you're among old-time veterans.

You're more likely to embarrass yourself if you mix up the expression "catch a lot of flak" with "give a lot of slack," which has almost the opposite meaning. You can't catch slack.

flammable/inflammable
See "inflammable/flammable."

flare/flair
See "flair/flare."

flaunt/flout
To flaunt is to show off: you flaunt your new necklace by wearing it to work. "Flout" has a more negative connotation; it means to treat with contempt some rule or standard. The cliché is "to flout convention." Flaunting may be in bad taste because it's ostentatious, but it is not a violation of standards.

flesh out/flush out
To "flesh out" an idea is to give it substance, as a sculptor adds clay flesh to a skeletal armature. To "flush out" a criminal is to drive him or her out into the open. The latter term is derived from bird-hunting, in which one flushes out a covey of quail. If you are trying to develop something further, use "flesh"; but if you are trying to reveal something hitherto concealed, use "flush."

floe/flow
Only ice floating on water produces a floe. Volcanoes produce lava *flows*.

floppy disk/hard disk
Floppy disks have disappeared from the computer world, but even when they

were common only in the earliest years were they literally floppy. The fact that a 3½" diskette was enclosed in a hard plastic case did not justify calling it a "hard disk." A hard disk is a high-capacity storage medium like the main disk inside your computer on which your programs, operating system, and data are stored.

flounder/founder

As a verb, "founder" means "to fill with water and sink." It is also used metaphorically of various kinds of equally catastrophic failures. In contrast, to flounder is to thrash about in the water (like a flounder), struggling to stay alive. "Flounder"

With his innovative swimming machine, Albert never floundered or foundered.

is also often used metaphorically to indicate various sorts of desperate struggle. If you're sunk, you've foundered. If you're still struggling, you're floundering.

flout/flaunt

See "flaunt/flout."

fluke

A fluke was originally a lucky stroke in billiards, and it still means a fortunate chance event. It is nonstandard to use the word to label an unfortunate chance event. There are lucky flukes, but no unlucky ones.

flush out/flesh out

See "flesh out/flush out."

flustrated, fustrated/frustrated

People often get flustered and mispronounce (and sometimes misspell) "frustrated" as "flustrated." Another common mispronunciation is "fustrated."

flys/flies

"Flys" is a misspelling of "flies" except when the word is being deliberately changed from its traditional spelling as in the name of the popular music group, The Flys.

focus around/focus on

The popular expression "focus around" makes little sense. An example: "Next quarter's advertising will focus around our line of computer games." It is presumably meant to convey something like "concentrate on a number of different items in a single category." But "focus on" better conveys the idea of a sharp focus. "Focus around" suggests a jittery, shifting view rather than determined concentration.

followup/follow up, follow-up
A doctor can follow up with a patient during a follow-up visit (note that the adjectival form requires a hyphen). Neither phrase should be turned into a single hyphenless word.

foolproof/full proof
See "full proof/foolproof."

foot/feet
You can use eight-foot boards to side a house, but "foot" conveys a plural sense only in this sort of adjectival phrase combined with a number (and usually hyphenated). The boards are eight feet (not foot) long. It's always *x* feet per second and *x* feet away.

footnotes/endnotes
About the time that computers began to make the creation and printing of footnotes extremely simple and cheap, style manuals began to urge a shift away from them to endnotes printed at the ends of chapters or at the end of a book or paper rather than at the foot of the page. I happen to think this was a big mistake; but in any case, if you are using endnotes, don't call them "footnotes."

for
Sentences like "I want for you to weed the garden" and "I asked for you to bring a dessert" are not formal English. You can improve either sort of expression by leaving out the "for."

for/fore/four
The most common member of this trio is the preposition "for," which is not a problem for most people. "Fore" always has to do with the front of something (it's what you shout to warn someone when you've sent a golf ball their way). "Four" is just the number "4."

for free/free
Some people object to "for free" because any sentence containing the phrase will read just as well without the "for," but it is standard English.

for goodness' sakes/for goodness' sake
Picky folks point out that since the mild expletive "for goodness' sake" is a euphemism for "for God's sake" the second word should not be pluralized to "sakes"; but heavens to Betsy, if little things like that are going to bother you, you'll have your dander up all the time.

for one/for one thing
People often say "for one" when they mean "for one thing": "I really want to

go to the movie. For one, Kevin Spacey is my favorite actor." (One what?) The only time you should use "for one" by itself to give an example of something is when you have earlier mentioned a class to which the example belongs: "There are a lot of reasons I don't want your old car. For one, there are squirrels living in the upholstery." (One reason.)

for sale/on sale
If you're selling something, it's *for* sale; but if you lower the price, it goes *on* sale.

for sell/for sale
If you have things to sell, they are for sale. Nothing is ever "for sell."

for sure/sure
In casual speech, when you agree with somebody's statement, you may say "for sure." Your date says, "That was outstanding tiramisù," and you, wanting to show how in tune you are, reply, "For sure!" You can also use the phrase to mean "for certain," as in "I couldn't tell for sure that the bench was wet until I sat on it."

But people often substitute this phrase when they should use plain old "sure," as in "I couldn't be for sure." That should be "I couldn't be sure."

forbidding/foreboding/formidable
"Foreboding" means "ominous," as in "The sky was a foreboding shade of gray" (i.e., predictive of a storm). The prefix "fore-" with an *E* often indicates futurity, e.g. "forecast," "foreshadowing," and "foreword" (a prefatory bit of writing at the beginning of a book, often misspelled "forword"). A forbidding person or task is hostile or dangerous: "The trek across the desert to the nearest latte stand was forbidding." The two are easily confused because some things, like storms, can be both foreboding and forbidding.

"Formidable," which originally meant "fear-inducing" ("Mike Tyson is a formidable opponent"), has come to be used primarily as a compliment meaning "awe-inducing" ("Gary Kasparov's formidable skills as a chess player were of no avail against Deep Blue").

See also "fearful/fearsome."

forceful/forcible/forced
These words sometimes overlap, but generally "forceful" means "powerful" ("he imposed his forceful personality on the lions") while "forcible" must be used instead to describe the use of force ("the burglar made a forcible entry into the apartment"). "Forced" is often used for the latter purpose, but some prefer to reserve this word to describe something that is done or decided upon as a result of outside causes without necessarily being violent: "a forced landing," "a forced smile," "forced labor."

forego/forgo
The *E* in "forego" tells you it has to do with going before. It occurs mainly

in the expression "foregone conclusion," a conclusion arrived at in advance. "Forgo" means to abstain from or do without. "After finishing his steak, he decided to forgo the blueberry cheesecake."

foreword/forward/forwards
See "forward/forwards/foreword."

forget/disremember
See "disremember/forget."

formally/formerly
These two are often mixed up in speech. If you are doing something in a formal manner, you are behaving formally; but if you previously behaved differently, you did so formerly.

former/late
See "late/former."

formidable
See "forbidding/foreboding/formidable."

forsee/foresee
"Foresee" means "to see into the future." There are lots of words with the prefix "fore-" that are future-oriented, including "foresight," "foretell," "forethought," and "foreword," all of which are often misspelled by people who omit the *E*.

forte
See "not my forte."

fortuitous/fortunate
"Fortuitous" events happen by chance; they need not be fortunate events, only random ones: "It was purely fortuitous that the meter reader came along five minutes before I returned to my car." Although fortunate events may be fortuitous, when you mean "lucky," use "fortunate."

"I think it's fortunate that we met, too."

"I think you misheard me, dear, I said it was 'fortuitous' that we met."

forward/back/up in time
See "back/forward/up in time."

forward/forwards/foreword
Although some style books prefer "forward" and "toward" to "forwards" and "towards," none of these forms is really incorrect, though the forms without the final *S* are perhaps a smidgen more formal. The same generally applies to

"backward" and "backwards." There are a few expressions in which only one of the two forms works: step forward, forward motion, a backward child. The spelling "foreword" applies exclusively to the introductory matter in a book.

foul/fowl
A chicken is a fowl. A poke in the eye is a foul.

founder/flounder
See "flounder/founder."

four/for/fore
See "for/fore/four."

fourty/forty
"Four" loses its *U* when it changes to "forty."

fowl swoop/fell swoop
Poor Macduff, learning that Macbeth has had his wife and children murdered, cries, "What, all my pretty chickens and their dam/At one fell swoop?" Thus enters the language a popular phrase meaning "terrible blow" (the image is of a ruthless hawk swooping down to slaughter helpless chicks).

The old meaning of "fell" to mean "savage," "cruel," or "ruthless" has otherwise pretty much died out, so that many people mistakenly substitute "foul" or "fowl" for "fell." "Fell" in this sense is related to words like "felon" and "felony."

The mangled form "swell foop" is a popular bit of humor which should at least remind you that the first word in the phrase has to rhyme with "swell."

fragments
See "sentence fragments."

framework/groundwork
You *lay* groundwork; you *erect*, *build*, or *construct* a framework.

Frankenstein
"Frankenstein" is the name of the scientist who creates the monster in Mary Shelley's novel. The monster itself has no name, but is referred to popularly as "Frankenstein's monster."

frankly
Sentences beginning with this word are properly admissions of something shocking or unflattering to the speaker; but when a public spokesperson for a business or government is speaking, it almost always precedes a self-serving statement. "Frankly, my dear, I don't give a damn" is correct; but "Frankly, I think the American people can make their own decisions about health care" is an abuse of language. The same contortion of meaning is common in related phrases. When you hear a public figure say, "to be completely honest with you," expect a lie.

free/for free
See "for free/free."

free gift
See "redundancies."

French dip with au jus/French dip
This diner classic consists of sliced roast beef on a more or less firm bun, with a side dish of broth in which to dip it. *Au jus* means "with broth," so adding "with" to "au jus" is redundant. In fancier restaurants, items are listed entirely in French with the English translation underneath:

> *Tête de cochon avec ses tripes farcies*
> Pig's head stuffed with tripe

Mixing the languages is hazardous if you don't know what the original means. "With au jus broth" is also seen from time to time. People generally know what a French dip sandwich is, and they'll see the broth when it comes. Why not just call it a "French dip"?

freshman/freshmen
"Freshman" is the singular noun: "Birgitta is a freshman at Yale." "Freshmen" is the plural: "Patricia and Patrick are freshmen at Stanford." But the adjective is always singular: "Megan had an interesting freshman seminar on Romanesque architecture at Sarah Lawrence."

from . . . to
"From soup to nuts" makes sense because soup was the traditional first course in a formal meal, nuts the last. Similarly "from A to Z" makes sense because these are the first and last letters of the alphabet. But this construction, which identifies the extremes of a spectrum or range, is often improperly used when no such extremes are being identified, as in "She tried everything from penicillin to sulfa drugs." These are not extremes, just examples of different sorts of drugs. Even worse is "He gave his daughter everything from a bicycle to lawn darts to a teddy bear." A range can't have more than two extremes. "He gave his daughter everything from paper dolls to a Cadillac" conveys the notion of a spectrum from very cheap to very expensive and is fine. Often when people are tempted to use "from . . . to" they would be better off using a different expression, as, for example, in this sentence: "She tried all sorts of medicines, including penicillin and sulfa drugs."

frustrated
See "flustrated, fustrated/frustrated."

Fujiyama
See "Mount Fujiyama/Fujiyama."

-ful/-fuls

It's one cupful, but two cupfuls, not "two cupsful." The same goes for "spoon-fuls" and "glassfuls."

full proof/foolproof

If you want to get credit for solving a complicated mathematical problem, you will have to provide a full proof. But if you're trying to make something as easy as possible, you want to make it *foolproof*—so simple even a fool couldn't screw it up.

fully well/full well

Back in the Middle Ages and Renaissance it was common for "full" to modify adverbs. The only instance in which this continues today is the traditional phrase "full well," mostly in "knowing full well." People who "correct" this to "knowing fully well" may have modern grammar on their side, but they sound as if they aren't acquainted with the standard idiom.

fulsome

In modern usage, "fulsome" has two inconsistent meanings. To some people it means "offensive, overdone," so "fulsome praise" to them would be disgustingly exaggerated praise.

To other people it means "abundant," and for them "fulsome praise" is glowingly warm praise.

The first group tends to look down on the second group, and the second group tends to be baffled by the first. Best to just avoid the word altogether.

functionality

You'll find "functionality" in dictionaries, but it's almost always used as a pre-tentious and inaccurate substitute for "function" or "usefulness."

furl/furrow

When you concentrate really hard so that furrows appear in your forehead, you furrow your brow—an expression that means "worry, puzzle over." When you lower a sail and wrap it tightly around the mast to secure it you furl it. If you can furl your brow you belong in a sideshow.

further/farther

See "farther/further."

fushia/fuchsia

The flowers known as "fuchsias" are named after German Renaissance botanist Leonhard Fuchs. Although the word is pronounced "FYOO-sha" in English, it should not be misspelled "fushia."

fustrated

See "flustrated, fustrated/frustrated."

g/q

Lower-case "q" strongly resembles lower-case "g" in many typefaces, and the two are often confused with each other and the resulting misspelling missed in proofreading, for instance "quilt" when "guilt" is intended.

gaff/gaffe

"Gaffe" means "embarrassing mistake," and should not be mixed up with "gaff": a large hook.

gall/gull

See "gull/gall."

gamut/gauntlet

To "run a gamut" or "run the gamut" is to go through the whole scale or spectrum of something. To "run the gauntlet" (also "gantlet") is to run between two lines of people who are trying to beat you. And don't confuse "gamut" with "gambit," a play in chess, and by extension, a tricky maneuver of any kind.

gander/dander

When you get really angry you "get your dander up." The derivation of "dander" in this expression is uncertain, but you can't replace it with "dandruff" or "gander." The only way to get a gander up is to awaken a male goose.

Gandhi/Ghandi

See "Ghandi/Gandhi."

gaol/goal

See "goal/gaol."

Good for a gander: the Egyptian goose.

gardener snake/garter snake

"Garter snake" is a traditional American term for small harmless snakes with stripes running lengthwise along their bodies, resembling old-fashioned garters. It is more broadly used for all manner of small non-venomous snakes. Many folks don't get the allusion, and call them "gardener snakes" instead. Although you may find these little critters in your yard, they are unlikely to do much gardening. For that you need earthworms.

garnish/garner

A garner was originally a granary, and to garner something is to gather it in. Today the word rarely has to do with agriculture: we garner attention, praise, awards, evidence, and sympathy.

To garnish something is to decorate it. You can garnish a pork chop by placing a sprig of rosemary next to it. Quite a few people use "garnish" when they should be using "garner."

gauge/gouge

"Gauge" is an unusual spelling in English, and the word frequently gets misspelled. Your spelling-checker will catch "gague" (believe it!), but won't catch "gouge," which occurs more often than you might think. It's pretty easy to find a "tire pressure gouge" for sale on the Web. If the word you want has an *A* sound in it, the spelling you want is "gauge."

gaurd/guard

Too bad the Elizabethan "guard" won out over the earlier, French-derived spelling "garde," but the word was never spelled "gaurd." The standard spelling is related to Italian and Spanish *guarda*, pronounced "GWAR-da."

gender

When discussing males and females, feminists wanting to remove references to sexuality from contexts which don't involve mating or reproduction revived an older meaning of "gender," which had come to refer in modern times chiefly to language, as a synonym for "sex" in phrases such as "Our goal is to achieve gender equality." Americans, always nervous about sex, eagerly embraced this usage, which is now standard. In some scholarly fields, "sex" is used to label biologically determined aspects of maleness and femaleness (reproduction, etc.) while "gender" refers to their socially determined aspects (behavior, attitudes, etc.); but in ordinary speech this distinction is not always maintained. It is disingenuous to pretend that people who use "gender" in the new senses are making an error, just as it is disingenuous to maintain that "Ms." means "manuscript" (that's "MS"). Nevertheless, I must admit I was startled to discover that the tag on my new trousers describes not only their size and color, but their "gender."

genius/brilliant

In standard English "genius" is a noun, but not an adjective. In slang, people often say things like "Telling Mom your English teacher is requiring the class to get HBO was genius!" The standard way to say this is "was brilliant."

genre

Often mispronounced "jaundra" and sometimes misspelled that way too. Say "ZHON-ruh."

gentle/gentile

Non-Jews are called "gentiles." It's all too easy to absentmindedly type "gentles" instead.

genuine

The pronunciation of "genuine" with the last syllable rhyming with "wine" is generally considered less classy than the more common pronunciation in which the last syllable rhymes with "won."

gerunds & pronouns

This is a subtle point, and hard to explain without using the sort of technical language I usually try to avoid; but if you can learn how to precede gerunds with possessive pronouns, your writing will definitely improve in the eyes of many readers.

Verb forms ending in "-ing" can function as nouns and are sometimes preceded by pronouns. Such verb/noun forms are called "gerunds." You'll often see sentences like this: "I didn't appreciate him returning the car with the gas tank empty." But "returning" is a gerund, so it should be preceded by a possessive pronoun: "I didn't appreciate his returning the car. . . ." Other examples of standard usage: "Their coming to my birthday party was a nice surprise." "I didn't like his being rude to his teacher." "They weeded the garden without our having to tell them to." "Coming," "being," and "having" are all gerunds, and require preceding possessive pronouns ("their," "his," and "our"). If a person's name appears just before the gerund, that too needs to be in the possessive form: "We're excited about Bob's winning the tournament."

Not all verb forms ending in "-ing" are gerunds. Some are present participles, and function as adjectives: "a sailing ship," "a running joke," "aching back." These can be preceded by possessive pronouns ("my aching back"), but few people are tempted to use a non-possessive pronoun in this context except in certain dialects ("me aching back").

Confused? Try this simple rule of thumb: if you have to put a pronoun or noun in front of an "-ing" word, try a possessive one first. If the "ing" word seems like a thing or an action that could be possessed, it's probably a gerund. If using a possessive form makes sense, go with it.

get access to/access

See "access/get access to."

get me

"I gotta get me a new carburetor," says Joe-Bob. Translated into standard English, this would be "I have to get myself a new carburetor." Even better: leave out the "myself."

Ghandi/Gandhi

Mohandas K. Gandhi's name has an *H* after the *D*, not after the *G*. Note that "Mahatma" ("great soul") is an honorific title, not actually part of his birth name. The proper pronunciation of the first syllable should rhyme more with "gone" than "can." Among Indians, his name is usually given a respectful suffix and rendered as *Gandhiji*, but adding *Mahatma* to that form would be honor-ific overkill.

gibe/jibe/jive

"Gibe" is a now rare term meaning "to tease." "Jibe" means "to agree," but is usually used negatively, as in "The alibis of the two crooks didn't jibe." The latter word is often confused with "jive," which derives from slang that originally meant to treat in a jazzy manner ("Jivin' the Blues Away") but also came to be associated with deception ("Don't give me any of that jive").

gift/give

Conservatives are annoyed by the use of "gift" as a verb. If the ad says "gift her with jewelry this Valentine's Day," she might prefer that you *give* it to her.

gig/jig

"The jig is up" is an old slang expression meaning "the game is over—we're caught." A musician's job is a gig.

gild/guild

You *gild* an object by covering it with gold; you can join an organization like the Theatre *Guild*.

gist/just, jest

See "just, jest/gist."

given name

See "last name/given name/first name."

goal/gaol

UK writers are increasingly using the American spelling "jail" instead of "gaol." This should be helpful for those who sometimes absentmindedly type "goal" when they mean to write "gaol."

goal/objective

Most language authorities consider "goal" to be a synonym of "objective," and some dismiss the popular bureaucratic phrase "goals and objectives" as a meaningless redundancy.

However, if you have to deal with people who insist there is a distinction, here is their usual argument: goals are general, objectives are more specific. If your goal is to create a safer work environment, your objective might be to remove the potted poison ivy plant from your desk. In education, a typical example would be that if your goal is to improve your French, one objective might be to master the subjunctive.

God/god

When "God" is the name of a god, as in Judaism, Christianity, and Islam, it needs to be capitalized like any other name ("Allah" is just Arabic for "God," and many modern Muslims translate the name when writing in English). When it is used as a generic term, as in "He looks like a Greek god," it is not capitalized.

If you see the word rendered "G*d" or "G-d," it's not an error, but a Jewish writer reverently following the Orthodox prohibition against spelling out the name of the deity in full.

goes

"So he goes 'I thought your birthday was tomorrow,' and I'm—like—'Well, duh!'" Perhaps this bizarre pattern developed in analogy to childish phrases such as "the cow goes 'moo'" and "the piggy goes 'oink, oink.'" Is there any young person unaware that the use of "go" to mean "say" drives most adults crazy? Granted, it's deliberate slang rather than an involuntary error; but if you get into the habit of using it all the time, you may embarrass yourself in front of a class by saying something witless like "So then Juliet goes 'A rose by any other name would smell as sweet.'"

going forward

Speakers in the business world and in government are fond of saying "going forward" to mean "from now on," "in the future," or even "now." It gives a sense of action, purpose, and direction that appeals to many people.

However, many other people find it pretentious and annoying, especially when it is used simply to indicate that the future is being talked about. Since in English our verbs do this job nicely, "going forward" is often superfluous. In a statement like "Going forward, we're going to have to budget more for advertising," the sentence would be just as clear and less cluttered if the first two words were dropped.

gone/went

This is one of those cases in which a common word has a past participle which is not formed by the simple addition of "-ed" and which often trips people up. "I should have went to the business meeting, but the game was tied in the ninth" should be "I should have gone. . . ." The same problem crops up with the two forms of the verb "to do." Say "I should have done my taxes before the IRS called" rather than "I should have did. . . ."

gonna/going to

How do you pronounce "going to" in phrases like "going to walk the dog"? "Gonna," right? Almost everyone uses this slurred pronunciation, but it's not acceptable in formal writing except when you're deliberately trying to convey the popular pronunciation. In very formal spoken contexts you might want to (not "wanna") pronounce the phrase distinctly.

good/well

You do something well, but a thing is good. The exception is verbs of sensation in phrases such as "the pie smells good," or "I feel good." Despite the arguments of nitpickers, this is standard usage. Saying "the pie smells well" would imply that the pastry in question had a nose. Similarly, "I feel well" is also acceptable, especially when discussing health; but it is not the only correct usage.

Percy's nose smelled well, but it didn't particularly smell good.

good-by/good-bye/ goodby/goodbye

All of these spellings are legitimate, but if you want to go with the most popular one, it's "goodbye." This spelling has the advantage of recalling the word's origins in phrases like "God be with ye."

got/gotten

In the UK, the old word "gotten" dropped out of use except in such stock phrases as "ill-gotten" and "gotten up," but in the US it is frequently used as the past participle of "get." Sometimes the two are interchangeable. However, "got" implies current possession, as in "I've got just five dollars to buy my dinner with." "Gotten," in contrast, often implies the process of getting hold of something: "I've gotten five dollars for cleaning out Mrs. Quimby's shed" emphasizing the earning of the money rather than its possession.

Phrases that involve some sort of process usually involve "gotten": "My grades have gotten better since I moved out of the fraternity." When you have to leave, you've got to go. If you say you've "gotten to go" you're implying someone gave you permission to go.

got to/have got to

"Gotta go now. Bye!" This is a common casual way to end a phone conversation. But it's good to remember that it's a slangy abbreviation of the more formal "I have got to go now." In writing, at least, remember the "have" before the "got" in this phrase meaning "have to." In fact, you can omit the "got" altogether and say simply "I have to go." For a slightly less formal effect, contract "have" thus: "I've got to go."

gouge/gauge

See "gauge/gouge."

government

Be careful to pronounce the first *N* in "government."

GP practice/general practice

"GP" stands for "general practitioner," so a "GP practice" is a "general practitioner practice," which isn't exactly redundant, but strikes some people as awkward. However, if you don't want to spell the phrase out, there doesn't seem to be a good substitute for "GP practice"—it won't bother many people.

graduate/graduate from
In certain dialects (notably that of New York City), it is common to say, "He is going to graduate high school in June" rather than the more standard "graduate from." When writing for a national or international audience, use the "from."

graffiti
Graffiti is an Italian plural form. One scrawl on a wall is a *graffito*. But few English speakers are aware of this distinction and say things like "there's a graffiti on the storefront." This is not usually considered incorrect, but people who know Italian may disapprove, so you might want to use the word only in the plural.

grammer/grammar
It's amazing how many people write to thank me for helping them with their "grammer." It's "grammar." The word is often incorrectly used to label patterns of spelling and usage that have nothing to do with the structure of language, the proper subject of grammar in the most conservative sense. Not all bad writing is due to bad grammar.

grasping for straws/grasping at straws
To grasp at straws is to make desperate but futile attempts to escape from a problem. The image is of a drowning person wildly thrashing about trying to find something to keep afloat with, madly grasping even a wisp of straw which is plainly incapable of doing the job. "Grasping *for* straws" suggests that the person is deliberately trying to find straws rather than blindly grabbing them.

gratis/gratuitous
If you do something nice without being paid, you do it "gratis." Technically, such a deed can also be "gratuitous"; but if you do or say something obnoxious and uncalled for, it's always "gratuitous," not "gratis."

"Of course it's gratis—all of my gratuitous remarks are gratis."

gray/grey
"Gray" is the American spelling, "grey" the British spelling of this color/colour. When it's part of a British name—like Tarzan's title, "Lord Greystoke"—or part of a place name—like "Greyfriars"—it should retain its original spelling even if an American is doing the writing.

greatful/grateful
Your appreciation may be great, but you express gratitude by being grateful.

grievous/grievous
There are just two syllables in "grievous," and it's pronounced "GRIEVE-us."

grill/grille
You cook on a *grill* (perhaps in a "bar and grill"), but the word for a metal framework over the front of an opening is most often *grille*. When speaking of intensive questioning "grill" is used because the process is being compared to roasting somebody over hot coals: "whenever I came in late, my parents would grill me about where I'd been."

grill cheese/grilled cheese
The popular fried sandwich is properly called "grilled cheese."

grisly/grizzly
"Grisly" means "horrible"; a "grizzly" is a bear. "The grizzly left behind the grisly remains of his victim." "Grizzled" means "having gray hairs," not to be confused with "gristly," full of gristle.

ground floor/first floor
See "first floor/ground floor."

ground zero
"Ground zero" refers to the point at the center of the impact of a nuclear bomb, so it is improper to talk about "building from ground zero" as if it were a place of new beginnings. You can start from scratch, or begin at zero, but if you're at ground zero, you're at the end. The metaphorical extension of this term to the site of the destruction of the World Trade Center towers is, however, perfectly legitimate.

groundwork/framework
See "framework/groundwork."

group (plural vs. singular)
When the group is being considered as a whole, it can be treated as a single entity: "The group was ready to go on stage." But when the individuality of its members is being emphasized, "group" is plural: "The group were in disagreement about where to go for dinner."

grow
We used to grow our hair long or grow tomatoes in the yard, but now we are being urged to "grow the economy" or "grow your investments." Business and government speakers have extended this usage widely, but it irritates traditionalists. Use "build," "increase," "expand," "develop," or "cause to grow" instead in formal writing.

guild/gild
See "gild/guild."

gull/gall
"How could you have the nerve, the chutzpah, the effrontery, the unmitigated *gall* to claim you didn't cheat because it was your girlfriend who copied from the Web when she wrote your paper for you?"

This sense of "gall" has nothing to do with seabirds, so don't say "How could you have the *gull?*"

gut-rending, heart-wrenching/gut-wrenching, heart-rending
To wrench is to twist; to rend is to tear. Upsetting events can be stomach- or gut-wrenching (agonizing) or heart-rending (heartbreaking, making you feel terribly sad), but many people confuse the two and come up with "heart-wrenching." "Gut-rending" is also occasionally seen.

gyp/cheat
Gypsies complain that "gyp" ("cheat") reflects bias; but the word is so well entrenched and its origin so obscure to most users that there is little hope of eliminating it from standard use any time soon.

Note that the people commonly called "Gypsies" strongly prefer the name *Rom* (plural form *Roma* or *Romanies*).

had/would have
See "would have/had."

had ought/ought
Just say, "She ought to come in before she drowns," not "had ought."

hadn't have/hadn't
Many people throw an extra "have" when they talk about things that might have happened otherwise: "If he hadn't have checked inside the truck first he wouldn't have realized that the floorboards were rusted out." This is often rendered "hadn't of" and pronounced "hadn'ta." In standard English, omit the second word: "If he hadn't checked inside the truck. . . ."

haggle/barter
See "barter/haggle."

hail/hale
One old meaning of the word "hale" is "to drag," especially by force. In modern usage it has been replaced with "haul" except in the standard phrase "hale into court." People who can't make sense of this form often misspell the phrase

"hail into court." To be hailed is to be greeted enthusiastically, with praise. People haled into court normally go reluctantly, not expecting any such warm reception.

hairbrained/harebrained
Although "hairbrained" is common, the original word "harebrained" means "silly as a hare (rabbit)" and is preferred in writing.

hallmark/earmarks
See "earmarks/hallmark."

hand and hand/hand in hand
"Poverty goes hand in hand with malnutrition." The image here is of the two subjects holding hands, one hand *in* the other. The phrase is very frequently misspelled "hand *and* hand," which does not convey the same sort of intimate connection.

handcart/dolly
See "dolly/handcart."

hangar/hanger
You park your plane in a *hangar* but hang up your slacks on a *hanger.*

hanged/hung
Originally these words were pretty much interchangeable, but "hanged" eventually came to be used pretty exclusively to mean "executed by hanging." Does nervousness about the existence of an indelicate adjectival form of the word prompt people to avoid the correct word in such sentences as "Lady Wrothley saw to it that her ancestors' portraits were properly hung"? Nevertheless, "hung" is correct except when capital punishment is being imposed or someone commits suicide.

hanging indents
Bibliographies are normally written using hanging indents, where the first line extends out to the left-hand margin, but the rest of the entry is indented:

> Hoffman, Andrew Jay. *Inventing Mark Twain: The Lives of Samuel Langhorne.* New York: William Morrow, 1997.

These are extremely easy to create on a word processor, but many people have never mastered the technique. Normally the left-hand margin marker at the top of the page consists of two small arrows. Drag the top one to the right to make a normal indent, the bottom one to create a hanging indent. In most programs, you have to hold down the Shift key while dragging the bottom marker to leave the top part behind. Don't get into the habit of substituting a carriage return and a tab or spaces to create hanging indents because when your work is transferred to a different computer the result may look quite different—and wrong.

Hanukkah, Chanukah
This Jewish holiday is misspelled in a host of ways, but the two standard spellings are "Hanukkah" (most common) and "Chanukah" (for those who want to remind people that the word begins with a guttural throat-clearing sound).

Happy Belated Birthday/Belated Happy Birthday
When someone has forgotten your birthday, they're likely to send you a card reading "Happy Belated Birthday." But this is a mistake. The birthday isn't belated; the wishes are.

Better-phrased cards read "Belated Happy Birthday." This form treats "Happy Birthday" as a phrase equivalent to something like "Late Congratulations." (If you sent out your holiday cards in early January you might wish someone a "Belated Merry Christmas.") Even clearer would be "Belated Happy Birthday Wishes," but most people seem to consider this too wordy.

harbringer/harbinger
The correct spelling is "harbinger."

hard disk/floppy disk
See "floppy disk/hard disk."

hardly
When Bill says, "I can't hardly bend over with this backache," he means he *can* hardly bend over, and that's what he should say. Similarly, when Jane says, "You can feed the cat without hardly bending over," she means "almost without bending over."

hardly never/hardly ever
The expression is "hardly ever" or "almost never."

hardy/hearty
These two words overlap somewhat, but usually the word you want is "hearty." The standard expressions are "a hearty appetite," "a hearty meal," a "hearty handshake," "a hearty welcome," and "hearty applause." "Hardy" turns up in "hale and hardy," but should not be substituted for "hearty" in the other expressions. "Party hearty" and "party hardy" are both common renderings of a common youth saying, but the first makes more sense.

harebrained/hairbrained
See "hairbrained/harebrained."

hark/hearken
One old use of the word "hark" was in hunting with hounds, meaning to turn the dogs back on their course, reverse direction. It was this use that gave rise to the expression "hark back." It refers to returning in thought to an earlier time or returning to an earlier discussion: "That tie-died shirt harks back to the days we used to go to rock festivals together."

The expression is not "hearkens back." Although "hark" and "hearken" can both mean "listen," only "hark" can mean "go back."

have got to/got to
See "got to/have got to."

hawk/hock
See "hock/hawk."

hay day/heyday
The period when something is in its prime is its "heyday." Your spelling checker should catch it if you misspell this word "hayday," but if you write "hay day," it won't.

he, she/him, her
See "him, her/he, she."

heading/bound
If you're reporting on traffic conditions, it's redundant to say "heading north-bound on I-5." It's either "heading north" or "northbound."

heal/heel
Heal is what you do when you get better. Your *heel* is the back part of your foot. Achilles' heel was the only place the great warrior could be wounded in such a way that the injury wouldn't heal. Thus any striking weakness can be called an "Achilles' heel." To remember the meaning of "heal," note that it is the beginning of the word "health."

healthy/healthful
Many argue "people are healthy, but vegetables are *healthful*." Logic and tradition are on the side of those who make this distinction, but I'm afraid phrases like "part of a healthy breakfast" have become so widespread that they are rarely perceived as erroneous except by the hyper-correct. On a related though slightly different subject, it is interesting to note that in English adjectives connected to sensations in the perceiver of an object or event are often transferred to the object or event itself. In the 19th century it was not uncommon to refer, for instance, to a "grateful shower of rain," and we still say "a gloomy landscape," "a cheerful sight," and "a happy coincidence."

hear/here
If you find yourself writing sentences like "I know I left my wallet hear!" you should note that "hear" has the word "ear" buried in it and let that remind you that it refers only to hearing and is always a verb (except when you are giving the British cheer "Hear! Hear!"). "I left my wallet here" is the correct expression. "Here" is where you are, never something you do.

heared/heard

In some dialects "heared" is substituted for "heard" in the past tense when spoken aloud. This is not acceptable standard English.

hearing-impaired/deaf

"Hearing-impaired" is not an all-purpose substitute for "deaf" since it strongly implies some residual ability to hear.

heart-rending, heart-wrenching

See "gut-rending, heart-wrenching/gut-wrenching, heart-rending."

heart-rendering/heart-rending

Your heart is "rent" (torn) when you experience something heart-rending, not "rendered."

hearty/hardy

See "hardy/hearty."

heavily/strongly

"Heavily" is not an all-purpose synonym for "strongly." It should be reserved for expressions in which literal or metaphorical weight or density is implied, like "heavily underlined," "heavily influenced," "heavily armed," or "heavily traveled." Not standard are expressions like "heavily admired" or "heavily associated with." People sometimes use "heavily" when they mean "heartily," as in "heavily praised."

Hebrew/Jew

See "Jew/Hebrew."

heighth/height

"Width" has a *TH* at the end, so why doesn't "height"? In fact it used to, but the standard pronunciation today ends in a plain *T* sound. People who use the obsolete form misspell it as well, so pronunciation is no guide. By the way, this is one of those pesky exceptions to the rule, "*I* before *E* except after *C*," but the vowels are seldom switched, perhaps because we see it printed on so many forms along with "age" and "weight."

help the problem/help solve the problem

People say they want to help the problem of poverty when what they really mean is that they want to help solve the problem of poverty. Poverty flourishes without any extra help, thank you. I guess I know what a "suicide help line" is, but I'd rather it were a "suicide prevention help line." I suppose it's too late to ask people to rename alcoholism support groups as sobriety support groups, but it's a shoddy use of language.

hence why/hence

Shakespeare and the Bible keep alive one meaning of the old word "hence":

"away from here" ("get thee hence"). There's no need to add "from" to the word, though you often see "from hence" in pretentious writing, and it's not likely to bother many readers.

But another sense of the word "hence" ("therefore") causes more trouble because writers often add "why" to it: "I got tired of mowing the lawn, hence why I bought the goat." "Hence" and "why" serve the same function in a sentence like this; use just one or the other, not both: "hence I bought the goat" or "that's why I bought the goat."

herbs/spices

People not seriously into cooking often mix up herbs and spices. Generally, flavorings made up of stems, leaves, and flowers are herbs; and those made of bark, roots, and seeds and dried buds are spices. An exception is saffron, which is made of flower stamens but is a spice. When no distinction is intended, the more generic term is "spice"; you have a spice cabinet, not a spice-and-herb cabinet, and you spice your food, even when you are adding herbs as well. The British pronounce the *H* in "herb" but Americans follow the French in dropping it.

Herb's favorite flavoring is neither herb nor spice: salt is a mineral.

here/hear

See "hear/here."

here's/here are

Sentences like "here's the gerbil" are shortened ways of saying "here is the gerbil." But "here's the gerbils" is wrong because "here's" is not a contraction of "here are." In speaking we might say "here're the gerbils," but we probably would not use the contracted form in writing unless we were trying to convey the effect of spoken English. Instead write "here are the gerbils."

See also "there's."

hero/protagonist

In ordinary usage "hero" has two meanings: "leading character in a story" and "brave, admirable person." In simple tales the two meanings may work together, but in modern literature and film the leading character or "protagonist" (a technical term common in literary criticism) may behave in a very unheroic fashion. Students who express shock that the "hero" of a play or novel behaves despicably reveal their inexperience. In literature classes avoid the word unless you mean to stress a character's heroic qualities. However, if you are discussing the main character in a traditional opera, where values are often simple, you may get by with referring to the male lead as the "hero"—but is Don Giovanni really a *hero*?

141

heroin/heroine

Heroin is a highly addictive opium derivative; the female main character in a narrative is a heroine.

See also "hero/protagonist."

her's

See "his and her's."

hesitant/reticent

See "reticent/hesitant."

hew and cry/hue and cry

If you were to accidentally whack your leg with a hatchet you might be said to hew it, and you would certainly be justified in crying.

Can't get enough of Joan of Arc?
Perhaps you have a heroine addiction.

But in the expression "hue and cry" "hue" means "shout" and is derived from an Old French verb *huer*, designating the shouts that soldiers or hunters make when they are on the assault. It's a bit redundant, like "screaming and shouting"; but the spelling in this expression is definitely the same as that of the word meaning "color": *hue.*

heyday/hay day

See "hay day/heyday."

highly looked upon/highly regarded

Many people, struggling to remember the phrase "highly regarded," come up with the awkward "highly looked upon" instead; which suggests that the looker is placed in a high position, looking down, when what is meant is that the looker is looking up to someone or something admirable.

hilarious/hysterical

See "hysterical/hilarious."

him, her/he, she

There is a group of personal pronouns to be used as subjects in a sentence, including "he," "she," "I," and "we." Then there is a separate group of object pronouns, including "him," "her," "me," and "us." The problem is that the folks who tend to mix up the two sets often don't find the subject/object distinction clear or helpful, and say things like "Her and me went to the movies."

A simple test is to substitute "us" for "her and me." Would you say "us went to the movies"? Obviously not. You'd normally say "we went to the movies," so when "we" is broken into the two persons involved it becomes "she and I went to the movies."

But you would say "the murder scene scared us," so it's correct to say "the murder scene scared her and me."

If you aren't involved, use "they" and "them" as test words instead of "we" and "us." "They won the lottery" becomes "he and she won the lottery," and "the check was mailed to them" becomes "the check was mailed to him and her."

See also "I/me/myself."

himself/hisself
See "hisself/himself."

Hindi/Hindu
Hindi is a language. Hinduism is a religion, and its believers are called "Hindus." Not all Hindus speak Hindi, and many Hindi-speakers are not Hindus.

hippy/hippie
A long-haired '60s flower child was a "hippie." "Hippy" is an adjective describing someone with wide hips. The *IE* is not caused by a *Y* changing to *IE* in the plural as in "puppy" and "puppies." It is rather a dismissive diminutive, invented by older, more sophisticated hipsters looking down on the new kids as mere "hippies." Confusing these two is definitely unhip.

his and her's
Possessive pronouns don't take apostrophes. It's not "hi's" (but you knew that), and it's not "her's," even in the popular phrase "his and hers."

Hispanic/Chicano/Latino
See "Chicano/Latino/Hispanic."

hisself/himself
In some dialects people say "hisself" for "himself," but this is nonstandard.

historic/historical
The meaning of "historic" has been narrowed down to "famous in history." One should not call a building, site, district, or event "historical." Sites may be of historical interest if historians are interested in them, but not just because they are old. In America "historic" is grossly overused as a synonym for "older than my father's day."

historic: an historic vs. a historic
You should use "an" before a word beginning with an *H* only if the *H* is not pronounced: "An honest effort." It's properly "a historic event" though many sophisticated speakers somehow prefer the sound of "an historic," so that version is not likely to get you into any real trouble.

hit and miss/hit or miss
Something done in a careless, haphazard way is done in a hit-or-miss fashion. The person acting doesn't seem to care whether the action is successful (a "hit") or unsuccessful (a "miss").

The variation "hit *and* miss" is very popular, but makes less sense. This form of the phrase has traditionally been used to describe certain mechanical devices; but that meaning is rare and antiquated. In almost all contexts, the better form is "hit *or* miss."

HIV virus

"HIV" stands for "human immunodeficiency virus," so adding the word "virus" to the acronym creates a redundancy. "HIV" is the name of the organism that is the cause of AIDS, not a name for the disease itself. A person may be HIV-positive (a test shows the person to be infected with the virus) without having yet developed AIDS (acquired immunodeficiency syndrome). HIV is the cause; AIDS the result.

hoard/horde

A greedily hoarded treasure is a hoard. A herd of wildebeests or a mob of people is a horde.

hock/hawk

People who pawn goods at a pawnshop *hock* them. That's why such places are sometimes called "hock shops."

Vendors who proclaim aloud the availability of their goods on the street hawk them. Such people are called "hawkers."

The latter word is used metaphorically of people or businesses aggressively promoting anything for sale. They are not "hocking their wares" (or worse, "hocking their wears"), but "hawking their wares."

hoi polloi

Hoi polloi is Greek for "the common people," but it is often misused to mean "the upper class" (does "hoi" make speakers think of "high" or "hoity-toity"?). Some urge that since "hoi" is the article, "the hoi polloi" is redundant; but the general rule is that articles such as "the" and "a" in foreign language phrases cease to function as such in place names, brands, and catch phrases except for some of the most familiar ones in French and Spanish, where everyone recognizes "la"—for instance—as meaning "the." "The El Niño" is redundant, but "the hoi polloi" is standard English.

hold/ahold

See "ahold/hold."

hold your peace/say your piece

Some folks imagine that since these expressions are opposites, the last word in each should be the same; but in fact they are unrelated expressions. "Hold your peace" means "maintain your silence," and "say your piece" means literally "speak aloud a piece of writing" but is used to express the idea of making a statement.

hole/whole

"Hole" and "whole" have almost opposite meanings. A hole is a lack of something, like the hole in a doughnut (despite the confusing fact that the little nubbins of fried dough are called "doughnut holes"). "Whole" means things like "entire," "complete," and "healthy" and is used in expressions like "the whole thing," "whole milk," "whole wheat," and "with a whole heart."

holistic/wholistic

See "wholistic/holistic."

holocaust

"Holocaust" is a Greek-derived translation of the Hebrew term *olah*, which denotes a sort of ritual sacrifice in which the food offered is completely burnt up rather than being merely dedicated to God and then eaten. It was applied with bitter irony by Jews to the destruction of millions of their number in the Nazi death camps. Although phrases like "nuclear holocaust" and "Cambodian holocaust" have become common, you risk giving serious offense by using the word in less severe circumstances, such as calling a precipitous decline in stock prices a "sell-off holocaust."

home page

On the World Wide Web, a "home page" is normally the first page a person entering a site encounters, often functioning as a sort of table of contents for the other pages. People sometimes create special pages within their sites introducing a particular topic, and these are also informally called "home pages" (as in "The Emily Dickinson Home Page"); but it is a sure sign of a Web novice to refer to all Web pages as home pages. Spelling "homepage" as a single word is common on the Web, but distinctly more casual than "home page."

homophobic

Some object to this word—arguing that it literally means "man-fearing," but the "homo" in "homosexual" and in this word does not refer to the Latin word for "man," but is derived from a Greek root meaning "same" while the "-phobic" means literally "having a fear of," but in English has come to mean "hating." "Homophobic" is now an established term for "prejudiced against homosexuals."

hone in/home in

You home in on a target (the center of the target is "home"). "Honing" has to do with sharpening knives, not aim.

Hoover

See "brand names."

hopefully

This word has meant "it is to be hoped" for a very long time, and those who insist it can only mean "in a hopeful fashion" display more hopefulness than realism.

horde/hoard
See "hoard/horde."

hors d'oeuvres
If you knew only a little French, you might interpret this phrase as meaning "out of work," but in fact it means little snack foods served before or outside of (*hors*) the main dishes of a meal (the *oeuvres*). English speakers have trouble mastering the sounds in this phrase, but it is normally rendered "or-DERVES," in a rough approximation of the original. Mangled spellings like "hors' dourves" are not uncommon. Actually, many modern food writers have decided we needn't try to wrap our tongues around this peculiar foreign phrase and now prefer "starters." They are also commonly called "appetizers."

hot water heater
See "redundancies."

"Let's see . . . not like that."

"Let's see . . . how to phrase this?"

how come/why
"How come?" is a common question in casual speech, but in formal contexts use "why?"

how to/how can I
You can ask someone how to publish a novel; but when you do, don't write "How to publish a novel?" Instead ask "How can I publish a novel?" or "How does someone publish a novel?" If you're in luck, the person you've asked will tell you how to do it. "How to" belongs in statements, not questions.

howsomever/however
"Howsomever" is a dialectical substitute for "however," to be avoided in formal English.

hue and cry/hew and cry
See "hew and cry/hue and cry."

humanism/humanist
People today often use "humanist" to refer to non-religious attitudes or even to atheism, but scholars know that the term originated to describe Renaissance writers who were often Catholic, rarely atheists, and that there is such a thing as humanistic religion. Careful writers avoid using this term loosely, remembering that in historical contexts it does not usually refer to a lack of religion. Renaissance humanists emphasized human abilities and achievements, but they often praised God for them.

146

humanity

When radio reporter Herb Morrison saw the airship Hindenberg burst into flames in 1937, he blurted "Oh, the humanity!" meaning something like "what terrible human suffering!" Writers who use this phrase today—usually jokingly— are referring back to this famous incident. Just be aware of this context if you're tempted to use the word "humanity" in this way yourself.

humus/hummus

The rotted plant matter you spread on your garden to enrich it is *humus*.

The chickpea spread you dip your pita into is *hummus* (or *hoummos*). Turks call it *humus*, but that spelling of the word is better avoided in English: your guests might suspect you are serving them dirt.

The silver bells and cockle shells helped somewhat, but Mary's garden really started growing when she switched from hummus to humus.

hundreds/century

"Eighteen hundreds," "sixteen hundreds" and so forth are not exactly errors; the problem is that they are used almost exclusively by people who are nervous about saying "nineteenth century" when, after all, the years in that century begin with the number eighteen. This should be simple: few people are unclear about the fact that this is the twenty-first century even though our dates begin with twenty. For most dates you can just add one to the second digit in a year and you've got the number of its century. It took a hundred years to get to the year 100, so the next hundred years, which are named "101," "102," etc. were in the second century. This also works for BC. The four hundreds BC are the fifth century BC. Using phrases like "eighteen hundreds" is a signal to your readers that you are weak in math and history alike.

hundreds/100's

See "100's/hundreds."

hyperdermic/hypodermic

Do you get a little hyper when you have to go to the doctor for a shot? The injection is made with a *hypodermic* needle. The prefix *hypo-* means "under," and the needle slides under your skin (your epidermis).

hyphen/minus

See "minus/hyphen."

hyphenation

The *Chicago Manual of Style* contains a huge chart listing various sorts of phrases that are or are not to be hyphenated. Consult such a reference source for a thorough-going account of this matter, but you may be able to get by with a few basic rules. An adverb/adjective combination in which the adverb ends in "-ly" is never hyphenated: "His necktie reflected his generally grotesque taste." Other sorts of adverbs are followed by a hyphen when combined with an adjective: "His long-suffering wife finally snapped and fed it through the office shredder." The point here is that "long" modifies "suffering," not "wife." When both words modify the same noun, they are not hyphenated. A "light-green suitcase" is pale in color, but a "light green suitcase" is not heavy. In the latter example "light" and "green" both modify "suitcase," so no hyphen is used.

Adjectives combined with nouns having an "-ed" suffix are hyphenated: "Frank was a hot-headed cop."

Hyphenate ages when they are adjective phrases involving a unit of measurement: "Her ten-year-old car is beginning to give her trouble." A girl can be a "ten-year-old" ("child" is implied). But there are no hyphens in such an adjectival phrase as "Her car is ten years old." In fact, hyphens are generally omitted when such phrases follow the noun they modify except in phrases involving "all" or "self" such as "all-knowing" or "self-confident." Fractions are almost always hyphenated when they are adjectives: "He is one-quarter Irish and three-quarters Nigerian." But when the numerator is already hyphenated, the fraction itself is not, as in "ninety-nine and forty-four one hundredths." Fractions treated as nouns are not hyphenated: "He ate one quarter of the turkey."

A phrase composed of a noun and a present participle ("-ing" word) must be hyphenated: "The antenna had been climbed by thrill-seeking teenagers who didn't realize the top of it was electrified."

These are the main cases in which people are prone to misuse hyphens. If you can master them, you will have eliminated the vast majority of such mistakes in your writing. Some styles call for space around dashes (a practice of which I strongly disapprove), but it is never proper to surround hyphens with spaces, though in the following sort of pattern you may need to follow a hyphen with a space: "Stacy's pre- and post-haircut moods."

See also the appendix, "Phrasal Verbs vs. Nouns."

hyphens & dashes

Dashes are longer than hyphens, but since some browsers do not reliably interpret the code for dashes, they are usually rendered on the Web as they were on old-fashioned typewriters, as double hyphens (like this: --). Dashes tend to separate elements, and hyphens to link them. Few people would substitute a dash for a hyphen in an expression like "a quick-witted scoundrel," but the opposite is common. In a sentence like "Astrud—unlike Inger—enjoyed vacations in Spain rather than England," one often sees hyphens incorrectly substituted for dashes.

When you are typing for photocopying or direct printing, it is a good idea to learn how to type a true dash instead of the double hyphen. In old-fashioned styles, dashes (but never hyphens) are surrounded by spaces — like this. With modern computer output, which emulates professional printing, this makes little sense. Skip the spaces unless your editor or teacher insists on them.

There are actually two kinds of dashes. The most common is the "em dash" (theoretically the width of a letter *M*—but this is often not the case). To connect numbers, it is traditional to use an "en dash" which is somewhat shorter, but not as short as a hyphen: "cocktails 5–7 P.M." All modern computers can produce en dashes, but few people know how to type them (try searching your program's help menu). For most purposes you don't have to worry about them, but if you are preparing material for print, you should learn how to use them.

In HTML code the code for an em dash is **—** and **–** is the code for an en dash.

hypocritical

"Hypocritical" has a narrow, very specific meaning. It describes behavior or speech that is intended to make one look better or more pious than one really is. It is often wrongly used to label people who are merely narrow-minded or genuinely pious. Do not confuse this word with "hypercritical," which describes people who are picky.

hypodermic/hyperdermic

See "hyperdermic/hypodermic."

hysterical/hilarious

People say of a bit of humor or a comical situation that it was "hysterical"— shorthand for "hysterically funny"—meaning "hilarious." But when you speak of a man being "hysterical" it means he is having a fit of hysteria, and that may not be funny at all.

I/me/myself

In the old days when people studied traditional grammar, we could simply say, "The first person singular pronoun is 'I' when it's a subject and 'me' when it's an object," but now few people know what that means. Let's see if we can apply some common sense here. The misuse of "I" and "myself" for "me" is caused by nervousness about "me." Educated people know that "Jim and me are goin' down to slop the hogs," is not elegant speech, not "correct." It should be "Jim and I" because if I were slopping the hogs alone I would never say "Me is going. . . ." If you refer to yourself first, the same rule applies: It's not "Me and Jim are going" but "I and Jim are going."

So far so good. But the notion that there is something wrong with "me" leads people to overcorrect and avoid it where it is perfectly appropriate. People will say "The document had to be signed by both Susan and I" when the correct statement would be, "The document had to be signed by both Susan and me."

All this confusion can easily be avoided if you just remove the second party from the sentences where you feel tempted to use "myself" as an object or feel nervous about "me." You wouldn't say, "The IRS sent the refund check to I," so you shouldn't say "The IRS sent the refund check to my wife and I" either.

Trying even harder to avoid the lowly "me," many people will substitute "myself," as in "the suspect uttered epithets at Officer O'Leary and myself." Conservatives often object to this sort of use of "myself" when "me" or "I" would do. It's usually appropriate to use "myself" when you have used "I" earlier in the same sentence: "I am not particularly fond of goat cheese myself." "I kept half the loot for myself." "Myself" is also fine in expressions like "young people like myself" or "a picture of my boyfriend and myself." In informal English, beginning a sentence with "myself" to express an opinion is widely accepted: "Myself, I can't stand dried parmesan cheese." In all of these instances you are emphasizing your own role in the sentence, and "myself" helps do that.

On a related point, those who continue to announce "It is I" have traditional grammatical correctness on their side, but they are vastly outnumbered by those who proudly boast "it's me!" There's not much that can be done about this now. Similarly, if a caller asks for Susan and Susan answers "This is she," her somewhat antiquated correctness may startle the questioner into confusion.

I/present writer
See "present writer/I."

i.e./e.g.
See "e.g./i.e."

-ic
In the Cold War era, anti-socialists often accused their enemies of being "socialistic," by which they meant that although they were not actually socialists, some of their beliefs were like those of socialists. But the "-ic" suffix is recklessly used in all kinds of settings, often without understanding its implications. Karl Marx was not "socialistic"; he was actually socialist.

ice tea/iced tea
Iced tea is not literally made of ice, it simply is "iced": has ice put in it.

idea/ideal
Any thought can be an idea, but only the best ideas worth pursuing are ideals.

idle/idol
Something or someone inactive is idle. The word can also mean "lazy" ("the

idle rich"). Unemployed workers are said to be idle, fired ones to have been idled. A car engine can idle.

Someone you admire or something you worship is an idol. But no matter how much you admire the former *Monty Python* actor, Eric Idle's name should not be misspelled "Eric Idol."

ie/ei
See "ei/ie."

if/whether
"If" is used frequently in casual speech and writing where some others would prefer "whether": "I wonder if you would be willing to dress up as a giant turnip for the parade?" Revise to "I wonder whether. . . ." "If" can't really be called an error, but when you are discussing two alternative possibilities, "whether" sounds more polished. (The two possibilities in this example are: 1) you would be willing or 2) you wouldn't. In sentences using "whether," "or not" is often understood.) Don't substitute the very different word "whither," which means "where."

if I was/if I were
The subjunctive mood, always weak in English, has been dwindling away for centuries until it has almost vanished. According to traditional thought, statements about the conditional future such as "If I were a carpenter . . ." require the subjunctive "were"; but "was" is certainly much more common. Still, if you want to impress those in the know with your usage, use "were." The same goes for other pronouns: "you," "she," "he," and "it." In the case of the plural pronouns "we" and "they" the form "was" is definitely nonstandard, of course, because it is a singular form.

Meet Rusty the red wood ant. His version of "If I Were a Carpenter" used to knock 'em dead at the coffee houses.

if not
"He was smart if not exactly brilliant." In this sort of expression, "if not" links a weaker with a stronger word with a related meaning. Other examples: "unattractive if not downright ugly," "reasonably priced if not exactly cheap," "interested if not actually excited."

But this sort of "if not" is often misused to link words that don't form a weaker/stronger pair: "obscure if not boring," "happy if not entertained," "anxious if not afraid." The linked terms in these examples do have some logical relationship, but they do not form a weaker/stronger pair.

ignorant/stupid
A person can be ignorant (not knowing some fact or idea) without being stupid (incapable of learning because of a basic mental deficiency). And those

who say, "That's an ignorant idea," when they mean "stupid idea" are expressing their own ignorance.

illicit/elicit
See "elicit/illicit."

Illinois
It annoys people from this state when people pronounce the final syllable in "Illinois" to rhyme with "noise." The final *S* in "Illinois" is silent.

illiterate/alliterate
See "alliterate/illiterate."

illusion/allusion
See "allusion/illusion."

imbedded/embedded
The proper spelling is "embedded."

imitate/emulate
See "emulate/imitate."

immaculate conception/virgin birth
The doctrine of "immaculate conception" (the belief that Mary was conceived without inheriting original sin) is often confused with the doctrine of the "virgin birth" (the belief that Mary gave birth to Jesus while remaining a virgin).

immanent/imminent/eminent
See "eminent/imminent/immanent."

immemorial/in memorial
See "in memorial/immemorial."

immigrate/emigrate
See "emigrate/immigrate."

immoral/amoral
See "amoral/immoral."

impact
One (very large) group of people thinks that using "impact" as a verb is just nifty: "The announcement of yet another bug in the software will strongly impact the price of the company's stock." Another (very passionate) group of people thinks that "impact" should be used only as a noun and considers the first group to be barbarians. Although the first group may well be winning the usage struggle, you risk offending more people by using "impact" as a verb than you will by substituting more traditional words like "affect" or "influence."

impassible/impassable

"Impassible" is an unusual word meaning "incapable of suffering" or "unfeeling." The normal word for the latter meaning is "impassive." But "impassible" is most often a spelling error for "impassable," referring to mountain ranges, blocked roads, etc.

impeach

To impeach a public official is to bring formal charges against him or her. It is not, as many people suppose, to remove the charged official from office. Impeachment must be followed by a formal trial and conviction to achieve that result.

A source you would never think of accusing of any wrongdoing is "unimpeachable."

impertinent/irrelevant

"Impertinent" looks as if it ought to mean the opposite of "pertinent," and indeed it once did; but for centuries now its meaning in ordinary speech has been narrowed to "impudent," specifically in regard to actions or speech toward someone regarded as socially superior. Only snobs and very old-fashioned people use "impertinent" correctly; most people would be well advised to forget it and use "irrelevant" instead to mean the opposite of "pertinent."

implicitly/explicitly

See "explicitly/implicitly."

imply/infer

These two words, which originally had quite distinct meanings, have become so blended together that most people no longer distinguish between them. If you want to avoid irritating the rest of us, use "imply" when something is being suggested without being explicitly stated and "infer" when someone is trying to arrive at a conclusion based on evidence. "Imply" is more assertive, active: I *imply* that you need to revise your paper; and based on my hints, you *infer* that I didn't think highly of your first draft.

important/large

See "large/important."

importantly/important

When speakers are trying to impress audiences with their rhetoric, they often seem to feel that the extra syllable in "importantly" lends weight to their remarks: "And more importantly, I have an abiding love for the American people." However, these pompous speakers are wrong. It is rarely correct to use this form of the phrase because it is seldom adverbial in intention. Say "more important" instead. The same applies to "most importantly"; it should be "most important."

in a mirror, darkly/through a mirror, darkly
See "through a mirror, darkly/in a mirror, darkly."

in accordance with/as per
See "as per/in accordance with."

in another words/in other words
"In other words" is the correct expression.

in case/incase
See "incase/in case."

in depth/indepth
See "indepth/in depth."

in fact/infact
See "infact/in fact."

in lieu of/in light of
"In lieu of" (with "lieu" often misspelled) means "instead of" and should not be used in place of "in light of" in sentences like the following: "In light of the fact that Fred has just knocked the doughnuts on the floor, the meeting is adjourned."

in mass/en masse
We borrowed the phrase en masse from the French: "The mob marched en masse to the Bastille." It does indeed mean "in a mass," and you can use that English expression if you prefer, but "in mass" is an error.

in memorial/immemorial
The word "immemorial" means "longer than anyone can remember." It occurs in modern English almost exclusively in the phrase "from time immemorial." People often hear the phrase as "in memorial," and that's how they misspell it.

in other words/another words
See "another words/in other words."

in proximity to/close proximity/close
See "close proximity/close/in proximity to."

in route/en route
En route is a French phrase meaning "on the way," as in "*En route* to the gallows, Lucky was struck by lightning." Don't anglicize this expression as "in route."

in shambles/a shambles
Your clothes are in tatters, your plans are in ruins, but you can console yourself that your room cannot be "in shambles."

The expression meaning "like a wreck" is "a shambles": "Your room is a shambles! It looks like a cyclone hit it."

A shambles used to be the counter in a meat stall and later, a bloody butchery floor. Settings like the throne room at the end of *Hamlet* or a disastrous battlefield strewn with body parts can be called "a shambles" in the traditional sense. Now the phrase usually means just "a mess."

in sink/in synch
"In synch" is short for "in synchronization" and has nothing to do with sinking.

in spite of/despite
Although "in spite of" is perfectly standard English, some people prefer "despite" because it is shorter. Be careful not to mix the two together by saying "despite of" except as part of the phrase "in despite of" meaning "in defiance of."

And note that unlike "despite," "in spite" should always be spelled as two separate words.

in store
Some people say things like "he is in store for a surprise on his birthday" when they mean he is in line for a surprise. The metaphor is not based on the image of going shopping in a store but of encountering something which has been stored up for you, so the correct form would be "a surprise is in store for him on his birthday."

in tact/intact
Often common two-word phrases are smooshed into a single word ("anymore," "alot," "everytime," "incase," "infact"). Here's an example where some people err in the other direction. When something survives undamaged, whole, it is not "in tact" but "intact"—one word, unbroken.

in terms of
Originally this expression was used to explain precise quantifiable relationships: "We prefer to measure our football team's success in terms of the number of fans attending rather than the number of games won." But it has for a long time now been greatly overused in all kinds of vague ways, often clumsily.

Here are some awkward uses followed by recommended alternatives:

"We have to plan soon what to do in terms of Thanksgiving." (*for*)

"What are we going to do in terms of paying these bills?" (*about*)

"A little chili powder goes a long way in terms of spicing up any dish." (*toward*)

"What do you like in terms of movies?" (*What kind of movies do you like?*)

in the fact that/in that
Many people mistakenly write "in the fact that" when they mean simply "in that" in sentences like "It seemed wiser not to go to work in the fact that the boss had discovered the company picnic money was missing." Omit "the fact." While we're at it, "infact" is not a word; "in fact" is always a two-word phrase.

in the mist/in the midst
When you are surrounded by something, you're in the midst of it—its middle. If you're in a mist, you're just in a fog.

in to/into
See "into/in to."

incase/in case
Just in case you haven't figured this out already: the expression "in case" is two words, not one. There is a brand of equipment covers sold under the InCase brand, but that's a very different matter, to be used only when you need something in which to encase your iPad.

incent/incentivize
Business folks sometimes use "incent" to mean "create an incentive," but it's not standard English. "Incentivize" is even more widely used, but strikes many people as an ugly substitute for "encourage."

incidence/incidents/instances
These three overlap in meaning just enough to confuse a lot of people. Few of us have a need for "incidence," which most often refers to degree or extent of the occurrence of something: "The incidence of measles in Whitman County has dropped markedly since the vaccine has been provided free." "Incidents," which is pronounced identically, is merely the plural of "incident," meaning "occurrences": "Police reported damage to three different outhouses in separate incidents last Halloween." Instances (not "incidences") are examples: "Semicolons are not required in the first three instances given in your query." Incidents can be used as instances only if someone is using them as examples.

incidently/incidentally
"Incidently" is an unusual spelling of "incidentally" that will be considered a spelling error by spelling checkers and by many people.

includes
When listing members of a group, use "includes" only if your list is incomplete. A baseball team includes a pitcher, a right fielder, and a catcher. If you are going to list every single member of a group, you can say it consists of, is composed of, or is made up of them—but not that it includes them.

incredible
The other day I heard a film reviewer praise a director because he created "in-

credible characters," which would literally mean unbelievable characters. What the reviewer meant to say, of course, was precisely the opposite: characters so lifelike as to seem like real people. Intensifiers and superlatives tend to get worn down quickly through overuse and become almost meaningless, but it is wise to be aware of their root meanings so that you don't unintentionally utter absurdities. "Fantastic" means "as in a fantasy" just as "fabulous" means "as in a fable." A "wonderful" sight should make you pause in wonder. Some of these words are worn down beyond redemption, however. For instance, who now expects a "terrific" sight to terrify? And the most overused of all these words—"awesome"—now rarely conveys a sense of awe.

See also "intensifiers."

incredulous/incredible
"When Jessica said that my performance at the karaoke bar had been incredible, I was incredulous." I hope Jessica was using "incredible" in the casual sense of "unbelievably good" but I knew I used "incredulous" to mean "unbelieving, skeptical," which is the only standard usage for this word.

indepth/in depth
You can make an "in-depth" study of a subject by studying it "in depth," but never "indepth." Like "a lot" this expression consists of two words often mistaken for one. The first, adjectival, use of the phrase given above is commonly hyphenated, which may lead some people to splice the words even more closely together. "Indepth" is usually used as an adverb by people of limited vocabulary who would be better off saying "profoundly" or "thoroughly." Some of them go so far as to say that they have studied a subject "indepthly." Avoid this one if you don't want to be snickered at.

Indian/Native American
Although academics have long promoted "Native American" as a more accurate label than "Indian," most of the people so labeled continue to refer to themselves as "Indians" and prefer that term. In Canada, there is a move to refer to descendants of the original inhabitants as "First Nations" or "First Peoples," but so far that has not spread to the US.

Indiana University/University of Indiana
See "University of Indiana/Indiana University."

indifferent/ambivalent
See "ambivalent/indifferent."

indite/indict
"Indite" is a rare word meaning "to write down."

Authorities indict a person charged with a crime. This act is called an "indictment." The *C* is not pronounced in these words, so that "indict" sounds exactly like "indite," but don't let that cause you to misspell them.

individual/person

Law-enforcement officers often use "individual" as a simple synonym for "person" when they don't particularly mean to stress individuality: "I pursued the individual who had fired the weapon at me for three blocks." This sort of use of "individual" lends an oddly formal air to your writing. When "person" works as well, use it.

infact/in fact

"In fact" is always two words.

infamous

"Infamous" means "famous in a bad way." It is related to the word "infamy." Humorists have for a couple of centuries jokingly used the word in a positive sense, but the effectiveness of the joke depends on the listener knowing that this is a misuse of the term. Because this is a very old joke indeed you should stick to using "infamous" only for people like Hitler and Billy the Kid.

See also "notorious."

infer/imply

See "imply/infer."

infinite

When Shakespeare's Enobarbus said of Cleopatra that "age cannot wither her, nor custom stale her infinite variety," he was obviously exaggerating. So few are the literal uses of "infinite" that almost every use of it is metaphorical. There is not an infinite number of possible positions on a chessboard, nor number of stars in the known universe. Things can be innumerable (in one sense of the word) without being infinite; in other words, things which are beyond the human capacity to count can still be limited in number. "Infinite" has its uses as a loose synonym for "a very great many," but it is all too often lazily used when one doesn't want to do the work to discover the order of magnitude involved. When you are making quasi-scientific statements you do a disservice to your reader by implying infinity when mere billions are involved.

inflammable/flammable

The prefix "in-" does not indicate negation here; it comes from the word "inflame." "Flammable" and "inflammable" both mean "easy to catch on fire," but so many people misunderstand the latter term that it's better to stick with "flammable" in safety warnings.

influencial/influential

If you have influence, you are "influential," not "influencial."

-ing

What's the point of urging people to pronounce the *G* in words ending in "-ing" when all manner of public leaders proudly proclaim they are "runnin' for office" and "savin' the planet"? Well, some people still care and think dropping the *G* sounds sloppy and unsophisticated.

ink pen/pen

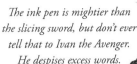

The ink pen is mightier than the slicing sword, but don't ever tell that to Ivan the Avenger. He despises excess words.

If there were any danger of confusing pens for writing with other kinds of pens (light-, sea-, pig-) the phrase "ink pen" might be useful, but it seems to be mainly a way of saying "not a pencil." Plain old "pen" will do fine.

input

Some people object to "input" as computer jargon that's proliferated unjustifiably in the business world. Be aware that it's not welcome in all settings; but whatever you do, don't misspell it "imput."

inquire/enquire

See "enquire/inquire."

insight/incite

An insight is something you have: an understanding of something, a bright idea about something.

To incite is to *do* something: to stimulate some action or other to be taken. You can never *have* an incite.

intact/in tact

See "in tact/intact."

install/instill

People conjure up visions of themselves as upgradable robots when they write things like "My Aunt Tillie tried to install the spirit of giving in my heart." The word they are searching for is "instill." You install equipment; you instill feelings or attitudes.

instances/incidence/incidents

See "incidence/incidents/instances."

instances/instants

Brief moments are "instants," and examples of anything are "instances."

insundry/and sundry

"Sundry" means "various" in modern English, so strictly speaking expressions like "various and sundry" and "all and sundry" are redundant; but many redundant expressions are standard in English, as are these. "Sundry" used to mean "different from each," which explains why the expression wasn't redundant when it first evolved. It was like "each and every": each single individual and all of them collectively.

159

The fact that "and sundry" now doesn't really add anything except a rhetorical flourish to the expression may help to explain why some folks mishear this phrase as "insundry."

insure/ensure/assure
See "assure/ensure/insure."

intact/in tact
See "in tact/intact."

integral
Often mispronounced "in-tra-gul" as if it were related to "intricate" instead of the more proper "in-tuh-grul," related to "integrate."

intend on/intend to
You can plan on doing something, but you intend to do it. Many people confuse these two expressions with each other and mistakenly say "intend on." Of course if you are really determined, you can be *intent* on doing something.

intense/intensive
If you are putting forth an intense effort, your work is "intense": "My intense study of Plato convinced me that I would make a good leader." But when the intensity stems not so much from your effort as it does from outside forces, the usual word is "intensive": "The village endured intensive bombing."

intensifiers
People are always looking for ways to emphasize how really, really special the subject under discussion is. (The use of "really" is one of the weakest and least effective of these.) A host of words have been worn down in this service to near-meaninglessness. It is good to remember the etymological roots of such words to avoid such absurdities as "fantastically realistic," "absolutely relative," and "incredibly convincing." When you are tempted to use one of these vague intensifiers consider rewriting your prose to explain more precisely and vividly what you mean: "Fred's cooking was incredibly bad" could be changed to "When I tasted Fred's cooking I almost thought I was back in the middle-school cafeteria."

See also "incredible."

intensive purposes/intents and purposes
This is another example of the oral transformation of language by people who don't read much. "For all intents and purposes" is an old cliché that won't thrill anyone, but using the mistaken alternative is likely to elicit guffaws.

interesting
The second syllable is normally silent in "interesting." It's nonstandard to pronounce the "ter," and definitely substandard to say "innaresting."

interface/interact
The use of the computer term "interface" as a verb, substituting for "interact," is widely objected to.

intergrate/integrate
There are lots of words that begin with "inter-" but this is not one of them. The word is "integrate" with just one *R*.

interment/internment
Interment is burial; internment is merely imprisonment.

intermural/intramural/extramural
"Intramural" means literally "within the walls" and refers to activities that take place entirely within an institution. When at Macbeth State University the Glamis Hall soccer team plays against the one from Dunsinane Hall, that's an intramural game. When MSU's Fighting Scots travel to go up against Cawdor U. in the Porter's Bowl, the game is "extramural" (outside the walls) or "intermural" (though the perfectly correct "intercollegiate" is more often used instead). "Intermural," meaning literally "between the walls," is constantly both said and written when "intramural" is meant.

Internet/intranet
"Internet" is the proper name of the network most people connect to, and the word needs to be capitalized. However "intranet," a network confined to a smaller group, is a generic term that does not deserve capitalization. In advertising, we often read things like "unlimited Internet, $35." It would be more accurate to refer in this sort of context to "Internet *access*."

interpretate/interpret
"Interpretate" is mistakenly formed from "interpretation," but the verb form is simply "interpret."

See also "orientate/orient."

into/in to
"Into" is a preposition that often answers the question, "where?" For example, "Tom and Becky had gone far into the cave before they realized they were lost." Sometimes the "where" is metaphorical, as in "He went into the army" or "She went into business." It can also refer by analogy to time: "The snow lingered on the ground well into April." In old-fashioned math talk, it could be used to refer to division: "Two into six is three." In other instances where the words "in" and "to" just happen to find themselves neighbors, they must remain separate words. For instance, "Rachel dived back in to rescue the struggling boy." Here "to" belongs with "rescue" and means "in order to," not "where." (If the phrase had been "dived back into the water," "into" would be required.)

Try speaking the sentence concerned aloud, pausing distinctly between "in" and "to." If the result sounds wrong, you probably need "into."

Then there is the '60s colloquialism that lingers on in which "into" means "deeply interested or involved in": "Kevin is into baseball cards." This is derived from usages like, "The committee is looking into the fund-raising scandal." The abbreviated form is not acceptable formal English, but is quite common in informal communications.

intricate/integral

An integral part of a machine, organization, or idea is a necessary, inseparable part of it. Many people mistakenly substitute "intricate" for "integral" in the phrase "an integral part."

A very simple bit of metal can be an integral part of an intricate machine.

intrigue

Something fascinating or alluring can be called "intriguing," but "intrigue" as a noun means something rather different: scheming and plotting. Don't say people or situations are full of intrigue when you mean they are intriguing. The name of the Oldsmobile car model called the Intrigue is probably based on this common confusion.

invested interest/vested interest

If you have a personal stake in something which causes you to be biased toward it, you have a *vested* interest in it. People discussing financial investment sometimes pun on this phrase by writing "invested interest," but most of the time when you see the latter spelling, it's just a mistake.

invite/invitation

"Invite" (accent on the second syllable) is perfectly standard as a verb: "Invite me to the birthday party and I'll jump out of the cake."

But "invite" (accent on the first syllable) as a noun meaning "invitation" is less acceptable: "I got an invite to my ex-wife's wedding." Though this form has become extremely popular, even in fairly formal contexts, it is safer to use the traditional "invitation."

invoke/evoke

See "evoke/invoke."

Iraq

Want to sound like a good old boy who doesn't give a hoot what foreigners think? Say "EYE-rack." But if you want to sound knowledgeable, say "ear-ROCK." Politicians who know better sometimes adopt the popular mispronunciation in order to sound more folksy and down to earth.

Similarly in standard English, Iran is not pronounced "eye-RAN" but "ear-RON."

On a related matter, the first syllable of "Italian" is pronounced just like the first syllable in "Italy," with an "it" sound. "Eye-talian" sounds distinctly uneducated.

ironic/sarcastic

See "sarcastic/ironic."

ironically/coincidentally

An event that is strikingly different from or the opposite of what one would have expected, usually producing a sense of incongruity, is ironic: "The sheriff proclaimed a zero-tolerance policy on drugs, but ironically flunked his own test." Other striking comings-together of events lacking these qualities are merely coincidental: "The lovers leapt off the tower just as a hay wagon coincidentally happened to be passing below."

irregardless/regardless

Regardless of what you have heard, "irregardless" is a redundancy. The suffix "-less" on the end of the word already makes the word negative. It doesn't need the negative prefix "ir-" added to make it even more negative.

irrelevant/impertinent

See "impertinent/irrelevant."

is, is

In speech, people often lose track in the middle of a sentence and repeat "is" instead of saying "that": "The problem with the conflict in the Balkans is, is the ethnic tensions seem exacerbated by everything we do." This is just a nervous tic, worth being alert against when you're speaking publicly.

However, when you begin a sentence with the phrase "What it is," it's normal, though awkward, to follow the phrase with another "is": What it is, is a disaster." This colloquialism is probably derived from expressions like this: "I'll tell you what it is; it is a disaster." In this case, each "is" has its own proper "it," whereas the condensed version sounds like a verbal stumble. If you would rather avoid this sort of "is, is" you can avoid using "what it is" and say something simple like "It's a disaster," or "The point is that it's a disaster."

Of course, I suppose it all depends on what you think the meaning of "is" is.

Islams/Muslims

Followers of Islam are called "Muslims," not "Islams." *Muslim* is now widely preferred over the older and less phonetically accurate *Moslem.*

The *S* in "Islam" and "Muslim" is unvoiced like the *S* in "saint." It should not be pronounced with a *Z* sound.

isle/aisle

See "aisle/isle."

isn't/aren't/ain't/am not

See "ain't/am not/isn't/aren't."

isn't it/innit

In South Asia you often hear people end sentences with "isn't it?" in contexts where traditional English would require "doesn't it," "won't it," "aren't you," and related expressions. In Britain and among American Indians, among others, this "invariant isn't" is reduced to "innit," and may be used even more broadly as a general emphatic exclamation at the end of almost any statement.

This interesting pattern is liable to puzzle, amuse, or annoy those who aren't used to it, isn't it?

Isreal/Israel
To remember how to spell "Israel" properly, try pronouncing it the way Israelis do when they're speaking English: "ISS-rah-el."

Israelite/Israeli
In modern English the term "Israelite" is usually confined to the people of ancient Israel, either of the kingdom of that name or—more broadly—any Jew of the Biblical era. Only modern citizens of the state of Israel are called "Israelis." Although the term most often refers to Jewish citizens of that state, it can also refer to Arab, Muslim, or Christian citizens of Israel.

Issac/Isaac
Words with a double *A* are rare in English, causing many to misspell the Biblical name "Isaac."

issues/problems
An "issue" used to be a matter for consideration or discussion. For instance, a group might discuss the issue of how best to raise funds for its scholarship program. But people could also disagree with each other by saying "I take issue [disagree] with you on that point."

But then mental health professionals began to talk about "child-rearing issues" and "relationship issues," and such. In this context the meaning of "issues" began to blur into that of "problems" and cross-pollinate with "take issue," leading ordinary folks to begin saying things like "I have tendonitis issues" or "I have issues with telemarketing." This very popular sort of expression is viewed with contempt or amusement by many traditionalists, who are truly appalled when it's extended to the inanimate world: "these laptops have issues with some wireless cards."

itch/scratch
Strictly speaking, you scratch an itch. If you're trying to get rid of a tingly feeling on your back, scratch it, don't itch it.

its/it's
The exception to the general rule that one should use an apostrophe to indicate possession is in possessive pronouns. Some of them are not a problem. "Mine" has no misleading "s" at the end to invite an apostrophe. And few people are tempted to write "hi's," though the equally erroneous "her's" is fairly common, as are "our's" and "their's"—all wrong, wrong, wrong. The problem with avoid-

ing "it's" as a possessive is that this spelling is perfectly correct as a contraction meaning "it is." Just remember one point and you'll never make this mistake again: "it's" always means "it is" or "it has" and nothing else.

There is one personal pronoun—uncommon in American English—which takes an apostrophe in its possessive form: "one," as in the title of Virginia Woolf's famous book, *A Room of One's Own*.

See also "apostrophes."

jack/plug
In electronics, a jack is a female part into which one inserts a plug, the male part. People get confused because "Jack" is a male name. The cyberpunk term (from William Gibson's *Neuromancer*) "jack in" should logically be "plug in," but we're stuck with this form in the science fiction realm.

Jacuzzi
See "brand names."

jam/jamb
The only common use for the word "jamb" is to label the vertical part of the frame of a door or window. It comes from the French word for "leg"; think of the two side pieces of the frame as legs on either side of the opening. For all other uses, it's "jam": stuck in a jam, traffic jam, logjam, jam session, etc.

Jo emerged from her latest jamb unscathed.

jealous/envious
See "envious/jealous."

jerry-built/jury-rigged
Although their etymologies are obscure and their meanings overlap, these are two distinct expressions. Something poorly built is "jerry-built." Something rigged up temporarily in a makeshift manner with materials at hand, often in an ingenious manner, is "jury-rigged." "Jerry-built" always has a negative connotation, whereas one can be impressed by the cleverness of a jury-rigged solution. Many people cross-pollinate these two expressions and mistakenly say "jerry-rigged" or "jury-built."

Jew/Hebrew
These terms overlap but are often distinguished in usage. In the older portions of the Bible the descendants of Abraham and Sarah are referred to as "He-

brews." Since the sixth century BCE Babylonian captivity and the return from exile, they have been known as "Jews," a name derived from the dominant remaining tribe of Judah. Modern Jews are seldom referred to as "Hebrews" but the language spoken in the state of Israel today, based on ancient Hebrew, is "Modern Hebrew." Although "Hebrew" has sometimes been used in a condescending or insulting manner to refer to modern Jews, it is not in itself an insulting term. However, it is normal when you have a choice to use "Jew" to refer both to people of the Jewish faith and to ethnic Jews, religious or not.

"Hewbrew" is a common misspelling of "Hebrew." If you're in the habit of ignoring names when they are flagged by your spelling checker, don't ignore this one.

Jew/Jewish
"Jew" as an adjective ("Jew lawyer") is an ethnic insult; the word is "Jewish." But people who object to "Jew" as a noun are being oversensitive. Most Jews are proud to be called Jews. The expression "to Jew someone down"—an expression meaning "to bargain for a lower price"—reflects a grossly insulting stereotype and should be avoided in all contexts.

jewelry
Often mispronounced "joolereee." To remember the standard pronunciation, just say "jewel" and add "-ree" on the end. The British spelling is much fancier: "jewellery."

jibe/jive/gibe
See "gibe/jibe/jive."

jig/gig
See "gig/jig."

job titles
The general rule is to capitalize a title like "President" only when it is prefixed to a particular president's name: "It is notable that President Grover Cleveland was the first Democratic president elected after the Civil War." Similar patterns apply for titles like "principal," "senator," "supervisor," etc.

And we pronounce this jewelry . . . marvelous!

But often the American president's title is used as a sort of substitute for his name, and routinely capitalized despite the objections of some style manuals: "The President pardoned the White House Thanksgiving turkey yesterday." And the British would never write anything other than "The Queen ate strawberries in the Royal Enclosure." The Pope is also usually referred to with a capital *P* when the specific individual is meant: "The Pope announced that he will visit Andorra next month." Following these common patterns is not likely to get you in trouble unless your editor has adopted a contrary rule.

If no specific individual is meant, then definitely use lower case: "We need to elect a homecoming queen"; "The next president will inherit a terrible budget deficit."

John Henry/John Hancock

John Hancock signed the Declaration of Independence so flamboyantly that his name became a synonym for "signature." Don't mix him up with John Henry, who was a steel-drivin' man.

John Hopkins/Johns Hopkins

The famous university and hospital named Johns Hopkins derive their peculiar name from their founder. "Johns" was his great-grandmother's maiden name. It is an error to call these institutions "John Hopkins."

John Hancock was a pen-drivin' man.

joint possessives

When writing about jointly owned objects, people often fret about where to place apostrophes. The standard pattern is to treat the two partners as a single unit—a couple—and put an apostrophe only after the last name: "John and Jane's villa," "Ben & Jerry's ice cream." Add more owners and you still use only one apostrophe: "Bob and Carol and Ted and Alice's party."

If each person owns his or her own item, then each owner gets an apostrophe: "John's and Jane's cars" (each of them separately owns a car).

But when you begin to introduce pronouns the situation becomes much murkier. "Jane and his villa" doesn't sound right because it sounds like Jane and the villa make a pair. The most common solution—"Jane's and his villa"—violates the rule about using the possessive form only on the last partner in the ownership. However, most people don't care and using this form won't raise too many eyebrows.

How about when you have two pronouns? "She and his villa" definitely won't work. "Her and his villa" might get by, but if you say "his and her villa" you inevitably remind people of the common phrase "his and hers" with a very different meaning: male and female, as in a sale on "his and hers scarves."

If you have time to think ahead, especially when writing, the best solution is to avoid this sort of construction altogether by rewording: "Jane and John have a villa outside Florence. *Their* villa is beautiful." "The villa owned by *Jane and him* is beautiful." "The villa is *Jane's and his.*" "The villa that *he and she* own is beautiful."

Things get tricky when using personal pronouns instead of names. Note that "I's" is not an acceptable substitute for "my." It's not "directions to my wife and I's house," but if you say "directions to my wife and my house" it sounds as if you were providing directions to your wife plus directions to your house. Stick with simpler constructions like "our house."

Other awkward examples you might want to avoid: "your and my shares" (better: "your share and mine"), "their and our shares" (better: their share and ours"), and "his and her shares" (not too bad, but "his share and hers" is better).

journey/sojourn
See "sojourn/journey."

judgement/judgment
In Great Britain and many of its former colonies, "judgement" is still the correct spelling; but ever since Noah Webster decreed the first *E* superfluous, Americans have omitted it. Many of Webster's crotchets have faded away (each year fewer people use the spelling "theater," for instance); but even the producers of *Terminator 2: Judgment Day* chose the traditional American spelling. If you write "judgement" you should also write "colour."

jukebox/jutebox
See "jutebox/jukebox."

jump-start/kick-start
See "kick-start/jump-start."

junta
The original and most sophisticated pronunciation of this Spanish-derived word for an unelected military government is "HOON-tah." Those who prefer an anglicized pronunciation say "JUNN-tuh." Those who give it a French accent by saying "ZHOON-tuh" are just plain wrong.

jury-rigged/jerry-built
See "jerry-built/jury-rigged."

just assume/just as soon
People sometimes write, "I'd just assume stay home and watch TV." The expression is "just as soon."

just, jest/gist
"Gist" means "essence," "main part." But expressions like "the gist of it" are most often used in modern speech to more vaguely refer to the general sense of a matter: "I didn't understand everything in the chapter, but I got the gist of it." This broadened sense will offend few people, but it's more of a problem if you replace this unusual word with a more familiar one like "just" or "jest."

just so happens/just happen
Traditionally the expression "just so happens" is used only with the subject "it,"

with the word "so" providing emphasis: "Thank you for inviting me to your softball game, but it just so happens to be on the same date as my wedding, as you very well know since you are supposed to be my best man." Expressions such as the following are popular but non-traditional: "I just so happen," "she just so happens," "they just so happen," etc. In each of these cases, the "so" should be omitted.

jutebox/jukebox

The word "juke" originated in southern black dialect, where it came to be associated with roadside drinking establishments, especially those which provided music for dancing. They were called "juke joints."

Coin-operated record players which replaced the live musicians were called "juke-boxes." The word is still in widespread use—often spelled without the hyphen—though classic jukeboxes are now rare.

"Jute" is a tough fiber derived from the bark of various plants, originally exported from Bengal. It is used in the manufacture of gunnysacks, canvas, ropes, floor mats, etc. It is not suitable for the construction of boxes.

karat/carat/caret/carrot

See "carat/caret/carrot/karat."

key

"Deceptive marketing is key to their success as a company." "Careful folding of the egg whites is key." This very popular sort of use of "key" as an adjective by itself to mean "crucial" sets the teeth of some of us on edge. It derives from an older usage of "key" as a metaphorical noun: "The key to true happiness is an abundant supply of chocolate." "Key" as an adjective modifying a noun is also traditional: "Key evidence in the case was mislaid by the police."

But adjectival "key" without a noun to modify it is not so traditional. If this sort of thing bothers you (as it does me), you'll have to grit your teeth and sigh. It's not going away.

Learn the combination—that's the key to opening the lock.

key/cay/quay

See "quay/cay/key."

kick-start/jump-start

You revive a dead battery by jolting it to life with a jumper cable: an extraordinary measure used in an emergency. So if you hope to stimulate a foundering economy, you want to jump-start it. Kick-starting is an old-fashioned and difficult way of starting a motorcycle, so it is an inappropriate label for a shortcut method of getting something going.

killed after/killed in, killed by, died after
Reporters often claim that accident victims have been killed after a collision with car or after some other catastrophe. What they really mean is that they were killed in the accident (if death was instantaneous), or by it, or that they died after it (if they lingered); and that's what they should say.

kind/kind of
See "that kind/that kind of."

kindergarden/kindergarten
The original German spelling of the word "kindergarten" is also standard in English.

kitty-corner/caddy-corner
See "caddy-corner/catty-corner, cater-corner, kitty-corner."

knelt/kneeled
See "-ed/-t."

knots per hour/knots
A knot equals one nautical mile per hour, so it makes no sense to speak of "knots per hour." Leave off "per hour" when reporting the speed of a vessel in knots.

know what I'm sayin'/you know
See "you know/know what I'm sayin'."

koala bear/koala
A koala is not a bear. People who know their marsupials refer to them simply as "koalas." Recent research, however, indicates that pandas are related to other bears.

*"You can call me a koala—
just don't call me late for eucalyptus!"*

kowtow/cowtow
See "cowtow/kowtow."

l/1
People who learned to type in the pre-computer era sometimes type a lowercase letter "l" when they need a number "1." Depending on the font being used, these may look interchangeable, but there are usually subtle differences

between the two. For instance, the top of a letter "l" is usually flat, whereas the top of a number "1" often slopes down to the left. If your writing is to be reproduced electronically or in print, it's important to hit that number key at the top left of your keyboard to produce a true number 1.

l/ll

There are quite a few words spelled with a double L in UK English which are spelled in the US with a single L. Examples include "woollen" (US "woolen"), "counsellor" (US "counselor"), "medallist" (US "medalist"), "jeweller" (US "jeweler"), "initialled" (US "initialed"), "labelled" (US "labeled"), "signalled" (US "signaled"), "totalled" (US "totaled").

Most of these won't cause Americans serious problems if they use the UK spelling, and a good spelling checker set to US English will catch them. But "chilli" looks distinctly odd to Americans when it turns up in the UK-influenced English of South Asian cookbooks. Americans are used to seeing it spelled "chili." (Of course Spanish speakers think it should be *chile*.)

lackadaisical/laxidaisical

See "laxidaisical/lackadaisical."

laid/layed

See "layed/laid."

laissez-faire

The mispronunciation "lazy-fare" is almost irresistible in English, but this is a French expression meaning "let it be" or, more precisely, "the economic doctrine of avoiding state regulation of the economy," and it has retained its French pronunciation (though with an English *R*): "lessay fare." It is most properly used as an adjective, as in "laissez-faire capitalism," but is also commonly used as if it were a noun phrase: "the Republican party advocates laissez-faire."

lamblast/lambaste

"Lambaste" has its roots in words having to do with beating, not blasting.

land lover/landlubber

"Lubber" is an old term for a clumsy person, and beginning in the 18th century sailors used it to describe a person who was not a good seaman. So the pirate expression of scorn for those who don't go to sea is not "land lover" but "landlubber."

languish/luxuriate

To languish is to wilt, pine away, become feeble. It always indicates an undesirable state. If you're looking for a nice long soak in the tub, what you want is not to *languish* in the bath but to *luxuriate* in it.

The word "languid" (drooping, listless) often occurs in contexts that might lead people to think of relaxation. Even more confusing, the related word "languorous" does describe dreamy self-indulgent relaxation. No wonder people mistakenly think they want to "languish" in the bath.

lapse/elapse
See "elapse/lapse."

large/important
In colloquial speech it's perfectly normal to refer to something as a "big problem," but when people create analogous expressions in writing, the result is awkward. Don't write "This is a large issue for our firm" when what you mean is "This is an important issue for our firm." Size and intensity are not synonymous.

larnyx/larynx
"Larynx" is often mispronounced and sometimes misspelled "larnyx."

last name/given name/first name
Now that few people know what a "surname" is, we usually use the term "last name" to designate a family name; but in a host of languages the family name comes first. For instance, "Kawabata" was the family name of author Kawabata Yasunari. For Asians, this situation is complicated because publishers and immigrants often switch names to conform to Western practice, so you'll find most of Kawabata's books in an American bookstore by looking under "Yasunari Kawabata." It's safer with international names to write "given name" and "family name" rather than "first name" and "last name."

Note that in a multicultural society the old-fashioned term "Christian name" (for "given name") is both inaccurate and offensive.

late/former
If you want to refer to your former husband, don't call him your "late husband" unless he's dead.

later/latter
Except in the expression "latter-day" (modern), the word "latter" usually refers back to the last-mentioned of a set of alternatives. "We gave the kids a choice of a vacation in Paris, Rome, or Disney World. Of course the latter was their choice." In other contexts not referring back to such a list, the word you want is "later."

Conservatives prefer to reserve "latter" for the last-named of no more than two items.

Latino/Chicano/Hispanic
See "Chicano/Latino/Hispanic."

laundry mat/laundromat
"Laundromat" was coined in the 1950s by analogy with "automat"—an automated self-service restaurant—to label an automated self-service laundry.

People unaware of this history often mistakenly deconstruct the word into "laundry mat" or "laundrymat."

laxidaisical/lackadaisical

"Alack!" originally meant something like "Alas!" It bore connotations of dissatisfaction or shame. "Alack the day!" meant at first "may the day be shamed in which this awful thing has happened." Later, it came to be abbreviated "lack-a-day" and used to express mere surprise.

The expression was gradually weakened, shifting from expressions of anguish to resigned despair, to languid indifference. The end result is the modern form "lackadaisical," which conveys a lack of enthusiasm—a casual, perfunctory way of doing things.

This final meaning suggests "laxness" to some people who then misspell the word "laxadaisical," but this is nonstandard.

lay/lie

You lay down the book you've been reading, but you lie down when you go to bed. In the present tense, if the subject is acting on some other object, it's "lay." If the subject is lying down, then it's "lie." This distinction is often not made in informal speech, partly because in the past tense the words sound much more alike: "He lay down for a nap," but "He laid down the law." If the subject is already at rest, you might "let it lie." If a helping verb is involved, you need the past participle forms. "Lie" becomes "lain" and "lay" becomes "laid": "He had just lain down for a nap," and "His daughter had laid the gerbil on his nose."

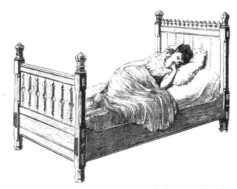

You may lay your thoughts to rest before you lie down.

layed/laid

Although "layed" is an extremely popular variant spelling of the past tense of transitive "lay," "laid" is the traditional spelling in all contexts. If your boss decides to lay you off, you are laid off. The hen laid an egg. You laid down the law.

LCD display/LCD

"LCD" stands for "liquid crystal display," so some argue it is redundant to write "LCD display" and argue you should use just "LCD" or "LCD screen" instead. But some in the industry argue that "LCD display" is the generic term for the category which comprises both LCD screens and LCD projectors.

However, if you want to avoid the redundancy in wording you can still refer more precisely to your laptop or TV as having an LCD screen.

Many people confuse this abbreviation with "LED," which stands for "light-emitting diode"—a much earlier technology. You will often see explanations even in technical contexts in which "LCD" is incorrectly defined as "liquid crystal diode." And it is misleading to call an LCD television screen which has LED backlighting an "LED screen."

leach/leech

Water leaches chemicals out of soil or color out of cloth; your brother-in-law leeches off the family by constantly borrowing money to pay his gambling debts (he behaves like a bloodsucking leech).

lead/led

When you're hit over the head, the instrument could be a *lead* pipe. But when it's a verb, "lead" is the present and "led" is the past tense. The problem is that the past tense is pronounced exactly like the above-mentioned plumbing material, so people confuse the two. ("Plumb," by the way, comes from a word meaning "lead.") In a sentence like "She led us to the scene of the crime," always use the three-letter spelling.

leant/leaned

See "-ed/-t."

leapt/leaped

See "-ed/-t."

leave/let

The colloquial use of "leave" to mean "let" in phrases like "leave me be" is not standard. "Leave me alone" is fine, though.

lectern/podium

See "podium/lectern."

led/lead

See "lead/led."

leech/leach

See "leach/leach."

leery/wary/weary

See "wary/weary/leery."

legend/myth

Myths are generally considered to be traditional stories whose importance lies in their significance, like the myth of the Fall in Eden; whereas legends can be merely famous deeds, like the legend of Davy Crockett. In common usage "myth" usually implies fantasy. Enrico Caruso was a legendary tenor, but

Hogwarts is a mythical school. Legends may or may not be true. But be cautious about using "myth" to mean "untrue story" in a mythology, theology, or literature class, where teachers can be quite touchy about insisting that the true significance of a myth lies not in its factuality but in its meaning for the culture that produces or adopts it.

lend/loan

"Loan me your hat" was just as correct everywhere as "lend me your ears" until the British made "lend" the preferred verb, relegating "loan" to the thing being lent. However, as in so many cases, Americans kept the older pattern, which in its turn has influenced modern British usage so that those insisting that "loan" can only be a noun are in the minority.

See also "borrow/loan."

lense/lens

Although the variant spelling "lense" is listed in some dictionaries, the standard spelling for those little disks that focus light is "lens."

less/fewer

See "amount/number."

less painless/less painful, more painful

Quite a few people accidentally say they want to make some process "less painless" when they mean "less painful." "Less painless" would be *more* painful.

lessen/lesson

Although not many people try to teach someone a "lessen," many people try to "lesson" their risks by taking precautions.

"Lessen" is something you do—a verb—and means to make smaller. "Lesson" is a noun, something you learn or teach. Remember this lesson and it will lessen your chances of making a mistake.

let/leave

See "leave/let."

let alone

"I can't remember the title of the book we were supposed to read, let alone the details of the story." In sentences like these you give a lesser example of something first, followed by "let alone" and then the greater example. But people often get this backwards, and put the greater example first.

The same pattern is followed when the expression is "much less": "I can't change the oil in my car, much less tune the engine." The speaker can much less well tune the engine than he or she can change the oil.

Another common expression which follows the same pattern uses "never mind," as in "I can't afford to build a tool shed, never mind a new house."

See also "little own/let alone."

let's/lets

The only time you should spell "let's" with an apostrophe is when it means "let us": "Let's go to the mall."

If the word you want means "allows" or "permits," no apostrophe should be used: "My mom lets me use her car if I fill the tank."

liable/libel

If you are likely to do something you are *liable* to do it; and if a debt can legitimately be charged to you, you are *liable* for it. A person who defames you with a false accusation *libels* you. There is no such word as "lible."

liaise

The verb "liaise," meaning to act as a liaison (intermediary between one group and another), has been around in military contexts since early in the 20th century; but recently it has broken out into more general use, especially in business, where it bothers a lot of people. Although dictionaries generally consider it standard English, you may want to avoid it around people irritated by business jargon.

library

The first *R* in "library" is often slurred or omitted in speech. It sometimes drops out in writing as well, and "librarian" is often turned into "libarian."

licence/license

In the UK, the noun is "licence": "here is my driving licence." But when it is a verb, the spelling is "license": "she is licensed to drive a lorry."

In contrast, Americans use the spelling "license" in all contexts and the spelling "licence" is considered a spelling error.

lie/lay

See "lay/lie."

lighted/lit

Don't fret over the difference between these two words; they're interchangeable.

lightening/lightning

Those bright flashes in the storm clouds indeed used to be referred to as "lightening," later as "light'ning," but now they are simply "lightning."

"Lightening" has a quite different meaning in modern English: making lighter, as in lightening your load or lightening the color of your hair.

light-year

"Light-year" is always a measure of distance rather than of time; in fact it is the distance that light travels in a year. "Parsec" is also a measure of distance, equaling 3.26 light-years, though the term was used incorrectly as a measure of time by Han Solo in *Star Wars*, as director George Lucas has since admitted.

like/as if

Since the 1950s, when it was especially associated with hipsters, "like" as a sort of meaningless verbal hiccup has been common in speech. The earliest uses had a sort of sense to them in which "like" introduced feelings or perceptions which were then specified: "When I learned my poem had been rejected I was, like, devastated." However, "like" quickly migrated elsewhere in sentences: "I was like, just going down the road, when, like, I saw this cop, like, hiding behind the billboard." This habit has spread throughout American society, affecting people of all ages. Those who have the irritating "like" habit are usually unaware of it, even if they use it once or twice in every sentence: but if your job involves much speaking with others, it's a habit worth breaking.

Recently young people have extended its uses by using "like" to introduce thoughts and speeches: "When he tells me his car broke down on the way to my party I'm like, 'I know you were with Cheryl because she told me so.'" To be reacted to as a grown-up, avoid this pattern. (*See also* "goes.")

Some stodgy conservatives still object to the use of "like" to mean "as," "as though," or "as if." Examples: "Treat other people like you want them to treat you" (they prefer "as you would want them to treat you"). "She treats her dog like a baby" (they prefer "she treats her dog as if it were a baby"). In expressions where the verb is implied rather than expressed, "like" is standard rather than "as": "she took to gymnastics like a duck to water."

In informal contexts, "like" often sounds more natural than "as if," especially with verbs involving perception, like "look," "feel," "sound," "seem," or "taste": "It looks like it's getting ready to rain" or "It feels like spring."

So nervous do some people get about "like" that they try to avoid it even in its core meaning of "such as": "ice cream flavors like vanilla and strawberry always sell well" (they prefer "such as vanilla . . ."). The most fanatical even avoid "like" where it is definitely standard, in such phrases as "behaved like a slob" ("behaved as a slob" is their odd preference).

like for/like

I would like you to remember that saying, "I'd like for you to take out the garbage," is not formal English. The "for" is unnecessary.

likeliness/likeness

Your portrait is your likeness, not your "likeliness."

The probability of something is its likeliness.

lion's share

Even though the original meaning of this phrase reflected the idea that the lion can take whatever he wants—typically all of the slaughtered game, leaving nothing for anyone else—in modern usage the meaning has shifted to "the largest share." This makes great sense if you consider the way hyenas and vultures swarm onto the leftovers from a typical lion's kill.

lip-sing/lip-synch

When you pretend you are singing by synchronizing your lip movements to a recording, you lip-synch—the vocal equivalent of playing "air guitar." Some people mistakenly think the expression is "lip-sing," and they often omit the required hyphen as well. Note that you can lip-synch to speech as well singing.

Many writers use the spelling "sync" rather than "synch." Users of each form tend to regard the other as weird, but in contemporary writing "sync" clearly prevails.

liquor

Although it may be pronounced "likker," you shouldn't spell it that way, and it's important to remember to include the *U* when writing the word.

LISTSERV

"LISTSERV" is the brand name of one kind of electronic mail-handling software for distributing messages to a list of subscribers. Other common brand names are "Majordomo" and "Listproc." You can subscribe to the poodle-fluffing list, but not the LISTSERV. People at my university, where only Mailman was used, often (and erroneously) referred to themselves as managers of "listservs." English teachers are frequently tripped up when typing "listserv" as part of a computer command; they naturally want to append an *E* on the end of the word. According to L-Soft, the manufacturer of LISTSERV, the name of its software should be set in all capital letters. See the LISTSERV Web site for details.

lit/lighted

See "lighted/lit."

"lite" spelling

Attempts to "reform" English spelling to render it more phonetic have mostly been doomed to failure—luckily for us. These proposed changes, if widely adopted, would make old books difficult to read and obscure etymological roots, which are often a useful guide to meaning. A few—like "lite" for "light," "nite" for "night," and "thru" for "through"—have attained a degree of popular acceptance, but none of these should be used in formal writing. "Catalog" has become an accepted substitute for "catalogue," but I don't like it and refuse to use it. "Analog" has triumphed in technical contexts, but humanists are still more likely to write "analogue."

literally

Like "incredible," "literally" has been so overused as a sort of vague intensifier that it is in danger of losing its literal meaning. It should be used to distinguish between a figurative and a literal meaning of a phrase. It should not be used as a synonym for "actually" or "really." Don't say of someone that he "literally blew up" unless he swallowed a stick of dynamite.

literature

Businesspeople like to refer to advertising brochures and instructional manuals as "literature." This drives writers and literary scholars nuts, but who else cares? If you should happen to be trying to sell a product to a bunch of English majors, don't offer them "literature" about it unless it was written by a distinguished author.

little/few

See "amount/number."

little own/let alone

When Tom writes "I don't even understand what you're saying, little own agree with it" he is misunderstanding the standard phrase "let alone." In the same context many people would say "never mind."

See also "let alone."

lived

In expressions like "long-lived," pronouncing the last part to rhyme with "dived" is more traditional, but rhyming it with "sieved" is so common that it's now widely acceptable.

load (number)

See "lots, plenty, load (number)."

loan/borrow

See "borrow/loan."

loan/lend

See "lend/loan."

loath/loathe

"Loath" rhymes with "both" and is a rather formal adjective meaning "reluctant," whereas "loathe" rhymes with "clothe" and is a common verb meaning "dislike intensely." Kenji is loath to go to the conference at Kilauea because he loathes volcanos.

login, log-in, log in

There is a strong tendency in American English to smoosh the halves of hyphenated words and phrases together and drop the hyphen, so we commonly see phrases such as "enter your login and password." This is a misuse of "login" since logging in involves entering both your ID and password, and "login" is not a proper synonym for "ID" alone, or "user name" (commonly truncated to the ugly "username"). Such mash-ups are influenced by the world of computer programming, where hyphens and spaces are avoided.

If you would prefer to use more standard English, it would be appropriate to use "log-in" as the adjectival phrase: "Follow the correct log-in procedure."

But the verb-plus-adverb combination should not be hyphenated: "Before viewing the picture of Britney you'll need to log in."

"Log on" and "log-on" mean the same thing as "log in" and "log-in" but are less common now.

logon/visit

You log on to a Web site by entering your ID and password. If you are merely encouraging people to visit a site which has no such requirement, it is misleading to ask them to "log on" to it. News reporters often get this wrong by reporting how many people "logged on" to a particular site when they mean "visited." "Visit" or just "go to" will do just fine.

LOL

The common Internet abbreviation "lol" (for "laughing out loud") began as an expression of amusement or satirical contempt: "My brother-in-law thought the hollandaise sauce was gravy and poured it all over his mashed potatoes (lol)." It has become much overused, often to indicate mere surprise or emphasis with no suggestion of humor: "The boss just told us we have to redo the budget this afternoon (lol)." And some people drop it into their prose almost at random, like a verbal hiccup. It is no longer considered hip or sophisticated, and you won't impress or entertain anyone by using it.

Note that this initialism has had two earlier meanings: "Little Old Lady" and "Lots Of Love."

long story short/to make a long story short

The traditional expression "to make (or cut) a long story short" is now commonly abbreviated by omitting the first phrase: "Long story short, I missed my plane." Although there's a certain appeal to the notion of abbreviating an expression about abbreviation, the shorter form sounds odd to people not used to it.

long-lived

See "lived."

lookit/look

"Lookit"—meaning "listen," "pay attention to what I'm going to say"— is casual slang, and is associated by many people with the speech of small children. Preceding a statement with "look" is not formal usage either, but it sounds more grown-up.

loosen/unloosen

See "unloosen/loosen."

lose/loose

This confusion can easily be avoided if you pronounce the word intended aloud. If it has a voiced *Z* sound, then it's "lose." If it has a hissy *S* sound, then it's "loose." Here are examples of correct usage: "He tends to lose his keys." "She lets her dog run loose." Note that when "lose" turns into "losing" it loses its *E*.

loser/looser
A person who's a failure is a *loser*, often a "real loser." If something is loosened, it becomes *looser*.

lots, plenty, load (number)
The expression "a lot" takes a singular verb when it refers to an amount of something that can't be counted: "a lot of water *has* gone over the dam." But it takes a plural verb when it refers to a countable number of things: "there *are* a lot of fish in the sea." "Lots" works the same way: "there *is* lots of room left in the theater, but for some reason lots of us *are* still waiting to be seated." Remember that "there's" is a contraction of "there is"; so instead of "there's a lot of flowers in the garden," say "there *are* a lot of flowers."

The same rule applies to "plenty" and "load." "There *is* plenty of turkey left," but "there *are* plenty of pecans in the pie." "Loads of dirty dishes *are* in the sink," so "there *is* loads of washing up to do."

low and behold/lo and behold
The "lo" is a sort of poetic synonym for "behold." Don't substitute the nonsensical "low."

lustful/lusty
"Lusty" means "brimming with vigor and good health" or "enthusiastic." Don't confuse it with "lustful," which means "filled with sexual desire."

luxuriant/luxurious
The word meaning "abundant" is "luxuriant," as in "luxuriant hair." "Luxurious" refers to luxury.

luxuriate/languish
See "languish/luxuriate."

-ly adjectives
A standard way to turn an adjective into an adverb is to add "-ly": "glad" becomes "gladly" and "huge" becomes "hugely." But when the adjectival form itself already ends in "-ly" it often feels awkward to create an adverbial form. If someone acts in a friendly manner do they behave "friendly" or "friendlily"? Did your daughter perform her dance solo "lovely" or "lovelily"? Most of us sense that these forms, though legitimate, are awkward, and try to avoid constructions that seem to require them. There are a variety of ways to do this: someone is friendly, a daughter gives a lovely performance.

MAC/Mac

Apple's Macintosh computers are usually referred to as "Macs" for short. Windows users unfamiliar with the usual way of rendering the name often write it as if it were an acronym, in all caps: "MAC."

But a MAC is something quite different. Every computer on a network has a Media Access Control number; so when your IT support person asks you for your "MAC address," don't say you don't have one just because you use Windows. Don't ask me how to find the MAC for your Windows computer though; I'm a Mac user.

macabre

"Macabre" is a French-derived word which in its original language has the final "ruh" sound lightly pronounced. Those who know this are likely to scorn those who pronounce the word "muh-COB." But this latter pronunciation is very popular and blessed by some American dictionaries, and those who prefer it sometimes view the French-derived pronunciation as pretentious. It's up to you whether you want to risk being considered ignorant or snooty.

maddening crowd/madding crowd

When Thomas Hardy titled one of his novels *Far from the Madding Crowd* he was quoting a phrase from Thomas Gray's 1750 poem "Elegy on a Country Churchyard" which used the archaic spelling "madding." The only reason to refer to "madding crowds" is to show how sophisticated you are, but if you update the spelling to "maddening" it will have the opposite effect: you'll look ignorant.

magic bullet/silver bullet

In modern English there are a number of specialized uses for the phrase "magic bullet," but the traditional term for a quick, effective solution to a difficult problem is "silver bullet." It is derived from the folk belief that bullets made of silver were especially effective against werewolves, vampires, and other supernatural monsters.

majority are/majority is

"Majority" is one of those words that can be either singular or plural. Common sense works pretty well in deciding which. If you mean the word to describe a collection of individuals, then the word should be treated as plural: "The majority of e-mail users are upset about the increase in spam." If the word is used to describe a collective group, then consider it singular: "A 90% majority is opposed to scheduling the next meeting at 6:00 A.M." If you are uncertain which you mean, then choose whatever form sounds best to you; it's not likely to bother many people.

"Majority" should be used only with countable nouns: "he ate the majority of the cookies," but not "he ate the majority of the pie." Instead say, "he ate most of the pie."

majorly/extremely

"Majorly," meaning "extremely," is slang and should not be used in formal writing, or even speech if you want to impress someone. "Brad was extremely [not 'majorly'] worried about the course final until he got around to reading the syllabus and found out there wasn't one."

make due/make do

When you try to get by with what you have, you make do.

make pretend/make believe

When you pretend to do something in a game of fantasy, you *make believe*.

mantle/mantel

Though they stem from the same word, a "mantle" today is usually a cloak, while the shelf over a fireplace is most often spelled "mantel."

manufacture/manufacturer

When your company makes stuff, it *manufactures* it; but the company itself is a *manufacturer*. Both in speech and writing the final *R* is often omitted from the latter word.

many/much

See "amount/number."

marinate on/meditate on

To add flavor and moisture to meats or other raw ingredients, you can soak them for a while in a flavored liquid *marinade* (note that the word for the liquid is spelled with a *D*). You *marinate* it (note that the word for the action is spelled with a *T*). You would rarely have a legitimate reason to use the phrase "marinate on." An example would be: "leave the chicken to marinate on the counter while you prepare the other ingredients."

When you ponder a subject thoughtfully, you meditate on it. So many people are misusing "marinate" when they mean "meditate" that some have concluded that they are related words with overlapping meanings. They urge people to think carefully about a subject by telling them to "marinate and meditate" on it. Letting thoughts soak into your consciousness has nothing to do with marinades.

"Were you daydreaming again?"

"What? Oh, no—I was just meditating on my marinated three-bean salad."

marital/martial

"Marital" refers to marriage, "martial" to war, whose ancient god was Mars. These two are often swapped, with comical results.

marshall/marshal

You may write "The Field Marshal marshalled his troops," but you cannot spell his title with a double *L*. A marshal is always a marshal, never a marshall.

Whether theirs was marital or martial bliss no one ever knew.

marshmellow/marshmallow

Your s'mores may taste mellow, but that gooey confection you use in them is not "marshmellow," but "marshmallow." It was originally made from the root of a mallow plant which grew in marshes.

mash potatoes/ mashed potatoes

You mash the potatoes until they become mashed potatoes.

mass/massive

When the dumb Coneheads on *Saturday Night Live* talked about consuming "mass quantities" of food they didn't know any better, but native Earth humans wanting an adjective rather than a noun should stick with "massive" unless they are trying to allude to SNL. "Mass" is often used by young people in expressions where "many" or even the informal "a lot of" would be more appropriate.

Expressions in which the noun "mass" can modify another noun, as in "mass migrations," are fine; but when you can use "massive" instead you should do so.

masseuse/masseur

"Masseuse" is a strictly female term; Monsieur Philippe, who gives back rubs down at the men's gym, is a "masseur." Because of the unsavory associations that have gathered around the term "masseuse," serious practitioners generally prefer to be called "massage therapists."

material/materiel

"Material" is a very common word, so it's not surprising that when people encounter the French-derived spelling "materiel" in military contexts ("supplying men and materiel"), they think it's a mistake and "correct" it to the more familiar "material." The equipment and supplies used by armies and other organizations are "materiel," which is never spelled with an *S* on the end.

mathmatics/mathematics

Don't subtract its second syllable from "mathematics." The British logically abbreviate this word to "maths," but Americans use plain "math."

may/might

Most of the time "might" and "may" are almost interchangeable, with "might" suggesting a somewhat lower probability. You're more likely to get wet if the forecaster says it may rain than if she says it might rain, but substituting one for the other is unlikely to get you into trouble—so long as you stay in the present tense.

But "might" is also the past tense of the auxiliary verb "may," and is traditionally required in sentences like "Chuck might have avoided arrest for the robbery if he hadn't given the teller his business card before asking for the money." When speculating that events might have been other than they were many speakers now substitute "may" for "might," but this annoys traditionalists.

When you are uncertain what has happened and are making a guess, then you may want to use "may": "I think he may have thought I would really like an oil change for my birthday."

As an aside: if you are an old-fashioned child, you will ask, "May I go out to play?" rather than "Can I go out to play?" Despite the prevalence of the latter pattern, some adults still feel strongly that "may" has to do with permission whereas "can" implies only physical ability. But then if you have a parent like this you've had this pattern drilled into your head long before you encountered this page.

me/I/myself

See "I/me/myself."

me either/me neither

Inside a longer sentence, "me either" can be perfectly legitimate: "whole-wheat pie crust doesn't appeal to me either." But by itself, meaning "neither do I," in reply to a previous negative statement, it has to be "me neither": "I don't like whole-wheat pie crust." "Me neither."

mean/median

To find the mean (or average) of a series of numbers, for example 1,2,3,4,5 & 6, add them all together for a total of 21; then divide by the number of numbers (6) to give the mean (or average) of 3.5.

In contrast, when half the data of a set are above a point and half below, that point is the median. The difference between mean and median can be quite significant, but one often sees the terms used wrongly even in technical contexts.

mean for/mean

"I didn't mean for you to see your present until I'd wrapped it." This sort of use of "mean for" is a casual pattern inappropriate in written or formal English. Instead, say "I didn't mean you to see your present. . . . "

meantime/meanwhile

Although most authorities now consider these words interchangeable, some people still prefer to use "meanwhile" when it stands alone at the beginning of a sentence: "Meanwhile the dog buried the baby's pacifier in the garden." They prefer "meantime" to be used only in the expression "in the meantime": "In the meantime, the dog chewed up my last tennis ball."

medal/metal/meddle/mettle

A person who proves his or her mettle displays courage or stamina. The word "mettle" is seldom used outside of this expression, so people constantly confuse it with other similar-sounding words.

media/medium

There are several words with Latin or Greek roots whose plural forms ending in *A* are constantly mistaken for singular ones. Radio is a broadcast medium. Television is another broadcast medium. Newspapers are a print medium. Together they are media. Following the tendency of Americans to abbreviate phrases, with "transistor radio" becoming "transistor" (now fortunately obsolete) and "videotape" becoming "video," "news media" and "communications media" have been abbreviated to "media." Remember that watercolor on paper and oil on black velvet are also media, though they have nothing to do with the news. When you want to get a message from your late Uncle Fred, you may consult a medium. The word means a vehicle between some source of information and the recipient of it. The "media" are the transmitters of the news; they are not the news itself.

See also "criteria/criterion" *and* "data/datum."

medieval ages/Middle Ages

The "eval" of "medieval" means "age," so by saying "medieval ages" you are saying "middle ages ages." Medievalists also greatly resent the common misspelling "midevil."

mediocre

Although some dictionaries accept the meaning of this word as "medium" or "average," in fact its connotations are almost always more negative. When something is distinctly not as good as it could be, it is mediocre. If you want to say that you are an average student, don't proclaim yourself mediocre, or you'll convey a worse impression of yourself than you intend.

meditate on/marinate on

See "marinate on/meditate on."

medium/median

That strip of grass separating the lanes going opposite directions in the middle of a freeway is a median. But if you're trying to achieve a balance between extremes, you're trying to strike a happy medium.

meet up

"Meet up with" and similar expressions (as in "let's meet up with them at the diner") is casual and slangy. In standard English, omit the "up with": "Let's meet them at the diner."

melted/molten

See "molten/melted."

memento/momento

See "momento/memento."

memorium/memoriam

The correct spelling of the Latin phrase is "in memoriam."

metal/medal/meddle/mettle

See "medal/metal/meddle/mettle."

metaphor

See "parallel/symbol."

meteor/meteorite/meteoroid

A chunk of rock out in space is a "meteoroid." If it plummets down through the earth's atmosphere, the resulting streak of light is called a "meteor." And if it lands on the ground, the chunk of stone is called a "meteorite."

Don't confuse meteors with comets, which are masses of ice and dust whose tails are produced not inside our atmosphere, but out in space. When a comet gets too close to the Sun its warmth and the pressure of the solar wind cause some of the comet to evaporate and stream out to form a tail.

methodology/method

A fondness for big words isn't always accompanied by the knowledge of their proper use. Methodology is about the methods of doing something; it is not the methods themselves. It is both pretentious and erroneous to write "The architect is trying to determine a methodology for reinforcing the foundation now that the hotel on top of it has begun to sink."

mfr./mfg.

"Mfr." is the abbreviation for "manufacturer" and "mfg." is the abbreviation for "manufacturing." Acme Mfg. Co. is a mfr. of roadrunner traps.

mic/mike

Until recently the casual term for a microphone was "mike," not "mic." Young people now mostly imitate the technicians who prefer the shorter "mic" label on their soundboards, but it looks distinctly odd to those used to the traditional term. There are no other words in English in which "-ic" is pronounced to rhyme with "bike"—that's the reason for the traditional "mike" spelling in the first place.

Middle Ages/medieval ages
See "medieval ages/Middle Ages."

middleaged/middle-aged
When you're in your teens, you're a teenager; but when you get older, you earn a hyphen: you become "middle-aged."

midrift/midriff
"Midriff" derives from "mid-" and a very old word for "stomach." Fashions which bare the belly expose the midriff. People think of the gap being created by scanty tops and bottoms as a rift, and mistakenly call it a "midrift" instead. In earlier centuries, before belly-baring was in, the midriff was also the piece of cloth which covered the area.

might/may
See "may/might."

might could/might, could
In some American dialects it is common to say things like "I might could pick up some pizza on the way to the party." In standard English, "might" or "could" are used by themselves, not together.

"Had ought," "hadn't ought," "shouldn't ought," and "might can" are similarly nonstandard.

might has well/might as well
You might as well get this one right: the expression is not "might *has* well" but "might *as* well."

might ought/might, ought
In some dialects it's common to say things like "you might ought to (pronounced "oughta") turn off the engine before changing the spark plugs." If you want to sound educated, you might want to avoid this combination. If you want to sound sophisticated you definitely ought to.

militate/mitigate
These are not very common words, but people who use them—especially lawyers—tend to mix them up. "Militate" is usually followed by "against" in a phrase that means "works against": "His enthusiasm for spectacular collisions militates against his becoming a really effective air traffic controller."

"Mitigate" means almost the opposite: to make easier, to moderate. "His pain at leaving was mitigated by her passionate kiss." It should not be followed by "against."

minature/miniature
Few people pronounce the second syllable in "miniature" distinctly, so it often

188

gets dropped in spelling.

mind of information/mine of information

A book, a person, or any other source stuffed with gems of useful knowledge is a *mine* of information, a metaphorical treasure trove of learning. The information involved may or may not be in someone's mind.

miner/minor

Children are minors, but unless they are violating child-labor laws, those who work in mines are *miners*.

miniscule/minuscule

The preferred spelling is "minuscule."

minister/administer

See "administer/minister."

minority

In the US the term "minority" frequently refers to racial minorities, and is used not only for groups, but for individuals. But many authorities object to calling a single person a minority, as in "We hired a minority for the job." Even phrases like "women and minorities" bother some people. They think it should be "members of minorities."

minuet/minute

Shakespeare's colleague and popular comic actor Will Kemp was famous for his stunt of dancing the jig from London to Norwich (about 80 miles). That's what I think of when I see real estate ads boasting "only five minuets from downtown!"

This is one of those silly typos that your spelling checker won't catch, because "minuet" is a real word.

"I told him I would dance if he would just wait one minuet."

minus/hyphen

When baffled computer users phone Support they may say they have a Model AB "minus" 231. In the model name "AB-231" the linking character is a hyphen, though "dash" will do. "Minus" makes no sense in such contexts, but is so common that support personnel have begun to adopt it too.

mischievious/mischievous

The correct pronunciation of this word is "MISS-chuh-vuss," not "miss-CHEE-vee-uss." Don't let that mischievous extra *I* sneak into the word.

mislead/misled

"Mislead" is the present tense form of this verb, but the past tense and past participle forms are "misled." When you mislead someone you have misled them. The spelling error most often occurs in the phrase "don't be mislead," especially in advertising. Although this phrase refers to the future, the helping verb "be" requires the participle "misled": "don't be misled."

misnomer

A misnomer is a mistake in naming a thing; calling a debit card a "credit card" is a misnomer. Do not use the term more generally to designate other sorts of confusion, misunderstood concepts, or fallacies, and above all do not render this word as "misnamer."

mispell/misspell

Your spelling checker should catch this one, but judging by the popularity of "mispell," "mispelled," and "mispelling" on the Web, it slips by many people. These words need two S's: one to end "mis-" and another to begin "-spell." So the words are "misspell," "misspelled," and "misspelling." This ranks as an embarrassing spelling mistake right up there with "writting."

misplaced stress

"We *will* be descending shortly *into* Denver," says the flight attendant, sounding very weird. People who have to repeat announcements by rote—including radio station-break announcers and others—often try to avoid sounding like monotonous robots by raising and lowering the pitch of their voices at random and stressing words not normally stressed: mostly prepositions and auxiliary verbs. One has to sympathize; imagine having to repeatedly lecture on seat-belt use to a plane full of people when you know for a fact the only adults on board likely not to know already how to fasten a buckle are too demented to understand what you're saying. But the absurd sing-song into which many of these folks fall is both distracting and irritating, making them sound like malfunctioning robots. Those who speak in natural voices, stressing main nouns, verbs, and adjectives where it makes sense, are much easier to listen to.

mitigate/militate

See "militate/mitigate."

mixed-up media/mixed media

Mixed media can be great; mixed-up media not so much.

Books are published, movies and musical recordings released, and plays and TV shows premiered.

Movies are shown, plays staged, and TV shows broadcast.

Technically recordings get deleted (from catalogues) or withdrawn rather than going out of print like books (which may also be remaindered: sold at discount, or worse—pulped). However, there is a strong tendency to use "out of print" for all kinds of media: CDs, DVDs, etc. Movies and stage shows close or end their runs, but only stage shows fold.

molten/melted

"Molten" is now usually used to describe hard materials like lava, glass, and lead liquefied by very high heat. Most other substances are "melted," though some people like to refer to "molten cheese" and a popular dessert is called "molten chocolate cake," perhaps to emphasize its gooey, lava-like character.

momentarily

"The plane will be landing momentarily," says the flight attendant, and the grumpy grammarian in seat 36B thinks to himself, "So we're going to touch down for just a moment?" Everyone else thinks, "Just a moment now before we land." Back in the 1920s when this use of "momentarily" was first spreading on both sides of the Atlantic, one might have been accused of misusing the word; but by now it's listed without comment as one of the standard definitions in most dictionaries.

momento/memento

A memento is something associated with a memory and has nothing to do with "moment."

money is no option/money is no object

The expression "money is no object" means that cost is no *obstacle*: you're willing to pay whatever is required to get what you want.

People who don't understand this unusual meaning of "object" often substitute "option," saying "money is no option," which makes no sense at all.

mongerer/monger

See "warmongerer/warmonger."

Mongoloid

"Mongoloid" is an outdated anthropological term referring to certain peoples from central and eastern Asia. Its use to label people with Down Syndrome is also dated and highly offensive. Avoid the term entirely. If you have cause to refer to people from Mongolia the proper term is "Mongolian."

mono e mono/mano a mano

"Mono e mono" is an error caused by mishearing the Spanish expression *mano a mano* which means not "man-to-man" but "hand-to-hand," as in hand-to-hand combat: one on one.

Moon/moon

See "Earth/earth/Moon/moon."

moot point/mute point

See "mute point/moot point."

moral/morale

If you are trying to make people behave properly, you are policing their morals;

if you are just trying to keep their spirits up, you are trying to maintain their morale. "Moral" is accented on the first syllable, "morale" on the second.

morals/morale/ethics
See "ethics/morals/morale."

morays/mores
The customs of a people are its *mores*. These may include its morals (ethics), but the word "mores" is not synonymous with "morals." Some eels are morays, but they aren't known particularly for their social customs, though both words are pronounced the same.

more/most
It is traditional to use "most" when comparing three or more things and "more" when comparing only two. "This is the more powerful of the two vacuum cleaners." "This is the most delicious entree on the menu." In casual speech this pattern is often ignored, but it's good to keep the distinction in mind when writing or speaking formally.

more than/over
See "over/more than."

moreso/more so
"More so" should always be spelled as two distinct words. It is also overused and misused. Wherever possible, stick with plain "more."

most always/almost always
"Most always" is a casual, slangy way of saying "almost always." The latter expression is better in writing. The same is true of "most every," "most all," and related expressions where the standard first word is "almost."

motherload/mother lode
Although you may dig a load of ore out of a mother lode, the spelling "motherload" is a mistake which is probably influenced by people thinking it means something like "the mother of all loads." A "lode" was originally a stream of water, but by analogy it became a vein of metal ore. Miners of precious metals dream of finding a really rich vein, which they refer to as a "mother lode," most often spelled as two words, though you also commonly see it spelled as one.

motion/move
When you make a motion in a meeting, say simply "I move," as in "I move to adjourn"; and if you're taking the minutes, write "Barbara moved," not "Barbara motioned" (unless Barbara was making wild arm-waving gestures to summon the servers to bring in the lunch). Instead of "I want to make a motion . . ." it's simpler and more direct to say "I want to move. . . ."

motor/engine
See "engine/motor."

Mount Fujiyama/Fujiyama
Yama means "mountain" in Japanese, so when you say "Mount Fujiyama" you are saying "Mount Fuji Mountain." The Japanese usually say *Fuji-san*, but "Fujiyama" or "Mount Fuji" is standard in English—just be aware that both sound "foreign" to Japanese native speakers.

Ms.
See "gender."

much/many
See "amount/number."

much differently/very differently
Say, "We consistently vote very differently," not "much differently." But you can say, "My opinion doesn't much differ from yours."

muchly/much
Drop the nonstandard "-ly" ending from "much," or substitute the word "very" when appropriate.

mucus/mucous
Mucous membranes secrete mucus. "Mucus" is the noun and "mucous" is the adjective. It's not only snotty biologists who insist on distinguishing between these two words.

multipart names
In many European languages family names are often preceded by a preposition (*de, da, di, von,* and *van* all mean "of"), an article (*le* and *la* mean "the") or both (*du, des, del, de la, della* and *van der* all mean "of the"). Such prefixes often originated as designators of nobility—or pretensions to it—but today they are just incidental parts of certain names.

In their original languages the two parts of the name are usually separated by a space, and the prefixed preposition or article is not capitalized unless it begins a sentence. If you take a college course involving famous European names you will be expected to follow this pattern. It's not "De Beauvoir" but "de Beauvoir"; not "Van Gogh" but "van Gogh." The only exception is when the name begins a sentence: "De Gaulle led the Free French," but "Charles de Gaulle had a big nose."

Some European names evolved into one-word spellings early on (Dupont, Lamartine, Dallapiccola), but they are not likely to cause problems because English speakers are usually unaware of the significance of their initial syllables.

When families bearing prefixed names move to the US, they often adapt their spelling to a one-word form. A well-known example is "DiCaprio."

French le Blanc becomes LeBlanc in America, and Italian di Franco becomes DiFranco. The name "de Vries" is spelled in English by various people bearing that name "De Vries," "DeVries," and "Devries." You have to check carefully to determine how a particular person prefers the name to be spelled. Library reference tools like *Who's Who* are more reliable than most Web sources.

The practice of retaining the capital letter inside the fused form is one peculiar to American English. Early books by famed science-fiction author Ursula K. Le Guin rendered her name "LeGuin" though later reprints go with the separated form, which we may assume is her preference. The fused form has the advantage of being easier for computers to sort into alphabetized lists. You will find many Web pages in which the names of Europeans are adapted to the one-word form, but this is a sign of a lack of sophistication.

Once you learn to properly separate the parts of a last name, you need to know how to alphabetize it. Put van Gogh under *V*, but Van Morrison under *M* ("Van" is his given name, not part of his family name). Ludwig van Beethoven, however, is under *B*, not *V*.

College students also need to know that most Medieval and many Renaissance names consist of a single given name linked to a place name to indicate where the person came from. Marie de France means simply "Marie of France," and she should never be referred to as simply "de France." After introducing her full name, refer to her as "Marie." Forget *The Da Vinci Code*; scholars refer to him as "Leonardo," never as "da Vinci."

multiply/times
See "times/multiply."

multiply by double/double, multiply by 2
If you are talking about making a number twice as large, the expression is "double" or "multiply by 2": "double your sales to multiply your income by 2."

You could properly say "increase by a 100%" to mean the same thing, but lots of people won't understand that.

And definitely do not confuse people by saying "multiply by double."

See also "divide by half/divide in half."

mumble jumbo, mumbo jumble/mumbo jumbo, mumble jumble
The original and by far the most common form of this expression referring to superstitions or needlessly complex and obscure language is "mumbo jumbo." "Mumble jumble" is far less common, but still accepted by the *Oxford English Dictionary* as a variant.

But the hybrid forms "mumble jumbo" and "mumbo jumble" are just mistakes.

murmer/murmur
Think of "murmur" as a gentle repetition of sounds like "blahblah."

music/singing

After my wife—an accomplished soprano—reported indignantly that a friend of hers had stated that her church had "no music, only singing," I began to notice the same tendency among my students to equate music strictly with instrumental music. I was told by one that "the singing interfered with the music" (i.e., the accompaniment). In the classical realm most listeners seem to prefer instrumental to vocal performances, which is odd given the distinct unpopularity of strictly instrumental popular music. People rejoice at the sound of choral works at Christmas but seldom seek them out at other times of the year.

After establishing that their singing was, indeed, music, they began in earnest.

Serious music lovers rightly object to the linguistic sloppiness that denies the label "music" to works by such composers as Palestrina, Schubert, and Verdi. From the Middle Ages to the late 18th century, vocal music reigned supreme, and instrumentalists strove to achieve the prized compliment of "sounding like the human voice." The dominance of orchestral works is a comparatively recent phenomenon.

In contrast, my students often call instrumental works "songs," being unfamiliar with the terms "composition" and "piece." All singing is music, but not all music is singing.

Muslims/Islams

See "Islams/Muslims."

must of/must have

"Must of" is an error for "must have."

See also "could of, should of, would of/could have, should have, would have."

mute point/moot point

"Moot" is a very old word related to "meeting," specifically a meeting where serious matters are discussed. Oddly enough, a moot point can be a point worth discussing at a meeting (or in court)—an unresolved question—or it can be the opposite: a point already settled and not worth discussing further. At any rate, "mute point" is simply wrong, as is the less common "mood point."

myriad of/myriad

Some traditionalists object to the word "of" after "myriad" or an "a" before, though both are fairly common in formal writing. The word is originally Greek, meaning "10,000," but now usually means "a great many." Its main function is as a noun, and the adjective derived from it shows its origins by being reluctant to behave like other nouns expressing amount, like "ton" as in "I've got a ton of work to do." In contrast: "I have myriad tasks to complete at work."

myself
See "I/me/myself."

myth/legend
See "legend/myth."

n'/'n'
In your restaurant's ad for "Big 'n' Juicy Burgers," remember that the apostrophes substitute for both omitted letters in "and"—the *A* and the *D*—so strictly speaking it's not enough to use just one, as in "Big n' Juicy."

By so doing, you'll improve on the usage of McDonald's, which has actually created the registered trademark "Big N' Tasty."

nail in the coffin
See "death nail/death knell, nail in the coffin."

naive/nieve
See "nieve/naive."

name, pronoun
In old English ballads, it is common to follow the name of someone with a pronoun referring to the same person. For instance: "Sweet William, he died the morrow." The extra syllable "he" helps fill out the rhythm of the line.

Though this pattern is rare in written prose it is fairly common in speech. If you say things like "Nancy, she writes for the local paper," people are less likely to think your speech poetic than they are to think you've made a verbal stumble. Leave out the "she."

The same pattern applies to common nouns followed by pronouns as in "the cops, they've set up a speed trap" (should be "the cops have set up a speed trap").

Native American/Indian
See "Indian/Native American."

nauseated/nauseous
Many people say, when sick to their stomachs, that they feel "nauseous"

(pronounced "NOSH-uss" or "NOZH-uss") but traditionalists insist that this word should be used to describe something that makes you *want* to throw up: something nauseating. They hear you as saying that you make people want to vomit, and it tempers their sympathy for your plight. Better to say you are "nauseated," or simply that you feel like throwing up.

naval/navel
Your bellybutton is your navel, and navel oranges look like they have one; all terms having to do with ships and sailing require "naval."

near/nearly
Some dialects substitute "near" for standard "nearly" in statements like "There weren't nearly enough screws in the kit to finish assembling the cabinet."

near miss
It is futile to protest that "near miss" should be "near collision." This expression is a condensed version of something like "a miss that came very near to being a collision" and is similar to "narrow escape." Everyone knows what is meant by it and almost everyone uses it. It should be noted that the expression can also be used in the sense of almost succeeding in striking a desired target: "His Cointreau soufflé was a near miss."

Gustav's quarter-in-the-eye trick: A near miss at every party.

neck in neck/neck and neck
When a race is very tight, it's described not as "neck *in* neck" but "neck *and* neck."

needs -ed/-ing
In some dialects it is common to say "my shoes need shined" instead of the standard "my shoes need shining" or "my shoes need to be shined."

neice/niece
Despite the fact that the rule "*I* before *E* except after *C*" holds true most of the time, many people have trouble believing that words with the "ee" sound in them should be spelled with an *IE*. The problem is that in English (and only in English), the letter *I* sounds like "aye" rather than "ee," as it does in the several European languages from which we have borrowed a host of words. If you had studied French in high school you would have learned that this word is pronounced "knee-YES" in that language, and it would be easier to remem-

ber. Americans in particular misspell a host of German-Jewish names because they have trouble remembering that in German *IE* is pronounced "ee" and *EI* is pronounced "aye." The possessors of such names are inconsistent about this matter in English. "Wein" changes from "vine" to "ween," but "Klein" remains "kline."

See also "ei/ie."

Nevada

"Nuh-VAH-duh" is a little closer to the original Spanish pronunciation than the way Nevadans pronounce the name of their home state, but the correct middle syllable is the same *A* sound as in "sad." When East Coast broadcasters use the first pronunciation, they mark themselves as outsiders.

never the less, not withstanding/nevertheless, notwithstanding

For six centuries we have been spelling "nevertheless" and "notwithstanding" as single words, and today it is definitely not standard to break them up into hyphenated or non-hyphenated multiword phrases.

nevermind/never mind

The standard spelling of this phrase is as two words: "never mind." The popularity of the alternative one-word form "nevermind" was certainly enhanced by its use in 1991 as the title of a bestselling Nirvana album. "Nevermind" can look immature or slangy to some readers. You can still be cool by imitating the vocabulary choice in the title of another famous album: *Never Mind the Bollocks: Here's the Sex Pistols.*

"The lad with the torn shirt and safety pins? That's just Johnny Rotten . . . never mind about him."

In expressions like "pay him no nevermind" where the word means "attention" it's always one word, but those expressions are both slangy and old-fashioned.

new beginning

See "redundancies."

new lease of life/new lease on life

Reinvigorated people are traditionally said to have been granted not a "new lease of life" but a "new lease on life." After all, you take out a lease on a house, right? Same thing.

next/this

If I tell you that the company picnic is next Saturday it would be wise to ask whether I mean this coming Saturday or the Saturday after that. People differ in how they use "next" in this sort of context, and there's no standard pattern; so it's worth making an extra effort to be clear.

In the UK the distinction is made clear by saying "Saturday next" or "Saturday week."

next store/next door

You can adore the boy next door, but not "next store."

next to last/penultimate

See "penultimate/next to last."

nicety/niceness

"Nicety" is a noun meaning "fine detail" and is usually used in the plural. You may observe the niceties of etiquette or of English grammar. It is not a noun describing someone who is nice. That is "niceness."

niece/neice

See "neice/niece."

nieve/naive

People who spell this French-derived word "nieve" make themselves look naive. In French there is also a masculine form: "*naif*"; and either word can be a noun meaning "naive person" as well as an adjective. "Nieve" is actually the Spanish word for "snow." "Naïveté" is the French spelling of the related noun in English. If you prefer more nativized spelling, "naivety" is also acceptable.

niggard

"Niggard" is a very old word in English meaning "miser" or "stingy person." Americans often mistakenly assume it is a variant on the most common insulting term for dark-skinned people. You may embarrass yourself by attacking a writer for racism when you see it in print; but since so many people are confused about this it might be better to use "miser" and "stingy" instead of "niggard" and "niggardly."

ninty/ninety

"Nine" keeps its *E* when it changes to "ninety."

nip it in the butt/nip it in the bud

To nip a process in the bud is to stop it from flowering completely. The hilariously mistaken "nip it in the butt" suggests stimulation to action rather than stopping it.

nite

See "'lite' spelling."

no sooner when/no sooner than

The phrase "No sooner had Paula stopped petting the cat when it began to yowl" should be instead "No sooner had Paula stopped petting the cat than it began to yowl."

no such a thing/no such thing

Some say "there's no such thing as bad publicity," but in phrases like this it's much less common to insert an "a" after "such" so that the phrase becomes "no such a thing."

This variation followed by a phrase beginning with "as" will probably not be noticed in most contexts, but it tends to sound more obviously nonstandard when the phrase stands by itself as a simple negation: "Eric told me the grocery store was handing out free steaks. No such a thing." It sounds better to most people to say instead "no such thing."

no where/nowhere

"Nowhere," like "anywhere" and "somewhere," is always one word.

Noble Prize/Nobel Prize

Nobel laureates may indeed be intellectual nobility, but the award they get is not the "Noble Prize" but the "*Nobel* Prize," named after founder Alfred Nobel.

none

There's a lot of disagreement about this one. "None" can be either singular or plural, depending on the meaning you intend and its context in the sentence. "None of the pie is left" is clearly singular. But "None of the chocolates is left" is widely accepted, as is "None of the chocolates are left." If it's not obvious to you which it should be, don't worry; few of your readers will be certain either.

Singular? Plural? After a few drinks, none was in a position to care.

nonplussed

"Nonplussed" means to be stuck, often in a puzzling or embarrassing way, unable to go further ("non" = "no" + "plus" = "further"). It does not mean, as many people seem to think, "calm, in control."

noone/no one

Shall we meet at Ye Olde Sandwyche Shoppe at noone? "No one" is always two separate words, unlike "anyone" and "someone."

normalcy vs. normality

The word "normalcy" had been around for more than half a century when President Warren G. Harding was assailed in the newspapers for having used it in a 1921 speech. Some folks are still upset; but in the US "normalcy" is a perfectly normal—if uncommon—synonym for "normality."

not

You need to put "not" in the right spot in a sentence to make it say what you intend. "Not all fraternity members are drunks" means some are, but "All fraternity members are not drunks" means none of them is.

not all

The combination of "not" and "all" can be confusing if you're not careful about placement. "All politicians are not corrupt" could theoretically mean that no politician is corrupt; but what you probably mean to say is "Not all politicians are corrupt." When "not all" is a minority, it's sometimes better to replace "not all" with "some." "The widescreen version is not available in all video stores" can be made clearer by saying "The widescreen version is not available in some stores."

not all that/not very

The slangy phrase "not all that," as in "The dessert was not all that tasty," doesn't belong in formal writing. "Not very" would work, but something more specific would be even better: "The pudding tasted like library paste."

not hardly/not at all

"Not hardly" is slang, fine when you want to be casual—but in a formal document? Not hardly!

not my forte

Some people insist that it's an error to pronounce the word "forte" in the expression "not my forte" as if French-derived "forte" were the same as the Italian musical term for "loud": "for-tay." But the original French expression is *pas mon fort*, which not only has no *E* on the end to pronounce—it has a silent *T* as well. It's too bad that when we imported this phrase we mangled it so badly, but it's too late to do anything about it now. If you go around saying what sounds like "that's not my fort," people won't understand what you mean.

However, those who use the phrase to mean "not to my taste" ("Wagnerian opera is not my forte") are definitely mistaken. Your forte is what you're good at, not just stuff you like.

notate/note

To notate a text is to write annotations about it. This technical term should not be used as a synonym for the simple verb "note." It is both pretentious and incorrect to write "notate the time you arrived in your log."

nothing (singular)

In formal English, "nothing" is always singular, even when it's followed by a phrase stating an exception which contains a plural noun: "Nothing but weeds

grows [*not* grow] in my yard" and
"nothing except desserts appeals [*not*
appeal] to Jennifer." This pattern is
seldom followed in more casual speech
and writing, but you can see its logic
if you move "nothing" to immediately
precede its verb: "Nothing appeals to
Jennifer except desserts."

notorious

"Notorious" means famous in a bad
way, as in "Nero was notorious for giving long recitals of his tedious poetry."
Occasionally writers deliberately use

*Freddie and Frankie Frog—
notorious for their lager binges.*

it in a positive sense to suggest irony or wit, but this is a very feeble and tired
device. Nothing admirable should be called "notorious."

The same goes for "notoriety," which also indicates a bad reputation.
See also "infamous."

now and days/nowadays

Although it used to be hyphenated on occasion as "now-a-days," this expression is nowadays usually rendered as a single unhyphenated word. Some folks
mistakenly think the expression is "now and days," which makes no sense.

nowheres

"Nowheres" is a common dialectical variant. In standard English the word is
"nowhere."

nuclear

This isn't a writing problem, but a pronunciation error. President Eisenhower
used to consistently insert a *U* sound between the first and second syllables,
leading many journalists to imitate him and say "nuk-yuh-lar" instead of the
correct "nuk-lee-ar." The confusion extends also to "nucleus." Many people
can't even hear the mistake when they make it, and only scientists and a few
others will catch the mispronunciation; but you lose credibility if you are an
anti-nuclear protester who doesn't know how to pronounce "nuclear." Here's
one way to remember: we need a new, clear understanding of the issues; let's
stop saying "Nuke you!"

number/amount

See "amount/number."

number of verb

In long, complicated sentences people often lose track of whether the subject is
singular or plural and use the wrong sort of verb. "The ultimate effect of all of
these phone calls to the detectives were to make them suspicious of the callers"

is an error because "effect," which is singular, is the subject. If you are uncertain about whether to go with singular or plural, condense the sentence down to its skeleton: "The effect . . . was to make them suspicious."

Another situation that creates confusion is the use of interjections like "along with," "as well as," and "together with," where they are often treated improperly as if they meant simply "and." "Aunt Hilda, as well as her pet dachshund, is coming to the party" (not "are coming").

A compound subject requires a plural verb even if the words which make it up are themselves singular in form: "widespread mold and mildew damage [not damages] the resale value of your house."

If the title of a work is in the plural, you still use a singular verb because it is just one work: "My copy of *Great Expectations* has the original illustrations in it." That much seems obvious; but it might not seem quite so obvious that *Plutarch's Lives* is a single work, or that *Shakespeare's Sonnets* is. Of course if you are not referring to the book as a whole but to the individual poems they are "Shakespeare's sonnets," and take a plural verb.

Amounts of money and periods of time are usually considered singular: ten dollars is not a lot of money to lend someone, and five years is a long time to wait to be repaid.

numbers

If your writing contains numbers, the general rule is to spell out in letters all the numbers from zero to nine and use numerals for larger numbers, but there are exceptions. If what you're writing is full of numbers and you're doing math with them, stick with numerals. Approximations like "about thirty days ago" and catch-phrases like "his first thousand days" are spelled out. Large round numbers are often rendered thus: "50 billion sold." With measurements, use numerals: "4 inches long." Try to avoid starting a sentence with a numeral. You can either spell out the number involved or rearrange the sentence to move the number to a later position.

Many style manuals apply the same rule to what are called "ordinal" numbers, like "first," "second," "fifth." Following this pattern, higher numbers spelled as numerals begin with "10th" and go on through numbers like "22nd" and "114th." But dates are usually rendered in numerals even if they are small. It's normally "July 4th" and "the 4th of July," though few people would object to "Fourth of July." The only reason to worry about this is if you are writing for an editor or teacher who has a particular preference for one of these patterns. You are more likely to get in trouble if you use numerals for small numbers than if you use spelled-out forms for large numbers: "my 1st trip to France" looks bad to more people than "the seventy-fifth time I've told you to take out the trash." And large round ordinal numbers are almost always spelled out: "the hundredth issue published," "the thousandth ticket sold," "the millionth visitor to the park."

See also "decade names."

numerous of/numerous, numbers of

"Numerous customers returned the garlic-flavored toothpaste." "Numbers of customers returned the toothpaste." "Many of the customers." Any of these is fine.

But "numerous of the customers"? Yuck.

nuptual/nuptial

"Nuptial" is usually a pretentious substitute for "wedding," but if you're going to use it, be sure to spell it properly. For the noun, the plural form "nuptials" is more traditional.

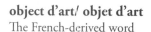

o/oh

See "oh/o."

o/zero

When reciting a string of numbers such as your credit card number it is common and perfectly acceptable to pronounce zero as "oh." But when dealing with a registration code or other such string of characters which mixes letters and numbers, it is important to distinguish between the number 0 and the letter O. In most typefaces a capital O is rounder, fatter, than a zero; but that is not always the case. What looks unambiguous when you type it may come out very unclear on the other end on a computer that renders your message in a different typeface.

In technical contexts, the distinction is often made by using zeros with slashes through them, but this can create as many problems as it solves: those unfamiliar with the convention will be confused by it, numbers using such characters may not sort properly, and slashed zeros created in some fonts change to normal zeros in other fonts.

"Just because she's French, Fifi thinks she's some kind of objet d'art."

If you work for a company that requires registration codes you do a disservice to your customers and yourself by including either zeros or O's in your codes where there is any possibility of confusion.

object d'art/ objet d'art

The French-derived word for an object of artistic value or a curio is *objet d'art* pronounced "ahb-ZHAY darr," (first syllable rhymes with "job"). It is often anglicized mistakenly to *object d'art*. People also mispronounce and misspell it *ojet d'art*, omitting the *B*. The correct plural form is *objets d'art*.

obsolescent/obsolete

Many people assume the word "obsolescent" must be a fancy form of "obsolete," but something obsolescent is technically something in the process of *becoming* obsolete. Therefore it's an error to describe something as "becoming obsolescent."

obtain/attain

See "attain/obtain."

obtuse/abstruse

See "abstruse/obtuse."

octopi/octopuses

"Octopi" is a slangy plural form of "octopus," but it's not the form used by marine biologists. Although some prefer "octopodes," this form is rare. The standard plural form is "octopuses."

odd

Expressions like "twenty-odd years," "a dozen-odd people," and "two hundred-odd mistakes" indicate that the exact number is unknown—perhaps a bit higher than the stated number. These expressions are usually written with a hyphen before the "odd." If you omit the hyphen, as in "a dozen odd people attended my birthday party," you risk giving the impression that the people who came were odd rather than that you can't be sure of the precise number of your guests.

oeuvre

In French *oeuvre* means "work" in many different ways. In English we use the word only in the specialized sense "the body of work produced by an individual creator." Unfortunately, "oeuvre" begins with a vowel sound we don't have in English and ends in a French *R* that also does not correspond to any English sound. The result is often grotesque mispronunciations like "oove." It's better to avoid foreign words like this if you haven't mastered the accent. "Body of work" or "output" will do fine.

of

"Of" is often shoved in where it doesn't belong in phrases like "not that big of a deal" and "not that great of a writer." Just leave it out.

of ___'s

Phrases combining "of" with a noun followed by *S* may seem redundant, since both indicate possession; nevertheless, "a friend of Karen's" is standard English, just as "a friend of Karen" and "Karen's friend" are.

ofcourse/of course

The misspelling of the two-word phrase "of course" as "ofcourse" should be caught by any good spelling-checker, but it seems to be extremely common.

off of

For most Americans, the natural thing to say is "Climb down off of (pronounced "offa") that horse, Tex, with your hands in the air"; but many UK authorities urge that the "of" should be omitted as redundant. Where British English reigns you may want to omit the "of" as superfluous, but common usage in the US has rendered "off of" so standard as to generally pass unnoticed, though some American authorities also discourage it in formal writing. But if "onto" makes sense, so does "off of." However, "off of" meaning "from" in phrases like "borrow five dollars off of Clarice" is definitely nonstandard.

offense/offence

In the US "offense" is standard; in the UK use "offence." The sports pronunciation accenting the first syllable should not be used when discussing military, legal, or other sorts of offense.

offline

When your computer is connected to the Internet, you are online. When you disconnect from the Internet, you are offline.

People who don't understand this often say of things they get from the Internet that they downloaded them "offline," evidently thinking that the word means "off of the Internet." Nothing can be uploaded or downloaded to a site when you are offline.

oft chance/off chance

"Oft" is just short for "often." Something that happens on an off chance is something that happens rarely, not often; so the expression is not "on the oft chance" but "on the off chance."

often

People striving for sophistication often pronounce the *T* in this word, but true sophisticates know that the masses are correct in saying "offen."

oggle/ogle

If you're being leered at lustfully you're being ogled (first vowel sounds like "OH")—not "oggled," even if you're being ogled through goggles. The word is probably related to the German word *äugeln*, meaning "to eye," from *Auge* ("eye").

oh/o

"O" is an older spelling of "oh" which survives today mostly in poetry. The title of the Canadian national anthem is "O Canada," not "Oh Canada."

Similarly, "America the Beautiful" begins "O beautiful for spacious skies." When not addressing some entity poetically, "oh" is fine.

OK/okay
This may be the most universal word in existence; it seems to have spread to most of the world's languages. Etymologists now generally agree that it began as a humorous misspelling of "all correct": "oll korrect." "OK" without periods is the most common form in written American English now, though "okay" is not incorrect.

Old English
Many people refer to any older form of English as "Old English," but this is properly a technical term for Anglo-Saxon, the original language in which *Beowulf* was written. Norman French combined with Old English to create Middle English, one form of which was used by Geoffrey Chaucer to write *The Canterbury Tales*. By Shakespeare's time the language is modern English, though it may seem antique to modern readers who aren't used to it.

There are many "Old English" typefaces which have nothing to do with the Old English language.

old fashion/old-fashioned
Although "old fashion" appears in advertising a good deal, the traditional spelling is "old-fashioned."

old wise tale/old wives' tale
An absurd superstition is an "old wives' tale": according to sexist tradition a story popular among credulous old ladies. It's not an "old wise tale" or—even worse—an "old wives' tail."

old-timer's disease/Alzheimer's disease
I've always thought that "old-timer's disease" was a clever if tasteless pun on "Alzheimer's disease," but many people have assured me that this is a common and quite unintentional error.

Some medical authorities prefer the form "Alzheimer disease," though that is seldom used by nonprofessionals.

on accident/by accident
Although you can do things *on* purpose, you do them *by* accident.

on sale/for sale
See "for sale/on sale."

on the contraire/au contraire, on the contrary, to the contrary
People who like to show off their French sometimes use the expression *au contraire* when they mean "on the contrary" or "to the contrary." People who don't know any better mix up French and English by saying "on the contraire."

"On the contrary" is the earliest form. It means "it's the opposite": "I thought you liked sweet pickles." "On the contrary, I prefer dills."

"To the contrary" means "to the opposite effect," "in opposition": "No matter what my neighbor says to the contrary, I think it's his dog that's been pooping on my petunias."

on the same token/by the same token

When we compare things with each other, we often say "on the one hand" and "on the other hand." These phrases mean "on this side" and "on the other side."

But it is a mistake to say "on the same token," meaning "in the same regard." The standard expression is "*by* the same token."

on to/onto

See "onto/on to."

once/ones

"Once" always has to do with time and answers the questions, "how many times?" or "when?" For instance: "I only played handball once." "Once I got my boot off, I saw my sock had a hole in it."

In contrast, "ones" have to do with things. In your tool collection, the *ones* you should keep handy are the *ones* you use most.

once and a while/once in a while

"Once and a while" is based on a mishearing of the traditional expression "once in a while."

1/l

See "l/1."

180 degrees/360 degrees

See "360 degrees/180 degrees."

100's/hundreds

It looks cheesy to spell "hundreds" as "100's"; and it isn't really logical because "100" doesn't mean "hundred"—it means specifically "one hundred."

one in the same/one and the same

The old expression "they are one and the same" is now often mangled into the roughly phonetic equivalent "one in the same." The use of "one" here to mean "identical with each other" is familiar from phrases like "Jane and John act as one." They are one; they are the same.

one of the (singular)

In phrases like "pistachio is one of the few flavors that appeals to me," formal grammar would require the verb to be plural ("appeal") rather than singular ("appeals") because "that" acts as the subject for the verb, and "that" in this sentence refers to "flavors." However, many sophisticated users of English allow for the singular verb in this case, though I would caution against the singular verb if you are taking a test on English grammar.

This is one of those occasions in English usage that lets you follow your ear to determine what works best. If you thought "let" would have worked better in that previous sentence, you would have formal grammar on your side, but using "lets" should not get you into trouble, either.

one of the only/one of the few

Although it has recently become much more popular, the phrase "one of the only" bothers some of us in contexts in which "one of the few" would traditionally be used. Be aware that it strikes some readers as odd. "One of only three groups that played in tune" is fine, but "one of the only groups that played in tune" is more likely to cause raised eyebrows.

one-dimensional/two-dimensional

Once upon a time most folks knew that "three-dimensional" characters or ideas were rounded, fleshed out, and complex; and "two-dimensional" ones were flat and uninteresting. It seems that the knowledge of basic geometry has declined in recent years, because today we hear uninteresting characters and ideas described as "one-dimensional." According to Euclid, no physical object can be one-dimensional (of course, according to modern physics, even two-dimensionality is only an abstract concept). If you are still bothered by the notion that two dimensions are one too many, just use "flat."

ones/one's

The possessive pronoun "one's" requires an apostrophe before the *S*, unlike "its," "hers," and other personal pronouns. Examples: "pull oneself up by one's own bootstraps," "a jury of one's peers," "minding one's own business."

A simple test: try inserting "anyone's" in place of "one's." If it works grammatically, you need the apostrophe in "one's" too. When "one's" is a contraction of "one is" it also requires an apostrophe: "no one's listening," "this one's for you."

The only times "ones" has no apostrophe are when it is being used to mean " examples" or "people" as in "ripe ones" or "loved ones," or in the informal arithmetical expression "the ones column."

ongoingly/currently, continuously

"Ongoingly" is not standard English. When something is occurring in an ongoing manner, you can speak of it as happening "currently" or "continuously."

online/on line/in line

The common adjective used to label Internet activities is usually written as one word: "online": "The online site selling banana cream pies was a failure." But it makes more sense when using it as an adverbial phrase to write two separate words: "When the teacher took her class to the library, most of them used it to go on line." The hyphenated form "on-line" is not widely used, but would be proper only for the adjectival function. However, you are unlikely to get into trouble for using "online" for all computer-related purposes.

As for real physical lines, New Yorkers and Bostonians wait "on line" (in queues), but most Americans wait "in line."

only

Writers often inadvertently create confusion by placing "only" incorrectly in a sentence. It should go immediately before the word or phrase it modifies. "I lost my only shirt" means that I had but one to begin with. "I lost only my shirt" means I didn't lose anything else. "Only I lost my shirt" means that I was the only person in my group to lose a shirt. Strictly speaking, "I only lost my shirt" should mean I didn't destroy it or have it stolen—I just lost it, but in common speech this is usually understood as being identical with "I lost only my shirt." Scrutinize your uses of "only" to make sure you are not creating unwanted ambiguities.

onto/on to

"Onto" and "on to" are often interchangeable, but not always. Consider the effect created by wrongly using "onto" in the following sentence when "on to" is meant: "We're having hors d'oeuvres in the garden, and for dinner moving onto the house." If the "on" is part of an expression like "moving on," it can't be shoved together with a "to" that just happens to follow it.

opaque

See "translucent/transparent/opaque."

op-ed

Although it looks like it might mean "opinion of the editor" the "op-ed" page is actually a page written by columnists or outside contributors to a newspaper, printed opposite the editorial page.

open/unlocked/unlatched

Many people refer to doors as being "open" when they mean to say they are merely unlocked. Telling people to leave a house open may mislead them into making the place more inviting to casual intruders than you intend if you really only want it to be unlocked. And you may unnecessarily alarm the driver if you report from the back seat of a car that one of the doors is open when you mean that it is merely unlatched.

opportunist

When applied to people, the label "opportunist" usually has negative connotations. It implies that the people so labeled take unprincipled, unfair advantage of opportunities for selfish ends. Opportunistic people are often also regarded as exploitative. The term is often used to label unscrupulous politicians who seek to manipulate voters in their favor by exploiting certain issues or opportunities in an unethical way.

Sports commentators who call the skillful interceptor of a pass in football an "opportunist" are misusing the word.

If you want to praise people for taking legitimate and skilled advantage of opportunities that spring up, it is better to call them "enterprising" or "quick-witted."

The specialized meaning of "opportunistic" in biology does not cause problems because the people who use the word in this sense know what it describes: the ability of a species to exploit a previously unexploited ecological niche.

oppose/appose
See "appose/oppose."

oppose to/opposed to, supposed to
Just as some people say "suppose to" when they mean "supposed to," others say "oppose to" when they mean "opposed to." You may be *opposed* to laugh tracks on TV comedy shows or wearing flip-flops at a wedding reception.

Some people go even further and get "oppose" and "suppose" all mixed up, saying things like "You're oppose to get the oil changed in the car every 5,000 miles." That should be "*supposed* to."

See also "use to/used to."

oppress/repress
Dictators commonly oppress their citizens and repress dissent, but these words don't mean exactly the same thing. "Repress" just means "keep under control." Sometimes repression is a good thing: "During the job interview, repress the temptation to tell Mr. Brown that he has toilet paper stuck to his shoe." Oppression is always bad, and implies serious persecution.

oral/aural
See "aural/oral."

oral/verbal
Some people insist that "verbal" refers to anything expressed in words, whether written or spoken, while "oral" refers exclusively to speech; but in common usage "verbal" has become widely accepted for the latter meaning. However, in legal contexts, an unwritten agreement is still an "oral contract," not a "verbal contract."

What they had went a bit beyond a verbal disagreement.

orders of magnitude
Many pretentious writers have begun to use the expression "orders of magnitude" without understanding what it means. The concept derives from the scientific notation of very large numbers in which each order of magnitude is ten times the previous one. When the bacteria in a flask have multiplied from some hundreds to some thousands, it is very handy to say that their numbers

have increased by an order of magnitude, and when they have increased to some millions, that their numbers have increased by four orders of magnitude.

Number language generally confuses people. Many seem to suppose that a 100% increase must be pretty much the same as an increase by an order of magnitude, but in fact such an increase represents merely a doubling of quantity. A "hundredfold increase" is even bigger: one hundred times as much. If you don't have a firm grasp on such concepts, it's best to avoid the expression altogether. After all, "Our audience is ten times as big now as when the show opened" makes the same point more clearly than "Our audience has increased by an order of magnitude."

Compare with "quantum leap."

ordinance/ordnance

A law is an ordinance, but a gun is a piece of ordnance.

Oregon

Oregon natives and other Westerners pronounce the state name's last syllable to sound like "gun," not "gone."

organic

The word "organic" is used in all sorts of contexts, often in a highly metaphorical manner; the subject here is its use in the phrase "organic foods" in claims of superior healthfulness. Different jurisdictions have various standards for "organic" food, but generally the label is applied to foods that have been grown without artificial chemicals or pesticides. Literally, of course, the term is a redundancy: all food is composed of organic chemicals (complex chemicals containing carbon). There is no such thing as an inorganic food (unless you count water and salt as foods). Natural fertilizers and pesticides may or may not be superior to artificial ones, but the proper distinction is not between organic and inorganic.

When it comes to nutrition, people tend to generalize rashly from a narrow scientific basis. After a few preservatives were revealed to have harmful effects in some consumers, many products were proudly labeled "No Preservatives!" I don't want *harmful* preservatives in my food, but that label suggests to me a warning: "Deteriorates quickly! May contain mold and other kinds of rot!" *Salt* is a preservative.

Oriental/Asian

In North America, "Oriental" when it refers to people is now generally considered old-fashioned, and many find it offensive. "Asian" is preferred, but not "Asiatic." It's better to write the nationality involved, for example "Chinese" or "Indian," if you know it. "Asian" is often taken to mean exclusively "East Asian," which irritates South Asian and Central Asian people.

In the UK, "Asian" usually refers exclusively to people of South Asian descent (from Pakistan, India, Sri Lanka, Bangladesh, etc.).

orientate/orient

Although it is standard in British English "orientate" is widely considered an error in the US, with simple "orient" being preferred.

The same pattern applies to "disorientate" vs. "disorient."

See also "interpretate/interpret."

ostensively/ostensibly

This word, meaning "apparently," is spelled "ostensibly."

ought/had ought

See "had ought/ought."

ourn/ours

"Ourn" is dialectical; "ours" is standard English. "Well, shoot!" says Jeb, "That may be the way some folks talk, but it ain't ourn."

outcast/outcaste

Believe it or not, these two similar words have very different origins. An "outcast" is someone who has been cast (thrown) out of a group, and may be used loosely of all kinds of loners.

An "outcaste" is technically a South Asian person who has been expelled from his or her caste, or a person who lacks a caste identification. Although this spelling can be used metaphorically, it is probably better to confine it to discussions of social relations in Hinduism and other South Asian contexts.

outlet/plug-in

See "plug-in/outlet."

over/more than

Some people insist that "over" cannot be used to signify "more than," as in "Over a thousand baton-twirlers marched in the parade." "Over," they insist, always refers to something physically higher: say, the blimp hovering over the parade route. This absurd distinction ignores the role metaphor plays in language. If I write "1" on the blackboard and "10" beside it, "10" is still the "higher" number. "Over" has been used in the sense of "more than" for over a thousand years.

over and out/out

There is an old tradition in two-way radio communication of saying "over" to indicate that the speaker is through talking and inviting the other person to speak. You are turning the air *over* to the person you're speaking with. When you're done speaking, you terminate the conversation by saying "out" (not "over and out").

For some reason, Hollywood and radio scriptwriters thought it was neat to conclude radio conversations with "over and out," but this would technically mean "You can talk now if you want, but I'm not going to be listening."

Today "over and out" lives on mostly as an ill-remembered allusion to those old movies and shows in song lyrics and punning headlines. Radio communication buffs, however, cringe when they hear it.

overdo/overdue

If you *overdo* the cocktails after work you may be *overdue* for your daughter's soccer game at 6:00.

over-exaggerated/exaggerated

"Over-exaggerated" is a redundancy. If something is exaggerated, it's already overstressed.

overhang indents

See "hanging indents."

oversee/overlook

When you *oversee* the preparation of dinner, you take control and manage the operation closely. But if you *overlook* the preparation of dinner you forget to prepare the meal entirely—better order pizza.

overtake/take over

When you catch up with the runners ahead of you in a marathon, you overtake them; but when you seize power, you take over the government.

Pacific/specific

See "specific/Pacific."

pair (number)

"This is a left-handed pair of scissors." "There is a pair of glasses on the mantelpiece." "Pair" is singular in this sort of expression. Note that we say, "That is a nice pair of pants," even though we also say, "Those are nice pants."

pair/pare/pear

When you peel an apple, you *pare* it. The resultant apple peelings are called "parings." "Pare" is also used metaphorically in phrases having to do with removing portions of something, such as "pare down the budget" or "pare your wish list to the three most important items." Many people overlook the meaning of this word and write instead "pair" or even "pear." You can pair apples with pears in a dessert, but to peel them you have to pare them.

Although it's not too surprising that cooks should mix up these spellings, it's astounding how often medical and scientific writers refer to substances that are "pared" with each other. A couple of medicines or treatments are *paired* with each other.

palate/palette/pallet

Your "palate" is the roof of your mouth, and by extension, your sense of taste. A "palette" is the flat board an artist mixes paint on (or by extension, a range of colors). A "pallet" is either a bed (now rare) or a flat platform onto which goods are loaded.

palm off/pawn off

See "pawn off/palm off."

par excellance/par excellence

Photoshop is the picture-editing software *par excellence*. We often italicize this phrase—meaning roughly "finest or most characteristic of its type," "exemplary"—to indicate it is French. The French pronounce the final syllable "-ahnss" (with a nasalized *N* which is hard for English-speakers to master), but that is no justification for misspelling the word as "excellance." Although they pronounce it differently, they spell "excellence" the same way we do.

parallel/symbol

Beginning literature students often write sentences like this: "He uses the rose as a parallel for her beauty" when they mean "a symbol of her beauty." If you are taking a literature class, it's good to master the distinctions between several terms relating to symbolism. An eagle clutching a bundle of arrows and an olive branch is a symbol of the US government in war and peace.

Students often misuse the word "analogy" in the same way. An analogy has to be specifically spelled out by the writer, not simply referred to: "My mother's attempts to find her keys in the morning were like early expeditions to the South Pole: prolonged and mostly futile."

A *metaphor* is a kind of symbolism common in literature. When Shakespeare writes "That time of year thou mayst in me behold/When yellow leaves, or none, or few, do hang/Upon those boughs which shake against the cold" he is comparing his aging self to a tree in late autumn, perhaps even specifically suggesting that he is going bald by referring to the tree shedding its leaves. This autumnal tree is a metaphor for the human aging process.

A *simile* resembles a metaphor except that "like" or "as" or something similar is used to make the comparison explicitly. Byron admires a dark-haired woman by saying of her, "She walks in beauty, like the night/Of cloudless climes and starry skies." Her darkness is said to be *like* that of the night.

An *allegory* is a symbolic narrative in which characters may stand for abstract ideas, and the story conveys a philosophy. Allegories are no longer popular, but the most commonly read one in school is Dante's *Divine Comedy* in which the poet Virgil is a symbol for human wisdom, Dante's beloved Beatrice is a symbol of divine grace, and the whole poem tries to teach the reader how to avoid damnation. Aslan in C. S. Lewis' Narnia tales is an allegorical figure meant to symbolize Christ: dying to save others and rising again (*aslan* is Turkish for "lion").

parallelism in a series

Phrases in a series separated by commas or conjunctions must all have the same grammatical form. "They loved mountain-climbing, to gather wild mushrooms, and first-aid practice" should be corrected to something like this: "They loved to climb mountains, gather wild mushrooms, and practice first aid" (all three verbs are dependent on that initial "to"). Fear of being repetitious often leads writers into awkward inconsistencies when creating such series.

parallelled/paralleled

The spelling of the past tense of "parallel" is "paralleled."

paralyzation/paralysis

Some people derive the noun "paralyzation" from the verb "paralyze," but the proper term is "paralysis."

parameters/perimeters

When parameters were spoken of only by mathematicians and scientists, the term caused few problems; but now that it has become widely adopted by other speakers, it is constantly confused with "perimeters." A parameter is most commonly a mathematical constant, a set of physical properties, or a characteristic of something. But the perimeter of something is its boundary. The two words shade into each other because we often speak of factors of an issue or problem being parameters, simultaneously thinking of them as limits; but this is to confuse two distinct, if related, ideas. A safe rule is to avoid using "parameters" altogether unless you are confident you know what it means.

paramount/tantamount

"Paramount" means "best," "top." Think of Paramount Pictures' trademark of a majestic mountain peak encircled with stars.

"Tantamount" means "equivalent."

"The committee's paramount concern is to get at the truth; your continued insistence that you don't remember any of the meetings you attended is tantamount to a confession of incompetence."

paranoid

The most common meaning of "paranoid" has to do with irrational fears of persecution, especially the unjustified fear that people are plotting against you. More generally it is applied to irrational fears of other kinds; but it is often misused of rational fears, as in "I know my Mom has been reading my blog, so I'm paranoid that she's found out what Jason and I did last Saturday night." That's not paranoia, but fully justifiable fear. It also doesn't make sense to use "paranoid" about mild worries

Don't be paranoid about the tiger—out-and-out fear would be more appropriate.

and fears. When you say you are paranoid, you should be conveying your own irrationality, not the risks you feel you are running.

parentheses
The most common error in using parenthesis marks (besides using them too much) is to forget to enclose the parenthetical material with a final, closing parenthesis mark. The second most common is to place concluding punctuation incorrectly. The simplest sort of example is one in which the entire sentence is enclosed in parentheses. (Most people understand that the final punctuation must remain inside the closing parenthesis mark, like this.) More troublesome are sentences in which only a clause or phrase is enclosed in parentheses. Normally a sentence's final punctuation mark—whether period, exclamation point, or question mark—goes outside such a parenthesis (like this). However, if the material inside the parenthesis requires a concluding punctuation mark like an exclamation point or question mark (but not a period!), that mark is placed inside the closing mark even though another mark is outside it. This latter sort of thing is awkward, however, and best avoided if you can help it.

For some reason, many writers have begun to omit the space before a parenthetic page citation, like this:(p. 17). Always preserve the space, like this: (p. 17).

parliment/parliament
Americans unfamiliar with parliamentary systems often mistakenly leave the second *A* out of "parliament" and "parliamentary."

part/apart
See "apart/a part."

partake/participate
"Partake" looks like it might mean "take part," and that's how many people mistakenly use it where they should say "participate." The main modern meaning of "partake" is "consume," especially in relation to food. One can partake of the refreshments at a party, but one can also partake of Twinkies at home alone, without any thought of sharing.

So don't ask people to "partake" in a planning process when you mean to ask them to participate.

pass/progress
See "progress/pass."

pass the muster/pass muster
When military troops are assembled for a review, they are mustered. A soldier who passes inspection is said to "pass muster." We use this phrase for all kinds of things and processes that must be approved, meet a certain standard. It is most often used in a negative sense, as in a flawed business plan than "doesn't pass muster."

The nonstandard form "pass the muster" may be influenced by the unrelated term "cut the mustard," which has a similar meaning. Don't believe those who insist that the latter phrase is a mistake for "cut the muster." And the expression is definitely not "pass the mustard."

See also "cut the muster/cut the mustard."

passed/past

If you are referring to a distance or a period of time before now, use "past": "the police car drove past the suspect's house" (distance) or "the team performed well in the past" (time). If you are describing the action of *passing*, however, you need to use "passed": "when John passed the gravy, he spilled it on his lap," "the teacher was astonished that none of the students had passed the test," "after a brief illness, he passed away." Remember that no matter however you have "passed the time" you have never "*past* the time," not even in the distant past.

"Past" can be an adjective, a noun, a preposition, or an adverb, but never a verb. If you need to write the past tense of the verb "to pass," use "passed."

passive voice

There are legitimate uses for the passive voice: "This absurd regulation was of course written by a committee." But it's true that you can make your prose more lively and readable by using the active voice much more often. "The victim was attacked by three men in ski masks" isn't nearly as striking as "Three men in ski masks attacked the victim." The passive voice is often used to avoid taking responsibility for an action: "My term paper was accidentally deleted" avoids stating the truth: "I accidentally deleted my term paper." Over-use of passive constructions is irritating, though not necessarily erroneous. But it does lead to real clumsiness when passive constructions get piled on top of each other: "No exception in the no-pets rule was sought to be created so that angora rabbits could be raised in the apartment" can be made clearer by shifting to the active voice: "The landlord refused to make an exception to the no-pets rule to allow Eliza to raise angora rabbits in the apartment."

past history

See "redundancies."

past time/pastime

An agreeable activity like knitting with which you pass the time is your pastime. Spell it as one word, with one *S* and one *T*.

patience/patients

Doctors have patients, but while you're waiting to see them you have to have patience.

pause for concern/cause for concern, pause

Something worrisome can give you pause, or cause for concern. But some people confuse these two expressions and say they have "pause for concern."

pawn off/palm off

Somebody defrauds you by using sleight of hand (literal or figurative) to "palm" the object you wanted and give you something inferior instead. The variant spelling "pawn off" is both long-established and very popular, but makes little logical sense.

pay the piper, face the music/face the piper

See "face the piper/pay the piper, face the music."

payed/paid

If you paid attention in school, you know that the past tense of "pay" is "paid" except in the special sense that has to do with ropes: "He payed out the line to the smuggler in the rowboat."

PC computer/PC

The phrase "PC computer" is a bit awkward and redundant since "PC" stands for "personal computer." The problem is that originally the label "PC" meant not personal computers generally, but computers compatible with the IBM PC introduced in 1981. By the time IBM adopted the abbreviation for a specific model there had been many earlier personal computers like the Commodore PET and the Apple II. Now IBM doesn't make PCs and none of today's popular personal computers is compatible with the original PC. The label is still used to distinguish between computers running some version of Microsoft's Windows operating system and the Macintosh computers made by Apple, even though Macs are certainly personal computers and the newer ones can also run Windows. No wonder people forget what "PC" stands for. If you want to use the abbreviation to indicate that your computer is not a Mac, "PC" alone will do, despite its literal inaccuracy.

peace/piece

It's hard to believe many people really confuse the meaning of these words, but the spellings are frequently swapped, probably out of sheer carelessness. "Piece" has the word "pie" buried in it, which should remind you of the familiar phrase "a piece of pie." You can meditate to find peace of mind, or you can get angry and give someone a piece of your mind. Classical scholars will note that *pax* is the Latin word for "peace," suggesting the need for an *A* in the latter word.

See also "hold your peace/say your piece."

peak/peek/pique

It is tempting to think that your attention might be aroused to a high point by "peaking" your curiosity; but in fact, "pique" is a French word meaning "prick," in the sense of "stimulate." The expression has nothing to do with "peek," either. Therefore the expression is "my curiosity was piqued."

An amazing number of people write about "mountain peeks." A peak is a summit; a peek is a glimpse.

peal out/peel out

Bells and thunderclaps peal out; but if your car "lays down rubber" in a squealing departure, the expression is "peel out" because you are literally peeling a layer of rubber off your tires.

pear

See "pair/pare/pear."

peasant/pheasant

See "pheasant/peasant."

pedal/peddle

If you are delivering newspapers from a bike you can pedal it around the neighborhood (perhaps wearing "pedal-pushers"), but when you sell them from a newsstand you peddle them.

pedal to the medal/pedal to the metal

When you depress the accelerator all the way so that it presses against the metal of the floorboards you put the pedal to the metal. You get no medals for speeding.

pen/ink pen

See "ink pen/pen."

pen/pin

In the dialect of many Texans and some of their neighbors "pen" is pronounced almost exactly like "pin." When speaking to an audience outside this zone, it's worth learning to make the distinction to avoid confusion.

penultimate/next to last

To confuse your readers, use the term "penultimate," which means "next to last," but which most people assume means "the very last." And if you really want to baffle them, use "antepenultimate" to mean "third from the end." Many people also mistakenly use "penultimate" when they mean "quintessential" or "archetypical."

peoples

In the Middle Ages "peoples" was not an uncommon word, but later writers grew wary of it because "people" has a collective, plural meaning which seemed to make "peoples" superfluous. It lived on in the sense of "nations" ("the peoples of the world") and from this social scientists (anthropologists in particular) derived the extended meaning "ethnic groups" ("the peoples of the upper Amazon Basin"). However, in ordinary usage "people" is usually understood to be plural, so much so that in the bad old days when dialect humor was popular having a speaker refer to "you peoples" indicated illiteracy. If you are not referring to national or ethnic groups, it is better to avoid "peoples" and use "people."

The possessive form "people's" is of course fine in sentences like "If elected, I will do the people's will."

See also "behaviors/behavior."

per/according to

Using "per" to mean "according to," as in "ship the widgets as per the instructions of the customer," is rather old-fashioned business jargon and is not welcome in other contexts. "Per" is fine when used in phrases involving figures like "miles per gallon."

per se/perse

See "perse/per se."

percent/per cent

In the US the two-word spelling "per cent" is considered rather old-fashioned and is rarely used; but in the UK and countries influenced by it, the two-word form is still standard, though use of "percent" is spreading fast even there.

percent decrease

When something has been reduced by one hundred percent, it's all gone (or if the reduction was in its price, it's free). You can't properly speak of reducing anything by more than a hundred percent (unless it's a deficit or debt, in which case you wind up with a surplus).

See also "orders of magnitude."

perciptation/precipitation

Rain, snow, hail, etc. are all forms of precipitation. This word is often misspelled and mispronounced as "perciptation."

peremptory/preemptory

See "preemptory/peremptory."

perimeters/parameters

See "parameters/perimeters."

permiscuous/promiscuous

The influence of "permissiveness" may influence this misspelling of "promiscuous."

pernickety/persnickety

The original Scottish dialect form was "pernickety," but Americans changed it to "persnickety" a century ago. "Pernickety" is generally unknown in the US though it's still in wide use across the Atlantic.

perogative/prerogative

"Prerogative" is frequently both mispronounced and misspelled as "perogative." It may help to remember that the word is associated with *p*rivileges of *p*recedence.

perpetuate/perpetrate

"Perpetrate" is something criminals do (criminals are sometimes called "perps" in slang). When you seek to continue something you are trying to "perpetuate" it.

perscription/prescription

"Prescription" is often mispronounced "perscription."

perse/per se

This legal term meaning "in, of, or by itself" is a bit pretentious, but you gain little respect if you misspell *per se* as a single word. Worse is the mistaken "per say."

persecute/prosecute

When you persecute someone, you're treating them badly, whether they deserve it or not; but only legal officers can prosecute someone for a crime.

persnickety/pernickety

See "pernickety/persnickety."

person/individual

See "individual/person."

personal/personnel

Employees are personnel, but private individuals considered separately from their jobs have personal lives.

personality

In show business personalities are people famous for being famous (mostly popular actors and singers); people with more substantial accomplishments like distinguished heads of state and Nobel Prize winners should not be referred to as "personalities" even when they appear on *The Tonight Show*.

perspective/prospective

"Perspective" has to do with sight, as in painting, and is usually a noun. "Prospective" generally has to do with the future (compare with "What are your prospects, young man?") and is usually an adjective. But beware: there is also a rather old-fashioned but fairly common meaning of the word "prospect" that has to do with sight: "As he climbed the mountain, a vast prospect opened up before him."

perspiration/prespiration

See "prespiration/perspiration."

persuade/convince

See "convince/persuade."

peruse

This word, which means "examine thoroughly" is often misused to mean "glance over hastily." Although some dictionaries accept the latter meaning, it is not traditional.

When it is used to mean "look through" it is not standard to add "through" to "peruse." It's not "peruse through the records" but "peruse the records."

perverse/perverted
The sex-related meanings of words tend to drive out all other meanings. Most people think of both "perverse" and "perverted" only in contexts having to do with desire; but "perverse" properly has the function of signifying "stubborn," "wrong-headed." Nothing erotic is suggested by this sort of thing: "Josh perversely insisted on carving wooden replacement parts for his 1958 Ford's engine." It's better to use "perverted" in relation to abnormal sexual desires; but this word also has non-sexual functions, as in "The bake-sale was perverted by Gladys into a fundraiser for her poker habit."

People sometimes mispronounce "pervert" as "PREE-vert."

phantom/fathom
Brianna exclaims confusedly, "I can't phantom why he thought I'd want a coupon for an oil change for Valentine's Day!" A phantom is a ghost, but a fathom is a nautical measure of depth. When you can't understand something—being unable to get to the bottom of it—you should say, "I can't fathom it." "Phantom" is not a verb.

phase/faze
See "faze/phase."

pheasant/peasant
When I visited the former Soviet Union I was astonished to learn that farm-workers were still called "peasants" there. In English-speaking countries we tend to think of the term as belonging strictly to the feudal era. However you use it, don't confuse it with "pheasant," a favorite game bird. Use the sound of the beginning consonants to remind you of the difference: pheasants are food, peasants are people.

phenomena/phenomenon
"Phenomena" is the plural form. It's "this phenomenon," but "these phenomena."

Philippines/Filipinos
The people of the Philippines are called "Filipinos." Don't switch the initial letters of these two words.

phoney/phony
The usual spelling in the US is "phony"; the usual spelling in the UK and in some countries influenced by it is "phoney."

phrasal verbs vs. nouns
Phrasal verbs make up a huge category of expressions in English that careless

users often misspell by substituting one-word noun forms for the standard two-word phrasal verb; for instance: it would have been a mistake for me to have written "Phrasal verbs makeup a huge category." It is fine to write "I didn't want to put on my makeup" ("makeup" is a noun) or "I had to take the makeup exam." (In this example "makeup" is a noun acting like an adjective modifying another noun—"exam." What kind of exam was it? A makeup exam.) Such nouns are often hyphenated, at least early in their history (it used to be common to write "make-up exam," and that is still fine); but there is a strong tendency for such hyphenated forms to evolve into single words. If both versions are current, the hyphenated form is usually the more formal one.

Most phrasal verbs consist of a verb and adverb combined. Note that some of the adverbs involved can also function as prepositions, but don't let this confuse you. In the phrase "cool down the broth" "down" is an adverb. Some do actually consist of a verb and a preposition, but these rarely cause problems. You aren't likely to write "would you lookafter my cat while I'm gone?"

If the word involved is immediately preceded by "a," "an," or "the," you probably need the one-word noun form. If it's immediately preceded by "to," you probably need the two-word phrasal verb. If you're tempted to use a one-word spelling elsewhere, try using a two-word or hyphenated form instead. If it looks better, it probably is.

See the appendix at the back of the book for an extensive list of phrasal verbs.

physical/fiscal

See "fiscal/physical."

physically challenged

See "differently abled, physically challenged/disabled."

pianist

The standard pronunciations of "pianist" are "peeANist" and "PEEanist." The latter is especially popular among musicians. The pronunciations of "piano" and "pianist" in which the first syllable sounds like "pie" are nonstandard.

picaresque/picturesque

"Picaresque" is a technical literary term you are unlikely to have a use for. It labels a sort of literature involving a *picaro* (Spanish), a lovable rogue who roams the land having colorful adventures. A landscape that looks as lovely as a picture is "picturesque."

pickup/pick up

The noun is spelled "pickup" as in "drive your pickup" or "that coffee gave me a pickup," or "we didn't have a real date; it was just a pickup." If it's a thing, use the single-word form. But if it's an action (verb-plus-adverb phrase) then spell it as two words: "pick up your dirty underwear."

There's also the adjectival form, which has to be hyphenated: "Jeremy tried out one of his corny pick-up lines on me at the bar." According to this rule, it should be a "pick-up game" but you're unlikely to get into trouble for writing "pickup game."

picture
The pronunciation of "picture" as if it were "pitcher" is common in some dialects, but not standard. The first syllable should sound like "pick."

piece/peace
See "peace/piece."

piety/religiosity
See "religiosity/piety."

pigeon English/pidgin English
"Pidgin" evolved from a Chinese mispronunciation of "business," and the original pidgin English developed as a simplified blend of Chinese and English used to facilitate international trade. Other similarly artificial blended languages have since also been called "pidgins." Although the spelling "pigeon" often occurred early on, the standard spelling today is "pidgin."

PIN number/PIN
Those who object to "PIN number" on the grounds that the *N* in "PIN" stands for "number" in the phrase "personal identification number" are quite right, but it may be difficult to get people to say anything else. "PIN" was invented to meet the objection that a "password" consisting of nothing but numbers is not a word. Pronouncing each letter of the acronym as "P-I-N" blunts its efficiency. Saying just "PIN" reminds us of another common English word, though few people are likely to think when they are told to "enter PIN" that they should shove a steel pin into the terminal they are operating. In writing, anyway, "PIN" is unambiguous and is better used without the redundant "number."

The same goes for "VIN number"; "VIN" stands for "Vehicle Identification Number." And "UPC code" is redundant because "UPC" stands for "Universal Product Code."

Similarly, "ISBN number" would logically mean "International Standard Book Number number." It's fine to say just "ISBN," and that's what most professionals in the book trade do.

pinned up/pent up
If you wear your heart on your sleeve I suppose you might be said to have "pinned up" emotions; but the phrase you want when you are suppressing your feelings is "pent-up emotions." Similarly, it's pent-up demand." "Pent" is a rare word; but don't replace it with "penned" in such phrases either.

pique/peak/peek
See "peak/peek/pique."

pit in my stomach/in the pit of my stomach

Just as you can love someone from the bottom of your heart, you can also experience a sensation of dread in the pit (bottom) of your stomach. I don't know whether people who mangle this common expression into "pit in my stomach" envision an ulcer, an irritating peach pit they've swallowed or are thinking of the pyloric sphincter; but they've got it wrong.

pith and vinegar/piss and vinegar

To say that people are "full of piss and vinegar" is to say that they are brimming with energy. Although many speakers assume the phrase must have a negative connotation, this expression is more often used as a compliment, "vinegar" being an old slang term for enthusiastic energy.

Some try to make this expression more polite by substituting "pith" for "piss," but this change robs it of the imagery of acrid, energetically boiling fluids and conjures up instead a sodden, vinegar-soaked mass of pith. Many people who use the "polite" version are unaware of the original.

plain/plane

Both of these words have to do with flatness. A flat prairie is a plain, and you use a plane to smooth flat a piece of wood.

"Plain" is also an adjective which can describe things that are ordinary, simple, or unattractive.

But whether you go the airport to catch a plane or meditate to achieve a higher plane of consciousness, the meanings that have to do with things high up are spelled "plane."

play against/verse

See "verse/play against."

plays a factor/plays a role

Some people say that an influential force "plays a factor" in a decision or change. They are mixing up two different expressions: "*is* a factor" and "*plays* a role."

playwrite/playwright

It might seem as if a person who writes plays should be called a "playwrite" but in fact a playwright is a person who has wrought words into a dramatic form, just as a wheelwright has wrought wheels out of wood and iron. All the other words ending in "-wright" are archaic, or we'd be constantly reminded of the correct pattern.

plead innocent

Lawyers frown on the phrase "plead innocent" (it's "plead guilty" or "plead not guilty"), but outside of legal contexts the phrase is standard English.

pleaded/pleated

A pleat is a sharp fold, so it's a *pleated* skirt, no matter how much your husband has pleaded you to wear it.

please RSVP/please reply

RSVP stands for the French phrase *répondez s'il vous plaît* ("reply, please"), so it doesn't need an added "please." However, since few people seem to know its literal meaning, and fewer still take it seriously, it's best to use plain English: "Please reply." And for those of you receiving such an invitation, yes, you have to let the host know whether you're coming or not, and no, you can't bring along the kids or other uninvited guests.

plenty (number)

See "lots, plenty, load (number)."

plug/jack

See "jack/plug."

plug-in/outlet

That thing on the end of an electrical cord is a plug, which goes into the socket of the wall outlet.

plural possessives

See "joint possessives."

plus/add

Some people continue a pattern picked up in childhood of using "plus" as a verb to mean "add," as in "You plus the 3 and the 4 and you get 7." "Plus" is not a verb; use "add" instead.

PM/AM

See "AM/PM."

podium/lectern

Strictly speaking, a podium is a raised platform on which you stand to give a speech; the piece of furniture on which you place your notes and behind which you stand is a lectern.

poinsetta/poinsettia

Those showy plants that appear in the stores around Christmas are "poinsettias," named after American diplomat John R. Poinsett who introduced them into the US from Mexico. The Latin ending "-ia" is seldom pronounced as spelled, but that's no justification for misspelling the word as "poinsetta."

point being is that

"The point being is that" is redundant; say just "the point is that" or "the point being that."

point in time/point, time

This redundancy became popular because it was used by astronauts seeking to distinguish precisely between a point in time and a point in space. Since most people use the expression in contexts where there is no ambiguity, it makes more sense to say simply "at this point" or "at this time."

point of you/point of view

Your viewpoint on a subject is your "point of view," not your "point of you." "Your" and "of you" mean the same thing, and combining the two makes little sense; but the expression really gets weird when it turns into "my point of you," "her point of you," "their point of you," etc.

pole/poll

A "pole" is a long stick. You could take a "poll" (survey or ballot) to determine whether voters want lower taxes or better education.

pompom/pompon

To most people that fuzzy ball on the top of a knit hat and the implement wielded by a cheerleader are both "pompoms," but to traditionalists they are "pompons," spelled the way the French—who gave us the word—spell it. A pompom, say these purists, is only a sort of large gun. Though you're unlikely to bother many people by falling into the common confusion, you can show off your education by observing the distinction.

poo-poo/pooh-pooh/pupu

The toddler with a soggy diaper proudly announces "I go poo-poo!"

The skeptic is inclined to pooh-pooh outlandish ideas. Don't mix up matter for skepticism with material for the septic system.

A selection of snacks served on a wooden platter in a Chinese restaurant is called a "pupu platter"—a custom and word that made its way to the mainland US from Hawaii.

populace/populous

The population of a country may be referred to as its "populace," but a crowded country is "populous."

pore/pour

When used as a verb, "pore" has the unusual sense of "scrutinize," as in "She pored over her receipts." If it's coffee or rain, the stuff pours.

portentious/portentous

People being pretentious get confused about "portentous," which is related to "portents"—omens.

portray/protray

See "protray/portray."

posses/possess

Posses chase after bank robbers. If you own something, you *possess* it.

possessed of/possessed by/possessed with

If you own a yacht, you're possessed *of* it. If a demon takes over your body, you're possessed *by* it. If that which possesses you is more metaphorical, as in the case of an executive determined to get ahead, he or she can be possessed *by* or *with* the desire to win.

posterity/prosperity

See "prosperity/posterity."

pour/pore

See "pore/pour."

PPS/PSS

See "PSS/PPS."

practice/practise

In the United Kingdom, "practice" is the noun, "practise" the verb; but in the US the spelling "practice" is commonly used for both, though the distinction is sometimes observed. "Practise" as a noun is, however, always wrong in both places: a doctor always has a "practice," never a "practise."

practicable/practical

"Practical" and "practicable" overlap a bit in meaning; but by far the most common word, and the one you will have the most use for, is "practical." The safest course is to save "practicable" for use only in describing something that it is possible to accomplish. If you're not sure which to use, stick with "practical."

Something impractical is not smart or efficient, but something impracticable is just plain impossible to do.

practicle/practical

Some words end in "-icle" and others in "-ical" without the result being any difference in pronunciation. But when you want somebody really practical, call on good old Al.

pray/prey

If you want a miracle, pray to God. If you're a criminal, you prey on your victims.

"Good Old Al" demonstrates one of his highly practical machines.

Incidentally, it's "praying mantis," not "preying mantis." The insect holds its forefeet in a position suggesting prayer.

precede/proceed

"Precede" means "to go before." "Proceed" means "to go on." Let your companion precede you through the door, then proceed to follow her. Interestingly, the second *E* is missing in "procedure."

precedence/precedents

Although these words sound the same, they work differently. The pop star is given precedence over the factory worker at the entrance to the dance club. "Precedents" is just the plural of "precedent": "If we let the kids adopt that rattlesnake as a pet and agree to let them take it for a walk in Death Valley, we'll be setting some bad precedents."

precipitate/precipitous

Both of these adjectives are based on the image of plunging over the brink of a precipice, but "precipitate" emphasizes the suddenness of the plunge, "precipitous," the steepness of it. If you make a "precipitate" decision, you are making a hasty and probably unwise one. If the stock market declines "precipitously," it goes down sharply.

precurse/foretell, foreshadow, preface, anticipate, precede

Tempted to "precurse" that guy who looks like he might be going to cut into the lane ahead of you? Until recently "precurse" as a verb was a rare archaic word, but lately people have been using it to mean "be a precursor to." Use a more ordinary and precise word like "foretell," "foreshadow," "preface," "anticipate," or "precede."

predicts/calls for

See "calls for/predicts."

predominate/predominant

"Predominate" is a verb: "In the royal throne room, the color red predominates." "Predominant" is an adjective: "The predominant view among the touts is that Fancy Dancer is the best bet in the third race."

predominately/predominantly

"Predominantly" is formed on the adjective "predominant," not the verb "predominate"; so though both forms are widely accepted, "predominantly" makes more sense.

preemptory/peremptory

"Peremptory" (meaning "imperative") is often misspelled and mispronounced "preemptory" through confusion caused by the influence of the verb "preempt," whose adjectival form is actually "preemptive."

preferably

Although some US dictionaries now recognize the pronunciation of "preferably" with the first two syllables pronounced just like "prefer"—first *E* long and the stress on the second syllable—the standard pronunciation is "PREFFer-ublee," with the first syllable stressed, just like in "preference." The alternative pronunciation sounds awkward to some people.

prejudice/prejudiced
People not only misspell "prejudice" in a number of ways, they sometimes say "he's prejudice" when they mean "he's prejudiced."

    See also "bias/biased."

pre-Madonna/prima donna
The leading soprano in an opera is the *prima donna* (Italian for "leading lady"). As an insult, "prima donna" implies that the person under discussion is egotistical, demanding, and doesn't work well as part of a team.

    Don't write "pre-Madonna" unless you intend to discuss the era before the singer Madonna became popular.

premier/premiere
These words are, respectively, the masculine and feminine forms of the word for "first" in French; but they have become differentiated in English. Only the masculine form is used as an adjective, as in "Tidy-Pool is the premier pool-cleaning firm in Orange County." The confusion arises when these words are used as nouns. The prime minister of a parliamentary government is known as a "premier." The opening night of a film or play is its "premiere."

    "Premiere" as a verb is common in the arts and in show business ("The show premiered on PBS"), but it is less acceptable in other contexts ("The state government premiered its new welfare system"). Use "introduced" or, if real innovation is involved, "pioneered."

premise/premises
Some people suppose that since "premises" has a plural form, a single house or other piece of property must be a "premise," but that word is reserved for use as a term in logic meaning something assumed or taken as given in making an argument. Your lowly one-room shack is still your "premises. "

preplan
See "redundancies."

prepone
South Asian speakers have evolved the logical word "prepone" to mean the opposite of "postpone": to move forward in time. It's a handy word, but users of it should be aware that those unfamiliar with their dialect will be baffled by it.

preposition, ending a sentence with a
See "ending a sentence with a preposition."

prepositions (repeated)

In the sentence "Alex liked Nancy, with whom he shared his Snickers bar with" only one "with" is needed—eliminate either one. Look out for similarly duplicated prepositions.

Incidentally, an often-cited example of this pattern is from Paul McCartney's "Live and Let Die": "this ever-changing world in which we live in"; but if you listen closely, you'll hear instead a quite correct "this ever-changing world in which we're livin'." Americans have a hard time hearing the soft British *R* in "we're."

prepositions (wrong)

One of the clearest indications that a person reads little and doesn't hear much formal English is a failure to use the standard preposition in a common expression. You aren't ignorant to a fact; you're ignorant of it. Things don't happen on accident, but by accident (though they do happen "on purpose"). There are no simple rules governing preposition usage: you just have to immerse yourself in standard English in order to write it naturally.

See also "different than/different from/different to."

prerogative/perogative

See "perogative/prerogative."

prescribe/proscribe

You recommend something when you prescribe it, but you forbid it when you proscribe it. The usually positive function of "pro-" confuses many people.

prescription/perscription

See "perscription/prescription."

present writer/I

Formal writers used to avoid writing "I" when referring to themselves by using instead the phrase "the present writer." This practice is generally discouraged by modern editors, and is considered awkward and old-fashioned. Simple "I" works fine and calls less attention to itself so long as it's not repeated too often.

For a moment Jack was confused—was he being attacked by a bear presently or currently?

presently/currently

Some argue that "presently" doesn't mean "in the present."

It means "soon." If you want to talk about something that's happening right now, they urge you to say it's going on "currently."

preservatives
See "organic."

prespiration/perspiration
"Perspiration" is often mispronounced and even misspelled "prespiration." The first syllable should sound like "purse."

presumably/assumably
See "assumably/presumably."

presumptious/presumptuous
"Presumptive" has an *I* in it, but "presumptuous" does not.

pretty/somewhat
It's pretty common to use "pretty" to mean "somewhat" in ordinary speech; but it should be avoided in formal writing, where sometimes "very" is more appropriate. The temptation to use "pretty" usually indicates the writer is being vague, so changing to something more specific may be an even better solution: "a pretty bad mess" might be "chocolate syrup spilled all over the pizza which had been dumped upside down on the carpet."

preventive/preventative
It is sometimes argued that "preventive" is the adjective, "preventative" the noun. I must say I like the sound of this distinction, but in fact the two are interchangeable as both nouns and adjectives, though many prefer "preventive" as being shorter and simpler. "Preventative" used as an adjective dates back to the 17th century, as does "preventive" as a noun.

prey/pray
See "pray/prey."

primer
When this word is used in the US to mean "elementary textbook" it is pronounced with a short *I*: "primmer" (rhymes with "dimmer"). All other meanings are pronounced with a long *I*: "prymer" (rhymes with "timer").

primevil/primeval
The existence of a music group and a comic book using the deliberately punning misspelling "Primevil" helps to further confusion about this word. Something ancient and primitive is "primeval." The "-eval" sequence comes from a root having to do with ages, as in "medieval." It has nothing to do with the concept of evil. The word can also be spelled "primaeval."

principal/principle
Generations of teachers have tried to drill this one into students' heads by

reminding them, "The principal is your pal." Many don't seem convinced. "Principal" is a noun and adjective referring to someone or something which is highest in rank or importance. (In a loan, the principal is the more substantial part of the money, the interest is—or should be—the lesser.) "Principle" is only a noun and has to do with law or doctrine: "The workers fought hard for the principle of collective bargaining."

prioritize

Many people disdain "prioritize" as bureaucratic jargon for "rank" or "make a high priority."

priority

It is common to proclaim, "In our business, customer service is a priority," but it would be better to say "a high priority," since priorities can also be low.

proactive

See "reactionary/reactive."

probably

The two *B*'s in this word are particularly difficult to pronounce in sequence, so the word often comes out as "probly" and is even occasionally misspelled that way. When even the last *B* disappears, the pronunciation "prolly" suggests drunken slurring or, at best, an attempt at humor.

problematic

"Problematic" has various traditional meanings: "presenting a problem," "difficult to resolve," "doubtful." But among academics it has become a sort of all-purpose negative expressing disapproval: "the depiction of married women in early American comic strips such as Maggie in *Bringing Up Father* is problematic," (i.e., I have a problem with this, I object to it). Not only is this not a traditional function of the word; it transfers a political or personal objection into the Platonic realm of Truth, allowing the speaker to avoid personal responsibility for the objection being made.

Similarly, "problematize" means "to make into a problem," not "to consider as a problem."

problems/issues

See "issues/problems."

proceed/precede

See "precede/proceed."

prodigy/progeny/protégé

Your progeny are your kids, though it would be pretty pretentious to refer to them as such. If your child is a brilliantly outstanding person he or she may be a child prodigy. In fact, anything amazingly admirable can be a prodigy. But a person that you take under your wing in order to help promote his or her career is your protégé.

Avoid misspelling or mispronouncing "prodigy" as "progidy."

program/programme

"Program" is the spelling for all uses in the US, but in the UK the spelling "programme" is used for broadcasts and schedules of various kinds (musical programme, programme of studies, theatre programme). However, in all computer-related contexts, the UK standard spelling is like the US one: "program."

progress/pass

Events may progress in time, but time itself does not progress—it just passes.

promiscuous/permiscuous

See "permiscuous/promiscuous."

prone/supine

"Prone" (face down) is often confused with "supine" (face up). "Prostrate" technically also means "face down," but is often used to mean simply "devastated."

See also "prostate/prostrate."

pronounciation/pronunciation

"Pronounce" is the verb, but the *O* is omitted for the noun: "pronunciation." This mistake ranks right up there in incongruity with "writting."

pronouns & gerunds

See "gerunds & pronouns."

proof is in the pudding/proof of the pudding is in the eating

This common truncated version of an old saying conjures up visions of poking around in your dessert looking for prizes, but "the proof of the pudding is in the eating" means that you don't really know that your dessert has come out right until you taste it.

The proof wasn't in the pork chop, either, but Robert held on to hope he'd find it in the pudding.

prophecy/prophesy

"Prophecy," the noun, (pronounced "PROF-a-see") is a prediction. The verb "to prophesy" (pronounced "PROF-a-sigh") means to predict something. When a prophet prophesies he or she utters prophecies.

Outside of Bob Dylan's lyrics, writers and critics do not "prophesize." They prophesy.

proscribe/prescribe
See "prescribe/proscribe."

prosecute/persecute
See "persecute/prosecute."

prospective/perspective
See "perspective/prospective."

prosperity/posterity
Your descendants—those who come after you—are posterity. Your posterior comes behind your front, right? Your posterity comes along behind you in time. In contrast, prosperity is financial well-being. But some people mix these up by saying "I am taking photos of our house construction for prosperity" when they mean "for posterity."

prostate/prostrate
The gland men have is called the "prostate." "Prostrate" is an adjective meaning "lying face downward."

protagonist/hero
See "hero/protagonist."

protagonist/proponent
People have been using "protagonist" to mean "proponent" for a long time, but people who know the word's origin—including most English teachers—object that "protagonist" refers to the main character of a work of fiction. An advocate of a certain course of action, they feel, should be called a "proponent."

protray/portray
There are a lot of words in English that begin in "pro-." This is not one of them. When you make a portrait, you portray someone.

proved/proven
For most purposes either form is a fine past participle of "prove," though in a phrase like "a proven talent" where the word is an adjective preceding a noun, "proven" is standard.

PSS/PPS
In the old days before personal computers, when people wanted to add something to a letter they had already ended, they would add a "postscript" (from Latin *post scriptum*, meaning "that which comes after the writing"). These postscripts were introduced with the label "PS" or "P.S."

When they wanted to add something else after the postscript, it was labeled "PPS" for "post postscript." But many people trying to follow this pattern today mistakenly write "PSS" instead.

Since modern technology makes it so easy to revise and add to texts, in most cases it's better to just go back and insert the additional material at an appropriate point in the main body of the writing. "PSS" makes you look not only ignorant, but lazy.

psychologist/psychiatrist/psychotherapist/psychoanalyst

A *psychologist* is a person who has studied the mind and earned a PhD or PsyD. Although some definitions state that psychologists have undergone clinical training but cannot prescribe medicines, there are research psychologists who are not engaged in clinical work at all, but merely do experiments to discover how our minds work. Some of their work can concern animal rather than human minds.

A *psychiatrist* is technically an MD who specializes in the treatment of mental problems and can prescribe medicines. They are licensed medical doctors, and get irritated when they are called "psychologists" and when psychologists are called "psychiatrists."

Psychotherapist is not a technical term, and may be used by anyone claiming to offer therapy for mental problems. That someone is called a "psychotherapist" tells you nothing about his or her qualifications. But qualified clinical psychologists and psychiatrists can be properly called "psychotherapists."

A *psychoanalyst* is a very specific kind of psychotherapist: a licensed practitioner of the methods of Sigmund Freud.

publically/publicly

There's no particular logic to the spelling of "publicly." Maybe it would help to remember not to include wastefully unnecessary letters at the public expense.

pundint/pundit

"Pundit" is one of those words we get from India, like "bungalow" and "thug." It comes from *pandit*, meaning "scholar," "learned person." The first premier of India, Jawaharlal Nehru, was often referred to respectfully as "Pandit Nehru."

In English it has come to refer to opinionated commentators on public affairs, but it is often mispronounced and misspelled "pundint" or "pundant."

purposely/purposefully

If you do something on purpose (not by accident), you do it purposely. But if you have a specific purpose in mind, you are acting *purposefully.*

---

q/g

See "g/q."

quantum leap

The thing about quantum leaps is that they mark an abrupt change from one state to a distinctly different one, with no in-between transitional states being possible. It makes sense to use "quantum leap" to refer to an abrupt, radical qualitative change, but less sense for a simple large increase. It's probably better to leave "quantum leap" to the subatomic physicists unless you know what you're talking about.

quash/squash

See "squash/quash."

quay/cay/key

You tie your boat up at a quay built next to the shore; you can take your boat out to explore a cay or key—a small island or reef. Cays and keys are natural; quays are always built by human beings.

question/ask

When you question someone, you may ask a series of questions trying to arrive at the truth: "The police questioned Tom for five hours before he admitted to having stolen the pig." "Question" can also mean "challenge": "His mother questioned Timmy's claim that the cat had eaten all the chocolate chip cookies." But if you are simply asking a question to get a bit of information, it is not appropriate to say "I questioned whether he had brought the anchovies" when what you really mean is "I asked whether he had brought the anchovies."

queue

If you're standing in a queue you'll have plenty of time to ponder the unusual spelling of this word. Remember, it contains two *U*'s.

queue/cue

See "cue/queue."

quick claim/quitclaim

The term for a legal document relinquishing a legal claim to some property is a "quitclaim deed." It is not a "quick claim," and "quitclaim" is a single word.

quiet/quite

This is probably caused by a slip of the fingers more often than by a slip of the mental gears, but one often sees "quite" (very) substituted for "quiet" (shhh!). This is one of those common errors your spelling checker will not catch, so look out for it.

quotation marks

The examples below are set off in order to avoid confusion over the use of single and double quotation marks.

There are many ways to go wrong with quotation marks. They are often used ironically:

> She ran around with a bunch of "intellectuals."

The quotation marks around "intellectuals" indicate that the writer believes that these are in fact so-called intellectuals, not real intellectuals at all. The ironic use of quotation marks is very much overdone, and is usually a sign of laziness indicating that the writer has not bothered to find the precise word or expression necessary.

Advertisers unfortunately tend to use quotation marks merely for emphasis:

"FRESH" TOMATOES
59 CENTS A POUND

The influence of the more common ironic usage tends to make the reader question whether these tomatoes are really fresh. Underlining, bold lettering, all caps—there are several less ambiguous ways to emphasize words than placing them between quotation marks.

In American usage, single quotation marks are used normally only for quoted words and phrases within quotations.

> Angela had the nerve to tell me "When I saw 'BYOB' on
> your invitation, I assumed it meant 'Bring Your Old Boy-
> friend.'"

British usage has traditionally been to reverse this relationship, with single quotation marks being standard and double ones being used only for quotations within quotations. (The English also call quotation marks "inverted commas," though only the opening quotation mark is actually inverted—and flipped, as well.) However, usage in the UK is shifting toward the US pattern, (see, for instance, *The Times* of London); though the printing of fiction tends to adhere to the older British pattern, where US students are most likely to encounter it.

Single quotation marks are also used in linguistic, phonetic, and philosophical studies to surround words and phrases under discussion; but the common practice of using single quotation marks for short phrases and words and double ones for complete sentences is otherwise an error.

> Block quotations like this should not be surrounded by any
> quotation marks at all. (A passage should consist of at least
> three lines of verse or five lines of prose to justify a block
> quotation.) Normally you should leave extra space above
> and below a block quotation.

When quoting a long passage involving more than one paragraph, quotation marks go at the beginning of each paragraph, but at the end of only the final one. Dialogue in which the speaker changes with each paragraph has each speech enclosed in its own quotation marks.

Titles of books and other long works that might be printed as books are usually italicized (except, for some reason, in newspapers); but the titles of short poems, stories, essays, and other works that would be more commonly printed within larger works (anthologies, collections, periodicals, etc.) are enclosed in quotation marks.

There are different patterns for regulating how quotation marks relate to other punctuation. Find out which one your teacher or editor prefers and use it, or choose one of your own liking, but stick to it consistently. One widely accepted authority in America is the *Chicago Manual of Style*, whose guidelines are outlined below. English, Canadian, Australian and other writers in British-influenced countries should be aware that their national patterns will be quite different, and variable.

In standard American practice, commas are placed inside quotation marks:

> I spent the morning reading Faulkner's "Barn Burning,"
> which seemed to be about a pyromaniac.

Periods are also normally placed inside quotation marks (with the exception of terms that appear in single quotation marks in linguistic, phonetic, and philosophical studies, as mentioned earlier). Colons and semicolons, however, are preceded by quotation marks.

If the quoted matter ends with a question mark or exclamation point, it is placed inside the quotation marks:

> John asked, "When's dinner?"

But if it is the enclosing sentence which asks the question, then the question mark comes after the quotation marks:

> What did she mean, John wondered, by saying "as soon as
> you make it"?

Similarly:

> Fred shouted, "Look out for the bull!"

but

> When I was subsequently gored, all Timmy said was, "This
> is kinda boring"!

It is unfortunately true that many standard character sets—including ASCII and basic HTML—lack true quotation marks which curl to enclose the quoted matter, substituting instead ugly "inch" or "ditto" marks. If you are writing HTML for the Web, you need to turn off the "smart quotes" feature in your word processor which curls quotation marks and apostrophes. Leaving curled quotation marks and apostrophes in text intended for the Web causes ugly gibberish which will make your writing hard to read.

If you would like to include proper curled quotation marks and apostrophes in your HTML code you can write **“** (curled double open quote), **”** (curled double close quote), **‘** (curled single open quote), and **’** (curled close quote). Most contemporary browsers can properly interpret these codes, though they used to cause trouble for people using older browser versions.

See also "apostrophes."

quote

A passage doesn't become a quote (or—better—"quotation") until you've quoted it. The only time to refer to a "quote" is when you are referring to someone quoting something. When referring to the original words, simply call it a "passage."

racism

The *C* in "racism" and "racist" is pronounced as a simple *S* sound. Don't confuse it with the "SH" sound in "racial."

rack/wrack

If you are racked with pain or you feel nerve-racked, you are feeling as if you were being stretched on that medieval instrument of torture, the rack. You rack your brains when you stretch them vigorously to search out the truth like a torturer. "Wrack" has to do with ruinous accidents, so if the stock market is wracked by rumors of imminent recession, it's wrecked.

raise/raze

To *raze* a building is to demolish it so thoroughly that it looks like it's been scraped right off the ground with a razor. To *raise* a building is just the opposite: to erect it from the ground up.

raise/rear

Old-fashioned writers insist that you raise crops and rear children, but in modern American English children are usually "raised."

rampart/rampant

"Rampant" is an adjective which originally meant a posture seen in animals on coats of arms: rearing up on their hind legs, but in modern times it mainly means "wild" or "very widespread." Some people confuse this word with "rampart," a noun denoting a barricade or fortification.

Crime, disease, and greed may all be rampant, but not "rampart."

ran/run

Computer programmers have been heard to say "the program's been ran," when what they mean is "the program's been run."

random

Kyle can choose the shirt he'll wear for the day at random—they're all orange.

This sort of use of "at random" to mean "by chance," is perfectly standard. (Kyle should get some new shirts, though.)

Less widely accepted are a couple of slangy uses of the word, mostly by young people. In the first, "random" means "unknown," "unidentified" as in "some random guy told me at the party that I reminded him of his old girlfriend."

The other is to use random to mean "weird," "strange," as in "The party at Jessica's was so random, not what I was expecting at all!" Evidently in this expression randomness is being narrowed down to unlikelihood and that is in turn being connected with strangeness, though randomness in real life is usually quite ordinary and boring.

Use of either of these two expressions in formal speech or writing is likely to annoy or confuse your audience.

rapport

Many more people hear this word, meaning "affinity," than read it, judging by the popularity of various misspellings such as "rapore" and "rapoire." If you get along really well with someone, the two of you have rapport.

rate of speed/rate, speed

Lots of people like to say things like "traveling at a high rate of speed." This is a redundancy. Say instead "traveling at a high rate" or "traveling at high speed."

rather/sooner

See "sooner/rather."

ratio

A ratio is a way of expressing the relationship between one quantity and another. If there is one teacher to fifty students, the teacher/student ratio is one to fifty, and the student/teacher ratio fifty to one. If a very dense but wealthy prince were being tutored by fifty teachers, the teacher/student ratio would be fifty to one, and the student/teacher ratio would be one to fifty. As you can see, the order in which the numbers are compared is important.

If you are campaigning for more individual attention in the classroom, you want a *higher* number of teachers, but a *lower* student/teacher ratio.

rational/rationale

"Rational" is an adjective meaning "reasonable" or "logical": "Ivan made a rational decision to sell his old car when he moved to New York." "Rational" rhymes with "national."

"Rationale" is a noun which most often means "underlying reason": "His rationale for this decision was that it would cost more to pay for parking than the car was worth." "Rationale" rhymes with "passion pal."

rationale/rationalization

When you're explaining the reasoning behind your position, you're presenting your *rationale*. But if you're just making up some lame excuse to make your position appear better—whether to yourself or others—you're engaging in *rationalization*.

ravaging/ravishing/ravenous

To ravage is to pillage, sack, or devastate. The only time "ravaging" is properly used is in phrases like "When the pirates had finished ravaging the town, they turned to ravishing the women." Which brings us to "ravish": meaning to rape or rob violently. A trailer court can be ravaged by a storm (nothing is stolen, but a lot of damage is done), but not ravished. The crown jewels of Ruritania can be ravished (stolen using violence) without being ravaged (damaged).

To confuse matters, people began back in the 14th century to speak metaphorically of their souls being "ravished" by intense spiritual or aesthetic experiences. Thus we speak of a "ravishing woman" (the term is rarely applied to men) today not because she literally rapes men who look at her but because her devastating beauty penetrates their hearts in an almost violent fashion. Despite contemporary society's heightened sensitivity about rape, we still remain (perhaps fortunately) unconscious of many of the transformations of the root meaning in words with positive connotations such as "rapturous."

Originally, "raven" as a verb was synonymous with "ravish" in the sense of "to steal by force." One of its specialized meanings became "devour," as in "The lion ravened her prey." By analogy, hungry people became "ravenous" (as hungry as beasts), and that remains the only common use of the word today.

If a woman smashes your apartment up, she ravages it. If she looks stunningly beautiful, she is ravishing. If she eats the whole platter of hors d'oeuvres you've set out for the party before the other guests come, she's ravenous.

RBI/RBIs

Some people reason that since "RBI" stands for "runs batted in," there is no need for an additional *S* to indicate a plural, and speak of "120 RBI." However, though somewhat illogical, it is standard to treat the initialism as a word and say "RBIs." In writing, one can add an optional apostrophe: "RBI's." Definitely nonstandard is the logical but weird "RsBI."

The same pattern applies to other such plural initialisms as "WMDs" ("weapons of mass destruction"), "POWs" ("prisoners of war"), and "MREs" ("meals ready to eat"); but "RPMs" ("revolutions per minute") is less widely accepted.

reactionary/reactive

Many people incorrectly use "reactionary" to mean "acting in response to some outside stimulus." That's "reactive." "Reactionary" actually has a very narrow meaning; it is a noun or adjective describing a form of looking backward that goes beyond conservatism (wanting to prevent change and maintain present conditions) to reaction—wanting to recreate a lost past. The advocates of restoring Czarist rule in Russia are reactionaries. While we're on the subject, the term "proactive" formed by analogy with "reactive" seems superfluous to many of us. Use "active," "assertive," or "positive" whenever you can instead.

readably/readily

Some people mistakenly say of something easily available that it is "readably available." The original expression has nothing to do with reading; it is "readily available," ready at hand.

real/really

The correct adverbial form is "really" rather than "real," but even that form is generally confined to casual speech, as in, "When you complimented me on my speech I felt really great!" To say "real great" instead moves the speaker several steps downscale socially. However "really" is a feeble qualifier. "Wonderful" is an acceptable substitute for "really great" and you can give a definite upscale slant to your speech by adopting the British "really quite wonderful." Usually, however, it is better to replace the expression altogether with something more precise: "almost seven feet tall" is better than "really tall." To strive for intensity by repeating "really" as in "That dessert you made was really, really good" demonstrates an impoverished vocabulary.

realize/realise

"Realize" is the dominant spelling in the US, and "realise" in the UK. Spelling checkers often try to enforce these patterns by labeling the other spelling as an error, but it is good to know that most dictionaries list these as acceptable spelling variants.

realms of possibility/realm of possibility

We say of something that is not impossible that it is "within the realm of possibility," or "within the realm of the possible." The plural form "realms" is so popular in the worlds of fantasy fiction and gaming that it is understandable that many people would refer to "realms of possibility," but the realm of the possible contains everything that is possible. That's what its name means. The idea of plural possibilities is already inherent in the word "realm."

When even serious physicists speculate about multiple "universes" the concept of multiple realms of possibility may sound all right, but it's neither logical nor traditional.

realtor

For some reason, this word is often mispronounced as "real-a-ter" instead of the proper "ree-ul-ter." Incidentally, realtors insist that this is a term originally trademarked by the National Association of Real Estate Boards (now renamed the National Association of Realtors), that it must be capitalized, and that all non-members of that association are mere "real estate associates." Common usage, however, calls both "real estate agents," despite their protests.

reap what you sew/reap what you sow

When you plant seeds you sow them. Galatians 6:7 says, "A man reaps what he sows" (harvests what he plants, gets what he deserves). This agricultural metaphor gets mangled frequently into "you reap what you sew." At best, you might rip what you sew; but you probably wouldn't want to tell people about it.

rear/raise

See "raise/rear."

reason because

We often hear people say things like, "the reason there's a hole in the screen door is because I tripped over the cat on my way out." The phrase "is because" should be "is that." If you wanted to use "because," the sentence should be phrased, "There's a hole in the screen door because I tripped over the cat." Also, the expression "the reason being is" should be simply "the reason being."

The similarly redundant common expression "the reason why" is generally regarded as standard now, although some people still object to it.

rebelling/revolting

Even though "rebel" and "revolt" mean more or less the same thing, in modern English people who are *revolting* are usually disgusting, rather than taking up arms against the government. To prevent incongruous associations, use "rebelling" to label the actions of those who conduct uprisings and save "revolting" to label things that make you want to upchuck.

rebut/refute

When you *rebut* someone's argument you argue against it. To *refute* someone's argument is to prove it incorrect. Unless you are certain you have achieved success, use "rebut."

recent/resent

There are actually three words to distinguish here. "Recent," always pronounced with an unvoiced hissy *S* and with the accent on the first syllable, means "not long ago," as in, "I appreciated your recent encouragement." "Resent" has two different meanings with two different pronunciations, both with the accent on the second syllable. In the most common case, where "resent" means "feel annoyed at," the word is pronounced with a voiced *Z* sound: "I resent your implication that I gave you the chocolates only because I was hoping you'd share them with me." In the less common case, the word means "to send again," and is pronounced with an unvoiced hissy *S* sound: "The e-mail message bounced, so I resent it." So say the intended word aloud. If the accent is on the second syllable, "resent" is the spelling you need.

recognize

In sloppy speech, this often comes out "reck-uh-nize." Sound the *G*.

record
See "tape, record."

recreate/reinvent
The expression "no need to reinvent the wheel" loses much of its wit when "recreate" is substituted for the original verb. While we're at it, "recreate" does not mean "to engage in recreation." If you play basketball, you may be exercising, but you're not recreating.

recuperate/recoup
If you are getting over an illness, you are recuperating; but if you insist on remaining at the roulette table when your luck has been running against you, you are seeking to recoup your losses.

recurring/reoccurring
See "reoccurring/recurring."

rediculous/ridiculous
You may ridicule ideas because you find them ridiculous, but not *red*iculous.

redo it over/redo it, do it over
"Redo it over" is redundant; say either "redo it" or "do it over." The only time this phrase makes sense is in the phrase "redo it over and over again."

redundancies
There are many examples of redundancies in these pages: phrases which say twice what needs to be said only once, like "past history." Advertisers are particularly liable to redundancy in hyping their offers: "as an added bonus" (as a bonus), "preplan" (plan), and "free gift" (but look out for the shipping charges!). Two other common redundancies that are clearly errors are "and plus" (plus) and "end result" (result). But some other redundancies are contained in phrases sanctioned by tradition: "safe haven," "hot water heater," "new beginning," and "tuna fish."

reeking havoc/wreaking havoc
"Reeking" means "smelling strongly," so that can't be right. The phrase simply means "working great destruction." "Havoc" has always referred to general destruction in English, but one very old phrase incorporating the word was "cry havoc," which meant to give an army the signal for pillage. To "play havoc with" means the same thing as to "wreak havoc." Avoid as well the mistaken "wreck havoc."

refer/allude
See "allude/refer."

refer back
Some people argue that "refer back" is redundant, but you can refer ahead as well as back. "Refer back" is standard usage.

reference

Nouns are often turned into verbs in English, and "reference" in the sense "to provide references or citations" has become so widespread that it's generally acceptable, though some teachers and editors still object.

See also "vague reference."

refrain/restrain

"Restrain" is a transitive verb: it needs an object. Although "refrain" was once a synonym for "restrain" it is now an intransitive verb: it should not have an object. Here are examples of correct modern usage: "When I pass the dough-nut shop I have to restrain myself" ("myself" is the object). "When I feel like throwing something at my boss, I usually refrain from doing so." You can't *refrain* yourself or anyone else.

refute/rebut

See "rebut/refute."

refute/reject

To *refute* someone's argument is to prove it incorrect. If you attempt no such proof but simply disagree with an argument the word you want is "reject."

regard/regards

Business English is deadly enough without scrambling it. "As regards your downsizing plan . . ." is acceptable, if stiff. "In regard to" and "with regard to" are also correct. But "in regards to" is nonstandard. You can also convey the same idea with "in respect to" or "with respect to."

regardless/irregardless

See "irregardless/regardless."

regime/regimen

Some people insist that "regime" should be used only in reference to govern-ments, and that people who say they are following a dietary regime should instead use "regimen"; but "regime" has been a synonym of "regimen" for over a century, and is widely accepted in that sense.

However "regiment" is an error in this sense. The only way you could follow a strict regiment would be to march behind a highly disciplined military unit. Your diet or exercise routine is not a "regiment."

regretfully/regrettably

Either word can be used as an adverb to introduce an expression of regret, though conservatives prefer "regrettably" in sentences like "Regrettably, it rained on the 4th of July." Within the body of a sentence, however, "regret-fully" may be used only to describe the manner in which someone does something: "John had to regretfully decline his beloved's invitation to go hang-gliding because he was terrified of heights." If no specified person in the sentence is doing the regretting, but the speaker is simply asserting "it is to be regretted," the word is "regrettably": "Their boss is regrettably stubborn."

reign/rein

A king or queen reigns, but you rein in a horse. The expression "to give rein" means to give in to an impulse as a spirited horse gives in to its impulse to gallop when you slacken the reins. Similarly, the correct expression is "free rein," not "free reign."

reinvent/recreate

See "recreate/reinvent."

reknown/renown

When you won the national spelling bee you achieved great *renown* (fame). Now you are a *renowned* speller (notice the "-ed" ending on the adjectival form).

Many people mistakenly suppose that because "renown" has to do with being well known the word should be spelled "reknown," but in fact it is derived from the French word *nom* and has to do with gaining a name. In French, fame is *renomée*.

relevant/revelant

See "revelant/relevant."

religion

Protestants often refer incorrectly to "the Catholic religion." Catholicism is a faith or a church. (Only Protestants belong to "denominations.") Both Catholics and Protestants follow the Christian religion.

religion believes/religion teaches

People often write things like "Buddhism believes" when they mean to say "Buddhism teaches" or "Buddhists believe." Religions do not believe, they are the objects of belief.

religiosity/piety

The main modern use of "religiosity" is to describe exaggerated or ostentatious showing off of one's religiousness. A better word to label the quality of being truly religious is "piety."

remotely close

"Not even remotely close" is a fine example of an oxymoron. An idea can be "not even remotely correct," but closeness and remoteness are opposites; and it doesn't make sense to have one modify the other. There are lots of lists of oxymorons on the Web, but they mostly mix jokey editorializing ("military intelligence" and "Microsoft Works") with true oxymorons. Good for a laugh, but not providing much guidance to writers.

renumeration/remuneration

Although "remuneration" looks as if it might mean "repayment" it usually means simply "payment." In speech it is often confused with "renumeration," which would mean re-counting (counting again).

reoccurring/recurring

It might seem logical to form this word from "occurring" by simply adding a *RE-* prefix— but the most common form is "recurring." The root form is "recur" rather than "reoc-cur." Although the forms with an *O* are legiti-mate, many style guides recommend against

Saying "remuneration" was no problem for Nancy and Mary, who never misplaced their N's and M's.

them. For some reason "recurrent" is seldom transformed into "reoccurrent."

repel/repulse

In most of their meanings these are synonyms, but if you are disgusted by someone, you are repelled, not repulsed. The confusion is compounded by the fact that "repellent" and "repulsive" mean the same thing. Go figure.

reply back/reply

"Reply back" is redundant because "reply" already conveys the idea of get-ting back to someone. The same is true of "answer back" except in the rather old-fashioned use of the phrase to describe the behavior of a lippy kid rudely refusing to submit to the wishes of parents or teachers.

report into/report on

You can conduct an investigation into a matter, like a scandal or a crime; but the result is a report *on* or *of* your findings. You don't make a report *into* any-thing. You could eliminate "into" altogether by using the simpler "investigate" instead.

repress/oppress

See "oppress/repress."

repungent/repugnant, pungent

"Repungent" is an amusing mash-up of "repugnant" (disgusting) and "pun-gent" (strong, especially used of smells). It is used for repulsive smells; and though it is vivid, it's not standard English and may get you laughed at.

request/ask

If you want something you can request it or you can ask for it. Many people like "request" because it sounds more formal, more elegant; but to other people it just sounds pretentious. There are many instances in which plain old "ask" works better: "I'm asking my buddies to go camping with me"; "She asked him to walk the dog." Except on wedding invitations, try to avoid "request" where "ask" will do as well.

resent/recent
See "recent/resent."

resign/re-sign
Athletes who renew their contracts *re-sign* with their teams (note the hyphen). If they were to *resign* they would do the opposite—leave.

resignate/resonate
When an idea gives you good vibes it resonates with you: "His call for better schools resonates with the voters." Not *resignates—resonates.*

resister/resistor
A *resistor* is part of an electrical circuit; a person who resists something is a *resister.*

respect/aspect
See "aspect/respect."

respiratory
Even health professionals tend to mispronounce this word by smooshing the second and third syllables into one. This word has several possible pronunciations, but "resp-uh-tory" is not one of them. However you say it, try to at least hint at all five syllables.

respond back/respond, reply
It's possible that some people think they have to write "respond back" to distinguish a reply from other kinds of responses, like groaning and cursing, or chucking a request in the wastebasket; but most of the time the context makes perfectly clear that "respond" means "answer" and the "back" is redundant. Or you can just say "reply."

restauranter/restaurateur
In standard English, the title for the owner of a restaurant is "restaurateur" (note: no *N*).

retch/wretch
If you vomit, you *retch*; if you behave in a wretched manner or fall into wretched circumstances, you are a *wretch.*

reticent/hesitant
"Reticent" most often means "reluctant to speak." It can also mean "reserved" or "restrained," though conservatives prefer to use it to apply only to speech. If you're feeling nervous about *doing* something, you're hesitant: "I'm hesitant about trying to ride a unicycle in public." "Hesitant" is by far the more common word; so if you hesitate to choose between the two, go with "hesitant."

retrospective/retroactive

"Retrospective" has to do with looking back, as is shown by the similarity of its middle syllable to words like "spectacles." A retrospective exhibit looks back at the earlier work of an artist.

"Retroactive," on the other hand, refers to actions, and is about making a current change applicable to the past, especially in law. Retroactive punishment is generally considered unjust. For instance, the city council can't pass an ordinance retroactively punishing you for having sung off-key in the karaoke bar on Main Street last Saturday night.

return back/return

"Return back" is a redundancy. Use just "return," unless you mean to say instead "turn back."

revelant/relevant

"Relevant" matters are *related* to the subject at hand. "Revelant" is both spoken and written frequently when "relevant" is intended.

revenge/avenge

See "avenge/revenge."

revert/reply

The most common meaning of "revert" is "to return to an earlier condition, time, or subject." When Dr. Jekyll drank the potion he reverted to the brutish behavior of Mr. Hyde. But in South Asia it has become common to use "revert" instead of "reply," writing when people want you to get back to them about something: "revert to me at this address." In standard English this would literally mean they are asking you to become them, so it is best to stick with "reply" when dealing with non-South Asian correspondents. Even some South Asians disapprove of this use of "revert."

revert back

Since "revert" means "go back," many people feel that "revert back" is a pointless redundancy. "Revert" all by itself is better.

revolting/rebelling

See "rebelling/revolting."

revolve/rotate

In ordinary speech these two words are often treated as interchangeable, though it's "revolving credit account" and "rotating crops." Scientists make a sharp distinction between the two: the earth revolves (orbits) around the sun but rotates (spins) around its axis.

revolve around/center around/center on

See "center around/center on/revolve around."

revue/review

You can attend a musical *revue* in a theatre, but when you write up your reactions for a newspaper, you're writing a *review*.

rhetorical questions

A rhetorical question implies its own answer; it's a way of making a point. Examples: "Aren't you ashamed of yourself?" "What business is it of yours?" "How did that idiot ever get elected?" "What is so rare as a day in June?" These aren't questions in the usual sense, but statements in the form of a question.

Many people mistakenly suppose that any nonsensical question, or one which cannot be answered, can be called a rhetorical question. The following are not proper rhetorical questions: "What was the best thing before sliced bread?" "If a tree falls in the forest and no one hears it, does it make a sound?" "Who let the dogs out?"

Sometimes speakers ask questions so they can then proceed to answer them: "Do we have enough troops to win the war? It all depends on how you define victory." The speaker is engaging in rhetoric, but the question asked is not a rhetorical question in the technical sense. Instead this is a mock-dialogue, with the speaker taking both roles.

ridged/rigid

Only things with ridges are ridged, like mountain ranges or a plowed field. Backs lifting heavy loads, strict regulations, and things or ideas which are stiff, inflexible, or uncompromising are *rigid*.

riffle/rifle

To rifle something is to steal it. The word also originally had the sense of "to search thoroughly," often with intent to steal. But if you are casually flipping through some papers, you *riffle* through them.

right/rite/write

"Write" has to do with writing, whether on a piece of paper or to a hard drive.

A "rite" is a ritual.

Everything else is "right," right?

right of passage/rite of passage

The more common phrase is "rite of passage"—a ritual one goes through to move on to the next stage of life. Learning how to work the combination on a locker is a rite of passage for many entering middle school students. A "right of passage" would be the right to travel through a certain territory, but you are unlikely to have any use for the phrase.

ring its neck/wring its neck

Wring the chicken's neck; and after you've cooked it, ring the dinner bell.

ringer/wringer

Old-fashioned washing machines lacked a spin cycle. Instead, you fed each piece of wet clothing between two rotating cylinders which would wring the excess water out of the cloth. This led to the metaphorical saying according to which someone put through an ordeal is said to have been put "through the wringer."

Few people remember those old wringer washers, and many of them now mistakenly suppose the spelling of the expression should be "through the ringer." This error has been reinforced by the title of a popular album by the band Catch 22: *Washed Up and Through the Ringer.*

Rio Grande River/Rio Grande

Rio is Spanish for "river," so "Rio Grande River" is a redundancy. Just write "Rio Grande." Non-Hispanic Americans have traditionally failed to pronounce the final *E* in "Grande," but they've learned to do it to designate the large size of latte, so perhaps it's time to start saying it the proper Spanish way: "REE-oh GRAHN-day." Or to be really international we could switch to the Mexican name: "Rio Bravo."

risky/risqué

People unfamiliar with the French-derived word "risqué" ("slightly indecent") often write "risky" by mistake. Bungee-jumping is risky, but nude bungee-jumping is *risqué.*

Angela's flying wheel routine: a little bit risky, a little bit risqué.

rite

See "right/rite/write."

rite of passage/right of passage

See "right of passage/rite of passage."

road to hoe/row to hoe

Out in the cotton patch you have a tough row to hoe. This saying has nothing to do with road construction.

rob/steal

When you rob a bank, you steal its money. You can't rob the money itself. The stuff taken in a robbery is always "stolen," not "robbed."

rod iron, rot iron/wrought iron

Wrought iron has been worked (wrought) by hammering and bending, often into elaborate shapes. It is distinguished from cast iron, where the iron takes on the shape of the mold the molten metal was poured into.

There is such a thing as "rod iron"—iron shaped into rods—but this is a rare specialized term. Most instances of this form are erroneous spellings of "wrought iron," as are all instances of "rot iron."

rogue/rouge

You can create an artificial blush by using *rouge*, but a scoundrel who deserves to be called a *rogue* is unlikely to blush naturally. Many people write about "rouge software" when they mean "rogue software."

role/roll

An actor plays a *role*. Bill Gates is the entrepreneur's *role model*. But you eat a sausage on a *roll* and *roll* out the barrel. To take attendance, you call the *roll*.

rollover/roll over

A rollover used to be only a serious highway accident, but in the computer world this spelling has also been used to label a feature on a Web page which reacts in some way when you roll the trackball of a mouse over it without having to click. It also became an adjective, as in "rollover feature." However, when giving users instructions, the correct verb form is "roll over"—two words: "roll over the photo of our dog to see his name pop up."

Since most people now use either optical mice or trackpads the term "rollover" has become technically obsolete, but it persists.

Romainian/Romanian

The ancient Romans referred to what we call "the Roman Empire" as Romania (roh-MAHN-ee-ya). The country north of Bulgaria borrowed this ancient name for itself. Older spellings—now obsolete—include "Roumania" and "Rumania." But although in English we pronounce "Romania" roh-MAIN-ee-ya, it is never correct to spell the country's name as "Romainia," and the people and language are referred to not as "Romainian" but as "Romanian."

Ancient Romans were citizens of the Roman empire, and today they are inhabitants of the city of Rome (which in Italian is *Roma*). Don't confuse Romans with Romanians.

romantic

If you are studying the arts, it's important to know that the word "romantic" is used in such contexts to mean much more than "having to do with romantic love." It originated in the Middle Ages to label sensational narratives written in romance languages—rather than Latin—depicting events like the fall of King Arthur's Round Table (in French, novels are still called *romans* whether they depict love affairs or not). In literature and art it often refers to materials that are horrifying, exotic, enthralling, or otherwise emotionally stimulating to an extreme degree. A romantic art song is as likely to be about death as about love.

rondezvous/rendezvous

The first syllable of "rendezvous" rhymes with "pond" but is not spelled like it. It comes from a word related to English "render" and is hyphenated in French: *rendez-vous*. In English the two elements are smooshed together into one: "rendezvous."

roomate/roommate
You have to crowd two *M*'s into "roommate."

root/rout/route
You can *root* for your team (cheer them on) and hope that they utterly smash their opponents (create a *rout*), then come back in triumph on *Route* 27 (a road).

rot iron
See "rod iron, rot iron/wrought iron."

rouge/rogue
See "rogue/rouge."

rough/ruff
See "ruff/rough."

row to hoe/road to hoe
See "road to hoe/row to hoe."

rubbage
Although the generally obsolete form "rubbage" persists in some dialects, many people will assume if you use it that you are confusing "rubbish" with "garbage."

Rueben/Reuben
Diner owners who put "Rueben sandwiches" on their menus may rue the day they did so when they encounter a customer who cares about the correct spelling of this classic American concoction of corned beef, sauerkraut, Swiss cheese, and Russian dressing on rye bread. Although the origin of the sandwich is obscure, being credited to several different restaurateurs, all of them spelled their name "Reuben," with the *E* before the *U*.

ruff/rough
The slangy spelling "ruff" for "rough" is not appropriate in formal writing, but your spelling-checker won't flag it because "ruff" has a traditional meaning of its own, denoting a frilled collar.

run/ran
See "ran/run."

rural
In some US dialects, the second *R* in "rural" is not pronounced, so that it sounds like "ROO-ull" or even "rull." The dominant standard pronunciation sounds both *R*'s, to rhyme with "plural."

rye/wry
"Wry" means "bent, twisted." Even if you don't have a wry sense of humor you may crack a wry smile. No rye is involved.

sacred/scared

This is one of those silly typos which your spelling checker won't catch: gods are sacred, the damned in Hell are scared.

sacreligious/sacrilegious

Doing something sacrilegious involves committing sacrilege. Don't let the related word "religious" trick you into misspelling the word as "sacreligious."

Joyce the angel in full-speed descent— it's a fine line between sacred and scary.

safe haven

See "redundancies."

safety deposit box/safe deposit box

Those who prefer "safe deposit box" feel that the box in question is a container for the safe deposit of goods; it is not a box in which to deposit your safety. But manufacturers and dealers in this kind of safe are split in their usage. Just be aware that some people feel that "safety deposit" is an error whereas no one is likely to look down on you for saying "safe deposit box."

said/spoke

See "spoke/said."

sail/sale/sell

These simple and familiar words are surprisingly often confused in writing. You sail a boat which has a sail of canvas. You sell your old fondue pot at a yard sale.

salchow/sowcow

See "sowcow/salchow."

sale

See "for sale/on sale" *and* "sail/sale/sell."

salsa sauce/salsa

Salsa is Spanish for "sauce," so "salsa sauce" is redundant. Here in the US, where people now spend more on salsa than on ketchup (or catsup, if you prefer), few people are unaware that it's a sauce. Anyone so sheltered as not to be aware of that fact will need a fuller explanation: "chopped tomatoes, onions, chilies, and cilantro."

same difference

This is a jokey, deliberately illogical slang expression that doesn't belong in formal writing.

sameo sameo/same old same old

Many people who don't understand the expression "same old same old" (meaning "the same old thing") misspell it as "sameo sameo" or "same-o same-o."

samwich/sandwich

In some dialects, "sandwich" is pronounced "samwich." In standard English the first syllable is pronounced exactly the way it's spelled, like the word for sand at a beach.

sang/sung

In modern English the normal past tense form of "sing" is "sang." It's not "she sung the anthem" but "she sang the anthem." "Sung" is the past participle, used only after a helping verb: "She has sung the anthem. Play ball!"

sarcastic/ironic

Not all ironic comments are sarcastic. Sarcasm is meant to mock or wound. Irony can be amusing without being maliciously aimed at hurting anyone.

"I suppose you prefer irony to sarcasm—just like all the others."

satellite

Originally a satellite was a follower. Astronomers applied the term to smaller bodies orbiting about planets, like our moon. Then we began launching artificial satellites. Since few people were familiar with the term in its technical meaning, the adjective "artificial" was quickly dropped in popular usage. So far so bad. Then television began to be broadcast via satellite. Much if not all television now wends its way through a satellite at some point, but in the popular imagination only broadcasts received at the viewing site via a dish antenna aimed at a satellite qualify to be called "satellite television." Thus we see motel signs boasting:

AIR CONDITIONING,* SATELLITE

People say things like, "The fight's going to be shown on satellite." The word has become a pathetic fragment of its former self. The technologically literate speaker will avoid these slovenly abbreviations.

---

* At least motels have not yet adopted the automobile industry's truncation of "air conditioning" to "air."

saw/seen

In standard English, it's "I've seen" not "I've saw." The helping verb "have" (abbreviated here to "'ve") requires "seen." Any time you use a helping verb to introduce it, the word you need is "seen": "Mine eyes have seen the glory of the coming of the Lord."

In the simple past (no helping verb), the expression is "I saw," not "I seen." "I've seen a lot of ugly cars, but when I saw that old beat-up Rambler I couldn't believe my eyes." Or "I saw the game on TV."

say/tell

You *say*, "Hello, Mr. Chips," to the teacher and then *tell* him about what you did last summer. You can't "tell that" except in expressions like "go tell that to your old girlfriend."

say your piece/hold your peace

See "hold your peace/say your piece."

says that/expresses that

See "expresses that/says that."

scan/skim

Those who insist that "scan" can never be a synonym of "skim" have lost the battle. It is true that the word originally meant "to scrutinize," but it has now evolved into one of those unfortunate words with two opposite meanings: to examine closely (now rare) and to glance at quickly (much more common). It would be difficult to say which of these two meanings is more prominent in the computer-related usage, to "scan a document."

That said, it's more appropriate to use "scan" to label a search for specific information in a text, and "skim" to label a hasty reading aimed at getting the general gist of a text.

scarcely

"Scarcely" is a negative adverb and shouldn't have another negative word used with it. "She couldn't scarcely afford the bus fare" should be "She could scarcely afford the bus fare."

scared/sacred

See "sacred/scared."

sceptic/skeptic

Believe it or not, the British spellings are "sceptic" and "scepticism"; the American spellings are "skeptic" and "skepticism."

schizophrenic

In popular usage, "schizophrenic" (and the more slangy and now dated "schizoid") indicates "split between two attitudes." This drives people with training in psychiatry crazy. "Schizo-" does indeed mean "split," but it is used here to mean "split off from reality." Someone with a Jekyll-and-Hyde personality is suffering from "multiple personality disorder" (or, more recently, "dissociative identity disorder"), not "schizophrenia."

sci-fi/science fiction/SF

"Sci-fi," the widely used abbreviation for "science fiction," is objectionable to most professional science fiction writers and scholars, and to many fans. Some of them scornfully designate alien monster movies and other trivial entertainments "sci-fi" (which they pronounce "skiffy") to distinguish them from true science fiction. The preferred abbreviation in these circles is "SF." The problem with this abbreviation is that to the general public "SF" means "San Francisco."

"The Sci-Fi Channel" (now the "SyFy Channel") has exacerbated the conflict over this term. If you are a reporter approaching a science fiction writer or expert you immediately mark yourself as an outsider by using the term "sci-fi."

scone/sconce

If you fling a jam-covered biscuit at the wall and it sticks, the result may be a "wall scone"; but if you are describing a wall-mounted light fixture, the word you want is *sconce*.

"So then I said to her, 'Scone? Tastes more like a sconce to me.'"

Scotch/Scots

Scottish people generally refer to themselves as "Scots" or "Scottish" rather than "Scotch." "Scotch" is whisky (or in the US, "whiskey.")

Scotch free/scot free

Getting away with something "scot free" has nothing to do with the Scots (or Scotch). The *scot* was a medieval tax; if you evaded paying it you got off *scot free*. Some people wrongly suppose this phrase alludes to Dred Scott, the American slave who unsuccessfully sued for his freedom. The phrase is "scot free": no *H*, one *T*.

scrapegoat/scapegoat

Leviticus 16:5–10 describes an ancient ritual in which a goat was symbolically laden with the sins of the people and driven out into the desert to the demon

Azazel. In early English translations confusion led to this goat being called a "scapegoat" (for "escaped goat"). A person or cause being sacrificed as a victim to spare others is therefore referred to as a scapegoat. You load the burdens on; you don't scrape them off.

scratch/itch

See "itch/scratch."

sea change

In Shakespeare's *The Tempest*, Ariel deceitfully sings to Ferdinand:

> Full fathom five thy father lies;
> Of his bones are coral made;
> Those are pearls that were his eyes:
> Nothing of him that doth fade
> But doth suffer a sea-change
> Into something rich and strange.

Gerard swept the elephant, figuring he'd get around to scraping the goat later.

This rich language has so captivated the ears of generations of writers that they feel compelled to describe as "sea changes" not only alterations that are "rich and strange," but, less appropriately, those that are simply large or sudden. Always popular, this cliché has recently become so pervasive as to make "sea" an almost inextricable companion to "change" whatever its meaning. In its original context, it meant nothing more complex than "a change caused by the sea." Since the phrase is almost always improperly used and is greatly overused, it has suffered a swamp change into something dull and tiresome. Avoid the phrase; otherwise you will irritate those who know it and puzzle those who do not.

seam/seem

"Seem" is the verb, "seam" the noun. Use "seam" only for things like the line produced when two pieces of cloth are sewn together or a thread of coal in a geological formation.

She sewed a seam, or so it seemed.

seasonable/seasonal/ unseasonable/unseasonal

"Seasonable" means "appropriate to the season." In North America hot summer days are seasonable. Untypical weather is unseasonable. "Seasonal" is used to label something that changes with the season. Holiday sales in December and visits to water parks are seasonal, not seasonable. However, "Unseasonal" is not a standard form. When it is used, the writer usually means "unseasonable."

second of all/second

"First of all" makes sense when you want to emphasize the primacy of the first item in a series, but it should not be followed by "second of all," where the expression serves no such function. And "secondly" is an adverbial form that makes no sense at all in enumeration (neither does "firstly"). As you go through your list, say simply "second," "third," "fourth," etc.

seen/saw

See "saw/seen."

segway/segue

When you shift to a new topic or activity, you *segue*. Many people unfamiliar with the unusual Italian spelling of the word misspell it as "segway." This error is being encouraged by the deliberately punning name used by the manufacturers of the Segway Human Transporter.

seize the day/cease the day

See "cease the day/seize the day."

select/selected

"Select" means "special," "chosen because of its outstanding qualities." If you are writing an ad for a furniture store offering low prices on some of its recliners, call them "selected recliners," not "select recliners," unless they are truly outstanding and not just leftovers you're trying to move out of the store.

self-steam/self-esteem

If you bask in the sauna, you may self-steam. But the expression labeling people's opinions of their own worth is "self-esteem."

"Self-esteem" is also sometimes misspelled "self of steam."

self-titled/eponymous

See "eponymous/self-titled."

self-worth/self-esteem

To say that a person has a low sense of self-worth makes sense, though it's inelegant. But people commonly truncate the phrase, saying instead, "He has low self-worth." This would literally mean that he isn't worth much rather than that he has a low opinion of himself. "Self-esteem" sounds much more literate.

sell

See "sail/sale/sell."

semicolons

See "colons/semicolons."

semiweekly/biweekly
See "biweekly/semiweekly."

sense/since
"Sense" is a verb meaning "feel" ("I sense you near me") or a noun meaning "intelligence" ("have some common sense!"). Don't use it when you need the adverb "since" ("since you went away," "since you're up anyway, would you please let the cat out?").

sense of false hope/false sense of hope
If you're trying to lull someone into hopefulness you don't want to give them a sense of false hope. Rather, you want to make them feel really hopeful, although such hope is unjustified. So what you should say is "a false sense of hope."

The same goes for similar expressions such as "false sense of security," "false sense of confidence," and "false sense of privacy."

sensor/censor/censure/censer
See "censor/censure/sensor/censer."

sensual/sensuous
"Sensual" usually relates to physical desires and experiences and often means "sexy." But "sensuous" is more often used for aesthetic pleasures, like "sensuous music." The two words do overlap a good deal. The leather seats in your new car may be sensuous; but if they turn you on, they might be sensual. "Sensual" often has a slightly racy or even judgmental tone lacking in "sensuous."

sentence fragments
There are actually many fine uses for sentence fragments. Here's a brief scene from an imaginary Greek tragedy composed entirely of fragments:

> *Menelaus:* Aha! Helen!
> *Helen (startled):* Beloved husband!
> *Menelaus:* Slut!
> *Paris (entering, seeing Menelaus):* Oops. 'Bye.
> *Menelaus:* Not so fast! *(stabs Paris).*
> *Paris:* Arrggh!

But some people get into trouble by breaking a perfectly good sentence in two: "We did some research in newspapers. Like the *National Inquirer*." The second phrase belongs in the same sentence with the first, not dangling off on its own.

A more common kind of troublesome fragment is a would-be sentence introduced by a word or phrase that suggests it's part of some other sentence: "By picking up the garbage the fraternity had strewn around the street the weekend before got the group a favorable story in the paper." Just lop off "by" to convert this into a proper complete sentence.

seperate/separate
"Separate" has two *A*'s separated by an *R*.

sergeant of arms/sergeant at arms
The officer charged with maintaining order in a meeting is the "sergeant at arms," not "*of* arms."

service/serve
A mechanic services your car and a stallion services a mare, but most of the time when you want to talk about the goods or services you supply, the word you want is "serve": "Our firm serves the hotel industry."

set/sit
In some dialects people say "come on in and set a spell," but in standard English the word is "sit." You set down an object or a child you happen to be carrying; but those seating themselves sit. If you mix these two up it will not sit well with some people.

setup/set up
Technical writers sometimes confuse "setup" as a noun ("check the setup") with the phrase "set up" ("set up the experiment").

several/various
See "various/several."

SF/sci-fi/science fiction
See "sci-fi/science fiction/SF."

shall/will
"Will" has almost entirely replaced "shall" in American English except in legal documents and in questions like "Shall we have red wine with the duck?"

shan't/shall not
The use of the contraction "shan't" for "shall not" is more common in the UK than in the US, where it may strike readers as a bit old-fashioned. Americans are more likely to say "will not" in the same contexts.

shear/sheer
You can cut through cloth with a pair of shears, but if the cloth is translucent it's *sheer*. People who write about a "shear blouse" do so out of sheer ignorance.

sheath/sheaf
If you take your knife out of its sheath (case) you can use it to cut a sheaf (bundle) of wheat to serve as a centerpiece.

Shepard/shepherd
"Shepard" can be a family name, but the person who herds the sheep is a "shepherd."

sherbert/sherbet

The name for these icy desserts is derived from Turkish/Persian *sorbet*, but the *R* in the first syllable seems to seduce many speakers into adding one in the second, where it doesn't belong. A California chain called "Herbert's Sherbets" had me confused on this point for years when I was growing up.

shimmy/shinny

You shinny—or shin (climb)—up a tree or pole; but on the dance floor or in a vibrating vehicle you shimmy (shake).

shined/shone

The transitive form of the verb "shine" is "shined." If the context describes something shining on something else, use "shined": "He shined his flashlight on the skunk eating from the dog dish." You can remember this because another sense of the word meaning "polished" obviously requires "shined": "I shined your shoes for you."

When the shining is less active, many people would use "shone": "The sun shone on the tomato plants all afternoon." But some authorities prefer "shined" even in this sort of context: "The sun shined on the tomato plants all afternoon."

If the verb is intransitive (lacks an object) and the context merely speaks of the act of shining, the past tense is definitely "shone": "The sun shone all afternoon" (note that nothing is said here about the sun shining *on* anything).

shock/electrocute

See "electrocute/shock."

shoe-in/shoo-in

This expression purportedly comes from the practice of corrupt jockeys holding their horses back and shooing a preselected winner across the finish line to guarantee that it will win. A "shoo-in" is now an easy winner, with no connotation of dishonesty. "Shoe-in" is a common misspelling.

shone/shined

See "shined/shone."

shone/shown

"Shone" is the past tense of "shine": "long after sunset, the moon still shone brightly in the sky."

"Shown" is a past tense form of "show": "foreign films are rarely shown at our local theater."

It was considered a shoo-in for the footwear competition.

shook/shaken

Elvis Presley couldn't have very well sung "I'm all shaken up," but that is the grammatically correct form. "Shook" is the simple past tense of "shake," and quite correct in sentences like "I shook my piggy bank but all that came out was a paper clip." But in sentences with a helping verb, you need "shaken": "The quarterback had shaken the champagne bottle before emptying it on the coach."

shot in the arm/ boost in the arm

See "boost in the arm/shot in the arm."

should/would

Where a British person might say "I should like an apple" an American would be more likely to say "I would like an apple." In the US, "should" is largely confined to the meaning "ought to."

His unpopular act included grammatically correct hits of the fifties, all with harp accompaniment: "All Shaken Up," "Whom Do You Love," "There Is a Whole Lot of Shaking Going On," etc.

should of

See "could of, should of, would of/could have, should have, would have."

shoulder on/soldier on

Soldiers are expected to do their duty despite all obstacles, and that's why we say that a person who perseveres soldiers on. But because "soldier" is rarely used as a verb in modern English, many people mix this expression up with a more common one involving pushing through crowds: to shoulder through. People shouldering are being pushy, usually in an obnoxious way. People who soldier on are admirably determined to carry on despite difficulties.

show-stopper/deal-breaker

Originally a "show-stopper" (now often spelled without the hyphen as one or two words) was a sensational musical number which created so much applause that the show had to be temporarily halted. By extension, anything making a sensationally positive impact could be called "show-stopping."

Computer programmers flipped the meaning by labeling a bug that brings a program to a halt a "showstopper." Now the word is commonly used as a synonym for "deal-breaker" in government and business. The negative meaning is now so pervasive that it can't be called an error, but be aware that those who know only the show-business meaning may regard you as ignorant if you use it in this way.

shrunk/shrank

The simple past tense form of "shrink" is "shrank" and the past participle is "shrunk"; it should be "Honey, I *Shrank* the Kids," not "Honey, I *Shrunk* the Kids." (Thanks a lot, Disney.)

"Honey, I've shrunk the kids" would be standard, and also grammatically acceptable is "Honey, I've shrunken the kids" (though deplorable from a child-rearing point of view).

shutter to think/shudder to think

When you are so horrified by a thought that you tremble at it, you shudder to think it.

sick/sic

The command given to a dog, "sic 'em," derives from the word "seek." The 1992 punk rock album titled *Sick 'Em* has helped popularize the common misspelling of this phrase. Unless you want to tell how you incited your pit bull to vomit on someone's shoes, don't write "sick 'em" or "sick the dog."

The standard spelling of the "-ing" form of the word is "siccing."

In a different context, the Latin word *sic* ("thus") inserted into a quotation is an editorial comment calling attention to a misspelling or other error in the original which you do not want to be blamed for but are accurately reproducing: "She acted like a real pre-Madonna (*sic*)." When commenting on someone else's faulty writing, you really want to avoid misspelling this word as *sick*.

Although it's occasionally useful in preventing misunderstanding, *sic* is usually just a way of being snotty about someone else's mistake, largely replaced now by "lol." Sometimes it's appropriate to correct the mistakes in writing you're quoting; and when errors abound, you needn't mark each one with a *sic*—your readers will notice.

Sierra Nevada Mountains/Sierra Nevadas

Sierra is Spanish for "sawtooth mountain range," so knowledgeable Westerners usually avoid a redundancy by simply referring to "the Sierra Nevadas" or simply "the Sierras." Transplanted weather forecasters often get this wrong.

Some object to the familiar abbreviation "Sierras," but this form, like "Rockies" and "Smokies" is too well established to be considered erroneous.

sight/site/cite

See "cite/site/sight."

signaled out/singled out

When a single individual is separated out from a larger group, usually by being especially noticed or treated differently, that individual is being "singled out." This expression has nothing to do with signaling.

silicon/silicone

Silicon is a chemical element, the basic stuff of which microchips are made. Silicones are plastics and other materials containing silicon, the most commonly discussed example being silicone breast implants. Less used by the general public is "silica": an oxide of silicon.

silver bullet/magic bullet

See "magic bullet/silver bullet."

simile

See "parallel/symbol."

simplistic

"Simplistic" means "overly simple" and is always used negatively. Don't substitute it when you just mean to say "simple" or even "very simple."

since/because

Some assert that "since" must always refer only to time, but since the 14th century, when it was often spelled "syn," it has also meant "seeing that" or "because."

since/sense

See "sense/since."

singing/music

See "music/singing."

single quotes

In standard American writing, the only use for single quotation marks is to designate a quotation within a quotation. Students are exposed by Penguin Books and other publishers to the British practice of using single quotes for normal quotations and become confused. Some strange folkloric process has convinced many people that while entire sentences and long phrases are surrounded by conventional double quotation marks, single words and short phrases take single quotation marks. "Wrong," I insist.

See also "quotation marks."

Sir/Dame

The English titles "Sir" and "Dame" should never be used with a last name only. It's "Sir Paul McCartney" or "Sir Paul," but never "Sir McCartney." Similarly, it's "Dame Helen Mirren" or "Dame Helen," but not "Dame Mirren."

sister-in-laws/sisters-in-law

Your spouse's female siblings are not your sister-in-laws, but your sisters-in-law. The same pattern applies to brothers-in-law, fathers-in-law, and mothers-in-law.

sit/set
See "set/sit."

site/cite/sight
See "cite/site/sight."

skiddish/skittish
If you nervously avoid something you are not "skiddish" about it; the word is "skittish."

skim/scan
See "scan/skim."

slash/backslash
See "backslash/slash."

slaughter
See "decimate/annihilate, slaughter, etc."

slight of hand/sleight of hand
"Sleight" is an old word meaning "cleverness, skill," and the proper expression is "sleight of hand." It's easy to understand why it's confused with "slight" since the two words are pronounced in exactly the same way.

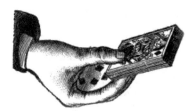

His sleight-of-hand skills were not slight.

slog it out/slug it out
Slogging is a slow, messy business, typically tramping through sticky mud or metaphorically struggling with other difficult tasks. You might slog through a pile of receipts to do your taxes. If you are engaged in a fierce battle with an adversary, however, you slug it out, like boxers slugging each other. There is no such expression as "slog it out."

sluff off/slough off
You use a loofah to *slough* off dead skin.

snuck/sneaked
In American English "snuck" has become increasingly common as the past tense of "sneak." This is one of many cases in which people's humorously self-conscious use of dialect has influenced others to adopt it as standard and it is now often seen even in sophisticated writing in the US. But it is safer to use the traditional form: "sneaked."

so/very
Originally people said things like, "I was so delighted with the wrapping that I couldn't bring myself to open the package." But then they began to lazily say,

"You made me so happy," no longer explaining just how happy that was. This pattern of using "so" as a simple intensifier meaning "very" is now standard in casual speech, but is out of place in formal writing, where "very" or another intensifier works better. Without vocal emphasis, the "so" conveys little in print.

so fun/so much fun
Strictly a young person's usage: "That party was so fun!" If you don't want to be perceived as a gum-chewing airhead, say "so much fun."

so much that, to the point that/to where
See "to where/so much that, to the point that."

so to speak/sorta speak
See "sorta speak/so to speak."

soar/sore
By far the more common word is "sore," which refers to aches, pains, and wounds: sore feet, sore backs, sores on your skin. The more unusual word used to describe the act of gliding through the air or swooping up toward the heavens is spelled "soar." This second word is often used metaphorically: eagles, spirits, and prices can all soar. If you know your parts of speech, just keep in mind that "soar" is always a verb, and "sore" can be either a noun ("running sore") or an adjective ("sore loser") but never a verb. In archaic English "sore" could also be an adverb meaning "sorely" or "severely": "they were sore afraid."

social/societal
"Societal" as an adjective has been in existence for a couple of centuries, but has become widely used only in the recent past. People who imagine that "social" has too many frivolous connotations of mere partying often resort to it to make their language more serious and impressive. It is best used by social scientists and others in referring to the influence of societies: "societal patterns among the Ibo of eastern Nigeria." Used in place of "social" in ordinary speech and writing it sounds pretentious.

socialize
People socialize at a party or on Facebook. Socialist governments socialize their economies. Sociologists speak of people being socialized into particular customs or groups. Animals can also be socialized. These are the main standard uses of "socialize."

But people in the business world have developed a new meaning for "socialize": to get people to agree with. Examples: "have them socialize the material with their work groups," "we need to socialize the idea." To nonspeakers of business jargon this sounds pretentious and silly.

sojourn/journey
Although the spelling of this word confuses many people into thinking it

means "journey," a sojourn is actually a temporary stay in one place. If you're constantly on the move, you're not engaged in a sojourn.

soldier on/shoulder on
See "shoulder on/soldier on."

sole/soul
The bottom of your foot is your sole; your spirit is your soul.

some where/somewhere
"Somewhere," like "anywhere" and "nowhere," is always one word.

somebody/someone
Can "somebody" or "someone" be plural nouns? No. They are always singular.

A sentence like "When somebody runs a red light, they risk causing an accident" is just an example of singular "they."

See also "they/their (singular)."

somebody's else/somebody else's
The expression is not "somebody's else," but "somebody else's."

somersault/summersault
See "summersault/somersault."

sometime/some time
"Let's get together sometime." When you use the one-word form, it suggests some indefinite time in the future. "Some time" is not wrong in this sort of context, but it is required when being more specific: "Choose some time that fits in your schedule." "Some" is an adjective here modifying "time." The same pattern applies to "someday" (vague) and "some day" (specific).

sometimes/not always
Expressions like "not always," "don't always," and "aren't always" overlap in meaning with "sometimes," but don't belong in the same phrase with this word—they're redundant.

"Sometimes I don't always feel like jogging" doesn't make any sense. Say either "sometimes I don't feel like jogging" or "I don't always feel like jogging."

someways/somehow
"Someways" Mark managed to catch his beard in his jacket zipper." "Someways" in this sense is slangy. "Somehow" is standard.

somewhat/pretty
See "pretty/somewhat."

somewhat of a/somewhat, something of a
An "a" is most commonly inserted after "something of" rather than after "somewhat": "She is somewhat awkward," and "He is something of a klutz." "Somewhat of a" will strike some readers as a little odd.

270

somewheres/somewhere
You may hear someone say things like "the yeast is somewheres in the baking aisle." The spelling "somewheres" is not standard; use "somewhere" instead.

song/work or composition
When you're writing that cultural event report based on last night's symphony concert, don't call the music performed "songs." Songs are strictly pieces of music which are sung—by singers. Instrumental numbers may be called "works," "compositions," or even "pieces." Be careful, though: a single piece may have several different movements; and it would be wrong to refer to the Adagio of Beethoven's *Moonlight Sonata* as a "piece." It's just a piece of a piece.

See also "music/singing."

sooner/rather
"I'd sooner starve than eat what they serve in the cafeteria" is less formal than "I'd rather starve."

sooner than later/sooner rather than later
The traditional expression "sooner rather than later" is now commonly abbreviated to the less logical "sooner than later." The shorter form is very popular, but is more likely to cause raised eyebrows than the similarly abbreviated expression "long story short."

See also "long story short/to make a long story short."

sort after/sought after
Something popular which many people are searching for is "sought after." If you are sorting a thing, you've presumably already found it. When this phrase precedes a noun or noun phrase which it modifies, it has to be hyphenated: "*Action Comics* #1 is a much sought-after comic book because it was the first to feature Superman."

sort of
"Sort of" is not only slangy, it is often vague. "Dinner was sort of expensive" does not convey nearly as much as "The bill for dinner came to more than he earned in a week." The same applies to the similarly vague "kind of."

sorta speak/so to speak
The expression "sorta speak" seems to be quite common. Some people will "correct" you by saying it should be pronounced and written "sort of speak."

But neither form is standard. When you use an expression that is not meant entirely literally, or is slang or informal, you may follow it with "so to speak" or "in a manner of speaking." It is most appropriately used to acknowledge that you have just expressed an idea in an unusual fashion.

Some people use it to label statements that are simply untrue, but that is stretching the expression too far.

Examples of standard usage: "They had money to burn, so to speak." "He

271

went ballistic, so to speak." "In my college years I was an academic nomad, so to speak."

Other similar expressions are "as it were," "in a manner of speaking," and "figuratively speaking."

A much less common but more amusing misspelling than "sorta speak" is "soda speak."

sound byte/sound bite

A "sound bite" is a brief snippet of recorded speech, usually used in the context of news reporting. The term originated around 1980, long before the recording of such snippets on personal computers was common; so those who argue that the correct spelling is "sound byte" are mistaken.

soup du jour of the day/soup of the day

Soupe du jour (note the *E* on the end of *soupe*) means "soup of the day." If you're going to use French to be pretentious on a menu, it's important to learn the meaning of the words you're using. Often what is offered is *potage*, anyway. Keep it simple, keep it in English, and you can't go wrong.

sour grapes

In a famous fable by Aesop, a fox declared that he didn't care that he could not reach an attractive bunch of grapes because he imagined they were probably sour anyway. You express sour grapes when you put down something you can't get: "Winning the lottery is just a big headache anyway." The phrase is misused in all sorts of ways by people who don't know the original story and imagine it means something more general like "bitterness" or "resentment."

souse chef/sous chef

"It was better than usual, I thought."

"Yes, well . . . I hear the sous chef wasn't soused for a change!"

What's a "souse chef"? Is it the fellow who adds a dash of brandy to your dessert?

No, it's just a misspelling of *sous chef*, a French phrase meaning "assistant chef." The first word is pronounced just like "sue."

sowcow/salchow

There's a fancy turning jump in ice skating named after Swedish figure skater Ulrich Salchow, but every Winter Olympics millions of people think they hear the commentators saying "sowcow" and that's how they proceed to misspell it.

spaces after a period

In the old days of typewriters using only monospaced fonts in which a period occupied as much horizontal space as any other letter, it was standard to double-space after each one to clearly separate each sentence from the following one. However, when justified variable-width type is set for printing, it has always been standard to use only one space between sentences. Modern computers produce type that is more like print, and most modern styles call for only one space after a period. This is especially important if you are preparing a text for publication which will be laid out from your electronic copy. If you find it difficult to adopt the one-space pattern, when you are finished writing you can do a global search-and-replace to find all double spaces and replace them with single spaces.

spaded/spayed
If you have sterilized your dog, you've spayed it; save the spading until it dies.

span/spun
Don't say "the demon span her head around." The past tense of "spin" in this sense is spun.

spare of the moment/spur of the moment
You don't see people wearing spurs much any more, which may explain why some are vague about the significance of metaphorical spurs. Anything that prompts you to do something can be a spur to action. We say of people that are prompted in this way that they are "spurred on" by fear, ambition, greed, or some other cause.

So a momentary impulse which causes you to act without advance planning can result in a decision made "on the spur of the moment."

Then there is the expression "spare moment": "When I was getting the kids ready for school I couldn't spare a moment to clean up the mess the dog made in the kitchen; would you please do it?"

This latter pattern seems to lead some people to mistakenly imagine that the expression is "on the *spare* of the moment."

"Yes, that is a specific ocean. We call it the Atlantic."

specie/species
In both the original Latin and in English "species" is the spelling of both the singular and plural forms. *Amphiprion ocellaris* is one species of clownfish. Many species of fish are endangered by overfishing.

Specie is a technical term referring to the physical form of money, particularly coins.

specific/Pacific
An astonishing number of people mispronounce "Pacific" as "specific."

speed

See "rate of speed/rate, speed."

spelt/spelled

See "-ed/-t."

spices/herbs

See "herbs/spices."

spiritualism/spirituality

The most common meaning of "spiritualism" is belief in the possibility of communication with the spirits of the dead.

A better term for other religious beliefs and activities is "spirituality," as in "I'm going to the ashram to explore my spirituality."

spit and image/spitting image

According to the *Oxford English Dictionary*, the earlier form was "spitten image," which may have evolved from "spit and image." It's a crude figure of speech: someone else is enough like you to have been spat out by you, made of the very stuff of your body. In the early 20th century the spelling and pronunciation gradually shifted to the less logical "spitting image," which is now standard. It's too late to go back. There is no historical basis for the claim sometimes made that the original expression was "spirit and image."

split infinitives

For the hyper-critical, "to boldly go where no man has gone before" should be "to go boldly. . . ." It is good to be aware that the insertion of one or more words between "to" and a verb is not strictly speaking an error, and is often more expressive and graceful than moving the intervening words elsewhere. But so many people are offended by split infinitives that it is better to avoid them except when the alternatives sound strained and awkward.

spoke/said

Novice writers of fictional dialogue sometimes become wary of repeating "said" too often, resulting in odd constructions like this: "'You've got gravy on your shirt,' she spoke."

You can speak a language or speak with someone, but you can't speak a speech.

If you get tired of "said" you could have your characters whisper, shout, hiss, or grumble; but you shouldn't be afraid of having them simply say things. It won't bore your readers; they won't even notice.

sprain/strain

So did you sprain your leg or strain it? It will take someone with medical training to say for sure. Technically, a sprain is a ligament injury and a strain is tendon or muscle injury. But don't fret about the distinction if you're trying to explain to your friends why you may not be able to finish a hike; they won't hold it against you if your "sprain" turns out to be a "strain."

spree

It used to be that a spree was mainly understood as a wild drinking carouse, with the emphasis on spontaneity and abandon. Then it was used metaphorically, as in a "shopping spree."

American journalists began to write of "killing sprees" by murderers recklessly killing people at random ("spree" fits so nicely in headlines).

But they go too far when they refer to terrorist bombing sprees. Targeted, purposeful acts like these lack the element of spontaneity and disorder that characterize a spree. Do they mean perhaps a *spate*?

spur of the moment/
spare of the moment

See "spare of the moment/spur of the moment."

squash/quash

You can squash a spider or a tomato; but when the meaning you intend is "to suppress," as in rebellions or (especially) legal motions, the more sophisticated term is "quash."

Ted was terrific at tennis, but always got quashed at squash.

squoze/squeezed

The standard past tense of "squeeze" is not "squoze" but "squeezed." Even most people who write "squoze" know this, and use it jokingly.

staid/stayed

"Staid" is an adjective often used to label somebody who is rather stodgy and dull, a stick-in-the-mud. But in modern English the past tense of the verb "stay" is "stayed": "I stayed at the office late hoping to impress my boss."

stain glass/stained glass

The proper spelling is "stained."

stake/steak

See "steak/stake."

stalactites/stalagmites

There's an old joke that will help you keep these straight. Remember "ants in the pants": the *mites* go up and the *tights* come down.

stamp/stomp

See "stomp/stamp."

stance/stand

When you courageously resist opposing forces, you take—or make—a stand. The metaphor is a military one, with the defending forces refusing to flee from the attacker. Your stance, on the other hand, is just your position—literal or figurative—which may not be particularly militant. A golfer wanting to improve her drives may adopt a different stance, or your stance on cojack may be that it doesn't belong on a gourmet cheese platter; but if you organize a group to force the neighbors to get rid of the hippo they've tethered in their front yard, you're taking a stand.

standalone/stand-alone

Despite the fact that it's been slow to appear in traditional dictionaries, the adjective "standalone"—meaning "independent"—has become hugely popular in recent years. There are standalone electronic devices, standalone computer applications, and standalone businesses. Authors known mainly for writing books in a series who decide to write a single work unconnected with any series are said to have written a standalone novel.

You're more likely to find what you're looking for in dictionaries under the hyphenated spelling "stand-alone." Formal edited English still usually prefers this version. There is a strong tendency for such hyphenated forms as "on-line" to get smooshed together into one-word spellings (for instance, "online" is now standard as an adjective). That process is clearly happening with "stand-alone," but it's safer to use the hyphen unless you know for sure that the audience you are writing for prefers the unhyphenated form: write "stand-alone device," etc.

Rendering this adjectival form as two unhyphenated words ("a stand alone device") is just a mistake.

states/countries

Citizens of the United States, where states are smaller subdivisions of the country, are sometimes surprised to see "states" referring instead to foreign countries. Note that the US Department of State deals with foreign affairs, not those of US states. Clearly distinguish these two uses of "state" in your writing.

stationary/stationery

When something is standing still, it's *stationary*. That piece of paper you write a letter on is *stationery*. Let the *E* in "stationery" remind you of "envelope."

staunch/stanch

Some people—and not a few usage guides—insist that although you can be a

One key to good penmanship is stationary stationery.

276

staunch friend you *stanch* the flow of blood from a wound. But "staunch" has been a standard spelling for the word with the latter meaning from its origin in the 14th century, and is today more popular than "stanch."

The two words spelled "staunch" are logically related through a root meaning "watertight": you are tight with your allies and friends, clinging firmly to them; and you close a wound tightly to halt the bleeding. Even people who write "stanch" often pronounce it "stawnch."

stayed/stood
See "stood/stayed."

steak/stake
"Stake" has many meanings, but the only time to use "steak" is when you are talking about a hunk of meat.

steal/rob
See "rob/steal."

step foot/set foot
When you want to say that you refuse to enter some location, the traditional expression is not "step foot," but "set foot": "I refuse to set foot in my brother-in-law's house while he lets his vicious pit bull run around inside."

stereo
"Stereo" refers properly to a means of reproducing sound in two or more discrete channels to create a solid, apparently three-dimensional sound. Because in the early days only fanciers of high fidelity (or hi-fi) equipment could afford stereophonic sound, "stereo" came to be used as a substitute for "high fidelity" and even "record player." Stereo equipment (for instance a cheap mp3 player) is not necessarily high fidelity equipment. Visual technology creating a sense of depth by using two different lenses can also use the root "stereo," as in "stereoscope."

still in all/still and all
The phrase "still and all" means something like "all things considered." Now ("still"), after having taken all relevant facts into account. . . . So it's not "still in all" but "still and all."

stint/stent
When the time to work comes, you've got to do your stint; but the medical device installed to keep an artery open is a "stent." Even people in the medical profession who should know better often use "stint" when they mean "stent."

stoled/stole
The past tense of "steal" is "stole." Tom stole the pig. The only time you can be stoled is when someone drapes a stole on you.

stomp/stamp

"Stomp" is colloquial, casual. A professional wrestler stomps his opponent. In more formal contexts "stamp" is preferred. But you will probably not be able to stamp out the spread of "stomp."

stood/stayed

In standard English, "stayed" is the past tense of "stay," and "stood" is the past tense of "stand." If you speak a dialect which uses "stood" for the past tense of "stayed" and want to switch to standard usage, try changing your sentence to the present tense to check: "I stood still" becomes "I stand still." But "I stood up past midnight" becomes "I stay up," not "I stand up." So you should say "I stayed up past midnight" and "I stayed in the best hotel in town."

The popular saying "I shoulda stood in bed" conjures up an amusing image, but it's not a model for standard usage.

straddled with/saddled with

To straddle is to stand or sit with legs spread. Sometimes "straddle" is used figuratively of someone who avoids taking a firm stand on an issue: the cautious politician straddled the issue of immigration.

To be burdened with something is to be *saddled* with it. You straddle your horse, and it is in turn saddled with the burden of carrying you.

straight/strait

The old word "strait" ("narrow, tight") has survived only as a noun in geography referring to a narrow body of water ("the Bering Strait") and in a few adjectival uses such as "straitjacket" (a narrowly confining garment) and "strait-laced" (literally laced up tightly, but usually meaning narrow-minded). Its unfamiliarity causes many people to mistakenly substitute the more common "straight."

See also "dire straights/dire straits."

straightened/straitened

When things get tight and your options are narrowed down, you may have to live in straitened circumstances or on a straitened budget.

Many people mistakenly use "straightened" in such expressions.

See also "dire straights/dire straits."

strain/sprain

See "sprain/strain."

strength

It is nonstandard to pronounce "strength" as if it were spelled "strenth." The same goes for "length." Make sure to sound the "eng" in the middle of these words.

stress on/feel stress

"Stress on" is commonly misused to mean "to experience stress" as in "I'm stressing on the term paper I have to do." Still informal, but better, is "I'm stressed about. . . ." In a more formal context you could express the same idea by saying "I'm anxious about. . . ."

It is perfectly fine, however, to say that you place stress on something, with "stress" being a noun rather than a verb.

stricken/struck

Most of the time the past participle of "strike" is "struck." The exceptions are that you can be stricken with guilt, a misfortune, a wound, or a disease; and a passage in a document can be stricken out. The rest of the time, stick with "struck."

strike a cord/strike a chord

Something that strikes a chord with you catches your attention because something about it corresponds to something in yourself. The metaphor refers to a chord played on a piano, with one note in yourself harmonizing nicely with a note in that which you are experiencing to create a pleasing chord.

The objects being struck are piano strings, not cords.

striped/stripped

Naked people are stripped. Walls whose paint has been removed are stripped. When the thread of a screw is damaged, it is stripped.

Zebras and skunks are striped.

If you object to wearing formal striped trousers, they may be stripped off.

strong suite/strong suit

"Strong suit" is an expression derived from card-playing, in which hearts, diamonds, clubs, and spades are the suits. When you put your best foot forward you play your strong suit.

strongly/heavily

See "heavily/strongly."

stupid/ignorant

See "ignorant/stupid."

subject to/subjected to

"I was told I could board the airplane subject to a security scan."

"At the airport I was subjected to a humiliating search."

Does it help you to distinguish between these expressions to know that "subject" in the first example is an adverb and "subjected" in the second example is a verb? Didn't think so.

Although these two expressions can sometimes be switched with only a slight change in meaning, they are not equivalent. To be subjected to some sort of treatment is to actually be treated in that way, usually in an objectionable way.

But to be *subject* to a regulation, to taxes, to discussion, to inspection, to any sort of condition, is to be liable to it. In some contexts, the conditional action is mandatory: "Shipment will be made subject to approval of your charge card." In others, the conditional action may be theoretical, not uniformly enforced: "This Web page is subject to change." Many people mistakenly use "subjected to" in this sort of context.

subjunctive
See "if I was/if I were."

submittal/submission
"Submittal" is the act of submitting; it should not be used to describe the thing being submitted, as in "clip a five-dollar bill to your submittal and it will receive our earliest attention." In almost all cases "submission" is clearer and more traditional than "submittal."

subscribe/ascribe
See "ascribe/subscribe."

substance-free
An administrator at our university once announced that his goal was a "substance-free" campus, which I suppose fit in with the fad of the period for "virtual education." What he really meant was, of course, a campus free of illegal drugs and alcohol, designated "controlled substances" in the law. This is a very silly expression, but if he'd just said "sober and straight" he would have sounded too censorious. How about "drug- and alcohol-free"?

substitute with/substitute for
You can substitute pecans for the walnuts in a brownie recipe, but many people mistakenly say "substitute with" instead, perhaps influenced by the related expression "replace with." It's always "substitute for."

subtle/suttle
See "suttle/subtle."

succeed/secede
If you advocate withdrawing formally from a nation or other organization, you want to *secede*.

If you're successful at this or anything else, you *succeed*.

suffer with/suffer from
Although technical medical usage sometimes differs, in normal speech we say that a person suffers from a disease rather than suffering with it.

sufficeth

"Sufficeth" is just an old spelling of "suffices," commonly used in the King James translation of the Bible and other Renaissance religious texts. People often use it in a joking manner to give their writing a semi-Biblical air, especially in the phrase "it sufficeth to say." But they sound clumsy rather than clever when they omit the "it" and begin the phrase thus "Sufficeth to say. . . ." "Sufficeth" is a verb; it requires a subject.

suit/suite

Your bedroom suite consists of the bed, the nightstand, and whatever other furniture goes with it. Your pajamas would be your bedroom suit.

sulking/skulking

That guy sneaking furtively around the neighborhood is skulking around; that teenager brooding in his bedroom because he got grounded is *sulking*. "Sulking around" is not a traditional phrase.

"Aw . . . don't sulk, Rusty. I'm sure we could get more tennis balls if we skulk around in the bushes some more."

summary/summery

When the weather is warm and summery and you don't feel like spending a lot of time reading that long report from the restructuring committee, just read the summary.

summersault/somersault

"Summersault" is a common variant, but the standard spelling is "somersault."

sung/sang

See "sang/sung."

suped up/souped up

The car you've souped up may be super, but it's not "suped up."

supercede/supersede

"Supersede," meaning "to replace," originally meant "to sit higher" than, from Latin *sedere*, "to sit." In the 18th century, rich people were often carried about as they sat in sedan chairs. Don't be misled by the fact that this word rhymes with words having quite different roots, such as "intercede."

supine/prone

See "prone/supine."

supposably, supposingly, supposively/supposedly

"Supposedly" is the standard form. "Supposably" can be used only when the meaning is "capable of being supposed," and then only in the US. You won't get into trouble if you stick with "supposedly."

suppose to/supposed to
Because the *D* and the *T* are blended into a single consonant when this phrase is pronounced, many writers are unaware that the *D* is even present and omit it in writing. You're supposed to get this one right if you want to earn the respect of your readers.

See also "use to/used to."

supremist/supremacist
A neo-Nazi is a white supremacist, not "supremist."

sure/for sure
See "for sure/sure."

surfing the Internet
"Channel-surfing" developed as an ironic term to denote the very unathletic activity of randomly changing channels on a television set with a remote control. Its only similarity to surfboarding on real surf has to do with the aesthetic of "going with the flow." The Internet could be a fearsomely difficult place to navigate until the World Wide Web was invented; casual clicking on Web links was naturally quickly compared to channel-surfing, so the expression "surfing the Web" was a natural extension of the earlier expression. But the Web is only one aspect of the Internet, and you label yourself as terminally uncool if you say "surfing the Internet." (Cool people say "Net" anyway.) It makes no sense to refer to targeted, purposeful searches for information as "surfing"; for that reason I call my classes on Internet research techniques "scuba-diving the Internet."

surplus neckline/surplice neckline
Medieval priests in chilly Northern European churches wore an extra-large cassock over a fur-lined gown. This garment came to be known as a *surplice* (from Latin *super pelliceum*: "over fur").

Even those few who might have heard of the priestly garment are not likely to make the connection when discussing the surplice neckline on women's clothing because the secular women's garment has an overlapping V-neck whereas most surplices worn in churches today have square or rounded necklines.

So it's not surprising that a large number of people mistakenly refer to the women's garment style as a "surplus neckline." The only surplus involved in these items is the amount of flesh revealed by them.

suspect/suspicious
If your boss thinks you may have dipped into petty cash to pay your gambling debts, you may be *suspect* (or "a suspect"). But if you think somebody else did it, you are *suspicious* of them. Confusingly, if the police suspect you of a crime, you can be described as a "suspicious person" and if you constantly suspect others of crimes, you can also be called "suspicious."

But "suspect" is not so flexible. A suspect is a person somebody is suspicious of, never the person who is doing the suspecting. It never makes sense to say "I am suspect that. . . ."

suttle/subtle
It's a not-so-subtle hint to the reader that your spelling is weak if you misspell "subtle" as "suttle."

swam/swum
The regular past tense of "swim" is "swam": "I swam to the island." However, when the verb is preceded by a helping verb, it changes to "swum": "I've swum to the island every day." The "'ve" stands for "have," a helping verb.

syllabi/syllabus
"Syllabi" is the plural of "syllabus," but you can also say "syllabuses." Don't call a single course schedule a "syllabi."

symbol/parallel
See "parallel/symbol."

sympathy/empathy
See "empathy/sympathy."

systematic/systemic
By far the more common word and the one you should use if you are in doubt is "systematic." It refers to things that are arranged or dealt with according to some system or organized method. "Gerry systematically sorts his socks into piles: those that are still wearable and those that are too smelly."

Often "systematic" and "systematically" are used metaphorically to imply that something is done so consistently that it almost seems there must be a system behind it: "Tom systematically leaves the toilet seat up." If you need a synonym for "consistent," the word you need is "systematic."

"Systemic" is a much rarer scientific and technical term referring to parts of a body or system. It is frequently used in medicine and biology. A systemic disease affects many parts of the body. A systemic herbicide may be sprayed on the leaves of a weed, but it spreads down to its roots to kill the whole plant. A systemic problem in banking affects many parts of the banking system.

If you're talking about how something is done according to a system, the word you want is "systematic."

If you're talking about something happening to or inside of a system, the word you want is "systemic."

-t/-ed
See "-ed/-t."

table

In the UK if you table an issue you place it on the table for discussion; but in the US the phrase means the opposite: you indefinitely postpone discussing the issue.

tact/tack

The expression "take a different tack" has nothing to do with tactfulness and everything to do with sailing, in which it is a direction taken. One tacks—abruptly turns—a boat. To "take a different tack" is to try another approach.

tad bit/tad, bit

A "tad" was originally a small boy, but this word evolved into the expression "a tad" meaning "very small" or "very slightly": "The movie was a tad long for my taste."

Some people combine this with the equivalent expression "a bit" and say "a tad bit." This is redundant. Just say "a bit" or "a tad."

take/bring

See "bring/take."

take and

In some dialects, it's common to emphasize an action by preceding the verb with "take and" (past tense "took and"): "When he got mad he would take and pound his fist into the wall." This expression is not used in formal English, and usually occurs in writing only when the author is trying to convey an impression of unsophisticated speech. The same goes for "went and": "After I told him I didn't get a bicycle for my birthday he went and bought me a unicycle instead."

taken back/taken aback

When you're startled by something, you're taken aback by it. When you're reminded of something from your past, you're taken back to that time.

tape, record

As time goes on, we are less and less likely to record sound or video onto a physical electromagnetic tape. More and more often, such recordings are made onto computer hard drives or solid-state devices. Yet the word "tape" lives on to label the activity involved. We say we are going to tape an interview, tape a dance recital, or tape a new greeting for our voice mail, even when no tape is involved. The problem is that the word "record" is a little too unspecific to be substituted in all contexts for "tape," so we fall back on this obsolete but handy word instead.

I'm not sure what can be done about this, but it bothers me. Now it can bother you too.

tattle-tail/tattle-tale
Somebody who reveals secrets—tattling, telling tales—is a tattle-tale, often spelled as one word: "tattletale."

taught/taut
Students are taught, ropes are pulled taut.

taunt/taut/tout
I am told that medical personnel often mistakenly refer to a patient's abdomen as "taunt" rather than the correct "taut." "Taunt" ("tease" or "mock") can be a verb or noun, but never an adjective. "Taut" means "tight, distended," and is always an adjective. "Taut" is also occasionally misspelled "taught."

Don't confuse "taunt" with "tout," which means "promote," as in "Senator Bilgewater has been touted as a Presidential candidate." You tout somebody you admire and taunt someone that you don't.

teenage/teenaged
Some people object that the word should be "teenaged"; but unlike the still nonstandard "ice tea" and "stain glass," "teenage" is almost universally accepted now.

teeth/teethe
When your baby's teeth are just beginning to come in, you can say she has begun to "teethe" (rhymes with "breathe"). Don't spell this verb form as "teeth" (rhymes with "wreath"). That's the noun form, the word for what emerges during teething.

tell/say
See "say/tell."

temblor/tremblor
See "tremblor/temblor."

tempera/tempura
A sort of paint used in art—traditionally including eggs as an ingredient—is *tempera*.

Eggs are also sometimes used in *tempura*, a batter which is used to coat fried ingredients in Japanese cooking.

But don't be tempted to feed your friends tempera.

tenant/tenet
These two words come from the same Latin root, *tenere*, meaning "to hold," but they have very different meanings. "Tenet" is the rarer of the two, meaning a belief that a person holds: "Avoiding pork is a tenet of the Muslim faith." In contrast, the person leasing an apartment from you is your tenant. (She holds the lease.)

tender hooks/tenterhooks

A "tenter" is a canvas-stretcher, and
to be "on tenterhooks" means to
be as tense with anticipation as a
canvas stretched on one.

*There's no such thing as a tender hook—
that's the first thing you learn in trout school.*

tense

See "verb tense."

tentative

This is often all-too-tentatively pronounced "tennative." Sound all three *T*'s.

than/then

When comparing one thing with another you may find that one is more appealing "than" another. "Than" is the word you want when doing comparisons. But if you are talking about time, choose "then": "First you separate the eggs; then you beat the whites." Alexis is smarter than I, not "then I."

thanks God/thank God

I suppose if you wanted to express your gratitude directly to the deity you might appropriately say "Thanks, God, for helping our team win the big game." More appropriate is something more formal, like "Thank you, God" or "Thanks be to God." In any case, the general expression when it's not specifically meant as a prayer is not "thanks God," but "thank God." Not "*Thanks* God Emily hit a homer in the last inning," but "*thank* God" she did.

thankyou/thank you, thank-you

When you are grateful to someone, tell them "thank you." Thanks are often called "thank-yous," and you can write "thank-you notes." But the expression should never be written as a single unhyphenated word.

that/than

People surprisingly often write "that" when they mean "than" in various standard phrases. Examples: "harder that I thought," "better safe that sorry," and "closer that they appear." In all these cases, "that" should be "than."

that/what

See "what/that."

that/which

I must confess that I do not myself observe the distinction between "that" and "which." Furthermore, there is little evidence that this distinction is or has ever been regularly made in past centuries by careful writers of English. However, a small but impassioned group of authorities has urged the distinction; so here is the information you will need to pacify them.

If you are defining something by distinguishing it from a larger class of which it is a member, use "that": "I chose the lettuce that had the fewest wilted leaves." When the general class is not being limited or defined in some way, then "which" is appropriate: "He made an iceberg Caesar salad, which didn't taste quite right." Note the comma preceding "which" in the previous sentence.

that/who
See "who/that."

that kind/that kind of
Although expressions like "that kind thing" are common in some dialects, standard English requires "of" in this kind of phrase.

thaw/unthaw
See "unthaw/thaw."

the/ye
See "ye/the."

the both of them/both of them
You can say "the two of them," as in "the two of them make an interesting couple"; but normally "the" is not used before "both," as in "both of them have purple hair."

The Ukraine/Ukraine
Some country names are preceded by an article—like "The United States" and "La France"—but most are not. Sometimes it depends on what language you are speaking: in English we call the latter country simply "France," and "La Republica Argentina" is just "Argentina" although in the 19th century the British often referred to it as "The Argentine."

When the region formerly known as "The Ukraine" split off from the old Soviet Union, it declared its preference for dropping the article, and the country is now properly called simply "Ukraine."

their/there/they're
See "they're/their/there."

their/they (singular)
See "they/their (singular)."

their's/theirs
Like the related possessive pronouns "ours," "his," and "hers," "theirs" does not take an apostrophe.

theirselves/themselves
There is no such word as "theirselves" (and you certainly can't spell it "theirselfs" or "thierselves"); it's "themselves." And there is no correct singular form of this non-word; instead of "theirself" use "himself" or "herself."

them/those

One use of "them" for "those" has become a standard catch phrase: "How do you like them apples?" This is deliberate dialectical humor. But "I like them little canapés with the shrimp on top" is gauche; say instead "I like those little canapés."

then/than

See "than/then."

theory

In ordinary speech, a theory is just a speculation. The police inspector in a Miss Marple mystery always has a theory about who committed the murder which turns out to be wrong.

But in science the word "theory" plays a very different role. What most of us call "theories" are termed "hypotheses" until enough evidence has been accumulated to validate them and allow them to assume the status of theories: scientifically acceptable explanations of phenomena. Examples: the theory of gravity, the wave theory of light, chaos theory.

Foes of evolutionary science often insist that the theory of evolution is invalid because it is "only a theory." This merely demonstrates their lack of knowledge of scientific usage and hence will not impress any scientifically literate person.

there/their/they're

See "they're/their/there."

therefor/therefore

The form without a final *E* is an archaic bit of legal terminology meaning "for." The word most people want is "therefore."

there's

People often forget that "there's" is a contraction of "there is" and mistakenly say "there's three burrs caught in your hair" when they mean "there're" ("there are"). Use "there's" only when referring to one item. "There's" can also be a contraction of "there has," as in "There's been some mistake in this bill, clerk!"

Remember if you don't contract "there is" that it also can only be used with something singular following. It's not "There is many mistakes in this paper" but "there *are* many mistakes in this paper."

these are them/these are they

Although only the pickiest listeners will cringe when you say "these are them," the traditionally correct phrase is "these are they," because "they" is the predicate nominative of "these." However, if people around you seem more comfortable with "it's me" than "it's I," you might as well stick with "these are them."

these kind/this kind
In a sentence like "I love this kind of chocolates," "this" modifies "kind" (singular) and not "chocolates" (plural), so it would be incorrect to change it to "I love these kind of chocolates." Only if "kind" itself is pluralized into "kinds" should "this" shift to "these": "You keep making these kinds of mistakes!"

these ones/these
By itself, there's nothing wrong with the word "ones" as a plural: "surrounded by her loved ones." However, "this one" should not be pluralized to "these ones." Just say "these." The same pattern applies to "those."

they/their (singular)
Using the plural pronoun to refer to a single person of unspecified gender is an old and honorable pattern in English, not a newfangled bit of degeneracy or a politically correct plot to avoid sexism (though it often serves the latter purpose). People who insist that "Everyone has brought his own lunch" is the only correct form ignore the usage of centuries of fine writers. A good general rule is that only when the singular noun does not specify an individual can it be replaced plausibly with a plural pronoun: "Everybody" is a good example. We know that "everybody" is singular because we say "everybody is here," not "everybody are here," yet we tend to think of "everybody" as a group of individuals, so we usually say "everybody brought their own grievances to the bargaining table." "Anybody" is treated similarly.

However, in many written sentences the use of singular "their" and "they" creates an irritating clash even when it would pass unnoticed in speech. It is wise to shun this popular pattern in formal writing. Often expressions can be pluralized to make the "they" or "their" indisputably proper: "All of them have brought their own lunches." "People" can often be substituted for "each." Americans seldom avail themselves of the otherwise very handy British "one" to avoid specifying gender because it sounds to our ears rather pretentious: "One's hound should retrieve only one's own grouse." If you decide to try "one," don't switch to "they" in mid-sentence: "One has to be careful about how they speak" sounds absurd because the word "one" so emphatically calls attention to its singleness. The British also quite sensibly treat collective bodies like governmental units and corporations as plural ("Parliament have approved their agenda"), whereas Americans insist on treating them as singular.

See also "collective plural."

they're/their/there
Many people are so spooked by apostrophes that a word like "they're" seems to them as if it might mean almost anything. In fact, it's always a contraction of "they are." If you've written "they're," ask yourself whether you can substitute "they are." If not, you've made a mistake. "Their" is a possessive pronoun like "her" or "our": "They eat their hotdogs with sauerkraut."

289

Everything else is "there." "*There* goes the ball, out of the park! See it? Right *there*! *There* aren't very many home runs like that." "Thier" is a common misspelling, but you can avoid it by remembering that "they" and "their" begin with the same three letters. Another hint: "there" has "here" buried inside it to remind you it refers to place, while "their" has "heir" buried in it to remind you that it has to do with possession.

Although "there's" is a standard abbreviation of "there is" it is nonstandard to use "ther're" as a written abbreviation of "there are." People who use this nonstandard form often mistakenly use "they're" ("they're a lot of people coming to the party") or even "their" ("their a lot of people").

think on/think about
An archaic form that persists in some dialects is seen in statements like "I'll think on it" when most people would say "I'll think about it."

this day and age/today's day and age
See "today's day and age/this day and age."

this here, that there/this, that
The expressions "this here" and "that there" immediately before a noun are nonstandard. In standard English it's not "this here dog" or "that there cat," but "this dog" and "that cat." Less casual is "this dog here" when you are emphasizing the exact item you are indicating as contrasted with others.

Of course "this here" and "that there" have standard uses when they are not followed by a noun: "put that there," "I left this here on purpose," "I'll say this here and now," "there's a space for this here."

this kind/these kind
See "these kind/this kind."

those/them
See "them/those."

though/thought/through
Although most of us know the differences between these words, people often type one of them when they mean another. Spelling checkers won't catch this sort of slip, so look out for it.

360 degrees/180 degrees
When you have turned 360 degrees you've completed a circle and are back where you started. So if you want to describe a position that's diametrically opposed to another, the expression you want is not "360 degrees away" but "180 degrees away."

threw/through
"Threw" is the past tense of the verb "throw": "The pitcher threw a curve

ball." "Through" is never a verb: "The ball came through my living room window." Unless your sentence involves someone throwing something—even figuratively, as in "she threw out the idea casually"—the word you want is "through."

throne/thrown

A throne is that chair a king sits on, at least until he gets thrown out of office.

through a mirror, darkly/ in a mirror, darkly

When it came time to choose a fine ale, the good king was never thrown for a loop.

Here's an error with a very distinguished heritage.

When in 1 Corinthians 13:12 Paul tries to express the imperfection of mortal understanding, he compares our earthly vision to the dim and wavery view reflected by a typical Roman-era polished bronze mirror. Unfortunately, the classic King James translation rendered his metaphor rather confusingly as "For now we see through a glass, darkly." By the time of the Renaissance, mirrors were made of glass and so it was natural for the translators to call the mirror a "glass," though by so doing they obscured Paul's point. Why they should have used "through" rather than the more logical "in" is unclear; but it has made many people think that the image is of looking through some kind of magical glass mirror like that in Lewis Carroll's *Through the Looking Glass*.

Although most other translations use more accurate phrasing ("as in a mirror," "a blurred image in a mirror," etc.), the King James version is so influential that its misleading rendering of the verse is overwhelmingly more popular than the more accurate ones. It's not really an error to quote the King James version, but if you use the image, don't make the mistake of suggesting it has to do with a dirty window rather than a dim mirror.

throws of passion/throes of passion

A dying person's final agony can be called their "death throes." The only other common use for this word is "throes of passion." "Throws" are wrestling moves or those little blankets you drape on the furniture.

thru

See "'lite' spelling."

thusfar/thus far

Some common phrases get fused in people's mind into single words. The phrase "thus far" is frequently misspelled "thusfar." Hardly anybody writes "sofar" instead of "so far"—just treat "thus far" in the same way.

thusly/thus

"Thusly" has been around for a long time, but it is widely viewed as nonstandard. It's safer to go with plain old "thus."

tic/tick

The word for a spasmodic twitch or habitual quirk of speech or behavior is spelled the French way: "tic." You may have to worry about Lyme disease if you get a bite from a tick on your face, but that spasm in your left cheek whenever the teacher calls on you is a facial *tic*.

tie me over/tide me over

That little something that enables you to get through the dry spell between tides (or any other periods of plenty), *tides* you over.

tilde

See "accent marks."

till/until

Since it looks like an abbreviation for "until," some people argue that this word should always be spelled "'til" (though not all insist on the apostrophe). However, "till" has regularly occurred as a spelling of this word for over 800 years; it's actually older than "until." It is perfectly good English.

timber/timbre

You can build a house out of timber, but that quality which distinguishes the sound produced by one instrument or voice from others is *timbre*, usually pronounced "TAM-bruh," so the common expression is "vocal timbre."

time period

The only kinds of periods meant by people who use this phrase are periods of time, so it's a redundancy. Say simply "time" or "period."

times/multiply

School children struggling with their times tables often say that they "times" one number by another. It's "2 times 2," but the mathematical operation being performed is not "timesing."

Some unfortunate folks carry this childish vocabulary into adulthood, continuing to use "times" as a verb meaning "multiply." If you're old enough to handle three-syllable words you can manage this one.

times smaller

Mathematically literate folks object to expressions like "my paycheck is three times smaller than it used to be" because when used with whole numbers "times" indicates multiplication and should logically apply only to increases in size. Say "one third as large" instead.

tirimisù/tiramisù
Tiramisù is Italian for "pick me up," and is the name of a popular modern Italian dessert, commonly misspelled as *tirimisù*, which gives it a slightly Japanese air. The Japanese love *tiramisù*, but although they sometimes make it with green tea rather than coffee this misspelling isn't their fault.

titled/entitled
See "entitled/titled."

to/too/two
People seldom mix "two" up with the other two; it obviously belongs with words that also begin with *TW*, like "twice" and "twenty" that involve the number 2. But the other two are confused all the time. Just remember that the only meanings of "too" are "also" ("I want some ice cream too.") and "in excess" ("Your iPod is playing too loudly."). Note that extra *O*; it should remind you that this word has to do with adding more on to something. "To" is the proper spelling for all the other uses.

to home/at home
In some dialects people say, "I stayed to home to wait for the mail," but in standard English the expression is "stayed *at* home."

to the contrary
See "on the contraire/au contraire, on the contrary, to the contrary."

to the manor born/to the manner born
Hamlet complains of the drunken carousing at Elsinore to his friend Horatio, who asks, "Is it a custom?" Hamlet replies that it is and adds, "but to my mind,—though I am native here and to the manner born,—it is a custom more honour'd in the breach than the observance."

"As if to the manner born" is used to praise someone's skill: "Reginald drives the Maserati as if to the manner born" (as if he were born with that skill).

To the Manor Born was the punning title of a popular BBC comedy, which greatly increased the number of people who mistakenly supposed the original expression had something to do with being born on a manor. Perhaps because of the poetically inverted word order in "manner born" the expression tends to occur in rather snooty contexts. Nevertheless, the correct expression is "to the manner born."

to where/so much that, to the point that
Complains Fred, "Mac kept borrowing my tools to where I couldn't finish fixing the front porch." This sort of use of "to where" to mean "so much that"

You can sharpen the pencil lead to a point; just don't sharpen it to the point that it falls off.

or "to the point that" is not standard English. The meaning is more about when than where.

today's day and age/this day and age

The traditional expression is "in this day and age," meaning "right at this moment and during a considerable stretch of time around this moment." "Today's day" is redundant: "today" already has "day" in it.

today's modern society/today

People seeking to be up to the minute often indulge in such redundancies as "in today's modern society" or "in the modern society of today." This is empty arm-waving which says nothing more than "now" or "today." A reasonable substitute is "contemporary society." Such phrases are usually indulged in by people with a weak grasp of history to substitute for such more precise expressions as "for the past five years" or "this month."

See also "beginning of time."

toe a fine line/tread a fine line, toe the line

When you tread (or walk) a fine line, you are trying to keep your balance between two alternatives, rather as if you were walking carefully along a narrow tightrope. Neighbors have to tread a fine line between being friendly and being nosy. A related expression is "there is a fine line between" two alternatives: "there's a fine line between enthusiasm and fanaticism." In this case you aren't traveling along the line, but crossing over it. The fineness of the line suggests how subtly the two alternatives blend into each other. The first expression is used when you're being cautious; the second is used when you're observing how close two alternatives are to each other.

The expression "toe the line" means something rather different. It describes toes obediently and conscientiously lined up for review, military style. It refers to situations in which you are trying to be very careful to follow the rules, do precisely the right thing. Strict parents make their children toe the line.

It does not involve the emphasis on alternatives referred to by the other expressions. Envision yourself standing in front of a line like the starting line for a race. Such a line need not be particularly fine. What is emphasized here is the straightness of the line. But many people confuse "tread a fine line" with "toe the line" and use the mangled expression "toe a fine line."

See also "tow the line/toe the line."

toe-headed/tow-headed

Light-colored rope is called "tow" and someone with very blond hair is called a "tow-head." Tow-headed children are cute, but a toe-headed one would be seriously deformed.

tolled/told

Some people imagine that the expression should be "all tolled" as if items were being ticked off to the tolling of a bell or it involved the paying of a toll, but in fact this goes back to an old meaning of "tell": "to count." You could "tell over" your beads if you were counting them in a rosary. "All told" means "all counted." This older meaning of "tell" is the reason that people who count money out behind bank windows are called "tellers."

tongue and cheek/tongue in cheek
When people want to show they are kidding or have just knowingly uttered a falsehood, they stick their tongues in their cheeks, so it's "tongue in cheek," not "tongue and cheek."

tooken/took/taken
"Hey, Tricia! Ted couldn't find his parrot so he's tooken your toucan to show and tell!" "Tooken" is a non-standard form of "taken."

In fact, there are two past-tense forms of "take" which shouldn't be mixed up with each other. For the simple past you need "took": "Beau took a course in acoustics." But if a helping verb precedes it, the word you need is "taken": "he has taken some other courses too."

torchiere/torchère
Consumers and dealers who call tall floor lamps *torchieres* undoubtedly think they're being sophisticated, but the French word is simple *torchère* (originally meaning "torch-holder"). Because of widespread confusion about this word you'll have to search for both spellings on the Web when you're shopping.

tore/torn
Is the road in front of your house "all tore up"? In some dialects that's what people say. But for standard English speakers what happens to stuff is that it gets *torn up*. That guy who tore up your love letter left you feeling torn up.

torturous/tortuous
A path with a confusing proliferation of turns is tortuous (from a French root meaning "twisted"). But "torturous" (meaning painful or unpleasant, like torture) is very frequently confused with it. So often has "tortuous logic" (tangled, twisted logic) been misspelled as "torturous logic" that it has given rise to a now independent form with its own meaning, "tortured logic." Few people object to the latter; but if you want to describe your slow progress along a twisting path, the word you want is "tortuous."

touch bases/touch base
Although in baseball a home-run hitter has to touch all four bases while whizzing past, when you propose to linger with someone long enough to compare notes you do all your chatting at a single base. The expression is "let's touch base."

touché

In formal fencing matches, when someone is hit by an opponent's sword it is traditional for the person hit to cry out *touché* (French for "touched") to acknowledge that fact. In other contexts, we may say *touché* when somebody scores a point against us in an argument, or otherwise skewers us verbally.

It is inappropriate to cry *touché* when you think you are the one who has skewered your opponent. *Touché* is not a synonym for "gotcha!"

tounge/tongue

"Tounge" is a common misspelling of "tongue."

tout/taunt/taut

See "taunt/taut/tout."

tow the line/toe the line

"Toe the line" has to do with lining your toes up on a precise mark, not with pulling on a rope.

However, if you have to take your kids along when you visit friends, you have them not in *toe*, but in *tow*.

toward/towards

These two words are interchangeable, but "toward" is more common in the US and "towards" in the UK.

Some people, probably influenced by "forwards," write "torwards" instead of the correct "towards."

track home/tract home

Commuters from a tract home may well feel that they are engaged in a rat race, but that does not justify them in describing their housing development as a "track." "Tract" here means an area of land on which inexpensive and uniform houses have been built. Incidentally, note that the phrase is "digestive tract," not "digestive track."

tradegy/tragedy

Not only do people often misspell "tragedy" as "tradegy," they mispronounce it that way too. Just remember that the adjective is "tragic" to recall that it's the *G* that comes after the *A*. Also common is the misspelling "tradgedy."

tragedy/travesty

"Travesty" has farcical connotations; it's actually related to "transvestite." A disaster that could be described as a farce or a degraded imitation may be called a travesty: "The trial—since the defense lawyer slept through most of it—was a travesty of justice." A tragedy is an altogether more serious matter.

translucent/transparent/opaque

Although technically anything that light can shine through is translucent, most writers now reserve this word for substances that don't clearly display what is on the other side. A frosted window-pane, a thin rice-paper screen, or a sheet of tissue paper may be called "translucent." A clear window or camera lens is transparent. "Sheer" fabric can be either translucent or transparent. Better check before you go out in public.

"Opaque" is the opposite of "translucent." Anything solid through which light cannot pass is opaque.

tread a fine line

See "toe a fine line/tread a fine line, toe the line."

tremblor/temblor

Earthquake experts call each vibration produced by an earthquake a "temblor," derived from the Spanish word for "tremble." It's not surprising that many people turn this word into "tremblor," but journalists and others who may have experts among their readers would be wise to stick with "temblor."

tripple/triple

Don't double the *P* in "triple." Don't be confused by the fact that Triple Sec is a tipple (alcoholic drink).

trite and true/tried and true

Ideas that are trite may well be true; but the expression is "tried and true": ideas that have been tried and turned out to be valid.

troop/troupe

A group of performers is a *troupe*. Any other group of people, military or otherwise, is a *troop*. A police officer, member of a mounted military group or similar person is a *trooper*, but a gung-ho worker is a real *trouper*.

Troops are normally groups, despite the current vogue among journalists of saying things like "two troops were wounded in the battle" when they mean "two soldiers." "Two troops" would be two groups of soldiers, not two individuals.

The popularity of this use of "troop" is encouraged by the fact that the various branches of the US military services insist that only members of the Army should be called "soldiers." Marines, Air Force personnel, and Navy sailors all object to being called "soldiers" but there is no other traditional generic term for an unknown military person. When the branch of the service is known the writer would do better to refer to an individual by the appropriate branch label. "Troops" is more justifiable when referring to a mixed group—say, of Marines and Army personnel: "the President ordered 15,000 more troops into the region."

troubling, worrisome/concerning

See "concerning/worrisome, troubling."

trudge/dredge/drudge

See "dredge/drudge/trudge."

truely/truly

"True" has to give up its final *E* when it changes into "truly."

trustee/trusty

A member of an organizational board is a trustee; a trusted convict is a trusty.

try and/try to

Although "try and" is common in colloquial speech and will usually pass unremarked there, in writing try to remember to use "try to" instead of "try and."

tuna fish

See "redundancies."

turn into/turn in to

Probably out of simple absentmindedness, an amazing number of Web pages of educational institutions call for people to fill out a form and "turn it into" some office or official. "Turn into" means "transform into." Your fairy godmother can turn a pumpkin into a coach.

The way to instruct someone to submit a document is "turn in to," with a space between the "in" and the "to": "turn your application in to the registrar."

Once you have your coach, you can turn into a driveway; but you cannot turn a form into a registrar unless you have very advanced origami skills.

tussled/tousled

Even if your hair gets messed up in a tussle with a friend, it gets *tousled*, not *tussled*.

two/to/too

See "to/too/two."

two to tangle/two to tango

A 1952 pop song popularized the phrase "it takes two to tango"; and it was quickly applied to everything that required two parties, from romance to fighting. Later, people baffled by hearing the phrase used of conflicts, imagined that the proper word must be "tangle." Perhaps if they had remembered the fierce choreography of Parisian *apache* dancing they would not have been so confused. "It takes two to tangle" will seem the normal

"And that, class, is how we spell 'horse.' Now we will move on to math and prove once and for all that it takes two to tango."

phrase to some people, a clever variation to a few, and an embarrassing mistake to many people you might want to impress.

two-dimensional/one-dimensional
See "one-dimensional/two-dimensional."

UFO
"UFO" stands for "unidentified flying object," so if you're sure that a silvery disk is an alien spacecraft, there's no point in calling it a "UFO." I love the sign in a Seattle bookstore labeling the alien-invasion section: "Incorrectly Identified Flying Objects."

And now for a few correctly identified flying objects . . .

ugly American
The term "ugly American"—used to describe boorish people from the US insensitive to those in other countries—bothers fans of the 1958 novel *The Ugly American*, whose title character was actually sensitive and thoughtful—he just *looked* ugly. The popularizers of this phrase hadn't read the book, and judged its message too quickly by its title.

Ukraine/The Ukraine
See "The Ukraine/Ukraine."

ulterior/alterior
See "alterior/ulterior."

umlaut
See "accent marks."

unchartered/uncharted
"Unchartered" means "lacking a charter," and is a word most people have little use for. "Uncharted" means "unmapped" or "unexplored," so the expression meaning "to explore a new subject or area" is "enter uncharted territory." Similarly, it's uncharted regions, waters, and paths.

unconscience/unconscious
Do people confuse the unconscious with conscience because the stuff fermenting in one's unconscious is often stuff that bothers one's conscience? Whatever the cause, there is no such word as "unconscience." And while we're on the subject, "subconscious" is not used in Freudian psychology; it implies some-

thing that is merely not consciously thought of, rather than something that is suppressed. The term is, however, used by Jungians.

under the guise that/under the guise of

Phishing e-mails try to extract valuable information from you so they can rob you *under the guise of* protecting your online security. They are disguising their theft as protection. There are other related phrases, mostly ending in "that," such as "under the pretext that" and "with the excuse that"; but "under the guise" requires "of," usually followed by a gerund ending in "-ing."

under weigh/under way

The original expression for getting a boat moving has nothing to do with weighing anchor and is "getting under way," but so many sophisticated writers get this wrong that you're not likely to get into trouble if you imitate them.

When "underway" is used elsewhere as an adjective or adverb, by far the most common spelling is as a single word, as in "our plans are underway"; though some authorities argue that the adverbial form should be spelled as two words: "under way."

The spectacle of the peculiar weighing-in ceremony was forgotten once the boxing match was underway.

underestimated

Enthusiastic sportscasters often say of a surprisingly talented team that "they cannot be underestimated" when what they mean is "they *should* not be underestimated."

underlining/underlying

You can stress points by underlining them, but it's "underlying" in expressions like "underlying story," "underlying motive," and "underlying principle."

undermind/undermined

Some people believe in a mystical overmind, but not even they believe in an "undermind." The word is "undermined." If you dig under a castle wall to prepare to breach its defenses, you are undermining it, digging a mine under it. The metaphor applies to all sorts of weakening of opposing positions, most often in arguments.

undo/undue

The noun "undo" is the opposite of "do." You undo your typing errors on a computer or undo your shoelaces to go wading.

The adjective "undue" is the opposite of "due" and means "unwarranted" or "improper." It is used in phrases like "undue influence," "undue burdens," and "undue expense."

undoubtably/undoubtedly
Doubtless the spelling of "presumably" influences the misspelling "undoubtably." The word is "undoubtedly." When something is undoubtedly true, it is undoubted.

uninterested/disinterested
See "disinterested/uninterested."

unique
See "very unique/unique."

University of Indiana/Indiana University
There is no such place as "the University of Indiana"; it's "Indiana University." I should know; I went there.

unkept/unkempt
"Unkempt" is an old version of "uncombed." The standard expression for a sloppy-looking person is not "unkept," but "unkempt."

unlike
When you're linking two phrases with "unlike" you need to keep them in grammatically parallel forms: "Unlike Cecile, Gareth likes persimmons." This sentence parallels two people: Cecile and Gareth. But "unlike at home, my boss won't let me wear sandals" is incorrect because "at home" and "my boss" aren't grammatically parallel. You'd have to change this to "at home" and "at work" or something similar.

unloosen/loosen
Think about it. "Unloosen" would mean "tighten." The word is "loosen."

unpleased/displeased
"Unpleased" is considered archaic; the standard modern word for your reaction to something you don't like is "displeased."

However "unpleasing" is still current to describe something that fails to please: "the arrangement of 'Silent Night' for truck air horns was unpleasing." But "displeasing" is more common.

unquote/endquote
See "endquote/unquote."

unrest
Journalists often use this mild term to describe all manner of civil disorders, but it's silly to call mayhem or chaos merely "unrest" when there are bullets flying about and bodies lying in the streets.

unseasonable/unseasonal
See "seasonable/seasonal/unseasonable/unseasonal."

unthaw/thaw
"Unthaw" is another illogical negative. Use "thaw."

until/till
See "till/until."

untracked/on track
When things begin running smoothly and successfully, they get "on track." Some people oddly substitute "untracked" for this expression, perhaps thinking that to be "tracked" is to be stuck in a rut.

up in time/back/forward
See "back/forward/up in time."

upmost/utmost
"Upmost" can mean "uppermost," referring to something on top. But usually this word is a mistake for "utmost," meaning "most extreme." "Utmost" is related to words like "utter," as in "The birthday party was utter chaos."

upto/up to
Not upto alot lately? You might use some of your spare time memorizing the fact that "up to" is a two-word phrase, as is "a lot."

urine analysis/urinalysis
The technical term for the test you use to kick the druggies off the team is not "urine analysis" but "urinalysis."

us/we
"We" is a subject form, "us" an object. We do things; things are done to or for us.

If this doesn't help, you can try a couple of simple tests. If you are clear about the difference between "I" and "me," try making your sentence singular. "We" becomes "I" in the singular and "us" becomes "me."

"Our mothers and us are going shopping" becomes "my mother and me are going shopping"—which is wrong. So the sentences should read "My mother and I are going shopping" and "Our mothers and we are going shopping."

But if that doesn't seem obvious, try eliminating everything but the pronoun and the verb: "Us are going shopping" should be "we are going shopping."

Test a sentence like "us girls have sold more calendars than the guys" by reducing it to "us have sold." This sounds wrong. It should be "We girls have sold."

But "they gave us girls the prize" is correct because "they gave us the prize" is also correct.

use/usage

"Use" and "usage" overlap somewhat, but they are not entirely synonymous. Many people treat "usage" as if it were just a fancier form of "use" in phrases like "make usage of," where "make use of" is the standard expression. As a rule of thumb, if either "use" or "usage" seems appropriate, go with "use."

use to/used to

Because the *D* and the *T* are blended into a single consonant when this phrase is pronounced, many writers are unaware that the *D* is even present and omit it in writing.

See also "suppose to/supposed to."

used to could/used to be able

"I used to could lift a hay-bale with my teeth," says Jeb, meaning "I used to be able to."

utilize/use

The best use for "utilize" is to mean "make use of": "Ryan utilized his laptop in the library mainly as a pillow to rest his head on." In most contexts, "use" is simpler and clearer. Many readers consider "utilize" pretentious.

* * *

vague reference

Vague reference is a common problem in sentences where "this," "it," "which," or other such words don't refer back to any one specific word or phrase, but a whole situation. "I hitchhiked back to town, got picked up by an alien space-craft, and was subjected to humiliating medical experiments, which is why I didn't get my paper done on time." In conversation this sort of thing goes unnoticed, but more care needs to be taken in writing. There are lots of ways to reorganize this sentence to avoid the vague reference. You could replace "which is why" with "so," for instance.

Sometimes the referent is only understood and not directly expressed at all: "Changing your oil regularly is important, which is one reason your engine burned up." The "which" refers to an implied *failure* to change the oil regularly, but doesn't actually refer back to any of the specific words used earlier in the sentence.

Sometimes there is no logical referent: "In the book it says that Shakespeare was in love with some 'dark lady.'" This is a casual way of using "it" that is not acceptable in formal written English. Write instead "Arthur O. Williams says in *The Sonnets* that Shakespeare. . . ."

A reference may be ambiguous because it's not clear which of two referents is meant: "Most women are attracted to guys with a good sense of humor unless they are into practical jokes." Does "they" refer to "women" or "guys"? It would be clearer if the sentence said, "Most women are attracted to guys with a good sense of humor, though not usually to practical jokers."

vain/vane/vein

When you have vanity you are conceited: you are vain. "You're so vain you probably think this song is about you." This spelling can also mean "futile," as in "All my love's in vain" (fruitless). Note that when Ecclesiastes says that "all is vanity" it doesn't mean that everything is conceited, but that everything is pointless.

A vane is a blade designed to move or be moved by gases or liquid, like a weathervane.

A vein is a slender thread of something, like blood in a body or gold in a mine. It can also be a line of thought, as in "After describing his dog's habit of chewing on the sofa, Carlos went on in the same vein for several minutes."

valance/valence

A decorative hanging cloth is a valance. Unless you are a chemist or someone else dealing with the technical aspects of combining things you're unlike to have a need for the word "valence."

vale of tears/veil of tears

See "veil of tears/vale of tears."

valuble/valuable

Few of us pronounce the second *A* in "valuable" distinctly; just be sure to include it when writing the word.

vapid/vacuous

"Vapid" is used to describe something flavorless, weak, flat. Many people confuse this word with "vacuous," which describes things which are unintelligent, lacking serious content. A boring speech may be vapid even though it's learned, and a lively speech may be vacuous even though it's exciting. A dull person may be vapid, but it is not standard usage to refer to a person as vacuous—only their speech, thoughts, etc., can be so described. To avoid the most common error involving these words, just remember that something vapid isn't stupid, it's bland.

various/several

Many people say, "She heard from various of the committee members that they wanted to cancel the next meeting." "Several of the committee members" would be better.

vary/differ

See "differ/vary."

vary/very

"Vary" means "to change." Don't substitute it for "very" in phrases like "very nice" or "very happy."

veil of tears/vale of tears

The expression "vale of tears" goes back to pious sentiments that consider life on earth to be a series of sorrows to be left behind when we go on to a better world in heaven. It conjures up an image of a suffering traveler laboring through a valley ("vale") of troubles and sorrow. "Veil of tears" is poetic sounding, but it's a mistake.

vein/vain/vane

See "vain/vane/vein."

vendor

Some writers are turning "vendor" into a verb meaning "to sell," writing things like, "he was vendoring comic books on eBay." Since "vend" is already a verb meaning "sell" and "vendor" is normally a noun, this sounds very odd to many readers.

Other people use forms of the word to mean "to be certified as a vendor": "Persons wishing to be vendored must complete the appropriate form." This process is also referred to as "vendorization."

This pattern is probably inspired by the widespread use of "vendor" to label suppliers on commercial Web sites. Instead of thinking of vendors as mere merchants, dealers, or sellers, some special quality is being attributed to them.

None of this is standard English.

veracious/voracious

If you are extremely hungry, you may have a "voracious" appetite (think of the *O* as an open mouth, ready to devour anything). "Veracious" is an unusual word meaning "truthful, honest" (think about the *E* in "verify"). A truthful person has "veracity." "Voracity," meaning "extreme appetite," is a rare word you are unlikely to have a use for; "voraciousness" is more common.

verb (number)

See "number of verb."

verb tense

If the situation being described is an ongoing or current one, the present tense is needed, even in a past-tense context: "Last week she admitted that she is really a brunette" (not "was").

Pairs of verbs that go together logically have to be kept in the same tense. "Patricia described her trip to China and writes that the Great Wall really impressed her." Since "described" is in the past tense, and the writing contains her descriptions, "writes" should be "wrote."

Lots of people get into trouble with sentences that describe a hypothetical situation in the past: "If he would have packed his own suitcase, he would have noticed that the cat was in it." That first "would have" should be a simple "had": "If he had packed his own suitcase he would have noticed that the cat was in it." Also "The game would have been more fun if we had [not "would have"] won." This sort of construction consists of two parts: a hypothetical cause in the past and its logical effect. The hypothetical cause needs to be put into the past tense: "had." Only the *effect* is made conditional: "would have." Note that in the second example above the effect is referred to before the cause.

Students summarizing the plot of a play, movie, or novel are often unfamiliar with the tradition of doing so in the present tense: "Hester embroiders an 'A' on her dress." Think of the events in a piece of fiction as happening whenever you read them—they exist in an eternal present even if they are narrated in the past tense. Even those who are familiar with this pattern get tripped up when they begin to discuss the historical or biographical context of a work, properly using the past tense, and forget to shift back to the present when they return to plot summary. Here's how it's done correctly: "Mark Twain's days on the Mississippi were long past when he wrote *Huckleberry Finn*, but Huck's love for life on the river clearly reflects his youthful experience as a steamboat pilot." The verb "reflects" is in the present tense. Often the author's activity in writing is rendered in the present tense as well: "Twain depicts Pap as a disgusting drunk." What about when you are comparing events that occur at two different times in the same narrative? You still have to stick to the present: "Tom puts Jim through a lot of unnecessary misery before telling him that he is free." Just remember when you go from English to your history class that you have to shift back to the past tense for narrating historical events: "Napoleon lost the battle of Waterloo."

verbage/verbiage

"Verbiage" is an insulting term usually meant to disparage needlessly wordy prose. Don't use it to mean simply "wording." There is no such word as "verbage."

verbal/oral

See "oral/verbal."

verse/play against

Some young people use "verse" as a verb meaning "to play against," as in "I'll verse you at basketball after school." Computer gamers are particularly fond of virtual opponents *versing* each other. Presumably this bit of slang derives from the word "versus," but it's not standard English and is likely to confuse outsiders.

verses/versus

The "vs." in a law case like "Brown vs. The Board of Education" stands for Latin *versus* (meaning "against"). Don't confuse it with the word for lines of poetry—"verses"—when describing other conflicts, like the upcoming football game featuring Oakesdale versus Pinewood.

Note that in formal legal contexts the abbreviation is usually just "v.," as in "Brown v. The Board of Education."

very/so
See "so/very."

very/vary
See "vary/very."

very differently/much differently
See "much differently/very differently."

very sort of, very kind of
"He's very sort of buffed." Wha . . ? He can't be very buffed and only sort of buffed at the same time. It's an error to follow the phrase "very sort of" with an adjective (a quality, such as "rich," "happy," "conscientious").

It's all right to say "very sort of" when "very" means "exact, precise," and the phrase is followed by an noun (a thing or person): "the very sort of pastry I can't resist," "the very sort of boss I can't stand."

Less common is the equally confused expression "very kind of" as in "he's very kind of charming when he's trying to impress women."

Of course "very kind of" is fine in appreciative comments where "kind" is an adjective meaning "generous," "helpful," like "it was very kind of you to shovel Mrs. Mukherjee's front walk."

very unique/unique
"Unique" singles out one of a kind. That "un" at the beginning is a form of "one." A thing is unique (the only one of its kind) or it is not. Something may be almost unique (there are very few like it), but nothing is "very unique."

vice versa/visa versa
See "visa versa/vice versa."

vice-like/vise-like
In the US and Canada the clamp fastened to a workbench is a vise, but a vice is a moral flaw or bad habit. So in North America a person with an overly firm handshake has a vise-like grip. Writing of a "vice-like" grip invites racy jokes at your expense.

However "vice" is the spelling of both words in UK English, and the Oxford English Dictionary defines "vice-like" as "firmly tenacious or compressive."

vichyssoise
Waiters in restaurants offering this potato-leek cream soup often mispronounce it "vish-ee-SWAH" in a mistaken attempt to sound authentically French.

Setting aside the fact that this soup was invented in New York, French final consonants are not silent when they are followed by an *E*. The correct pronunciation is "vee-shee-SWAHZ."

vicious/viscous circle/cycle

The term "vicious circle" was invented by logicians to describe a form of fallacious circular argument in which each term of the argument draws on the other: "Democracy is the best form of government because democratic elections produce the best governments." The phrase has been extended in popular usage to all kinds of self-exacerbating processes such as this: "Poor people often find themselves borrowing money to pay off their debts, but in the process create even more onerous debts which in their turn will need to be financed by further borrowing." Sensing vaguely that such destructive spirals are not closed loops, people have transmuted "vicious circle" into "vicious cycle." The problem with this perfectly logical change is that a lot of people know what the original "correct" phrase was and are likely to scorn users of the new one. They go beyond scorn to contempt, however, toward those poor souls who render the phrase as "viscous cycle." Don't use this expression unless you are discussing a Harley-Davidson in dire need of an oil change.

video/film

Many of us can remember when portable transistorized radios were ignorantly called "transistors." We have a tendency to abbreviate the names of various sorts of electronic technology (*see* "stereo" and "satellite"), often in the process confusing the medium with the content. Video is the electronic reproduction of images and applies to broadcast and cable television, prerecorded videocassette recordings (made on a videocassette recorder, or VCR), and related technologies. MTV appropriated this broad term for a very narrow meaning: "videotaped productions of visual material meant to accompany popular music recordings." This is now what most people mean when they speak of "a video," unless they are "renting a video," in which case they mean a videocassette or DVD recording of a film. (Incidentally, people in the video trade prefer not to call Blu-Ray discs "DVDs," reserving that label for the lower definition sort of video disc.) One also hears people referring to theatrical films that they happened to have viewed in videotaped reproduction as "videos." This is simply wrong. A film is a film (or movie), whether it is projected on a screen from 35 or 70 mm film or broadcast via the NTSC, SECAM or PAL standard. Orson Welles' *Citizen Kane* is not now and never will be a "video."

villian/villain

Villainous misspellings of "villain" have lain in wait to trip up unwary writers for many years.

vinegarette/vinaigrette

Naïve diners and restaurant workers alike commonly mispronounce the classic French dressing called "vinaigrette" as if it were "vinegarette." To be more sophisticated, say "vin-uh-GRETT" (the first syllable rhymes with "seen").

vintage point/vantage point
The spot from which you have a good view is a vantage point.

viola/voila
A *viola* is a flower or a musical instrument. The expression which means "behold!" is *voila*. It comes from a French expression literally meaning "look there!" In French it is spelled with a grave accent over the *A*, as *voilà*, but when it was adopted into English, it lost its accent. Such barbarous misspellings as "vwala" are even worse, caused by the reluctance of English speakers to believe that *OI* can represent the sound "wah," as it usually does in French.

Voila! A viola.

"Wallah" is a Hindi word for a worker, and "Walla" is half of the name of the Washington State city of Walla Walla.

virgin birth/immaculate conception
See "immaculate conception/virgin birth."

visa versa/vice versa
This expression, meaning "just the opposite," begins with "vice" (Latin for "turn"). The expression has nothing to do with charges on your Visa card.

visable/visible
To make things clearly visible, you need both your eyes, and both its *I*'s.

visit/logon
See "logon/visit."

visually impaired
Many people mistakenly suppose that "visually impaired" is a more polite term than "blind." But the distinction between these two is simpler: a person without eyesight is blind; a person with vision problems stopping short of total or legal blindness is visually impaired.

vitae/vita
Unless you are going to claim credit for accomplishments you had in previous incarnations, you should refer to your "vita," not your "vitae." All kidding aside, the *AE* in *vitae* supposedly indicates the genitive rather than the plural (that is, *vitae* in this case works like a possessive form to modify "curriculum"), but the derivation of *vita* from *curriculum vitae* is purely speculative (see the *Oxford English Dictionary*), and *vitae* on its own makes no sense grammatically.

Résumé, by the way, is a French word with both *E*'s accented. It literally means "summary." In English one often sees it without the accents or with only the second accent, neither of which is a serious error. But if you're trying to show how multilingual you are, remember the first accent.

vocal chords/vocal cords

The musical meaning of "chords" influences some folks to misspell "vocal cords." The "cords" in question are long, thin muscles that look like pieces of fat string.

vocation/avocation

See "avocation/vocation."

voila/viola

See "viola/voila."

volumn/volume

There are a few unusual words in English ending in *MN* in which the *N* is silent, such as "hymn" and "column," but "volume" is not one of them.

volumptuous/voluptuous

Given the current mania for slim, taut bodies, it is understandable—if amusing—that some folks should confuse voluptuousness with lumpiness. In fact, "voluptuous" is derived from Latin *voluptas*, which refers to sensual pleasure and not to shape at all. A voluptuous body is a luxurious body.

voracious/veracious

See "veracious/voracious."

vunerable/vulnerable

"Vulnerable" is often mispronounced, and sometimes misspelled, without its first *L*.

"Yes, I suppose I'm 'vunerable,' but why the sloppy pronunciation?"

"Well, all my life people have been telling me to get the L out!"

wail/whale

One informal meaning of "whale" is "to beat." Huck Finn says of Pap that "He used to always whale me when he was sober."

Although the vocalist in a band may wail a song, the drummer *whales* on the drums; and lead guitarists when they thrash their instruments wildly *whale* on them.

Although this usage dates back to the 18th century and used to be common in Britain and America, it is now confined mostly to the US, and even there people often mistakenly use "wail" for this meaning.

wait on/wait for

In some dialects it's common to say that you're waiting *on* people or events when in standard English we would say you're waiting *for* them. Waiters wait on people, so it's all right to say "I'm tired of waiting on you hand and foot"; but you shouldn't say "I'm waiting on you down here at the police station; bring the bail money so I can come home."

wake

In the US the reception following a funeral is now often called a "wake" although traditionally that term was applied to the period of staying up at night watching over the dead body before the funeral. Since historically "wake" has been used in many broad senses involving celebration—not always necessarily at night—it's not surprising to find it being extended even further in this way. But if you want to sound more sophisticated, use the term "reception" for the gathering after a funeral.

Urban legend has it that the term has some connection with the possibility that the deceased might "wake up." To the contrary, it's the mourners who do the waking at a wake, not the corpse.

walk the talk/walk the walk

Aristotle's followers are said to have discussed philosophy while walking about with him—hence their name: "peripatetics." I suppose they could have been said to "walk the talk."

For the rest of us, the saying is "if you're going to talk the talk, you've got to walk the walk"—a modern version of old sayings like "actions speak louder than words" and "practice what you preach." Another early form of the expression was "walk it like you talk it."

Many people now condense this to "walk the talk," which makes a sort of sense (act on your speech), but strikes those who are more familiar with the original form as confused.

wander/wonder

If you idly travel around, you wander. If you realize you're lost, you wonder where you are.

want that . . . should/want . . . to

When someone wants someone else to do something, the expression is not "she wants that you should do it" but "she wants you to do it." Similarly, it's "I want you to do it," "we want you to do it," etc.

warmongerer/warmonger

"Monger" is a very old word for "dealer." An ironmonger sells metal or hardware, and a fishmonger sells fish. Warmongers do not literally sell wars, but they advocate and promote them. For some reason lots of people tack an unneeded extra "-er" onto the end of this word. Why would you say "mongerer" when you don't say "dealerer"?

warrantee/warranty

Confused by the spelling of "guarantee," people often misspell the related word "warrantee" rather than the correct "warranty." "Warrantee" is a rare legal term that means "the person to whom a warrant is made." Although "guarantee" can be a verb ("we guarantee your satisfaction"), "warranty" cannot. The rarely used verb form is "to warrant."

wary/weary/leery

People sometimes write "weary" (tired) when they mean "wary" (cautious), which is a close synonym with "leery." "Leery" in the psychedelic era was often misspelled "leary," but since Timothy Leary faded from public consciousness, the correct spelling has prevailed.

was/were

In phrases beginning with "there" many people overlook the need to choose a plural or singular form of the verb "to be" depending on what follows. "There *were* several good-looking guys at the party" (plural). "There *was* one of them who asked for my phone number" (singular).

wash

In my mother's Oklahoma dialect, "wash" was pronounced "warsh," and I was embarrassed to discover in school that the inclusion of the superfluous *R* sound was considered ignorant. This has made me all the more sensitive now that I live in Washington to the mispronunciation "Warshington." Some people tell you that after you "warsh" you should "wrench" ("rinse").

waver/waiver

Wave bye-bye. Ride the wave. Do the wave. We all know what a wave is, right? The verb "waive," whose root meaning is "abandon," is less familiar. When you give up a legal right, you waive it; and the document you sign to do so is called not a "waver" but a "waiver."

Tony's contraption allowed him to wash and rinse in style, however you pronounce it.

wax

An unusual use of the word "wax" is "to change manner of speaking," as in "she waxed eloquent on the charms of New Jersey" or "he waxed poetic on virtues of tube amplifiers." These expressions mean that she became eloquent and he became poetic. It is an error to say instead "she waxed eloquently" or "he waxed poetically."

way more/far more/much more

Young people frequently use phrases like "way better" to mean "far better" or "very much better." In formal writing, it would be gauche to say that Impressionism is "way more popular" than Cubism instead of "much more popular."

ways/way

In some dialects it's common to say, "You've got a ways to go before you've saved enough to buy a Miata," but in standard English it's "a *way* to go."

we/us

See "us/we."

weak/week

People often absentmindedly write "last weak" or "next weak." Less often they write "I feel week." These mistakes will not be caught by a spelling checker.

"Weak" is the opposite of "strong." A week is made up of seven days.

weary/leery/wary

See "wary/weary/leery."

weather/wether/whether

The climate is made up of "weather"; whether it is nice out depends on whether it is raining or not. A wether is just a castrated sheep. Such a sheep wearing a bell is a "bellwether," and that's the correct spelling for the same word when it means "an indicator of change."

Web

See "World Wide Web."

weiner/wiener

The Vienna sausage from the city the Austrians call *Wien* inspired the American hot dog, or wiener. Americans aren't used to the European pronunciation of *IE* as "ee" and often misspell the word as "weiner."

well/good

See "good/well."

wench/winch

"Wench" began as a general term for a girl or woman, and over the centuries acquired a variety of meanings, including female servant, lower-class female, and prostitute. It is mostly used today as a jokingly affectionate archaic allusion to Shakespearean ribaldry.

The hoisting or hauling mechanism attached to a tow truck is a *winch* (and it's not on a "toe truck").

If a woman can lift your car, she's not a wench—she's an Amazon!

Wensday/Wednesday

Wednesday was named after the Germanic god "Woden" (or "Wotan"). Almost no one pronounces this word's middle syllable distinctly, but it's important to remember the correct spelling in writing.

went/gone

See "gone/went."

we're/were

"We're" is a contraction of the phrase "we are": the apostrophe stands for the omitted letter *A.* "Were" is simply a plural past-tense form of the verb "are." To talk about something happening now or in the future, use "we're"; but to talk about something in the past, use "were." If you can't substitute "we are" for the word you've written, omit the apostrophe.

"We *were* going to go to the party as a prince and princess, but Derek cut himself shaving, so *we're* going instead as a vampire and her victim."

were/where

Sloppy typists frequently leave the *H* out of "where." Spelling checkers do not catch this sort of error, of course, so look for it as you proofread.

wet your appetite/whet your appetite

It is natural to think that something mouth-watering "wets your appetite," but actually the expression is "whet your appetite"—sharpen your appetite, as a whetstone sharpens a knife.

wether/whether/weather

See "weather/wether/whether."

whacky/wacky

Although the original spelling of this word meaning "crazy" was "whacky," the current dominant spelling is "wacky." If you use the older form, some readers will think you've made a spelling error.

what/that

In some dialects it is common to substitute "what" for "that," as in "You should dance with him what brought you." This is not standard usage.

wheat/whole wheat

Waiters routinely ask, "Wheat or white?" when bread is ordered, but the white bread is also made of wheat. The correct term is "whole wheat," in which the whole grain, including the bran and germ, has been used to make the flour. "Whole wheat" does not necessarily imply that no white flour has been used in the bread; most whole wheat breads incorporate some white flour.

wheelbarrel/wheelbarrow

One very old meaning of the word "barrow" is an open container for carrying people or goods. The earliest barrows were carried by two people holding handles on either end. Add a wheel to one end and you have a *wheel*barrow which can be handled by a single person. The word is also sometimes applied to two-wheeled versions.

The word has nothing to do with barrels.

Yes, it rolls like a wheel, but it's just a barrel.

whenever/when

"Whenever" has two main functions. It can refer to repeated events: "Whenever I put the baby down for a nap the phone rings and wakes her up." Or it can refer to events of whose date or time you are uncertain: "Whenever it was that I first wore my new cashmere sweater, the baby spit up on it." In some dialects (notably in Northern Ireland and Texas) it is common to substitute "whenever" for "when" in statements about specific events occurring only once and whose date is known: "Whenever we got married, John was so nervous he dropped the ring down my décolletage." This is nonstandard. If an event is unique and its date or time known, use "when."

where/were

See "were/where."

where (and prepositions)

When you are asking about a location someone is coming from you need to use the preposition "from" with "where": "Where are you coming from?" But when you are discussing a destination instead of a point of departure, don't add a preposition. It's not "Where are you going to?" but "Where are you going?"

Similarly, when asking about the location of a place, "at" should not be used after "where." It's not "Where is the movie theater at?" but "Where is the movie theater?"

where it's at

This slang expression gained widespread currency in the 1960s as a hip way of stating that the speaker understood the essential truth of a situation: "I know where it's at." Or more commonly, "You don't know where it's at." It is still heard from time to time with that meaning, but the user risks being labeled as a quaint old baby boomer. However, standard usage never accepted the literal sense of the phrase. Don't say, "I put my purse down and now I don't know where it's at," unless you want to be regarded as uneducated. "Where it is" will do fine; the "at" is redundant.

315

whereabouts are/whereabouts is

Despite the deceptive *S* on the end of the word, "whereabouts" is normally singular in meaning because it means "location." However, it commonly takes a plural verb: "Its whereabouts are unknown." But the Associated Press prefers a singular verb: "Its whereabouts is unknown." Many authorities disagree, and most will accept either form. Of course if you were simultaneously referring to two or more persons having separate whereabouts it would require a plural verb: "The whereabouts of several members of the team were unknown."

whether/if

See "if/whether."

whether/weather/wether

See "weather/wether/whether."

whether/whether or not

"Whether" works fine on its own in most contexts: "I wonder whether I forgot to turn off the stove?" But when you mean "regardless of whether," it has to be followed by "or not" somewhere in the sentence: "We need to leave for the airport in five minutes whether you've found your teddy bear or not."

See also "if/whether."

which/that

See "that/which."

while away/wile away

See "wile away/while away."

whilst/while

Although "whilst" is a perfectly good traditional synonym of "while," in American usage it is considered pretentious and old-fashioned.

whim and a prayer/wing and a prayer

A 1943 hit song depicted a bomber pilot just barely managing to bring his shot-up plane back to base, "comin' in on a wing and a prayer" (lyrics by Harold Adamson, music by Jimmy McHugh). Some people who don't get the allusion mangle this expression as "a whim and a prayer." Whimsicality and fervent prayerfulness don't go together.

whimp/wimp

The original and still by far the most common spelling of this common bit of slang meaning "weakling, coward" is "wimp." If you use the much less common "whimp" instead, people may regard you as a little wimpy.

whip cream/whipped cream

You whip cream until it becomes *whipped* cream; and that's what you should write on the menu.

whisky/whiskey
Scots prefer the spelling "whisky"; Americans follow instead the Irish spelling, so Kentucky bourbon is "whiskey."

whit/wit
See "wit/whit."

who/that
There are many instances in which the most conservative usage is to refer to a person using "that": "All the politicians that were at the party later denied even knowing the host" is actually somewhat more traditional than the more popular "politicians who." An aversion to "that" referring to human beings as somehow diminishing their humanity may be praiseworthily sensitive, but it cannot claim the authority of tradition. In some sentences, "that" is clearly preferable to "who": "She is the only person I know of that prefers whipped cream on her granola." In the following example, to exchange "that" for "who" would be awkward: "Who was it that said, 'A woman without a man is like a fish without a bicycle'?"*

who/whom
"Whom" has been dying an agonizing death for decades—you'll notice there are no Whoms in Dr. Seuss's Whoville. Many people never use the word in speech at all. However, in formal writing, critical readers still expect it to be used when appropriate. The distinction between "who" and "whom" is basically simple: "who" is the subject form of this pronoun and "whom" is the object form. "Who was wearing that awful dress at the Academy Awards banquet?" is correct because "who" is the subject of the sentence. "The M.C. was so startled by the neckline that he forgot to whom he was supposed to give the Oscar" is correct because "whom" is the object of the preposition "to." So far so good.

Now consider this sort of question: "Who are you staring at?" Although strictly speaking the pronoun should be "whom," nobody who wants to be taken seriously would use it in this case, though it is the object of the preposition "at." "Whom" is very rarely used even by careful speakers as the first word in a question, and many authorities have now conceded the point.

There is another sort of question in which "whom" appears later in the sentence: "I wonder whom he bribed to get the contract?" Here an old gender-biased but effective test for "whom" can be used. Try flipping that "whom he bribed" phrase around and rewrite it using "he" or "him." Clearly "He bribed he" is incorrect; you would say "he bribed him." Where "him" is the proper word in the paraphrased sentence, use "whom."

Instances in which the direct object appears at the beginning of a sentence are tricky because we are used to having subjects in that position and are

---

*Commonly attributed to Gloria Steinem, but she attributes it to Irina Dunn.

strongly tempted to use "who": "Whomever Susan admired most was likely to get the job." (Test: "She admired *him*." Right?)

Where things get really messy is in statements in which the object or subject status of the pronoun is not immediately obvious. For example, "The police gave tickets to whoever had parked in front of the fire hydrant." The object of the preposition "to" is the entire noun clause, "whoever had parked in front of the fire hydrant," but "whoever" is the subject of that clause, the subject of the verb "had parked." Here's a case where the temptation to use "whomever" should be resisted.

Confused? Just try the "he or him" test, and if it's still not clear, go with "who." You'll bother fewer people and have a fair chance of being right.

whole/hole
See "hole/whole."

a whole 'nother/a completely different
It is one thing to use the expression "a whole 'nother" as a consciously slangy phrase suggesting rustic charm and a completely different matter to use it mistakenly. The *A* at the beginning of the phrase is the common article "a" but is here treated as if it were simultaneously the first letter of "another," interrupted by "whole."

whole wheat/wheat
See "wheat/whole wheat."

whole-hardily/wholeheartedly
If you want to convey your hearty congratulations to someone, you do so not "whole-hardily" but "wholeheartedly"—with your whole heart.

wholely/wholly
"Whole" loses its concluding *E* when it changes to "wholly."

wholistic/holistic
This trendy word is correctly spelled "holistic."

who's/whose
This is one of those cases where it is important to remember that possessive pronouns never take apostrophes, even though possessive nouns do (*see* "its/it's). "Who's" always and forever means only "who is," as in "Who's that guy with the droopy mustache?" or "who has," as in "Who's been eating my porridge?" "Whose" is the possessive form of "who" and is used as follows: "Whose dirty socks are these on the breakfast table?"

whose-ever/whoever's
In speech people sometimes try to treat the word "whoever" as two words when it's used in the possessive form: "Whose-ever delicious plums those were in the

refrigerator, I ate them." Occasionally it's even misspelled as "whoseever." The standard form is "whoever's," as in "Whoever's plums those were. . . ."

why/how come
See "how come/why."

wile away/while away
"Waiting for my physical at the doctor's office, I whiled away the time reading the dessert recipes in an old copy of *Gourmet* magazine." The expression "while away the time" is the only surviving context for a very old meaning of "while" as a verb meaning "to spend time." Many people mistakenly substitute "wile," but to wile people is to lure or trick them into doing something—quite different from simply idling away the time.

will/shall
See "shall/will."

wimp/whimp
See "whimp/wimp."

winch/wench
See "wench/winch."

wing and a prayer/whim and a prayer
See "whim and a prayer/wing and a prayer."

-wise
In political and business jargon it is common to append "-wise" to nouns to create novel adverbs: "Revenue-wise, last quarter was a disaster." Critics of language are united in objecting to this pattern, and it is often used in fiction to satirize less than eloquent speakers.

wit/whit
If you still have all your wits about you, could it be said that your mental powers have diminished "not a wit"? No, for the traditional expression is "not a whit." "Whit" is an old word meaning "bit," surviving only in this and similar expressions like "not one whit."

within/among
"Within" means literally "inside of," but when you want to compare similarities or differences *between* things you may need "among" instead. It's not "There are some entertaining movies within the current releases," but "among the current releases." But you can use "within" by rewriting the sentence to lump the movies together into a single entity: "There are some entertaining movies within the current batch of releases." A batch is a single thing, and the individual films that make it up are within it.

without further adieu/without further ado

This familiar cliché introducing speakers and performing acts has nothing to do with saying *adieu* (goodbye) to them. It means "without further blather, fuss, or to-do." The last word is "ado."

woman/female

See "female/woman."

women/woman

The singular "woman" probably gets mixed up with the plural "women" because although both are spelled with an *O* in the first syllable, only the pronunciation of the *O* really differentiates them. Just remember that this word is treated no differently than "man" (one person) and "men" (more than one person). A woman is a woman—never a women.

wonderful

See "incredible."

wonderkind/wunderkind

We borrowed the term "wunderkind," meaning "child prodigy," from the Germans. We don't capitalize it the way they do, but we use the same spelling. When writing in English, don't half-translate it as "wonderkind."

wont/won't

People often leave the apostrophe out of "won't," meaning "will not." "Wont" is a completely different and rarely used word meaning "habitual custom." Perhaps people are reluctant to believe this is a contraction because it doesn't make obvious sense like "cannot" being contracted to "can't." The *Oxford English Dictionary* suggests that "won't" is a contraction of a nonstandard form: "woll not."

Quite a few confused folks substitute "want" for "wont," leading to mangled expressions such as "such is my want."

work or composition/song

See "song/work or composition."

working progress/work in progress

If your project isn't finished yet, it's not a "working progress" but a "work in progress."

World Wide Web

"World Wide Web" is a name that some of us feel needs to be capitalized, like "Internet." It is made up of Web pages and Web sites (or, less formally, Websites).

world-renown/world-renowned

Your hamburgers may have world renown, but they are world-renowned hamburgers.

worrisome, troubling/concerning

See "concerning/worrisome, troubling."

worse comes to worse/worst comes to worst

The traditional idiom is "if worst comes to worst." The modern variation "worse comes to worst" is a little more logical. "Worse comes to worse" is just a mistake.

worser

If you look "worser" up in a dictionary, you're likely to find it labeled "archaic," which means that although Shakespeare and many other writers once used it, the word is no longer a part of standard English. Just use "worse" instead: "It just keeps getting worse and worse."

would have/had

People are often confused about how to discuss something that didn't happen in the past. It's standard usage to say "If I had remembered where I parked the car, I would have gotten home sooner." Notice that in the part of the sentence containing "if" the helping verb is "had" but in the other part of the sentence, which depends logically on the first, the verb "gotten" is preceded by "would have."

The same pattern applies when the "if" is in a later part of the sentence: "I would have gotten home sooner if I had remembered where I parked the car." Plain old "had" stays with the "if" clause (the second one) and "would have" goes in the other clause (the first one).

The problem is that people used to thinking of "would have" as marking non-events in the past often replace a correct "had" with an incorrect "would have": "If I would have remembered where I parked the car. . . ." This is non-standard.

Even worse, the same mistake is made in sentences where no "if" is involved: "The robber wished he would have given the bank clerk a fake ID when she asked for one." This should be "The robber wished he had given."

One reminder of the correct pattern is that "had" all by itself can replace "if . . . had": "Had I remembered where I parked the car. . . . "Would have" clearly can't be used in this way, so you need to stick with plain old "had."

would liked to have had/would have liked to have

"She would liked to have had another glass of champagne" should be "She would have liked to have another glass. . . ."

would of

See "could of, should of, would of/could have, should have, would have."

wrack/rack

See "rack/wrack."

wrangle/wangle

If you deviously manage to obtain something you wangle it: "I wangled an invitation to Jessica's party by hinting that I would be inviting her to our house on the lake this summer." But if you argue with someone, you wrangle with them: "Once I got to the party, Jessica's attitude irritated me so much that we wound up wrangling constantly during it." Of course cowboys wrangle cattle, and specialists wrangle other animal species in films.

wreaking havoc/reeking havoc

See "reeking havoc/wreaking havoc."

wreath/wreaths/wreathe/wreathes

One circle of greens is a wreath (rhymes with "teeth"). The plural is "wreaths" (rhymes with "heaths"). In both cases the *TH* is unvoiced (like the *TH* in "both").

To decorate something with wreaths is wreathe it (rhymes with "breathe" with a voiced *TH* like the one at the end of "bathe"). He or she wreathes it (also with a voiced *TH*).

wrecking bar/crowbar

See "crowbar/wrecking bar."

wreckless/reckless

This word has nothing to do with creating the potential for a wreck. Rather it involves not reckoning carefully all the hazards involved in an action. The correct spelling is therefore "reckless."

wretch/retch

See "retch/wretch."

wring its neck/ring its neck

See "ring its neck/wring its neck."

wringer/ringer

See "ringer/wringer."

write

See "right/rite/write."

write me

Many UK English speakers and some American authorities object strongly to the common American expression "write me," insisting that the correct expression is "write to me." But "write me" is so common in US English that I think few Americans will judge you harshly for using it. After all, we say "call me"— why not "write me"? But if you're an American trying to please foreigners or particularly picky readers, you might keep the "write me" phobia in mind.

If you disagree, please don't write me.

writting/writing

One of the comments English teachers dread to see on their evaluations is "The professor really helped me improve my writting." When "-ing" is added to a word that ends in a short vowel followed only by a single consonant, that consonant is normally doubled, but "write" has a silent *E* on the end to ensure the long *I* sound in the word. Doubling the *T* in this case would make the word rhyme with "flitting."

wrought iron

See "rod iron, rot iron/wrought iron."

xeriscape/zeroscape

See "zeroscape/xeriscape."

Xmas/Christmas

"Xmas" is not originally an attempt to exclude Christ from Christmas, but uses an abbreviation of the Greek spelling of the word "Christ" with the *X* representing the Greek letter *chi*. However, so few people know this that it is probably better not to use this popular abbreviation in religious contexts.

ya'll/y'all

"How y'all doin'?" If you are rendering this common Southernism in print, be careful where you place the apostrophe, which stands for the second and third letters in "you."

Note that "y'all" stands for "you all" and is properly a plural form, though some southern speakers treat it as a singular form and resort to "all y'all" for the plural. Most southerners reserve "all y'all" to mean "each and every one of you." Then there is the occasional case in which the speaker is addressing someone representing a store or other institution composed of several people: "Do y'all sell shop vacs?"

ye/the

Those who study the history of English know that the word often misread as "ye" in Middle English is good old "the" spelled with an unfamiliar character called a *thorn* which looks vaguely like a *Y* but which is pronounced "TH." So all those quaint shop names beginning with "Ye Olde" are based on a confusion: people never *said* "ye" to mean "the." However, if you'd rather be cute than historically accurate, go ahead. Very few people will know any better.

yea/yeah/yay

"Yea" is a very old-fashioned, formal way of saying "yes," used mainly in voting. It's the opposite of—and rhymes with—"nay." When you want to write the common casual version of "yes," the correct spelling is "yeah" (sounds like "yeh"). When the third grade teacher announced a class trip to the zoo, we all yelled "yay!" (the opposite of "boo!"). That was back when I was only *yay* big.

year end and year out/year in and year out

When something goes on continually, it is traditional to say it happens "year in and year out," meaning "from the beginning of the year to its end—and so on year after year."

The mistaken form "year end and year out" doesn't make sense because "year end" and "year out" both refer to the same part of the year, so no time span is being described.

yet/as of yet

See "as of yet/yet."

ying and yang/yin and yang

The pair of female and male terms in Chinese thought consists of "yin and yang," not "ying and yang."

yoke/yolk

The yellow center of an egg is its *yolk*. The link that holds two oxen together is a *yoke*; they are *yoked*.

you

The second person has perfectly legitimate uses, even when you are not directly addressing another specific person as I am doing in this sentence (I am addressing you, the reader). One example is the giving of directions: "to reach the Pegasus Coffee House, you drive west on Winslow Way to Madison, turn left to the end of Madison, then turn right onto Parfitt Way, and you'll see Pegasus on your left."

It is also commonly used in an indefinite way, where a more formal writer might use "one": "You can eat all you want at Tiny's salad bar."

It can be disorienting to switch from first person to second: "I always order pizza with extra cheese because you know that otherwise they're not going to give you enough." But sometimes such a switch works well to broaden the context of a sentence. For example: "I hate living in the dorm because other people always want to party when you're trying to study." The first part of the sentence is specifically about feelings of the speaker, but the second part is about a general pattern which affects many other people who can plausibly be referred to as "you."

Because the use of the second person conveys an intimate, casual tone, many teachers discourage its use in class essays, feeling that it gives an unsophisticated air to student prose. Be careful about using it in such essays unless you know that your teacher approves.

you better/you had better

In casual speech, it's common to say things like "you better make your bed before Mom comes home." But in writing and in formal speech, the expression is "you *had* better." Slightly less formal but still fine is the contracted version: "you'd better."

you can't have your cake and eat it too/
you can't eat your cake and have it too

The most popular form of this saying—"You can't have your cake and eat it too"—confuses many people because they mistakenly suppose the word "have" means "eat," as in "Have a piece of cake for dessert." A more logical version of this saying is "You can't eat your cake and have it too," meaning that if you eat your cake you won't have it any more. The point is that if you eat your cake right now you won't have it to eat later. "Have" means "possess" in this context, not "eat."

you have mail/you've got mail

See "you've got mail/you have mail."

you know/know what I'm sayin'

In casual speech it's fine to say things like "You know, I really liked that blouse you were wearing yesterday." But some people fall into the habit of punctuating their speech with "you know" so frequently that it becomes irritating to the listener. Most people do this unconsciously, not meaning anything by it. If you become aware that you have this habit your friends and colleagues will be grateful if you try to overcome it.

Hip-hop popularized a similar formula—"know what I'm sayin'?"—frequently used when there is little or no doubt about what is being said. It means something like "right?" It's time to retire this worn-out phrase—know what I'm sayin'?

you was

"I just knowed you was here when I seed your truck outside." "You" followed by "was" is nonstandard, and occurs in print mainly when the writer is trying to make the speaker sound uneducated. The standard verb to follow "you" is "were": "I knew you were here."

your/you

"I appreciate your cleaning the toilet" is more formal than "I appreciate you cleaning the toilet."

your/you're

"You're" is always a contraction of "you are." If you've written "you're," try substituting "you are." If it doesn't work, the word you want is "your." Your writing will improve if you're careful about this.

If someone thanks you, write back "you're welcome" for "you are welcome."

your guys's/your

Many languages have separate singular and plural forms for the second person (ways of saying "you"), but standard English does not. "You" can be addressed to an individual or a whole room full of people.

In casual speech, Americans have evolved the slangy expression "you guys" to function as a second-person plural, formerly used of males only but now extended to both sexes; but this is not appropriate in formal contexts. Diners in fine restaurants are often irritated by clueless waiters who ask "Can I get you guys anything?"

The problem is much more serious when extended to the possessive: "You guys's dessert will be ready in a minute." Some people even create a double possessive by saying "your guys's dessert. . . ." This is extremely clumsy. When dealing with people you don't know intimately, it's best to stick with "you" and "your" no matter how many people you're addressing.

yourself

In formal English it's safest to use "yourself" only after having earlier in the same sentence used "you." When the British reply to a query like "How are you?" with "Fine, and yourself?" they are actually pointing back to the "you" in the query.

It used to be common to address someone in British English as "Your good self" and some people have continued this tradition by creating the word "goodself," common especially in South Asia; but this is nonstandard.

youse/you

The plural form of "you" pronounced as "youse" is heard mainly in satire on the speech of folks from Brooklyn. It's not standard English, since "you" can be either singular or plural without any change in spelling or pronunciation.

you've got another thing coming/you've got another think coming

Here's a case in which eagerness to avoid error leads to error. The original expression is the last part of a deliberately ungrammatical joke: "If that's what you think, you've got another think coming."

you've got mail/you have mail

The "have" contracted in phrases like this is merely an auxiliary verb, not an expression of possession. It is not a redundancy. Compare: "You've sent the mail."

zeroscape/xeriscape

If you nuke your front lawn I suppose you might call it a "zeroscape," but the term for an arid-climate garden requiring little or no watering is "xeriscape" (xeri- is a Greek root meaning "dry").

zero-sum gain/zero-sum game

The concept of a zero-sum game was developed first in game theory: what one side gains the other loses. When applied to economics it is often contrasted with a "win-win" situation in which both sides can make gains without anyone losing. People who are unaware of the phrase's origins often mistakenly substitute "gain" for "game."

zoology

Both *O*'s in "zoo" are needed to create the "oo" sound in this word; but the same is not true of words like "zoology" and "zoologist." Here each *O* has its own sound: "oh" followed by "ah." The first two syllables rhyme with "boa."

Then there is a whole class of technical words like "zooplankton" where both *O*'s are pronounced "oh," though the second "oh" is pronounced so weakly it comes out more like "uh." But if you need to speak such words, you probably know how to pronounce them already.

Poor Zoe the zooplankton—
she could not even
pronounce her own name.

Category
Listings

❧

Commonly Confused Expressions

These entries explain words and expressions that are, in most cases, correct in some contexts. The trouble is that they are sometimes switched for one another.

abstruse/obtuse
accede/exceed
accept/except
adapt/adopt
administer/minister
admission/admittance
adopted/adoptive
advance/advanced
adverse/averse
advice/advise
aesthetic/ascetic
affect/effect
affluence/effluence
afterwards/afterwords
agnostic/atheist
aide/aid
alliterate/illiterate
allude/elude
allude/refer
allusion/illusion
allusive/elusive/illusive
altogether/all together
ambiguous/ambivalent
ambivalent/indifferent
amoral/immoral
ancestor/descendant

anecdote/antidote
anxious/eager
apart/a part
appraise/apprise
apropos/appropriate
arrant/errant
artisinal/artesian
ascribe/subscribe
aspect/respect
assure/ensure/insure
astrology/astronomy
attain/obtain
attribute/contribute
augur/auger
aural/oral
autobiography/biography
avenge/revenge
avocation/vocation
back/forward/up in time
backslash/slash
backup/back up
bailout/bail out
barter/haggle
bazaar/bizarre
bemuse/amuse
beside/besides

biweekly/semiweekly
block/bloc
blog/post
blunt/brunt
bonds/bounds
born/borne
borrow/loan
both/each
breach/breech
breakup/break up
breath/breathe
bring/take
Britain/Briton
broach/brooch
bullion/bouillon
cacao/cocoa
callous/callused
calls for/predicts
Calvary/cavalry
cannot/can not
caramel/Carmel
carousal/carousel
celibate/chaste
cement/concrete
ceremonial/ceremonious
choose/chose
chunk/chuck
cite/site/sight
clench/clinch
climactic/climatic
coiffeur/coiffure
coma/comma
compare to/compare with
complementary/complimentary
comprised of/composed of
confident/confidant/confidante
connote/denote
contaminates/contaminants
continual/continuous
contrary/contrast
convince/persuade
core/corps/corpse
council/counsel/consul
credible/credulous
crescendo/climax
crevice/crevasse
criteria/criterion
critique/criticize

crucifix/cross
cut and paste/copy and paste
damped/dampened
data/datum
dateline/deadline
decent/descent/dissent
defamation/deformation
defuse/diffuse
depravation/deprivation
depreciate/deprecate
desert/dessert
desirable/desirous
deviant/deviate
device/devise
devote/devout
dew/do/doo/due
differ/vary
dilemma/difficulty
disburse/disperse
disc/disk
discreet/discrete
disinterested/uninterested
dissemble/disassemble
dogma/doctrine
dolly/handcart
dominate/dominant
done/finished
doubt that/doubt whether/doubt if
douse/dowse
downfall/drawback
downgrade/degrade/denigrate
dozed/dosed
drastic/dramatic
dredge/drudge/trudge
dribble/drivel
drive/disk
e.g./i.e.
earmarks/hallmark
ecology/environment
economic/economical
elapse/lapse
elegy/eulogy
elicit/illicit
emergent/emergency
emigrate/immigrate
eminent/imminent/immanent
empathy/sympathy
emulate/imitate

endemic/epidemic
engine/motor
enormity/enormousness
entitled/titled
entomology/etymology
envelop/envelope
epic/epoch
epigram/epigraph/epitaph/epithet
equivocate/equate
error/err
espouse/expound/expand
ethics/morals/morale
evoke/invoke
exact same/exactly the same
exalted/exulted
exasperate/exacerbate
exorcise/exercise
explicitly/implicitly
extend/extent
extended, extensive
faithful/fateful
farther/further
fatal/fateful
fearful/fearsome
feint/faint
fiance/fiancee
first floor/ground floor
flak/flack
flaunt/flout
flesh out/flush out
floppy disk/hard disk
flounder/founder
forbidding/foreboding/formidable
forceful/forcible/forced
formally/formerly
fortuitous/fortunate
forward/forwards/foreword
framework/groundwork
freshman/freshmen
furl/furrow
g/q
gamut/gauntlet
gander/dander
gibe/jibe/jive
gig/jig
goal/objective
gratis/gratuitous
grill/grille

grisly/grizzly
group (plural vs. singular)
gull/gall
hanged/hung
hardy/hearty
heal/heel
healthy/healthful
herbs/spices
Hindi/Hindu
historic/historical
hold your peace/say your piece
homophobic
humus/hummus
hundreds/century
hysterical/hilarious
idea/ideal
idle/idol
if/whether
ignorant/stupid
immaculate conception/virgin birth
impertinent/irrelevant
imply/infer
importantly/important
in lieu of/in light of
in spite of/despite
incidence/incidents/instances
incredulous/incredible
inflammable/flammable
insight/incite
install/instill
instances/instants
intense/intensive
interment/internment
intermural/intramural/extramural
Internet/intranet
into/in to
intricate/integral
ironically/coincidentally
itch/scratch
jerry-built/jury-rigged
kick-start/jump-start
l/1
languish/luxuriate
last name/given name/first name
later/latter
lay/lie
lead/led
leave/let

legend/myth
lend/loan
let's/lets
lighted/lit
like/as if
likeliness/likeness
loath/loathe
lose/loose
loser/looser
lustful/lusty
MAC/Mac
mass/massive
masseuse/masseur
material/materiel
me either/me neither
medal/metal/meddle/mettle
media/medium
medium/median
mfr./mfg.
militate/mitigate
minus/hyphen
moral/morale
motion/move
mucus/mucous
nauseated/nauseous
nicety/niceness
one-dimensional/two-dimensional
open/unlocked/unlatched
oppress/repress
Oriental/Asian
overdo/overdue
oversee/overlook
overtake/take over
pair/pare/pear
palate/palette/pallet
parallel/symbol
parameters/perimeters
paramount/tantamount
partake/participate
passed/past
pawn off/palm off
peace/piece
peak/peek/pique
peal out/peel out
perpetuate/perpetrate
persecute/prosecute
personal/personnel
perspective/prospective

phantom/fathom
pheasant/peasant
phenomena/phenomenon
picaresque/picturesque
podium/lectern
pole/poll
poo-poo/pooh-pooh/pupu
populace/populous
pore/pour
posses/possess
practicable/practical
pray/prey
precede/proceed
precedence/precedents
precipitate/precipitous
predominate/predominant
predominately/predominantly
premier/premiere
prescribe/proscribe
presently/currently
pretty/somewhat
preventive/preventative
principal/principle
prodigy/progeny/protégé
progress/pass
prone/supine
prophecy/prophesy
prosperity/posterity
prostate/prostrate
psychologist/psychiatrist/
   psychotherapist/psychoanalyst
purposely/purposefully
quay/cay/key
question/ask
quiet/quite
rack/wrack
raise/rear
rampart/rampant
ran/run
rational/rationale
rationale/rationalization
ravaging/ravishing/ravenous
reactionary/reactive
real/really
rebelling/revolting
rebut/refute
recent/resent
recreate/reinvent

recuperate/recoup
refute/reject
regard/regards
regime/regimen
regretfully/regrettably
reign/rein
religiosity/piety
renumeration/remuneration
repel/repulse
request/ask
resign/re-sign
resister/resistor
restauranter/restaurateur
retch/wretch
reticent/hesitant
retrospective/retroactive
revolve/rotate
revue/review
ridged/rigid
riffle/rifle
risky/risqué
rob/steal
role/roll
rollover/roll over
root/rout/route
sail/sale/sell
sarcastic/ironic
saw/seen
say/tell
scan/skim
scone/sconce
seam/seem
seasonable/seasonal/
    unseasonable/unseasonal
self-worth/self-esteem
sense/since
sensual/sensuous
service/serve
set/sit
setup/set up
shall/will
sheath/sheaf
shimmy/shinny
silicon/silicone
since/because
social/societal
sojourn/journey
somewhat of a/somewhat, something of a

sooner/rather
spaded/spayed
spoke/said
sprain/strain
squash/quash
stalactites/stalagmites
states/countries
stint/stent
stomp/stamp
straight/strait
straightened/straitened
subject to/subjected to
submittal/submission
suit/suite
sulking/skulking
summary/summery
suspect/suspicious
syllabi/syllabus
tact/tack
taken back/taken aback
taught/taut
taunt/taut/tout
tenant/tenet
than/then
that/which
them/those
these kind/this kind
they're/their/there
360 degrees/180 degrees
throne/thrown
tic/tick
to/too/two
tolled/told
torturous/tortuous
toward/towards
troop/troupe
tussled/tousled
unchartered/uncharted
underlining/underlying
University of Indiana/
    Indiana University
vain/vane/vein
various/several
vary/very
verses/versus
video/film
viola/voila
wary/weary/leery

way more/far more/much more
ways/way
weather/wether/whether
were/where
who's/whose
women/woman
wont/won't

world-renown/world-renowned
wrangle/wangle
ye/the
yea/yeah/yay
yoke/yolk
your/you
your/you're

Of Foreign Origin

These entries explain words and phrases that are misspelled, mispronounced, or misused, often due to their foreign-language roots.

A.D.
academia
acapella, a capella/a cappella
accent marks
ad nauseum/ad nauseam
ala/à la
AM/PM
amature/amateur
apropos/appropriate
bazaar/bizarre
beaurocracy/bureaucracy
blonde/blond
bologna/baloney
bon a petite/bon appétit
bonafied/bona fide
bourgeois
cache/cachet
caddy-corner/catty-corner,
    cater-corner, kitty-corner
capeesh/capisce
Ceasar/Caesar
Celtic
chai tea/chai
chaise longue
chick/chic
cliché/clichéd
click/clique
coffee clutch/coffee klatsch, coffee klatch
coiffeur/coiffure
connaisseur/connoisseur
coupe de gras/coup de grace

crape/crepe
criteria/criterion
croissant
data/datum
de rigueur
deja vu
e.g./i.e.
ect./etc.
ensuite
-es
et al.
fiance/fiancee
French dip with au jus/French dip
genre
graffiti
hoi polloi
hors d'oeuvres
in mass/en masse
in route/en route
kindergarden/kindergarten
laissez-faire
liaise
macabre
mono e mono/mano a mano
Mount Fujiyama/Fujiyama
nieve/naive
not my forte
object d'art
oggle/ogle
par excellance/par excellence
peak/peek/pique

pernickety/persnickety
picaresque/picturesque
please RSVP/please reply
pompom/pompon
premier/premiere
PSS/PPS
pundint/pundit
Rio Grande River/
    Rio Grande
risky/risqué
rondezvous/rendezvous
salsa sauce/salsa
Sierra Nevada Mountains/Sierra Nevadas

soup du jour of the day/soup of the day
souse chef/sous chef
specie/species
tic/tick
tirimisù/tiramisù
torturous/tortuous
verses/versus
vinegarette/vinaigrette
viola/voila
vitae/vita
whisky/whiskey
Xmas/Christmas
ye/the

Grammar, Spelling & Style

These entries cover grammar, spelling, and style topics.

a/an
A.D.
accent marks
accidently/accidentally
acronyms & apostrophes
all
all ready/already
almost
alright/all right
altho/tho
AM/PM
amount/number
any
anymore/any more
anyone/any one
anyways/anyway
apostrophes
as far as/as far as . . . is concerned
assess
awhile/a while
backseat/back seat
backward/backwards
bad/badly
began/begun
better
between
between you and I/between you and me

bit/bitten
bologna/baloney
borrow/loan
both
both/each
boughten/bought
bouyant/buoyant
brang/brung/brought
breeches
by/'bye/buy
capitalization
catched/caught
cents
Church/church
cleanup/clean up
cliché /clichéd
coliseum/Colosseum
collective plural
colons/semicolons
commas
company names with apostrophes
conjunction, beginning
    a sentence with a
conversate/converse
crafts
crape/crepe
creeped/crept

dangling and misplaced modifiers
daylight savings time/daylight saving time
deal
dealed/dealt
decade names
definate/definite
degree titles
device/devise
dialogue/discuss
different than/different from, different to
differently abled, physically challenged/
   disabled
directions
disease names
done/did
don't/doesn't
do's and don'ts/dos and don'ts
double negatives
double possessive
dove/dived
drank/drunk
drug/dragged
each
ei/ie
either
either are/either is
ellipses
email/e-mail
ending a sentence with a preposition
equally as/equally, as
-er/-est
et al.
-eth
every (plural vs. singular)
everyday
everyone/every one
expatriot/expatriate
fastly/fast
federal (capitalization)
female/woman
first annual
first person
for
from . . . to
-ful/-fuls
gender
gerunds & pronouns
God/god

going forward
gone/went
good/well
good-by/good-bye/goodby/goodbye
got/gotten
got to/have got to
group (plural vs. singular)
had ought/ought
hadn't have/hadn't
hanging indents
heighth/height
here's/here are
him, her/he, she
historic: an historic vs. a historic
homophobic
hopefully
hyphenation
hyphens & dashes
I/me/myself
-ic
if I was/if I were
impact
Indian/Native American
individual/person
input
intensifiers
interface/interact
is, is
Islams/Muslims
its/it's
job titles
joint possessives
just so happens/just happen
l/1
lay/lie
less/fewer
like/as if
"lite" spelling
-ly adjectives
majority are/majority is
material/materiel
may/might
minus/hyphen
momentarily
multipart names
name, pronoun
near miss

normalcy vs. normality
not
not all
not all that/not very
not hardly/not at all
nothing (singular)
number of verb
numbers
of
of ___'s
off of
OK/okay
100's/hundreds
one of the (singular)
online/on line/in line
only
onto/on to
orientate/orient
over/more than
pair (number)
parallelism in a series
paralyzation/paralysis
parentheses
passive voice
peoples
phenomena/phenomenon
phrasal verbs vs. nouns
pickup/pick up
plural possessives
prepone
prepositions (repeated)
prepositions (wrong)
present writer/I
proved/proven
quotation marks
RBI/RBIs
reference
remotely close
sang/sung
saw/seen
scarcely
second of all/second
sentence fragments
shined/shone
shook/shaken
shrunk/shrank
single quotes

sister-in-laws/sisters-in-law
snuck/sneaked
so fun/so much fun
somebody/someone
spaces after a period
span/spun
specie/species
split infinitives
standalone/stand-alone
staunch/stanch
stoled/stole
stricken/struck
swam/swum
that/which
that kind/that kind of
The Ukraine/Ukraine
their's/theirs
theirselves/themselves
there's
these are them/these are they
these kind/this kind
these ones/these
they/their (singular)
thusly/thus
this here, that there/this, that
tripple/triple
vague reference
verb tense
very unique/unique
was/were
we're/were
what/that
whereabouts are/whereabouts is
whether/whether or not
whilst/while
who/that
who/whom
who's/whose
-wise
World Wide Web
would have/had
would liked to have had/
   would have liked to have
Xmas/Christmas
your/you
yourself
you've got mail/you have mail

Homonyms

These entries cover words that sound alike but are not spelled alike.

adviser/advisor
afterwards/afterwords
aide/aid
aisle/isle
all for not/all for naught
all ready/already
aloud/allowed
altar/alter
altogether/all together
anymore/any more
away/a way
axel/axle
bail/bale
ball/bawl
bare/bear
base/bass
block/bloc
boarders/borders
brake/break
breach/breech
by/'bye/buy
canon/cannon
capital/capitol
carat/caret/carrot/karat
cite/site/sight
cleanup/clean up
close/clothes
coarse/course
Colombia/Columbia
complement/compliment
complementary/complimentary
core/corps/corpse
council/counsel/consul
cue/queue
currant/current
dew/do/doo/due
dike/dyke
disc/disk
discreet/discrete
drier/dryer
dual/duel

dyeing/dying
eek/eke
eminent/imminent/immanent
fair/fare
faun/fawn
faze/phase
feint/faint
flair/flare
flak/flack
floe/flow
for/fore/four
forego/forgo
forward/forwards/foreword
foul/fowl
gaff/gaffe
gibe/jibe/jive
gild/guild
hairbrained/harebrained
hail/hale
hangar/hanger
hardy/hearty
heal/heel
hear/here
heroin/heroine
hippy/hippie
hoard/horde
hole/whole
incidence/incidents/instances
into/in to
its/it's
jam/jamb
leach/leech
lead/led
lessen/lesson
liable/libel
mantle/mantel
medal/metal/meddle/mettle
miner/minor
mucus/mucous
naval/navel
onto/on to

pair/pare/pear
palate/palette/pallet
passed/past
patience/patients
peace/piece
peak/peek/pique
pedal/peddle
plain/plane
pole/poll
populace/populous
pore/pour
pray/prey
precedence/precedents
premier/premiere
principal/principle
rack/wrack
raise/raze
reign/rein
resister/resistor
retch/wretch
revue/review
right/rite/write
ringer/wringer
role/roll
root/rout/route
rye/wry
sail/sale/sell
seam/seem
segway/segue
shear/sheer
shone/shown
sick/sic

slight of hand/sleight of hand
sluff off/slough off
soar/sore
sole/soul
staid/stayed
stationary/stationery
steak/stake
stomp/stamp
straight/strait
suit/suite
summary/summery
taught/taut
they're/their/there
threw/through
throne/thrown
tic/tick
to/too/two
tolled/told
troop/troupe
undo/undue
vain/vane/vein
vary/very
verses/versus
wail/whale
weak/week
weather/wether/whether
who's/whose
wile away/while away
without further adieu/without further ado
yea/yeah/yay
yoke/yolk
your/you're

Commonly Misspelled

These entries cover words that are commonly misspelled. See the end of this list for an added list of entries covering words to be especially careful with when running a spelling checker on your computer.

absorbtion/absorption
acapella, a capella/a cappella
accidently/accidentally
acrosst/accrossed/across
ad nauseum/ad nauseam
add/ad

adultry/adultery
adviser/advisor
afterwards/afterwords
ala/à la
all be it/albeit
all ready/already

alot/a lot
aloud/allowed
alright/all right
amature/amateur
ampitheater/amphitheater
angel/angle
anteclimax/anticlimax
anticlimatic/anticlimactic
any where/anywhere
apiece/a piece
appauled/appalled
arthuritis/arthritis
artical/article
ascared/scared
ashfault/asphalt
asterick/asterisk
athiest/atheist
augur/auger
away/a way
awe, shucks/aw, shucks
bail/bale
basicly/basically
bazaar/bizarre
boarders/borders
bon a petite/bon appétit
bonafied/bonafide
bought/brought
bouyant/buoyant
breach/breech
breath/breathe
broach/brooch
bullion/bouillon
by/'bye/buy
caddy-corner/catty-corner,
   cater-corner, kitty-corner
callous/callused
capeesh/capisce
capital/capitol
caramel/Carmel
Ceasar/Caesar
Champaign/Champagne
Check/Czech
chick/chic
chrispy/crispy
clamor/clamber
click/clique
climactic/climatic

close/clothes
closed-minded/close-minded
coma/comma
concensus/consensus
confident/confidant/confidante
Confusionism/Confucianism
congradulations/congratulations
connaisseur/connoisseur
conservativism/conservatism
copywrite/copyright
cortage/cortege
costumer/customer
council/counsel/consul
coupe de gras/coup de grace
cowtow/kowtow
crucifiction/crucifixion
cue/queue
daring-do/derring-do
de rigueur
decent/descent/dissent
defence/defense
definate/definite
deja vu
desert/dessert
device/devise
dew/do/doo/due
dialate/dilate
dieties/deities
dire straights/dire straits
disasterous/disastrous
disburse/disperse
disc/disk
disgression/discretion
diswraught/distraught
do respect/due respect
do to/due to
doctorial/doctoral
doggy dog world/dog-eat-dog world
donut/doughnut
drownding/drowning
duck tape/duct tape
due to the fact that/because
Earth/earth/Moon/moon
easedrop/eavesdrop
ect./etc.
-ed/-t
eek/eke

electorial college/electoral college
elicit/illicit
email/e-mail
embaress/embarrass
enviroment/environment
epitomy/epitome
everyone/every one
excape/escape
exceptional/exceptionable
excrable/execrable
exhileration/exhilaration
exorcise/exercise
expecially/especially
expresso/espresso
extend/extent
faun/fawn
Febuary/February
firey/fiery
fiscal/physical
fits to a tee/fits to a t
flak/flack
flustrated/frustrated
flys/flies
followup/follow up, follow-up
forsee/foresee
fourty/forty
fushia/fuchsia
gaurd/guard
gentle/gentile
genre
Ghandi/Gandhi
goal/gaol
government
grammer/grammar
gray/grey
greatful/grateful
grievious/grievous
hail/hale
Hanukkah, Chanukah
harbringer/harbinger
his and her's
hone in/home in
hors d'oeuvres
hyperdermic/hypodermic
ice tea/iced tea
imbedded/embedded
in sink/in synch

incase/in case
incidently/incidentally
indepth/in depth
indite/indict
infact/in fact
influencial/influential
input
intergrate/integrate
interment/internment
interpretate/interpret
into/in to
Isreal/Israel
Issac/Isaac
judgement/judgment
kindergarden/kindergarten
l/ll
lamblast/lambaste
larnyx/larynx
laxidaisical/lackadaisical
layed/laid
lense/lens
lessen/lesson
let's/lets
library
licence/license
lightening/lightning
liquor
LISTSERV
loser/looser
manufacture/manufacturer
marshmellow/marshmallow
mathmatics/mathematics
medal/metal/meddle/mettle
medieval ages/Middle Ages
memorium/memoriam
mic/mike
middleaged/middle-aged
minature/miniature
miner/minor
miniscule/minuscule
mischievious/mischievous
mispell/misspell
momento/memento
morays/mores
moreso/more so
murmer/murmur
mute point/moot point

n'/'n'
naval/navel
neice/niece
never the less, not withstanding/
    nevertheless, notwithstanding
nevermind/never mind
nieve/naive
ninty/ninety
no where/nowhere
Noble Prize/Nobel Prize
noone/no one
nuptual/nuptial
octopi/octopuses
ofcourse/of course
oggle/ogle
oh/o
old fashion/old-fashioned
ostensively/ostensibly
outcast/outcaste
parallelled/paralleled
parliment/parliament
past time/pastime
patience/patients
payed/paid
peace/piece
pedal/peddle
peoples
percipitation/precipitation
permiscuous/promiscuous
pernickety/persnickety
perogative/prerogative
perscription/prescription
perse/per se
phenomena/phenomenon
Philippines/Filipinos
phoney/phony
pickup/pick up
pigeon English/pidgin English
playwrite/playwright
poinsetta/poinsettia
pompom/pompon
poo-poo/pooh-pooh/pupu
posses/possess
practice/practise
practicle/practical
precede/proceed
predominately/predominantly

preemptory/peremptory
prejudice/prejudiced
premise/premises
presumptious/presumptuous
primevil/primeval
principal/principle
program/programme
pronounciation/pronunciation
protray/portray
publically/publicly
pundint/pundit
queue
quiet/quite
rapport
realize/realise
recent/resent
rediculous/ridiculous
reeking havoc/wreaking havoc
regard/regards
reign/rein
reknown/renown
renumeration/remuneration
reoccuring/recurring
reoccurring/recurring
resignate/resonate
resister/resistor
restauranter/restaurateur
revelant/relevant
right of passage/rite of passage
risky/risqué
rod iron, rot iron/wrought iron
rogue/ rouge
Romainian/Romanian
rondezvous/rendezvous
roomate/roommate
Rueben/Reuben
ruff/rough
rye/wry
sacred/scared
sacreligious/sacrilegious
safety deposit box/safe-deposit box
sameo sameo/same old same old
segway/segue
seperate/separate
shear/sheer
shepard/shepherd
sherbert/sherbet

sick/sic
skiddish/skittish
sluff off/slough off
some where/somewhere
sometime/some time
souse chef/sous chef
sowcow/salchow
spaded/spayed
stain glass/stained glass
stationary/stationery
straight/strait
summary/summery
summersault/somersault
supercede/supersede
supposably/supposingly/
    supposedly
suppose to/supposed to
supremist/supremacist
suttle/subtle
tattle-tail/tattle-tale
teenage/teenaged
tender hooks/tenterhooks
thankyou/thank you
that/than
theirselves/themselves
therefor/therefore
there's
they're/their/there
though/thought/through
thusfar/thus far
tic/tick
till/until
timber/timbre
tirimisù/tiramisù
to/too/two
tounge/tongue
toward/towards
track home/tract home
tradegy/tragedy
troop/troupe
truely/truly
tussled/tousled
unconscience/unconscious
undoubtably/undoubtedly
upmost/utmost
upto/up to
use to/used to

vain/vane/vein
valuble/valuable
veil of tears/vale of tears
veracious/voracious
verbage/verbiage
verses/versus
villian/villain
vinegarette/vinaigrette
viola/voila
visa versa/vice versa
visable/visible
vitae/vita
vocal chords/vocal cords
volumn/volume
volumptuous/voluptuous
vunerable/vulnerable
wander/wonder
warmongerer/warmonger
warrantee/warranty
wary/weary/leery
waver/waiver
weiner/wiener
Wensday/Wednesday
we're/were
were/where
wet your appetite/whet your appetite
whacky/wacky
whimp/wimp
whisky/whiskey
wholely/wholly
wholistic/holistic
who's/whose
wile away/while away
women/woman
wonderkind/wunderkind
wont/won't
world-renown/world-renowned
wreckless/reckless
writting/writing
ya'll/y'all
yea/yeah/yay
your/you're

**And be careful with these . . . your
    spelling checker won't catch them.**
accept/except
afterwards/afterwords

343

all be it/albeit
aloud/allowed
an/and
angel/angle
any where/anywhere
apiece/a piece
appose/oppose
away/a way
bail/bale
boarders/borders
bought/brought
breach/breech
broach/brooch
bullion/bouillon
canvas/canvass
capital/capitol
Champaign/Champagne
Check/Czech
closed-minded/close-minded
costumer/customer
cowered/coward
crape/crepe
cue/queue
dairy/diary
demure/demur
depravation/deprivation
dew/do/doo/due
disc/disk
do respect/due respect
duly/dully
everyone/every one
exited/excited
exorcise/exercise
extend/extent
gauge/gouge
grill/grille
gull/gall
hay day/heyday
humus/hummus
idle/idol

impassible/impassable
in memorial/immemorial
in tact/intact
lessen/lesson
let's/lets
loser/looser
manufacture/manufacturer
marital/martial
miner/minor
minuet/minute
morays/mores
naval/navel
never the less, not withstanding/
    nevertheless, notwithstanding
no where/nowhere
Noble Prize/Nobel Prize
pair/pare/pear
patience/patients
pedal/peddle
pleaded/pleated
quiet/quite
recent/resent
rod iron, rot iron/wrought iron
rouge/rogue
ruff/rough
rye/wry
sacred/scared
shear/sheer
sick/sic
some where/somewhere
sound byte/sound bite
straightened/straitened
striped/stripped
though/thought/through
tic/tick
timber/timbre
vain/vane/vein
verses/versus
we're/were
were/where

Mangled Expressions

These entries cover words and phrases that are prone to getting mangled.

access/get access to
actual fact/actually
agreeance/agreement
ahold/hold
ain't/am not/isn't/aren't
all and all / all in all
all be it/albeit
all goes well/augurs well
all of the sudden/all of a sudden
all the farther/as far as
along the same vein/in the same vein,
    along the same line
alot/a lot
anchors away/anchors aweigh
another words/in other words
any other number of/any number of other
any where/anywhere
anytime/any time
anyways/anyway
anywheres/anywhere
Arab/Arabic/Arabian
as
as best as/as best
as less as possible
assumably/presumably
awhile/a while
baited breath/bated breath
based around, based off of/based on
basises/bases
beat/bead
beckon call/beck and call
begs belief/beggars belief
belief toward/belief in
below table/table below
beyond the pail/beyond the pale
blindsighted/blindsided
boast your confidence/
    bolster your confidence
bonds/bounds
boost in the arm/shot in the arm
born out of/born of

boughten/bought
bounce/bounds
bran new/brand new
brang/brung/brought
build off of/build on
butt naked/buck naked
buttload/boatload
by far and away/by far, far and away
caddy-corner/catty-corner,
    cater-corner, kitty-corner
calm, cool, and collective/
    calm, cool, and collected
can goods/canned goods
card shark/cardsharp
carrot on a stick/
    the carrot or the stick
cast dispersions/cast aspersions
cease the day/seize the day
center around/center on/revolve around
center of attraction/center of attention
chalk-full/chock-full, chuck-full
cheap at half the price/
    cheap at twice the price
chock it up/chalk it up
chomp at the bit/champ at the bit
coat strings/coat tails
coffee clutch/coffee klatsch, coffee klatch
cold slaw/cole slaw
cope up/cope with
could care less/could not care less
could give a damn/couldn't give a damn
Cracker Jacks/Cracker Jack
cursing through veins/
    coursing through veins
curve your appetite/curb your appetite
cut and dry/cut and dried
cut of tea/cup of tea
cut the muster/cut the mustard
daylight savings time/daylight saving time
death nail/death knell, nail in the coffin
denied of/denied

dialogue/discuss
digestive track/digestive tract
disconcerning/concerning, discerning
do respect/due respect
down the pipe/down the pike
down the shoot/down the chute
drips and drabs/dribs and drabs
drug/dragged
duck tape/duct tape
due to the fact that/because
edge on/egg on
enamored by/enamored of
endquote/unquote
enjoy to/enjoy -ing
ever so often/every so often
every since/ever since
exception proves the rule
execute on/execute
extract revenge/exact revenge
face the piper/pay the piper,
      face the music
far and few between/few and far between
far be it for me/far be it from me
fine toothcomb/fine-tooth comb
firstable/first of all
flustrated, fustrated/frustrated
followup/follow up, follow-up
for sell/for sale
for sure/sure
fowl swoop/fell swoop
full proof/foolproof
fully well/full well
gardener snake/garter snake
grasping for straws/grasping at straws
grill cheese/grilled cheese
hand and hand/hand in hand
Happy Belated Birthday/
      Belated Happy Birthday
hardly never/hardly ever
heart-rendering/heart-rending
hence why/hence
hew and cry/hue and cry
highly looked upon/highly regarded
hit and miss/hit or miss
hock/hawk
how to/how can I
hyperdermic/hypodermic

in another words/in other words
in lieu of/in light of
in mass/en masse
in memorial/immemorial
in shambles/a shambles
in the fact that/in that
in the mist/in the midst
incase/in case
indepth/in depth
insundry/and sundry
intend on/intend to
invested interest/vested interest
Islams/Muslims
John Hopkins/Johns Hopkins
just, jest/gist
just assume/just as soon
jutebox/jukebox
killed after/killed in, killed by, died after
knots per hour/knots
koala bear/koala
land lover/landlubber
laundry mat/Laundromat
less painless/less painful, more painful
lip-sing/lip-synch
little own/let alone
long story short/
      to make a long story short
maddening crowd/madding crowd
magic bullet/silver bullet
majorly/extremely
make due/make do
make pretend/make believe
marinate on/meditate on
mash potatoes/mashed potatoes
mean for/mean
midrift/midriff
might has well/might as well
might ought/might, ought
mind of information/mine of information
mixed-up media/mixed media
money is no option/money is no object
mono e mono/mano a mano
most always/almost always
motherload/mother lode
multiply by double/double, multiply by 2
mumble jumbo, mumbo jumble/
      mumbo jumbo, mumble jumble

mute point/moot point
neck in neck/neck and neck
new lease of life/new lease on life
next store/next door
nip it in the butt/nip it in the bud
no sooner when/no sooner than
no such a thing/no such thing
no where/nowhere
nowheres
Noble Prize/Nobel Prize
now and days/nowadays
numerous of/numerous, numbers of
odd
oeuvre
oft chance/off chance
old wise tale/old wives' tale
old-timer's disease/Alzheimer's disease
on accident/by accident
on the same token/by the same token
once and a while/once in a while
one in the same/one and the same
one of the only/one of the few
ongoingly/currently, continuously
oppose to/opposed to, supposed to
pass the muster/pass muster
pause for concern/
    cause for concern, pause
pedal to the medal/pedal to the metal
perse/per se
pinned up/pent up
pit in my stomach/in the pit of my
    stomach
pith and vinegar/piss and vinegar
plays a factor/plays a role
plus/add
point of you/point of view
precurse/foretell, foreshadow,
    preface, anticipate, precede
pre-Madonna/prima donna
proof is in the pudding/
    proof of the pudding is in the eating
prosperity/posterity
PSS/PPS
quick claim/quitclaim
rate of speed/rate, speed
readably/readily
realms of possibility/realm of possibility

reap what you sew/reap what you sow
reeking havoc/wreaking havoc
regard/regards
renumeration/remuneration
repungent/repugnant, pungent
right of passage/rite of passage
ring its neck/wring its neck
ringer/wringer
road to hoe/row to hoe
rod iron, rot iron/wrought iron
safety deposit box/safe-deposit box
sameo sameo/same old same old
Scotch free/scot free
scrapegoat/scapegoat
self-steam/self-esteem
sense of false hope/false sense of hope
sergeant of arms/sergeant at arms
shoe-in/shoo-in
shoulder on/soldier on
show-stopper/deal-breaker
shutter to think/shudder to think
signaled out/singled out
skiddish/skittish
slight of hand/sleight of hand
slog it out/slug it out
sluff off/slough off
some where/somewhere
somebody's else/somebody else's
sometimes not always
somewheres/somewhere
sooner than later/sooner rather than later
sort after/sought after
sorta speak/so to speak
soup du jour of the day/soup of the day
span/spun
spare of the moment/spur of the moment
spit and image/spitting image
step foot/set foot
still in all/still and all
straight/strait
straddled with/saddled with
strike a cord/strike a chord
strong suite/strong suit
suped up/souped up
supposably, supposingly,
    supposively/supposedly
supremist/supremacist

surplus neckline/surplice neckline
tad bit/tad, bit
taken back/taken aback
tattle-tail/tattle-tale
tender hooks/tenterhooks
thanks God
through a mirror, darkly/
   in a mirror, darkly
throws of passion/throes of passion
thusfar/thus far
tie me over/tide me over
to the manor born/to the manner born
to where/so much that, to the point that
today's day and age/this day and age
toe-headed/tow-headed
tongue and cheek/tongue in cheek
touch bases/touch base
tow the line/toe the line
track home/tract home
tragedy/travesty
trite and true/tried and true
two to tangle/two to tango
unconscience/unconscious
under the guise that/under the guise of
under weigh/under way
undermind/undermined
unkept/unkempt
unthaw/thaw
untracked/on track

upmost/utmost
upto/up to
urine analysis/urinalysis
used to could/used to be able
veil of tears/vale of tears
veracious/voracious
vicious/viscous circle/cycle
vintage point/vantage point
warmongerer/warmonger
wet your appetite/whet your appetite
wheelbarrel/wheelbarrow
whim and a prayer/wing and a prayer
whip cream/whipped cream
a whole 'nother/a completely different
whole-hardily/wholeheartedly
who's ever/whoever's
wile away/while away
without further adieu/
   without further ado
worse comes to worse/
   worst comes to worst
year end and year out/year in and year out
ying and yang/yin and yang
your guys's/your
youse/you
you've got another thing coming/
   you've got another think coming
zeroscape/xeriscape
zero-sum gain/zero-sum game

Inexact Words & Phrases

These entries cover words and phrases that are used imprecisely.

about
accurate/precise
addicting/addictive
advocate for/advocate
African-American
aggravate vs. irritate
agnostic/atheist
all
alleged, allegedly
almost
American
apiece/a piece

apropos/appropriate
Arab/Arabic/Arabian
astrology/astronomy
attain/obtain
attribute/contribute
autobiography/biography
avenge/revenge
back/forward/up in time
backslash/slash
baldfaced, boldfaced/barefaced
barter/haggle
beginning of time

belief/believe
Bible
blatant
blog/post
brand names
Canadian geese/Canada geese
can't . . . too
careen/career
Caucasian
celibate/chaste
cement/concrete
chauvinist/male chauvinist, sexist
chemicals
Chicano/Latino/Hispanic
classic/classical
concerning/worrisome, troubling
connote/denote
conscience, conscious, consciousness
contrary/contrast
crescendo/climax
crevice/crevasse
criticism
croissant
crowbar/wrecking bar
crucifix/cross
debrief
deceptively
decimate/annihilate, slaughter, etc.
Democrat Party/Democratic Party
deviant/deviate
dialogue/discuss
differ/vary
dilemma/difficulty
disc/disk
disinterested/uninterested
dogma/doctrine
dolly/handcart
downfall/drawback
drastic/dramatic
e.g./i.e.
economic/economical
electrocute/shock
empathy/sympathy
emulate/imitate
endemic/epidemic
engine/motor
English/British
enormity/enormousness

envious/jealous
epic/epoch
epicenter
eponymous/self-titled
espouse/expound/expand
ethics/morals/morale
ethnic
evoke/invoke
exponential growth
expressed/express
floppy disk/hard disk
fluke
focus around/focus on
footnotes/endnotes
for sale/on sale
Frankenstein
frankly
fulsome
gender
goal/objective
ground zero
grow
gyp/cheat
hanged/hung
hardly
hearing-impaired/deaf
heavily/strongly
help the problem/help solve the problem
herbs/spices
hero/protagonist
highly looked upon/highly regarded
holocaust
home page
humanism/humanist
hundreds/century
hypocritical
-ic
ignorant/stupid
immaculate conception/virgin birth
impact
impeach
incidence/incidents/instances
includes
incredible
Indian/Native American
individual/person
infinite
intensifiers

intrigue
Israelite/Israeli
issues/problems
jack/plug
kick-start/jump-start
koala bear/koala
large/important
last name/given name/first name
late/former
later/latter
legend/myth
literally
logon/visit
mean/median
meantime/meanwhile
mediocre
meteor/meteorite/meteoroid
minus/hyphen
mixed-up media/mixed media
motion/move
mucus/mucous
music/singing
nauseated/nauseous
next/this
not
obsolescent/obsolete
Old English
one of the only/one of the few
one-dimensional/two-dimensional
only
op-ed
open/unlocked/unlatched
opportunist
oral/verbal
orders of magnitude
organic
Oriental/Asian
parallel/symbol
parameters/perimeters
paranoid
percent decrease
personality
perverse/perverted
podium/lectern
practicable/practical
pretty/somewhat

prioritize
priority
psychologist/psychiatrist/
    psychotherapist/psychoanalyst
quantum leap
real/really
refrain/restrain
religion
religion believes/religion teaches
religiosity/piety
report into/report on
revolve/rotate
rhetorical questions
romantic
satellite
schizophrenic
Scotch/Scots
select/selected
self-worth/self-esteem
simplistic
so/very
social/societal
song/work or composition
sort of
spiritualism/spirituality
sprain/strain
stance/stand
stereo
substance-free
substitute with/substitute for
surfing the Internet
tape, record
times smaller
troop/troupe
UFO
ugly American
underestimated
unrest
use/usage
vague reference
vapid/vacuous
video/film
wheat/whole wheat
whenever/when
-wise
ye/the

Pronunciation

These entries cover words and phrases prone to pronunciation problems.

absorbtion/absorption
academia
accede/exceed
accessory
acrosst/accrossed/across
analogous
anticlimatic/anticlimactic
artic/arctic
asterick/asterisk
athlete
avaidable/available
ax/ask
barb wire/bob wire/
   barbed wire
bologna/baloney
bourgeois
bouyant/buoyant
bow
breeches
cache/cachet
Celtic
chaise longue
Check/Czech
click/clique
comptroller
coupe de gras/coup de grace
crape/crepe
crick/creek
dialate/dilate
disasterous/disastrous
doctorial/doctoral
drownding/drowning
ecstatic
ect./etc.
-ed/-t
electorial college/electoral college
elicit/illicit
emigrate/immigrate
eminent/imminent/immanent
envelop/envelope
enviroment/environment

epitomy/epitome
excape/escape
exceptional/exceptionable
excrable/execrable
expecially/especially
expresso/espresso
Febuary/February
fiscal/physical
flustrated, fustrated/frustrated
genre
genuine
goal/gaol
gonna/going to
government
grievious/grievous
harbringer/harbinger
heighth/height
historic: an historic vs. a historic
hone in/home in
hors d'oeuvres
Illinois
-ing
integral
interesting
intergrate/integrate
interment/internment
interpretate/interpret
Iraq
Islams/Muslims
jewelry
junta
laissez-faire
lamblast/lambaste
larnyx/larynx
laxidaisical/lackadaisical
library
lived
loath/loathe
lose/loose
macabre
manufacture/manufacturer

minature/miniature
mischievious/mischievous
misplaced stress
morays/mores
Nevada
not my forte
nuclear
o/zero
offense/offence
oggle/ogle
Oregon
par excellance/par excellence
pen/pin
percipitation/precipitation
perogative/prerogative
perscription/prescription
perverse/perverted
pianist
picture
poinsetta/poinsettia
practicle/practical
preemptory/peremptory
preferably
prespiration/perspiration
primer

probably
prophecy/prophesy
racism
realtor
recent/resent
recognize
respiratory
restauranter/restaurateur
Rio Grande River/Rio Grande
rondezvous/rendezvous
rural
safety deposit box/safe-deposit box
samwich/sandwich
segway/segue
set/sit
specific/Pacific
strength
tentative
timber/timbre
valuble/valuable
volumptuous/voluptuous
vunerable/vulnerable
wash
Wensday/Wednesday
zoology

Problem Prepositions

These entries cover misused prepositions.

about
based around/based on
belief toward/belief in
between
bored of/bored with
born out of/born of
build off of/build on
center around/center on/
   revolve around
close proximity/close/in proximity to
compare to/compare with
contrasts/contrasts with
cope up/cope with
couple/couple of
depends/depends on
different than/different from/different to

emphasize on/emphasize
enamored by/enamored of
ending a sentence with a preposition
evidence to/evidence of
feelings for/feelings about
focus around/focus on
for free/free
for sure/sure
graduate/graduate from
intend on/intend to
like for/like
myriad of/myriad
of
of ___'s
off of
on accident/by accident

onto/on to
over/more than
possessed of/possessed by/
   possessed with
prepositions (repeated)
prepositions (wrong)
report into/report on
substitute with/substitute for

suffer with/suffer from
that kind/that kind of
think on/think about
to home/at home
try and/try to
wait on/wait for
where (and prepositions)
within/among

Redundancies

These entries cover questions of redundancy.

access/get access to
actual fact/actually
added bonus
and/or
and also/and, also
and plus
as of yet/yet
ATM machine/ATM
but . . . however/but, however
CD-ROM disk/CD-ROM
cents
chai tea/chai
close proximity/close/in proximity to
compare and contrast/compare
disembark the vessel/disembark
ect./etc.
end result
equally as/equally, as
fellow classmate/classmate
French dip with au jus/French dip
goal/objective
going forward
GP practice/general practice
heading/bound
hence why/hence
HIV virus
ink pen/pen
irregardless/regardless
is, is
LCD display/LCD
medieval ages/Middle Ages
Mount Fujiyama/Fujiyama

new beginning
of ___'s
off of
organic
over-exaggerated/exaggerated
past history
PC computer/PC
PIN number/PIN
please RSVP/please reply
point being is that
point in time/point, time
preplan
prepositions (repeated)
rate of speed/rate, speed
reason because
redo it over/redo it, do it over
redundancies
reply back/reply
respond back/respond, reply
return back/return
revert back
Rio Grande River/Rio Grande
safe haven
salsa sauce/salsa
Sierra Nevada Mountains/
   Sierra Nevadas
soup du jour of the day/soup of the day
tad bit/tad, bit
time period
today's day and age/this day and age
where it's at
you've got mail/you have mail

Commonly Misused Expressions

These entries cover words and phrases that are susceptible to being used in the wrong situations, for one reason or another.

abject
able to
about
abstruse/obtuse
actionable/doable
administrate/administer
adopted/adoptive
advocate for/advocate
aesthetic/ascetic
Afghan/Afghani
African-American
afterwards/afterwords
agnostic/atheist
ahold/hold
all of the sudden/all of a sudden
alleged, allegedly
allusive/elusive/illusive
almost
alternate/alternative
altogether/all together
alumnus/alumni
American
amongst/among
ancestor/descendant
and/or
antihero
apropos/appropriate
arrant/errant
as far as/as far as . . . is concerned
as follow/as follows
as of yet/yet
as per/in accordance with
as such
at all
attain/obtain
attribute/contribute
autobiography/biography
avenge/revenge
back/forward/up in time
backup/back up

backslash/slash
bailout/bail out
begs belief/beggars belief
begs the question
behaviors/behavior
being that/because
belief/believe
bias/biased
Bible
bicep/biceps
blatant
blog/post
borrow/loan
both/each
brainchild
breakup/break up
broach/brooch
broke/broken
brussel sprout/brussels sprout
bully pulpit
caring
Catch-22
chemicals
Chicano/Latino/Hispanic
classic/classical
come with
concerning/worrisome, troubling
concerted effort
conflicted/conflicting feelings
connote/denote
contaminates/contaminants
coronate/crown
cowered/coward
crevice/crevasse
criticism
critique/criticize
crucifix/cross
daylight savings time/
    daylight saving time
debrief

deceptively

decimate/annihilate, slaughter, etc.

defamation/deformation

Democrat Party/Democratic Party

demure/demur

denied of/denied

depends/depends on

desirable/desirous

deviant/deviate

devote/devout

dialogue/discuss

different than/different from, different to

differently abled, physically challenged/disabled

dilemma/difficulty

discretion is the better part of valor

dispose/dispose of

disremember/forget

disrespect

divide by half/divide in half

documentated/documented

dogma/doctrine

doubt that/doubt whether/doubt if

doubtlessly/doubtless

downfall/drawback

dozen of/dozen

drastic/dramatic

duly/dully

e.g./i.e.

each

early adopter

earmarks/hallmark

economic/economical

efforting/trying

either/or, neither/nor

either are/either is

eminent/imminent/immanent

emphasize on/emphasize

emulate/imitate

endemic/epidemic

engine/motor

enjoy to/enjoy -ing

enormity/enormousness

enthuse

envious/jealous

epic/epoch

epicenter

eponymous/self-titled

equivocate/equate

error/err

espouse/expound/expand

ethics/morals/morale

ethnic

everyday

everytime/every time

evidence to/evidence of

exalted/exulted

exorcise/exercise

expensive, cheap

explicitly/implicitly

exponential growth

expresses that/says that

extend/extent

extended, extensive

factoid

faithful/fateful

feint/faint

fiance/fiancee

finalize/finish, put into final form

first come, first serve/ first come, first served

floppy disk/hard disk

fluke

foot/feet

footnotes/endnotes

forward/forwards/foreword

frankly

freshman/freshmen

fulsome

functionality

furl/furrow

gander/dander

garnish/garner

genius/brilliant

get me

gift/give

goes

gone/went

good/well

got/gotten

graduate/graduate from

ground zero

grow

had ought/ought
hairbrained/harebrained
hanged/hung
hardly
hardly never/hardly ever
hardy/hearty
hark/hearken
heared/heard
hearing-impaired/deaf
heart-rendering/heart-rending
heavily/strongly
herbs/spices
hero/protagonist
Hindi/Hindu
hisself/himself
holocaust
home page
homophobic
how come/why
howsomever/however
humanity
hypocritical
if not
in route/en route
in shambles/a shambles
in store
in terms of
incent/incentivize
incidence/incidents/instances
infamous
infinite
interface/interact
intermural/intramural/extramural
into/in to
intrigue
invite/invitation
is, is
isn't it/innit
issues/problems
jack/plug
Jew/Hebrew
Jew/Jewish
key
laissez-faire
languish/luxuriate
last name/given name/first name
late/former
later/latter

let alone
liaise
light-year
like
like for/like
lion's share
literature
login, log-in, log in
logon/visit
LOL
lookit/look
lots, plenty, load (number)
luxuriant/luxurious
me either/me neither
medal/metal/meddle/mettle
mediocre
medium/median
meteor/meteorite/meteoroid
methodology/method
minority
misnomer
molten/melted
Mongoloid
more/most
moreso/more so
most always/almost always
motion/move
much differently/very differently
muchly/much
myriad of/myriad
near/nearly
needs -ed/-ing
nicety/niceness
niggard
nonplussed
not all
notate/note
notorious
octopi/octopuses
odd
offline
once/ones
one of the only/one of the few
one-dimensional/two-dimensional
op-ed
opportunist
orders of magnitude
ourn/ours

over and out/out

parallel/symbol

parameters/perimeters

paranoid

penultimate/next to last

per/according to

percent decrease

personality

peruse

perverse/perverted

plead innocent

plus/add

point in time/point, time

prepositions (wrong)

present writer/I

problematic

quantum leap

question/ask

quote

random

ratio

reason because

refrain/restrain

religion believes/religion teaches

revert/reply

revolve/rotate

riffle/rifle

satellite

schizophrenic

sci-fi/science fiction/SF

scone/sconce

sea change

sheath/sheaf

shined/shone

simplistic

Sir/Dame

socialize

somebody/someone

someways/somehow

sour grapes

spree

squoze/squeezed

stint/stent

stood/stayed

stress on/feel stress

stricken/struck

subject to/subjected to

substance-free

sufficeth

take and

taunt/taut/tout

theory

there's

360 degrees/180 degrees

tooken/took/taken

torturous/tortuous

tragedy/travesty

troop/troupe

try and/try to

underestimated

underlining/underlying

unrest

use/usage

utilize/use

vapid/vacuous

vendor

verse/play against

walk the talk/walk the walk

wax

whenever/when

within/among

would have/had

you can't have your cake and eat it too/
   you can't eat your cake and have it too

American English vs. British English

These entries cover differences between American and British English.

aide/aid

alternate/alternative

defence/defense

different than/different from/
   different to

-ed/-t

enquire/inquire
ensuite
goal/gaol
got/gotten
gray/grey
isn't it/innit
jewelry
judgement/judgment
licence/license
next/this
off of
offense/offence
orientate/orient
parallelled/paralleled
percent/per cent
phoney/phony

practice/practise
program/programme
quotation marks
realize/realise
sceptic/skeptic
shan't/shall not
should/would
single quotes
supposably/supposingly/supposedly
table
taunt/taut/tout
they/their (singular)
toward/towards
vice-like/vise-like
write me
yourself

Misheard Expressions

These entries cover problems that arise when writers write what they heard; or rather, what they *think* they heard.

abstruse/obtuse
aesthetic/ascetic
all and all / all in all
all goes well/augurs well
all of the sudden/all of a sudden
allude/elude
allusion/illusion
alterior/ulterior
ampitheater/amphitheater
anchors away/anchors aweigh
asterick/asterisk
augur/auger
ax/ask
barb wire/bob wire/barbed wire
bazaar/bizarre
beat/bead
beckon call/beck and call
better
bounce/bounds
brussel sprout/brussels sprout
calm, cool, and collective/
   calm, cool, and collected
can goods/canned goods

case and point/case in point
cease the day/seize the day
chock it up/chalk it up
cold slaw/cole slaw
contaminates/contaminants
could of, should of, would of/could have,
   should have, would have
cursing through veins/
   coursing through veins
curve your appetite/curb your appetite
cut and dry
cut of tea/cup of tea
death nail/death knell, nail in the coffin
deep-seeded/deep-seated
digestive track/digestive tract
do to/due to
doggy dog world/dog-eat-dog world
down the pipe/down the pike
down the shoot/down the chute
drips and drabs/dribs and drabs
duck tape/duct tape
easedrop/eavesdrop
eminent/imminent/immanent

entomology/etymology
error/err
exorcise/exercise
firstable/first of all
for goodness' sakes/for goodness' sake
furl/furrow
gardener snake/garter snake
grill cheese/grilled cheese
hand and hand/hand in hand
hew and cry/hue and cry
hock/hawk
ice tea/iced tea
in memorial/immemorial
in sink/in synch
in the mist/in the midst
intensive purposes/intents and purposes
just assume/just as soon
just, jest/gist
I/ll
land lover/landlubber
laundry mat/Laundromat
lip-sing/lip-synch
little own/let alone
low and behold/lo and behold
might has well/might as well
mind of information/
   mine of information
must of/must have
neck in neck/neck and neck
next store/next door
nip it in the butt/nip it in the bud
no sooner when/no sooner than
now and days/nowadays
oft chance/off chance
often
old wise tale/old wives' tale
old-timer's disease/Alzheimer's disease
once and a while/once in a while
one in the same/one and the same
oppose to/opposed to, supposed to
past time/pastime

pause for concern/
   cause for concern, pause
pawn off/palm off
point of you/point of view
pre-Madonna/prima donna
quick claim/quitclaim
rapport
reeking havoc/wreaking havoc
right of passage/rite of passage
road to hoe/row to hoe
rod iron, rot iron/wrought iron
safety deposit box/safe-deposit box
self-steam/self-esteem
sheath/sheaf
shimmy/shinny
shoulder on/soldier on
slight of hand/sleight of hand
sluff off/slough off
sort after/sought after
spit and image/spitting image
still in all/still and all
stint/stent
suppose to/supposed to
taken back/taken aback
taunt/taut/tout
tender hooks/tenterhooks
tie me over/tide me over
tongue and cheek/tongue in cheek
tow the line/toe the line
track home/tract home
undoubtably/undoubtedly
use to/used to
veil of tears/vale of tears
Wensday/Wednesday
whim and a prayer/wing and a prayer
wile away/while away
worse comes to worse/
   worst comes to worst
year end and year out/year in and year out
you've got another thing coming/
   you've got another think coming

Appendix:
Phrasal Verbs vs. Nouns

Note: What follows is not meant to be exhaustive. It does not cover every possible meaning of these expressions. The entries are just sample two-word and one-word forms in context to give you an idea of what might be suitable. Many one-word entries listed below are used in the UK mainly in hyphenated form, but I've followed general US patterns.

back down vs. backdown
Don't let him make you back down. The result would be a humiliating backdown.

back up vs. backup
Back up your data regularly; then you'll have a backup when your hard disk crashes.

bail out vs. bailout
If the government has to bail out a bank it may have to pass a bailout bill. The result is a government bailout.

beat up vs. beat-up
The thugs beat up the weaker kids. He drove a beat-up truck.

blast off vs. blastoff
The spaceship was ready to blast off. Blastoff occurred at dawn.

blow out vs. blowout
Blow out the candle. The party was a blowout.

blow up vs. blow-up, blowup
Blow up the building. A storm may blow up. A blow-up Santa Claus. Their disagreement led to a blowup. The blowup of the photo showed spinach between her teeth.

boil over vs. boilover
Don't let the milk boil over. You have to watch carefully to avoid a boilover.

break away vs. breakaway
Some states wanted to break away from the Union. The breakaway group decided to meet separately.

break down vs. breakdown
Break down this wall. Break down the argument so I can understand it. The problems in the company led to a complete breakdown.

break out vs. breakout
Escapees break out of prison. The guards try to prevent a breakout.

break up vs. breakup
I hope we don't break up over this. A breakup always hurts.

brush off vs. brushoff
Brush off the cat hair. Don't listen to that guy; give him the brushoff.

build up vs. buildup
Build up your bank account. Avoid bathtub scum buildup.

burn off vs. burnoff
I'm hoping that the fog will burn off. Burn off the fat. The shrubs were destroyed in the area of the burnoff.

buy in vs. buy-in
To raise the money, we had to get several investors to buy in. We needed to get buy-in from all the parties concerned.

buy off vs. buyoff
The gangsters tried to buy off the cops. The extra health insurance benefit was a buyoff for early retirees.

buy out vs. buyout
The big corporation intended to buy out its small competitors. The company offered a buyout to get some of its employees to quit.

call back vs. callback
Call back your dogs. If no one answers the first time a callback is required.

carry on vs. carry-on
You can carry on one small bag. We have to inspect your carry-on. Carry-on luggage has to fit in the overhead bin.

cash in vs. cash-in
After working for 48 years, he decided to cash in. We did a cash-in refinance.

cash out vs. cashout
Close down the business and cash out. I accepted a lump-sum cashout.

catch up vs. catch-up
Wait for me to catch up. We're not getting anywhere; we're just playing catch-up.

cave in vs. cave-in
The kids kept begging to go to Disney World until they got me to cave in. The miners were trapped by a cave-in.

change over vs. changeover
We want to change over to a Web-based billing system. Accounting will be in charge of the changeover.

check in vs. check-in
You must check in before boarding the plane. You must complete check-in before participating in the meeting. The check-in procedures have been simplified.

check out vs. checkout
Check out the book from the library. Check out the cute lifeguard. Wait in the checkout line. Checkout is at 10:00 AM.

check up vs. checkup
I thought I'd check up on how she was doing. Go to the doctor for a checkup.

chill out vs. chill-out, chillout
Relax, man; chill out! This is my chill-out time. I call this chillout music.

clamp down vs. clampdown
The city is going to clamp down on illegal parking. I've gotten five tickets since the clampdown began.

claw back vs. clawback
The government needs to claw back some of the revenues it lost last quarter. The clawback will hit the incomes of some poor families especially hard.

clean out vs. cleanout
Clean out the refrigerator. Remove the cleanout to clear the clogged sink drain.

click through vs. clickthrough
Click through to claim your free iPod. The ad had a high clickthrough rate.

close out vs. closeout
Let's close out our stock of VCRs. We can get rid of them in a closeout sale. I bought this sweater cheap on closeout.

come down vs. comedown
Come down and see us in Baja this winter. From CEO to janitor: what a comedown!

come on vs. come-on
He tried to come on to me. Come on, you know you really like washing the car. The enticing offer was just a come-on.

cool down vs. cool-down, cooldown
Cool down in the shade for a while. Allow some time for a cool-down period after running. Before working out, do a warmup; and afterward, a cooldown.

cop out vs. cop-out, copout
When it was his turn to wash the dishes he would always cop out. That lame excuse was a real cop-out (or copout).

crack down vs. crackdown
The coach is going to crack down on players using steroids. Management insisted on a crackdown.

cut back vs. cutback
I'm trying to cut back on French fries. School funding fell victim to a government cutback.

cut out vs. cut-out, cutout
Cut out the fat. He put a cut-out (or cutout) in the exhaust pipe. I received a cut-out valentine.

die off vs. die-off
The honeybees began to die off. When the meteor struck the earth it caused a huge die-off.

draw back vs. drawback
The threat of a beating caused him to draw back. The drawback of the plan was that they didn't have a car for the getaway.

draw down vs. drawdown
Draw down your savings to invest in my company. After the drawdown it wasn't clear that there was enough water left in the reservoir to supply the town for the summer.

dress up vs. dress-up, dressup
We'll dress up for the party. The girls like to play dress-up (or dressup).

drive by vs. drive-by
Drive by the house to see whether it looks occupied. It was a drive-by shooting.

drop off vs. drop-off

Drop off the cleaning on your way to work. There has been a drop-off in attendance. Use a cell phone drop-off location.

drop out vs. dropout

If you drop out of school, you'll regret it later. You don't want to be a dropout.

face off vs. face-off

They will face off against each other on the talk show. A hockey game begins with a face-off.

fall back vs. fallback

The soldiers had to fall back and regroup. Just in case we need a fallback (or a fallback alternative).

fall off vs. falloff

Quality began to fall off. There was a falloff in quality.

fix up vs. fix-up

Fix up the basement as a home theater. The only date he could get was a fix-up. A novel made up of related short stories is sometimes called a "fix-up."

flame out vs. flameout

When they entered the tournament I knew their team would flame out. The jet suffered a flameout. Their career ended in spectacular flameout.

flare up vs. flare-up, flareup

Dripping fat causes the charcoal to flare up. The conflict will flare up. Last winter there was a flare-up (or flareup) of flu cases.

fly by vs. flyby

In this fascinating class time will just fly by. The space probe was designed for a flyby of the Planet Mongo.

fly over vs. flyover

You'll fly over our house on your way to the airport. The Air Force Blue Angels staged a flyover to mark the beginning of Seafair. In the UK, an overpass is a flyover.

fold up vs. fold-up

Fold up the sheets before you put them away. We have a fold-up treadmill.

follow through vs. follow-through

He invited everybody to the birthday party but he failed to follow through by ordering a cake. The secret to a good golf swing is the follow-through.

freak out vs. freakout

Calm down, don't freak out. It was wild: a real freakout.

freeze out vs. freeze-out

The large investors tried to freeze out the small ones. He was victim of a freeze-out. She learned what a freeze-out plug is in auto shop.

gad about vs. gadabout

I like to gad about to different parties. My friends say that makes me a real gadabout.

get away vs. getaway

We want to get away for the winter. A trip to New Zealand seems like a good getaway.

give away vs. give-away, giveaway
I'm trying to give away my old VCR. The bank promised every new customer a give-away. Unfortunately their giveaway gifts turned out to be shares of their worthless stock. Her expression was a dead give-away (or giveaway).

give back vs. giveback
He had to give back the comic book. Management insisted on a health benefit giveback when it negotiated with the union.

go ahead vs. go-ahead
We decided to go ahead with the project. The city permit office gave us the go-ahead.

goof off vs. goof-off
I don't feel like working today; let's just goof off. That guy is a lazy goof-off.

hand out vs. handout
Hand out the cookies at snack time. He was begging for a handout. On every street corner there's somebody distributing handouts.

hang out vs. hangout
We don't have to go anyplace special; let's just hang out together. The Harbor Pub is a popular island hangout.

hang up vs. hangup
Hang up your coat. I have a real hangup about robocalls; I just hang up on them.

hold back vs. holdback
She couldn't hold back her tears. The lender insisted on a 20% holdback until the project was done.

hold out vs. holdout
Hold out for a better deal. Most of the partners agreed to the merger, but there was one holdout.

hook up vs. hook-up, hookup
Go out and see who you can hook up with. I wasn't really interested in him, he was just a casual hookup.

keep away vs. keepaway
I try to keep away from cheeseburgers. They were playing keepaway with his backpack.

kiss off vs. kiss-off
Just kiss off the ones you don't like. Give them the kiss-off.

knock down vs. knock-down
Knock down the furniture for shipping. I got it at a knock-down price. It was a knock-down, drag-out fight.

knock off vs. knockoff
Knock off the arguing with your sister. That isn't a real Coach bag; it's just a cheap knockoff.

lay off vs. layoff
The company wants to lay off more workers. This will be a devastating layoff.

lay out vs. layout
Lay out the body for the funeral. You'll have to lay out some serious money for that granite countertop. We need a more efficient kitchen layout.

let down vs. letdown

Let down your hair on your birthday. The bad review my boss gave me was a real letdown.

lie down vs. lie-down

Take your shoes off before you lie down on the bed. Why don't you have a good lie-down?

lift off vs. liftoff

The rocket is ready to lift off. We have achieved liftoff.

live in vs. live-in

They want a nanny to live in: a live-in nanny.

lock down vs. lockdown

Lock down the prison. The prison reacted to the riot with a lockdown.

lock up vs. lockup

Lock up the house when you go on vacation. Throw the mugger in the lockup.

log in vs. log-in, login

Log in to your account. Enter your log-in ID. Your log-in (or login) is complete.

log off vs. log-off or logoff

Log off when you leave the bank site. Complete your log-off (or logoff) by clicking here.

look in vs. look-in

Look in on me when you come by the hospital. The nurse gave me a quick look-in during her rounds.

look out vs. look-out

Look out for falling rocks. Pull over onto the look-out and admire the mountains. The bank robbers were caught because they forgot to use a look-out. If you don't want to use a password to secure your laptop, that's your look-out.

look up vs. lookup

You can look up the name of the first owner of your house in the local library. You can do a zip code lookup on the USPS site. The spreadsheet provides a useful lookup function.

make do vs. make-do

Since we can't afford to buy a new car right now, we'll just have to make do with the old one. The tarp works as a make-do tent.

make up vs. make-up, makeup

Make up your mind. Take the make-up exam. Put on makeup.

mark down vs. markdown

If they mark down the sweaters, I'll buy one. There was a big markdown on last year's model.

mark up vs. markup

Mark up the document. Mark up the merchandise. The markup on this face-cream is about 500%.

mash up vs. mashup

Mash up the carrots with the potatoes. Her recording is more a mashup than a remix of those songs.

mix up vs. mix-up
Mix up the paint for the doghouse. There had been a mix-up at the bank.

mop up vs. mop-up
Mop up the spilled milk. It was a mop-up operation.

opt out vs. opt-out
Opt out of the mailing list. The Direct Marketing Association offers an opt-out service.

pass through vs. pass-through
Can ultraviolet light pass through the lenses? There was a pass-through between the kitchen and dining room. What is the pass-through rate?

pay back vs. payback
Pay back the loan. The water balloon was payback for the wedgie.

pay off vs. pay-off, payoff
We hope to pay off our mortgage soon. Our investments are beginning to pay off. His gamble had a disappointing payoff (or pay-off).

phase out vs. phase-out
Let's phase out the old models next month. The phase-out is just about complete.

pick up vs. pickup
Pick up the trash and throw it in your pickup.

pig out vs. pig-out, pigout
Try not to pig out at the buffet. After last night's pigout (or pig-out) I need to go on a diet.

pin up vs. pin-up
Pin up the hem. A photo of Betty Grable in a swimsuit was a famous WWII pin-up (or pinup). She was a pin-up girl.

play back vs. playback
Play back the recording. On old tape recorders the record head was usually to the left of the playback head. We listened to the playback. Asha Bhosle is a famous playback singer in Bollywood movies.

plug in vs. plugin
Plug in the vacuum cleaner. This is a cool Photoshop plugin (or plug-in).

pop out vs. pop-out
The zits began to pop out all over her chin. The car has a pop-out windshield.

press on vs. press-on
If we're going to make base camp by sundown we need to press on. Before PageMaker, we used to create the headlines in our newsletter with press-on type.

pull apart vs. pull-apart
The teacher had to pull apart the two kids who were fighting. Our bakery makes really good pull-apart rolls. They make a whole-wheat pull-apart.

pull down vs. pull-down
Pull down the shades. Make your selection from the pull-down menu.

pull off vs. pull-off
Can the team pull off an upset next Saturday? You can get a great view from the next pull-off on the highway.

pull over vs. pullover

Pull over and let me drive for a while. Would you rather I knitted you a cardigan or a pullover? It was a pullover shirt.

push up vs. push-up

We got ready for the last push up the mountain. She did a one-handed push-up. She wore a push-up bra. She ate a push-up pop.

put down vs. put-down

Put down the gun. It was an insulting remark, a real put-down.

put on vs. put-on

Put on the kettle for tea. His pretence of indifference was just a put-on. It was a put-on expression.

ring back vs. ring-back

When you get my message, please ring back immediately. After dialing, you hear the ring-back tone.

rip off vs. rip-off, ripoff

Rip off the plastic wrapping to get at the game. They tried to rip off our design. Their version was a total rip-off. They charge rip-off prices.

roll back vs. roll-back, rollback

Roll back the prices. The store announced a price roll-back (or rollback).

roll over vs. rollover

The vans tended to roll over. Roll over your IRA into a Roth. Yesterday on the highway there were two collisions and a roll-over (or rollover). They put a rollover at the top of their home page.

rub down vs. rubdown

Rub down the beef with an herb mixture. After the game you need a rubdown.

run about vs. runabout

These lamps will run about $100 each. This kind of little car is called a runabout.

run around vs. runaround

I had to run around all morning to get everything ready for the party. When I asked him for a straight answer, he gave me the runaround.

run off vs. runoff

He decided to run off with the circus. Catch the runoff from the gutters.

run up vs. run-up

Run up the stairs. The scandal broke out during the run-up to the election.

screw up vs. screw-up, screwup

Screw up your courage. Try not to screw up. It was a terrible screwup (or screw-up). He was a notorious screwup (or screw-up).

sell off vs. sell-off

Sell off the rest of the stock. Concerns about the economy triggered a sell-off on Wall Street today.

send up vs. send-up

She wanted to send up typical romance novels. Her book was a send-up of the kind she liked least.

set aside vs. set-aside
Set aside some money for your vacation. To get the agricultural subsidy we made the old cornfield a set-aside.

set back vs. setback
The late spring snows set back our camping trip for several weeks. The loss of the grant was a real setback. The zoning ordinance prescribes a ten-foot setback.

set up vs. setup
You can set up your iPhone account at the store. Bring your own bottle and the restaurant will provide a setup for you. This was just a setup to trap unwary consumers.

shake down vs. shakedown
The gangsters tried to shake down the merchants for protection money. Some refused to give in to the shakedown.

show off vs. show-off
Let me show off our new kitchen. She's a real show-off.

shut in vs. shut-in
The dog was shut in all day. He was a sickly shut-in.

sign in vs. sign-in
Sign in at the registration desk. Here's the sign-in sheet.

sign on vs. sign-on
Sign on to the project. Television stations used to display a test pattern for fifteen minutes before sign-on.

sit down vs. sit-down
Sit down and have a cold one. Go to a sit-down restaurant.

sit in vs. sit-in
Sit in this chair. The students staged a sit-in protest. The college president denounced the sit-in.

sleep over vs. sleepover
If it gets too late, you can sleep over here. Their daughter invited six friends for a sleepover.

spin off vs. spin-off
You can spin off a new TV series from an old one, like *Frasier* from *Cheers*. *Crankshaft* is a spin-off from *Funky Winkerbean*.

spin out vs. spinout
Don't let your car spin out on the ice. The spinout sent the car into the ditch.

spit up vs. spitup
The baby spit up most of its lunch. My blouse was covered with spit-up.

start up vs. startup
Start up the engine. We need investors to fund our startup. They got a start-up grant.

stand out vs. standout
Mindy tends to stand out on the basketball court. She's a real standout.

stick up vs. stickup
Stick up these posters around town. This is a stickup!

strike out vs. strikeout
Strike out the first paragraph. There were three strikeouts in the first fifteen minutes of the game.

tag along vs. tagalong
Her little brother always wanted to tag along. She thought he was an irritating little tagalong.

take off vs. takeoff, take-off
Well, I think it's time for us to take off. Fasten your seatbelt before takeoff (or take-off).

take out vs. takeout
Take out the garbage. Let's eat takeout Thai food tonight.

take over vs. takeover
The vice president of the club will take over while Patricia is on vacation. That corporation staged a takeover of ours.

tear down vs. teardown
Tear down the old barn. We bought the place just for the lot; the house was a teardown.

tip off vs. tipoff, tip-off
He tried to tip off the police about the planned robbery. The police ignored the tip-off (or tipoff). I was busy buying a hotdog and missed the tip-off.

touch down vs. touchdown
The astronauts reported they would soon touch down on the moon. The plane skidded slightly on touchdown. The quarterback scored a touchdown.

touch up vs. touch-up
Touch up your make-up. She gave her make-up a quick touch-up.

trade in vs. trade-in
Let's trade in the old car. We should get a pretty good trade-in price.

trickle down vs. trickle-down
They hoped the money would trickle down to the people who needed it the most. But many people are skeptical about the trickle-down theory.

try out vs. tryout
They want to try out for field hockey. The tryout is tomorrow.

turn down vs. turndown
Turn down the covers on the bed. Turn down the offer. The economy went into a turndown (also known as a downturn).

turn on vs. turn-on
Turn on the lights. A pet chimpanzee can turn on you. She found his accent to be a real turn-on.

turn over vs. turnover
The engine wouldn't turn over. I like to have an apple turnover with my morning coffee. The bomb squad had a high turnover rate of personnel. There was just one turnover in the game's last quarter.

wake up vs. wake-up
I need to wake up early tomorrow to catch a plane. I need a wake-up call.

walk in vs. walk-in

I prefer to take a very short walk in the rain. Between appointments I manage to squeeze in the occasional walk-in. Our bedroom has a walk-in closet.

warm up vs. warm-up

Before playing, we need to warm up. Come early to give time for the warm-up. Wear a warm-up suit.

wash out vs. washout

I couldn't wash out the stain. You can't get here on the old road; there's been a washout at the first curve. The initially enthusiastic candidate turned out to be a real washout.

weigh in vs. weigh-in

All jockeys have to weigh in before the race. I'll see you at the weigh-in.

white out vs. whiteout, white-out

In the days before personal computers we used to white out our mistakes. We used a lot of liquid white-out. The huge snowstorm caused a total whiteout (or white-out).

wind up vs. windup

Wind up the kite string. Here's the windup, and the pitch—it's a strike!

work out vs. workout

Go to the gym to work out. Do your workout every day.

write down vs. writedown

Write down the telephone number. Our accountant said the property was overvalued and recommended a writedown.

write off vs. write-off

We had to write off the bad debts. We took a write-off on the loss.

write up vs. write-up

He said he would write up an account of the meeting. That was a great write-up about you in the paper.